D0298290

The Goalkeeper's
History *of* Britain

The Goalkeeper's History *of* Britain

PETER CHAPMAN

FOURTH ESTATE • *London*

First published in Great Britain in 1999 by
Fourth Estate Limited
6 Salem Road
London W2 4BU

Copyright © Peter Chapman 1999

1 3 5 7 9 10 8 6 4 2

A catalogue record for this book is available from the
British Library.

ISBN 1–84115–009–6

Typeset by Palimpsest Book Production Limited,
Polmont, Stirlingshire
Printed in Great Britain by Clays Ltd, St Ives plc

For Marie, Alex and Pepito,
my mum and dad,
Maria and Marie I.

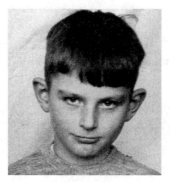

The photographs at the beginning of each chapter show Reg Matthews (p.1), Frank Swift (p.18), Jim Chapman (p.37), Gil Merrick (p.51), Bert Trautmann (p.69), Harry Gregg (p.84), Jack Kelsey (p.115), Lev Yashin (p.144), Pat Jennings (p.159), Alex Stepney (p.180), Gordon Banks (p.205), Jan Tomaszewski (p.228), Sepp Maier (p.248), Peter Shilton (p.273) and David Seaman (p.299). Page v shows Peter Chapman as a boy.

Photographs on pages 159, 180, 205, 228, 248, 273 and 299 reproduced by permission of Empics. Photograph on page 144 by Mstislav Botashev reproduced by permission of Nikolai Botashev, copyright Nikolai Botashev. All other photographs from the author's collection.

Acknowledgements

Special love and thanks to Marie for seeing it through, my parents and sister, whose help has been obvious, and Marie I for all her transatlantic support. Thank you to my late grandparents, to Keith and my aunts and uncles.

Thank you to Tim Whitfield and Clive Priddle for getting it off the ground; to Tottenham Hotspur historian Andy Porter, Manchester City historian John Maddocks, to Gordon Banks, Joe Corrigan, Ted Ditchburn and Alan Hodgkinson; and to Bromley public libraries (Anerley branch).

Thank you to the late Professor Chris Thorne.

'. . . a nation of goalkeepers'
Napoleon I, speaking of the British (later misquoted)

Chapter 1

A Determined *and* Heroic Defence

At the top of the street was a stretch of waste ground, a memorial in bumps and ruts to where the barrage balloon had flown. There hadn't been another one for miles. Attached by cable to an air force lorry, it was lowered during the day, my mum told me, to be checked for signs of damage and deflation by the two airmen in charge of it. They sent it up again at night, its job to deflect any bombers that had overshot their main targets of the City and the docks. It had played its part in what all reports said had been a determined and heroic defence.

Ten years after the end of the conflict, signs of it were all around. Numbers 8 and 10, which stood next to each other on the canal side of the street opposite us, were a half shell of their original selves. From a padlocked gate in the railings, steps ran down into a basement area virtually covered with rubble to the pavement level. The weed- and tree-strewn interiors were home to a colony of cats, large enough in size and number to scare off the packs of stray dogs that wandered the street and surrounding area. The cats were fed by Mrs Clements, the elderly lady who lived on the top floor of our house. Three times a day she would

1

rattle down four flights of stairs and across the road with tins of sour-smelling liver and fish relayed to her on their bikes by the competing catsmeat men of Frome Street and Camden Passage. In anticipation of her first delivery of the day, the cats would yowl through the pre-dawn hours.

A few doors down from us, all that remained of number 25 was a gap in the terrace. The 8 foot drop into what had been its basement was barred only by a few lengths of scaffold board and pole. The blind man on his way back home from work had no problem tapping his way past, but you wondered about the various male members of the Bray family who lived further down. On Saturday nights, they reeled and stumbled on their way home from post-licensing hours sessions in the York public house at the top of Duncan Street near the Angel. They shouted abuse at their wives, who attempted to remain a discreet distance in front of them.

Our street ran down from Colebrooke Row, which curved the quarter mile between City Road and Islington Green. Some Colebrooke Row houses had no railings around them, only stubs of iron a couple of inches long. My mum said they had been removed as soon as the war began, to be made into guns and ammunition. Both corners of Colebrooke Row and the street at our back, Gerrard Road, were wartime bombsites, used for bonfires on Guy Fawkes' night. The stretch of waste ground where the barrage balloon had flown was right opposite the bombsites but never used for the occasion. This was possibly out of respect for the priest and nuns of St John's, the red-brick Catholic church behind it, though no one openly made the religious connection. Irish and Italian families in the area threw rubbish and bits of unwanted furniture on the bonfires like everyone else.

Otherwise the Gerrard Road bombsites had no great use. They were certainly too rough for football or any other ball game. Encouraged by a fall of snow and reports that ice hockey was the fastest game in the world, I tried to emulate the Harringay Racers with two bits of wood knocked together by my grandad into a flat-bottomed stick. After two minutes trying to assert control over a few stones, I fell over and took a piece out of my right calf on some glass. I filled it with Germolene, a treatment my dad had applied after he had been bitten in the stomach one night by a large centipede when he was with the army in Sicily. A pink skin had formed over the hole in my leg by the morning. Harringay Racers disappeared no less miraculously soon after.

Playing with a ball in the street was largely confined to the walls of the houses at the very top. Both were used as factories and, for some reason long preceding the war, their windows had been bricked up. One belonged to Lowe's the printers. My mum, who had been trained as a bookbinder, worked there on and off for some years. Mr Lowe had the shape of the Michelin man and the public demeanour of the Laughing Policeman. In slimmer yet grimmer times he had been a soldier with the Czechoslovakian army. After the Germans had taken over his country in 1938, his unit underwent a stage-by-stage retreat to England. He, his wife and two young daughters lived on the floor above his factory. They were Jewish. Other than sensing that no one else in the street was, I had little idea what this meant.

Mr Lowe spoke several foreign languages, including 'Czechoslo-vakian' and Hungarian, all of which strangely failed him when it came to swearing at his clients. Despite the fact they were often his fellow central Europeans, he did this very loudly in English. One of his better customers sold holidays under the name and advertising banner of 'See Spain', an exotic destination unknown to anyone in the area. Few who sought his services to print their brochures and baggage labels paid unless he went physically to shake the money out of them. He had to go through this process on most Fridays to get enough money in the bank to pay the staff's wages.

He also swore at his staff but my mum and two or three other women who worked there – none of whom would have classi-fied themselves as liberal on the subject of industrially colourful language – seemed only mildly offended. Should he cast doubt on their parentage or liken them to parts of the anatomy rarely mentioned at the time, he could be a 'horrible man'. But to a degree he was excused the scorn which would be poured on locals who acted like this (the Saturday-night Brays, for example). It was assumed he could not have grasped the seriousness of what he was saying. It was the same if the people working for him were in his factory-come-house toilet at a time he wanted to use it. Mr Lowe would not retreat tactfully, as if relieving himself was the last thing on his mind, but wait outside and rattle on the door handle, shouting 'How lonk vill you be in dere?' He did not quite understand how we did things, which was to say, how they should be properly done.

This was entirely to the advantage of local kids when it came to playing up against his wall. He raised no objection. By contrast, the wall on the opposite corner we usually avoided. It belonged to a small engineering factory, populated by men in blue overalls who wore collars and ties beneath them as a symbol of the nation's industrial standing. The foreman, in his white overall, was vigilant about the noise of ball on brickwork and would come out to complain that his workers' concentration on their clanking machinery was being impaired. One day he caught me down the factory's basement area after I'd climbed the railings to retrieve a ball. He threatened to call the police. I had no doubt he would or, for such a crime, that Scotland Yard would turn up in force.

We lived with my grandparents. My grandad was from the Exmouth Market, near Saffron Hill and the Italian area, where his mother had leased a shop and sold roast meals. The vicar at the Holy Redeemer church opposite – High Anglican, with nuns, mass and sense of mission among the toiling poor – challenged her on why she opened on Sundays. 'Because it's my best day, vicar,' she said, 'like yours', which chased him off. She had the same effect on my great-grandfather when he drank or gambled, and he'd flee for weeks at a time to a sister in Bedfordshire.

My nan was born just off Theobald's Road in Holborn, a street or so back from the house where Disraeli lived. She spent much of her early life living in the City and Finsbury, near Smithfield Market and the Barbican, then later further north off the Goswell Road. Her grandmother was Italian, from a family she said sold ice cream – what they didn't sell in the day was kept under the bed at night. My nan's family was poor, not least because her father, a music printer, went blind when she was little, working by candlelight in the basement of the Adelphi Theatre in the Strand. When my grandparents married they moved across the Finsbury border into Islington, an advance of about a mile from their backgrounds.

My grandad earned most of his living in the years between the wars as a freelance bill poster, the mythical 'Bill Stickers'. He worked alone, cycling miles with pastebrush, bucket and bills to beyond Hammersmith in one direction and the Burdett and East India Dock Roads in the other. A policeman once commandeered a milkman's horse and cart to chase and arrest him in the Fulham Palace Road. The crowd outside a labour exchange shouted and converged on the policeman, who had to let him go. As big a threat was a rival cousin, whose gang would rip his work down. On one occasion they cornered him in a Finsbury mews and beat him up. Much of his bill posting work was for the *Sporting Life*. He also delivered papers and worked in Bouverie Street at the *News of the World* on Saturday nights, when the pay around Fleet Street's machine rooms was particularly good.

In the absence of pension plans, each time he saved up enough he would buy a house as a hedge against old age. The average Islington price in the 1920s and '30s was £200–350. He had three in our street, all on our side. Each was £50 dearer than houses bordering the Regent's Canal opposite because of the problem they had with rats clambering up from the towpath. He had four others in Carnegie Street, one road over from where the canal came out after its mile-long journey through the tunnel that ran from Colebrooke Row to Barnsbury. My grandma's oldest sister, Ada, who had played at the Collins music hall on Islington Green with Chaplin before he went to America ('not a nice man'; he never spoke to her or the others in the chorus line), had lived in one of them. So had her son Teddy, who was a little older than my mum and a favourite cousin. All my grandad's Carnegie Street houses, however, were destroyed one night in the bombing.

The London Blitz had started on a warm Saturday afternoon early in September 1940 when my mum and her sister were visiting Aunt Ada and cousin Teddy. He had a good job as a shop-fitter, which exempted him from military call-up since his skills were put to making rear-gunner placements on bombers. When the sirens sounded they didn't want to be caught away from home, so Teddy walked them down through Chapel Market and along the small street round the back of the Agricultural Hall – a large building where farmers used to exhibit their prize animals and which had the look of King's Cross railway station about it. At Upper Street by the Angel high pavement they stopped to watch the early moments of the raid. Planes were fighting to the south, away above the area of Moorgate and east over the docks. At the time it was a bit of a show. But the German planes were dropping incendiaries and, when it got darker, the sky over the City and river was alight. Then the real bombers came back.

In one of his broadcasts, Churchill – or the man who did his voice when he was away in the USA visiting Roosevelt – announced this as everyone's 'finest hour'. The family spent the initial month of raids in the basement, upright piano against the window. Stuck amid the machinery of the *News of the World* print room on the first night, my grandad wouldn't believe how bad it was until he'd experienced it himself on the second.

From shortly after the first siren at about seven in the evening, to not much before 7 a.m. when the all-clear sounded, the house shook. Bombs landing nearby were both terrifying and of some comfort. Once one had exploded close at hand, the next in the string dropped by that plane would, reliably, be away and beyond. Much worse was the device at some point in the middle distance. The bomb straight after it could be the one to fall on you. The British guns continually fired back. (My mum said the sound was like that, two years later, of the Allied guns opening up at Alamein.) Maybe briefly you'd doze off. When you found yourself still alive after the planes had gone, it was impossible to imagine that, on looking outside, you'd find anyone or anything else had survived.

In the mornings my mother, who was seventeen, and her sister, my aunt Olive, who was younger by a year, walked to work down the City Road, picking their way through a chaos of rubble and firemen's hoses. The City Road maternity hospital was among the bombed buildings one morning, its beds blown halfway out the windows. The teenagers worked at Waterlow's in Old Street, which printed foreign banknotes. After a day spent staring at the face of Chiang Kai-shek, they walked home, had their tea, put on a pair of slacks and prepared for another night.

My grandad spent weeks looking for a location to get them out to, then was reminded of his distant aunt whom his father used to run away to from Exmouth Market. The family, including my mum's one-year-old brother Keith, and other members like Great-aunt Ada, moved to about 50 miles away in Sandy, in Bedfordshire, where they found a place over a shop in the High Street.

Grandad stayed behind. Not wishing to join the crowd down the Angel tube, he offered to build a shelter in the backyard. Mrs Clements said she and her middle-aged children, Stanley and Lily, who lived with her on the top floor, would refuse to use it. So he converted the cupboard under the basement stairs. For a while the four of them shared this, crouched on two narrow benches. Stanley, who wore a detachable starched collar and was clerk to a firm of window cleaners in Camden Passage, sat with a suitcase on his knees packed for a hasty exit. He bemoaned my grandad's lack of similar preparation, and fretted he could hear the rattles of the air-raid patrol men signalling a gas alarm. Grandad soon opted for the relative peace and comfort of sleeping out the raids in the ground-floor parlour.

Number 25 succumbed quietly one night to an inextinguishable incendiary. When numbers 8 and 10 opposite went up, the blast blew the front parlour window over the room, but grandad was out working in Fleet Street. A bomb just along from the backyard took six houses out of the terrace in Gerrard Road. Two bombs which landed on the corners of Gerrard Road set off fears of a gas explosion and everyone was evacuated to Owen's boys' school, 300 yards away. Mrs Clements, Stanley and Lily left in such a rush they forgot to take their suitcase and any money and grandad had to buy them a cup of tea.

A few raids later a bomb dropped down a ventilation shaft into the basement of the girls' school on the other side of the Owen's playground. Many of the several hundred people sheltered there were killed either by the blast or by drowning when the water mains burst. Coming out of the Angel tube next morning on her monthly visit to make sure grandad was still intact, my nan said the scene was 'like a pit disaster'. Not that she knew it, but her youngest sister and one of my grandad's sisters, Mary, were still to be pulled out. Both walked away from it alive, Great-aunt Mary with a stick thereafter. Off-duty soldiers were taking advantage of the mayhem to throw their pass books into the smoke and debris to fake their own deaths.

Grandad's oldest sister, Polly, lived in Finsbury by the Iron-monger Row baths, an area not easy to survive in at the best of times. If you didn't know the precise address of the person you were visiting, it wouldn't have done any good inquiring of the locals – they'd assume you were the police or a debt-collector. On her own initiative Polly had gone down to the Northern line platforms at Old Street every night since a week before the war began. The tube was not officially being used for the purpose at the time, the government being reluctant to allow people underground during the raids lest they give the impression of a nation cowering in fear. Polly went down throughout the first twelve months of the 'phoney war' and, when the bombing started, was so petrified she almost had to be carried down. St Luke's church, the few feet across Ironmonger Row from her house, had been destroyed as she resurfaced after one raid. She died towards the end of the Blitz for no obvious reason. Her heart had been none too good, and my grandad said he was sure she'd been frightened to death.

Our street's great escape came when a 1,000-pound bomb struck the chimney stack on Siddy Bates's house at number 40. Had it hit and gone through the slates of the roof, much around the house would have gone with it. The sudden and looming presence of the barrage balloon might have jogged the bomb aimer's elbow the fraction required. I imagined the outcome. The bomb bounced off the stack – solid brickwork – and sailed into the air again. In a high arc, a tantalising parabola, the bomb flew towards the end of the 60-foot garden. But where would it land? Maybe an old, mythical goalkeeper stood down there, calmly watching as it dropped – flat cap, roll-neck jersey, positioned on his line, jumping at the last moment (actually giving little more than a nonchalant skip) to make sure the threat passed over. With his upstretched hand he'd have set the crossbar swaying up and down a couple of times, just to reassure all concerned he'd had it covered. Immediately beyond the garden and towpath the bomb fell into the canal, where it exploded beneath the brown and accommodating sludge. Next morning my grandma was on one of her visits. As she walked from the Angel tube, she said, the mud was splattered across the roadways, pavements and housefronts for streets around.

Her father died when the raids seemed to have come to an end. In his eighties, blind and in a wheelchair, he'd been either unwilling or unable to leave London and had sat out the bombing in his own private darkness in his house in one of the small Finsbury streets off Goswell Road. The family returned from Sandy for the funeral, Great-aunt Ada going to join her son Teddy, who had stayed on in Carnegie Street. Everyone assumed the bombing was more or less over, but the evening before the funeral saw one of the worst raids yet. Ada left quickly to go to the shelter at the end of the street but it was nearly full and there was nothing to sit on. Teddy ran back and was killed in a direct hit on the house.

From the Caledonian Road an air-raid patrol man saw him on the doorstep, coming out of the house carrying what he said looked like a chair. My mum and her sister were not allowed to see him. They later worked it out from what little they were told that he had been decapitated. His body was not in too much of a state, however, to deter whoever removed his wallet. It was assumed to have been one of the ARP men, 'good people as a rule' but in that area often market boys and bookies' runners. Great-aunt Ada was left to come to terms with the loss of her father and son within a few days of each other. She came back to Sandy two weeks later and the family met her at the station, none of them with any idea what to say. All she said was, 'We just have to start all over again.'

My mum and dad met soon after the family arrived in Sandy and were married fifteen months later. He had to be back at an army camp in the north of England the next day and was promptly sent to Africa and Italy for four years. She worked in the Naafi by the market square in Biggleswade, making 3,200 pounds of slab cake a day for the navy, army and air force. My dad said the army never saw any of it. After the war he moved back to Islington with her. War brides usually followed their husbands, but she had not exactly warmed to the country. Locals had sometimes wondered what Londoners were making all the fuss about and, worse, referred to the family as 'evacuees'. As my nan, in a rare state of vexation, was keen to point out, they had not left London like hundreds of thousands had as part of some state-dependent evacuation programme: 'We got ourselves out.' My father was also easily persuaded that demand for a bricklayer would be nowhere as high as in London.

I was born in the first week of the National Health Service in July 1948, in a stately home near Welwyn Garden City. The story had it that Lord Brocket, its former owner and a Member of Parliament in the 1930s, had been led astray by Sir Oswald Mosley,

Britain's moustachioed champion of fascism, after which the state required an act of noble penance. No mention of this was made on the plaque later put on the lobby wall: 'By the kindness of Lord Brocket', it said, he gave over his Hertfordshire home to expectant women who, but for the destruction of the maternity hospital in City Road, would have been accommodated nearer home. I was born in the room above the front door, once the chamber of Lord Palmerston before he sent in one British gunboat too many and became fatally entwined with a maid on Brocket Hall's billiard table. Lady Caroline Lamb, an earlier resident, served herself up naked from a large silver tureen on the birthday of her husband and prime minister, Lord Melbourne. While Melbourne was away on higher affairs of Georgian state, Byron probably passed through for a few grabbed moments of warmth and verse. My mother said it was a cold and sparse place. After the customary ten days of confining us there, and in the absence of ambulances or other transport, we took a taxi back to London.

At the upper end of the street, two adjoining houses lay between ours and the corner. They had been so shaken about by the bombs that two thick wooden props were placed diagonally from ground to the second floor to keep them up. Eventually the landlord accepted that the price of Islington property was never likely to rise and sold the freehold to the council, which promptly pulled the houses down. One of the families moved out to Ealing, where they had a garden. The demolition of the houses left ours at the top of the terrace. From here there was a sense of looking down and surveying the scene. The street sloped away gradually and became stranger the further it went. Our neighbours, up to about ten doors away, we knew reasonably well but even then people 'kept themselves to themselves'. Two hundred yards away Danbury Street divided the street in two and was rarely crossed. Before the war the lower half had been called Hanover Street, until the London County Council decreed the name should be confined to a byway in the more prestigious West End. The road was united, to local disapproval. Our upper part of the street was different and believed to be better than the lower half. There was little in common between us, so no point in pretending we had the same identity.

I had to cross Danbury Street to reach Hanover school. Opposite was the Island Queen pub, where barrels were delivered through the trap door in the pavement from a large cart pulled by dray horses. Its front doors were thrown open at all times of the day. It looked a black hole of a place, with only vague shapes visible as you glanced in. It wouldn't have done to look too long, since it was patronised by the very people from whom we kept ourselves to ourselves. Behind the school, around the banks of the canal, were the grey-bricked buildings of the British Drug Houses, the BDH. Viewed from our upper part of the street, they piled over the houses in the lower half like the bridge of a delapidated oil tanker. Chemicals in large green bottles bundled in straw and wire containers went into its entrance in Wharf Road. A smell akin to but several times more powerful than that produced when the gas board dug up the road rose out of it and over the school.

For our first couple of Empire Days we had to march in the infants' playground and salute the flag. This flew from the pole of the BDH building across the canal, beyond the lock-keepers' cottages. In my mum's time at the school, Empire Day was a stirring occasion, with kids dressed in assumed styles of the dependencies. Her girlfriend over the road who had bushy, curly hair went as the 'Wild Man of Borneo'. Now it was difficult to see the point, or the flag. It hung limp and damp, amid the more potent atmosphere let off by the BDH.

Shortly before the coronation, when my sister was born, my grandad had given my parents his house two doors away as a wedding anniversary present. He could neither handle nor afford the repairs any longer, so told my dad to take it and do it up. Before the war many houses had been occupied by single families but multi-occupancy became common as people bombed out of their homes were relocated. The family of four on the top floor were rehoused by the council, while the two old ladies in the property stayed. My parents had to persuade them to give up their gas mantles for electric light, which they'd refused as too expensive. Houses had been badly shaken in the war years. Even now it was a feature in the street for some people's front doorsteps to collapse in on them in their basement kitchens or bathrooms. With my grandad's help, it took my father two years working nights and weekends to get the house ready for us.

We moved into the kitchen and front room in the basement just before Christmas 1955 and my mum put up a tree. The bathroom beneath the front doorstep was very cold and it was easier to wash in the kitchen sink. The ground-floor front parlour where we slept was separated by two shutter doors from the room of one of the old ladies. On Saturday night she put on her hat and pin and went to the York for a drink (one or two, actually), and it was often after midnight before she'd shuffle back home, holding on to the railings where she could. At the end of our backyard and down was the Gerrard Road bombsite where languished the ghosts of six former dwellings. After heavy rain it filled with green slime and water to a depth of several feet. Known as 'the tank', it had the semi-official status of a poor-man's reservoir and the fire brigade would turn up at it every so often to run through manoeuvres with their pumps and hoses. Kids milled around and housewives came to their doorsteps with the excitement. The firemen left the 'tank' reduced to a mudflat, with old prams and lengths of cast-iron piping sticking out, until it gradually recovered its general swampiness and sought to infiltrate the backyards nearby.

Number 25, as an abandoned gap of rubble and scrubland, was particularly vulnerable. A brother and sister, Mario Maestri and Elena Salvoni, lived with their families one house along. My dad would be called in occasionally to put down damp courses and otherwise strengthen its flanking walls. One evening I went with him to watch Mario's new television. We didn't have one. Apart from my grandad's, Mario's was the only television I was aware of in the street. On it was the rare phenomenon of a BBC outside broadcast, and we caught the last quarter of an hour or so of a football game between England and West Germany in Berlin.

The match was in the stadium built by Hitler for the Olympics twenty years earlier, the one where, my dad told me, Jesse Owens won his medals and Hitler stormed out in fury. Hitler and the Germans, of course, had got their further come-uppance when they'd tried it on with us. From the comics I bought on Saturdays at the Polish newsagent in Danbury Street, I guessed this stadium must have been the only part of the German capital not left in ruins. But since the war's end we had been helping them get back on their feet and this game seemed to be a sign of our new friendship. It was the first post-war match between us in Germany. It was also the first football game I had ever seen.

The novelty was impaired by the Germans appearing to be all over us.

One man was doing miraculous things to defy them. His name was Matthews. Not Stanley, forty-one, the wizzened legend of the right-wing. In late May, the season of league fixtures was over by nearly three weeks and he was coaching in South Africa. This was another Matthews, the younger Reg, a goalkeeper. He was tall, beaky-nosed, with a haunted look and hunched shoulders that seemed to stick out of the back of his jersey. A kind of smudgy light grey on the screen, this was the 'traditional yellow' jersey worn by England keepers. Its colour was one of the variations on a theme that was part of football folklore. Wolverhampton Wanderers, for instance, said my dad, did not turn out in gold but 'old gold'. The England goalkeeper's jersey also came in 'coveted' or 'hallowed' yellow.

German attacks were arriving in waves on Matthews's goal. One shot, suddenly fired out of the mêlée on the edge of the England penalty area by a player the commentator identified as Fritz Walter, went with such force that it gave the impression of blowing Reg off his feet. As the camera jerked wildly left to follow it, he was horizontal, diving backwards and to his right, a yard from the ground, his arms thrust out the same distance. But momentarily suspended in this midair position, and with a snap as it hit his hands, he caught the ball cleanly.

The brilliance of it made me start and catch my breath. I had seen pictures of keepers in various moments of dramatic action, some diving to deflect shots with their fingertips around a goalpost or over the crossbar. In others they might be parrying the ball or, more rarely, seen in the act of punching it; my dad said it was 'continental' keepers who tended to be the punchers. But Reg did not tip the ball around or over his goal to give the opposition the minor satisfaction of winning a corner kick. Nor did he parry or punch the ball back into play to leave the German forwards with the chance of following up. His catch ended the danger in virtually the instant it had arisen.

The impact as he landed in the goalmouth might easily have been enough to dislodge the ball from his grasp and the air from his lungs. Having hit the ground it would have been understandable if he had stayed there a while, to gather his breath and thoughts, or take brief stock of any plaudits that might be on offer from his teammates or the crowd. 'Oh, and a *good* save by Matthews,' the commentator was saying.

'Good save,' murmured my dad, in appreciation but without getting too excited about it.

There was no time for us to reflect further. Matthews had sprung back on his feet, as if the film of the previous moment had been put into reverse or he'd been attached to a large rubber band. He was racing to the edge of his penalty area, bouncing the ball every fourth step as required by the rules of the game. As he dodged past his and the German players, he looked concerned to rid himself of the ball as quickly as possible and, with it, all evidence of his save. He seemed embarrassed by the whole affair, guilty for having attracted attention to himself. As he released the ball from his hands and punted it upfield, the BBC man was only just concluding his comment, '. . . young Reg Matthews of Coventry City'.

Coventry I had heard of. Just about all children had. Like London it had really suffered the Blitz. Other cities were hardly mentioned: Hull, Plymouth, Liverpool, Glasgow, Bristol, where relatives of my nan were bombed out twice before another direct hit killed them. Coventry was one of the rare nights in nine months of the Blitz, said my mum, that London had had off. She and the family had just arrived in Sandy when the bombers were overhead again, droning backwards and forwards. This time they flew on to the Midlands. Delivering his papers next day to the stand outside Old Street station, my grandad heard the man there complain what a bad night it had been. Next to no one – with the certain exception of Great-aunt Polly – had gone down the tube to take shelter and he'd hardly sold a thing. Coventry hadn't had much of a time of it either.

While London stood for defiance and heroic endurance, we learnt that Coventry, which had been flattened, embodied the spirit of rising again. It seemed exactly right that Reg Matthews of Coventry should be bouncing up and down against the might of Germany on the television in front of me. He and his city were what the newspapers and my comics called 'plucky', whatever that meant. But his club I'd not heard of. Coventry City were not one of the big teams, the Wolverhamptons, either of the Manchesters, the Arsenals, Blackpools, Preston North Ends and Burnleys in the top division of the English league. Nor were they in the Second. Reg's team were all the way down in the Third Division South, and even towards the tail-end of that. When the Fourth Division was set up three years later from the bottom halves of the Third Divisions North and South, Coventry City were founder members.

A goalkeeper from the humblest rung of the English football league was pitched against the Germans. Furthermore, the Germans were not any old foreign international team. They were holders of the World Cup, which they'd won two years earlier in Switzerland by beating no less than Puskas and the Hungarians. Reg Matthews could one week be up against the might of Gillingham at home, the next facing vengeful Germans away. From a foot-of-the-league battle with Bournemouth, he might suddenly have to face the flowing rhythms of Brazil. He had done, just over a fortnight earlier at Wembley, when England won 4–2 in the first game between the two countries.

Reg was typical of the British small guy, 'plucky' and plucked from a modest background to face whatever the world had to confront us with. Among the British national teams, England's goalkeepers weren't alone in affording their selectors the luxury of being able to reach down the divisions for someone of the highest calibre to defend the last line. Only Jack Kelsey of Arsenal and Wales was a keeper in the First Division. Ireland's Harry Gregg played for Doncaster Rovers and Scotland's Tommy Younger for Liverpool, both in the Second. When Gregg made his debut two years earlier, he'd been playing in Doncaster's third team. It all went to prove that while others claimed fancy titles – the 'World Cup' itself was an example – we didn't need to.

Reg Matthews's clearance upfield in Berlin found an England forward, who put in a shot on goal. It was not a particularly strong one. With a couple of brisk steps to his left, the German goalkeeper could have picked up the ball. He opted not to move his feet, however, and dived. Actually, it was more like a flop. He stopped the shot easily enough, and there on the ground lingered, hugging the ball to his chest. You could see a white number '1' on the back of his black jersey, facing the presumably grey Berlin sky. He kept glancing up, heightening the drama, soaking the moment for all, and much more than, it was worth. The misguided crowd cheered their appreciation and he even found time to smile in acknowledgement. 'It's a wonder he doesn't wave,' said my dad, no longer in an approving murmur but waving his own hand at the screen in disgust. 'There's the difference between us, you see. We get up and get on with it.'

When the German keeper finally did get on with it, I wished he hadn't. His forwards resumed their assault on Reg Matthews's goal, whereupon Walter materialised again to score. 'And it's Fritz Walter!' shouted the commentator. 'The Germans have scored!' His voice conveyed what I took to be a distinct state of alarm. He compounded mine by adding there were only five minutes to go.

There was nothing in my cultural heritage to prepare for the likelihood that the Germans might win. None of my comics, nor any film I had seen, had anything but a recurrent collection of Fritzs leering their way towards comfortable victory, till ultimately beaten by their deficiency of character. When down we got up, bounced bombs on water, sent in pilots with tin legs, or chased their battleships to distant Norwegian fjords and harbours in Latin America. We might have a tendency to get in tight situations ourselves – trapped on narrow beaches, for example – but it only needed a chirpy British private to wave a thumbs-up at the encircling Germans and say 'Not 'arf', for them to rush out with hands aloft yelling, 'Kamerad! Kamerad!'

Only five minutes to go was a time for us to be hitting the net, not them. But just as the unthinkable was having to be thought, the scoreline moved into vision, chalked by hand on what seemed like an old piece of black cardboard at the bottom of the screen: 'West Germany 1 England 3'.

'There we are, we're winning,' said Mario, who had noticed my concern (and who always supported England, even against Italy). Not having seen a game before, and because seven-year-olds did not instigate conversations in other people's houses, it had not occurred to me to ask the score.

'That's right,' said my dad, as unruffled by the goal as Mario. 'The Germans have never beaten us.' When I read reports of the game, it was true the Germans had dominated much of the play, but Reg Matthews had held things together at the back, while out on the field Duncan Edwards of Manchester United had created the few England attacks there had been. From nearly all of them we scored. The wider facts were that we had indeed, never lost to them. England and Germany had played four times – twice each at home and away – since their first match against each other in 1930. England had won three and drawn the other.

This helped explain the reaction of the German crowd. Far from regarding the goal as a late and meaningless consolation, they could hardly have cheered more when they'd beaten Puskas and the Hungarians those couple of years before in Berne. The TV picked out various areas of the Olympic stadium and the spectators involved in scenes of uproarious celebration. The camera swivelled sharply to catch the German commentator in similar rapture. 'The Germans are going mad,' said the BBC man, with more than a hint of a laugh and in tones which suggested that foreigners could be very funny people. The thought had occurred to me.

But their antics were understandable. In their historical rivalry with England, the Germans had adjusted to a low level of expectation. This goal was a goal, after all. It was the first, too, they had scored on home soil against England since the war. They had not won, they were not near achieving even a draw, but here in Berlin a German crowd had witnessed for themselves that they were at least back on the score sheet. The camera zoomed in on the crowd and people beamed, waved and roared straight back into it. They could have been shouting as one: 'We've had your aid and your Marshall Plan, and we've even won the World Cup. But now we've landed one back on you, you watch us really get going with that post-war revival.'

They had also not merely scored a goal against England. For almost ninety minutes the Germans had bombarded us, only to be kept out by a characteristic last line. Their solitary success was futile as far as the result was concerned but, at last, they had managed to get something past a typically great British goalkeeper. For a German or any foreign crowd, this was worth celebrating.

Chapter 2

More Flash *than* Harry

My dad had played in goal when he was at school: 'Always good with my own company,' he said. From a country family of seven brothers, his two nearest in age died very young and he was used to getting on with things on his own. At the age of eight he suffered paralysis and nearly died from what people came to believe was polio. Over a period of weeks he fought a lone and fevered battle with the question of whether he was to drop off this mortal coil. The family and the town doctor didn't expect him to survive. When he did, by their and his own reckoning, he had been those few yards beyond normal experience.

He liked goalkeeping for its occasional spectacular moments. At such times you went through the air knowing you were going to save what, to teammates and opposition alike, was an unstoppable shot bound for the corner of your net. The coordination of mind and body was enough to make you smile, even laugh, as you experienced it. But, overall, it was best not to flaunt things. They had to be done properly; in other words, not overdone. The best keepers were 'spectacular but safe'.

In British goalkeeping, the first half of the 1930s was the era of Harry Hibbs of Birmingham City. Over five years Harry won twenty-five caps for England, seeing off all challengers for the position. He presided over a period which consolidated the British tradition of goalkeeping, and one which built on foundations laid by two keepers whose heyday just preceded his own. The weighty *Encyclopaedia of Sport* I received one Christmas, published by Messrs Sampson Low, Marston and Co. for the children of the kingdom, dominions and empire, cast its magisterial gaze back some forty years to pronounce that 'among the greatest of all time' was Sam Hardy of Liverpool and Aston Villa. Hardy had been England's goalkeeper before and after the First World War and had a gift of calm judgement. As the opposition bore down on his goalmouth he was 'invariably in position when the shot was made'.

When Hardy was transferred to Aston Villa in 1912, he was succeeded at Liverpool by Elisha Scott, from the north of Ireland. Scott 'was strangely like him' and 'positioned well'. Over seventeen seasons to 1936 he played in thirty-one internationals, a number restricted because united Irish and (after partition) Northern Irish teams played games only within the British Isles. But Scott's appearances remained a record till the Spurs captain and half-back Danny Blanchflower outnumbered them in 1958, when Northern Ireland teams were travelling the continent and playing in World Cups. In Scott's time there was no need to travel for his skills to be put to the sternest test. 'At times he defied the might of England single-handed', said my encyclopaedia. There were few greater laurels it could have tossed at the man. British keepers were expected to be a match for the world; to defy England took something really special.

Both Hardy and Scott had another factor in common which qualified them for the ranks of the greatest. This was that they made no obvious claim for the title. They carried out their goalkeeping in a serious manner, motivated by the ideal of avoiding anything remotely extroverted. Much of Hardy's brilliance lay in the fact that he was 'hardly noticed on the field'. He was 'as unspectacular in goal as he was quiet and modest off it'. Scott, too, was 'modest and quiet' with 'nothing of the showman about him'.

Their way was in contrast to the keeper at the top of the profession in the period before them. At the turn of the century, the confidence of Victorian empire-building had swollen out of control in the shape of Billy 'Fatty' Foulke. Tall for his time at 6 feet or so, Foulke weighed in across a scale of 20–24 stone. In his career for Sheffield United, Chelsea and England, Foulke threw and otherwise put himself about, intimidating opponents and authorities alike. He stormed after referees to hammer on their dressing-room doors, if decisions had not gone his way. An increasingly bloated figure, his retirement was blessedly timed for Britain's approach to the First World War. Hardy and Scott provided the mould of those going to fight it. Millions filed into the trenches of France and Belgium to stand and wait, and to be 'invariably in position when the shot was made'. Sam and Elisha dutifully served the cause of being the first of the type: the British keeper as the goalmouth's humble 'custodian'.

Harry Hibbs followed in their stead, unflappably pursuing a one-club league and Cup career of over 400 games. His first international came in 1930, the year after some shocks to the system. As if the Wall Street Crash was not enough, England's first defeat abroad deepened the depression. It was one thing to be beaten by the Scots – twenty-four times between 1872 (when the first match between the two countries was staged) and 1929 made this reasonably common; it was quite novel to be humbled by the 'continentals'. In the game we had invented, Spain did the dirty, 4–3 in Madrid. This was equivalent to bullfighting's finest rolling up at Wembley from the *estancias* of Castille, to be humiliated by a squad of upstart *toreros* from the backstreets of Huddersfield. Previous English excursions abroad had been mainly confined to taking the steamer across the Channel to France or Belgium. We took our own matchballs to counter the likelihood of foreign jiggery-pokery. How the Spaniards had won the match was a source of national perplexity.

Hibbs was cannily suited to handle the uncertainties of the epoch, a man to lift the spirit by steadying the nerves. My encyclopaedia approved his style as a subtle variation from that commended by my father. Harry was 'safe rather than spectacular'. At 5 feet 9 inches, 'on the short side for a goalkeeper', he compensated by refining the brilliance of Sam Hardy to still higher levels. Hibbs was not just in position for assaults on his goal, but in the only possible position: 'He gave the impression that forwards were shooting straight at him.'

There was something very British about this knack. It was a natural detachment from the turmoil that enabled ultimate control of it. Britain in the 1930s had withdrawn into itself, in an understated, poor man's version of the old and sensible glories of 'Splendid Isolation'. As Harry Hibbs surveyed the scene from his goalmouth, the nation observed gathering continental chaos. Hitler and Mussolini strutted and pranced around. Britain did not have the faintest idea what to do. This could not be easily admitted, least of all to ourselves, so it was important to conjure up the sense of a nation being quietly 'there', in the right place should the need arise. Hibbs personified the being there. Like Britain, he was also particularly good whenever required to face the strutters and prancers. Harry's skills were most marked, said my encyclopaedia, 'against a continental side which included a showy keeper'.

This was possibly a reference to the Spanish goalkeeper, Ricardo Zamora, whom Hibbs and England came up against at Highbury in 1931. Revenge for the defeat two years earlier was duly extracted to the tune of a resounding 7–1. Zamora, who came with the reputation of being world-class, had a miserable game. What prompted more ridicule was the news that he earned £50 a week, compared with Hibbs's wage of £8 during the season and £6 in the summer break. But the implication that the England keeper was always at his best against a showy continental was stretching the point. His better games were not abroad. He was more comfortable at home, closer to base, something which was reflected in his style of play. In keeping with the times, Harry was not one to advance happily beyond his goalkeeper's area and into the broader reaches of the penalty box. By and large, he stuck firmly to his line.

In Hibbs's protective shadow, a new breed was emerging. Its members were obliged to display the classical certainties of the tradition, yet felt able to add a touch of goalkeeping rococo. In Glasgow, Jack Thomson of Celtic made his reputation when Scottish keepers were expected to be no less soberly dignified than those south of the border. 'There was little time for drama and histrionics,' said local writer Hugh Taylor. The keeper who tried to invest his game with colour was regarded with deep-rooted suspicion, he added, and had as much chance of a successful career 'as a bank clerk who went to work in sports jacket and flannels'.

Thomson could twist and change direction in midair. He also applied an extra thrust to his dives, to reach shots which would have been beyond others. This gift was compared to the hitch-kick later used by Jesse Owens, which won him the long-jump gold medal and world record in Berlin. All this, of course, could only be employed when the need for something spectacular arose. Thomson's talent was not confined to his agility. As Taylor noted, he held rather than punched or parried the hardest of shots and there was no keeper more reliable. He 'inspired tremendous confidence in the men in front of him, always watching play, combining rare, natural talent with a mathematical precision that took so many risks out of his often hazardous art'. Tragically, not all of them. He was a regular for Scotland, with eight caps by the age of twenty-two, but was killed in 1931 after diving and fracturing his skull at the feet of a Rangers forward at Ibrox Park.

Other young keepers who struck a popular chord followed. In 1932, Manchester City signed Frank Swift, aged seventeen. Goalkeeper for the third team, he was on ten shillings a week, so thought it financially wise to retain his job as coke-keeper at Blackpool gasworks. When City reached the 1933 Cup Final, he and a mate with a motor-cycle drove down to watch. Big for the time at 6 feet 2 inches and 13 stone 7 pounds, Swift squeezed into the sidecar. They left in the middle of the night in order to make the trip and, in the rain, managed to go off the road only once. Manchester City were more easily brushed aside, 3–0 by Everton. Swift soon found himself promoted in City's pecking order of keepers and, on £1 a week, able to give up the gasworks. He made his debut for the first team on Christmas Day. When he was knocked out early on by the opposition centre-forward, his trainer brought him round by mistakingly spilling half a bottle of smelling salts down his throat. But in the months after, it was injury to the regular first-team keeper that left Swift in line for selection, as City won their way through to the Cup Final again in 1934. As the time approached to face this year's opponents, Portsmouth, the prospect left him on top of the world one moment, he said, the next in fits of despondency. He told himself he was far too young to be playing at Wembley. With a 'terrible, sinking feeling', he saw the team sheet go up, with his name at the top of it.

He aimed to go to bed early the night before the game but

shared a room with his team captain, Sam Cowan, who sat bathing a poisoned big toe in a bowl of hot water. Cowan kept him talking till 3 a.m. Swift reckoned later this was to make him sleep late and have less time for pre-match nerves. They got the better of him in the Wembley dressing room. The sight of a jittery senior player having to have his laces tied, he said, turned him green. The trainer hauled Swift off to the washroom, gave him a slap round the face and a tot of whisky. He made it through the parade on to the pitch and presentation to George V. Just after the game started, Matt Busby, Manchester City's right-half, turned, shouted and passed back to him, to give him an early feel of the ball and calm him down.

Portsmouth scored after half an hour, for which Swift blamed himself. There'd been a brief shower of rain, which normally would have prompted him to put his gloves on. But he'd peered up the other end to see Portsmouth's keeper had left his in the back of the net. Not trusting his own judgement, Swift did, too, and paid for it when a shot across him from the right slithered through his fingers as he dived. In the dressing room at half-time, the Manchester City centre-forward, Fred Tilson, told Swift to stop looking so miserable about it. Tilson added he'd score twice in the second half, which he did. The second came with only four minutes to go. Suddenly Swift, aged nineteen, realised he might be on the point of winning a Cup Final.

The photographers sitting at the side of his goal began to count down the minutes and seconds for him. Seeing how tense he was, they may have been trying to be helpful. Equally, men of Fleet Street, they might have had their minds on the story. Swift started to lose control of his with about one minute remaining. With fifty seconds left he was thinking of his mother and if the Cup would take much cleaning. At forty seconds he worried whether the king would talk to him. At thirty seconds, Matt Busby smashed the ball into the crowd to waste time and a photographer shouted, 'It's your Cup, son'. As the whistle went he stooped to get his cap and gloves from the net, took a couple of steps out of it and 'everything went black'.

Swift was the favourite of millions of young fans thereafter. Among them was my dad, listening to the game on the wireless. He was to leave school at the end of that term, a month before his fourteenth birthday. For Swift at nineteen to be in a cup-winning team was enough in itself to make him a Kids' Own hero. His faint in the Wembley goalmouth only heightened this. Though he was a virtual Superboy of the day, he showed himself vulnerable to pressure like anyone else, a big kid after all. Laid out on the turf, he was brought round by cold water poured on his face and dabbed by the trainer's sponge. He was helped to his feet and limped across the pitch and up the steps to the Royal Box to get his medal from George V. The king spoke to him through what Swift described as a 'dizzy mist' and, at greater length than was customary, asked how he was, told him he played well and wished him good luck. The king sent a message the following week, via the Lord Lieutenant of the County of Lancashire, inquiring after Swift's health.

Throughout his career, Swift showed himself to be not only a large person, but also a large personality. He'd turn and wave to the crowd, acknowledge their shouts, even chat if the ball was at the other end. He applied an occasional flourish to his leaps or dives for the crowd's benefit. These were 'flash', though within limits. A dive when you could keep your feet, or a punch when a catch was feasible, was not the thing. Swift's principle, however, was that as long as it was safe, where was the harm in the bit of extra for effect?

Among British keepers, Swift pioneered the skills of throwing the ball, something he'd picked up from watching water polo. Crowds tended to feel short-changed by a keeper doing anything but clearing the ball out of his penalty area with a hefty boot. But Swift had enormous strength and huge hands – the length of the average person's foot – with which he could pick up or catch a ball single-handed. He'd hurl it over half the length of the pitch, and guide it far more accurately than could be accomplished with a hopeful punt. An extrovert character, it was one of the ways he imposed himself on the game. Swift was generally good at making himself known, not least to referees whose decisions he felt unable to go along with. Against the football hierarchy, he also became a vociferous campaigner for players' wages and conditions.

After his Cup medal, Swift's club career reached another peak when Manchester City won the league in 1937. Runners-up were Charlton Athletic, whose goalkeeper, Sam Bartram, had a similar personality and style. Not quite of Swift's physical dimensions, he was a tall and broad, red-haired character, who indulged in the flamboyant when opportunity arose. Much thanks to him, Charlton had climbed in successive seasons from the Third Division South, through the Second, to challenge for the First Division title itself. Swift and Bartram were identified as future rivals for a place in the England team and at one stage Bartram appeared the most likely contender. The season after Charlton ran Manchester City closely for the championship, he played for the Possibles against the Probables in an England trial.

Swift and Bartram had been born within weeks of each other a little before the start of the First World War. From, respectively, the industrial north-west and north-east, they grew up in regions feeling the worst of the post-war recession. The country's mood was also steeped in memories of one awful conflict and the strengthening conviction that a worse one was on the way. The Great War had had the wonders of the trenches and 'going over the top'; everyone knew the next war would bid goodbye to all that with mass aerial bombardment of the cities. Swift and Bartram were products of the widely-held view among ordinary people that there was little sane reaction but to laugh, make the best of it and pretend the worst was not going to happen. If ever the laughter had to be prompted a little, there were always characters around like Swift and Bartram to help its orchestration. Vaudeville keepers in their way, they played in response to popular demand.

In any of their off-duty pictures I later saw – team photos, head-and-shoulders portraits, or shots of them being introduced to one dignitary or another before a big game – they were always at least smiling. In accounts of their matches that I read or was told about, their presence dominated. Each was likely to rush from the keeper's 6-yard box, to the edge or beyond the penalty area to clear the ball, forsaking their hands and heading it if necessary. This was a way of doing things much more familiar to keepers on the continent. It brought the keeper out of his remote condition and into closer touch with his team. Both Swift and Bartram were students of the style of Harry Hibbs – now nearing the end of his career – and sought advice from him on how it was all meant to be done. But notes taken, they moved far beyond the role of humble 'custodian'.

Two weeks after my dad's nineteenth birthday the war was declared, an occasion as stressful at that age as playing in the Cup Final. After listening to Chamberlain's announcement, he went out in the back garden where his dad grew the vegetables and, as the phrase has it, broke down. His father followed and tried to help: 'That's OK, son, there's nothing to worry about,' he might have offered. 'I passed through the Menin Gate and the various battles of Ypres. Nasty explosion at the Somme, of course, and this open hip wound still plays up. But I survived – when most of the Beds and Herts were wiped out, they made me sergeant major for a day till reinforcements arrived.' But, in that moment, my Bedfordshire grandfather opted to stay quiet.

For two years my father's bricklaying had him on such essential works as building the Tempsford aerodrome. A Stuka came for a few minutes one afternoon and strafed the hundred or so of them working up the sheer face of the cooling towers at Barford. The bombing of London had prompted my mum's move to the country and they got married after he was called up into the Royal Signals. In Greenock he and several thousand others were put on ships which sailed west almost as far as Iceland. They weren't told where they were going, up to the point the boats turned to plunge south. Through the Bay of Biscay the weather was so rough the convoy's members were rarely in sight of each other. Maybe the conditions were a problem for the German U-boats as well. The next convoy out a fortnight or so later lost a third of its number. My dad's 'never saw a seagull'. Straight, more or less, from Sandy, Bedfordshire, he arrived at the Saharan fringes of North Africa, landing with the army in Algiers in 1942.

Across Algeria and Tunisia, the task of pushing back Rommel and his Afrika Korps allowed little opportunity for football or any other game but was carried out in a spirit not seen elsewhere in the war. The British troops viewed Rommel as a 'good bloke', a German but a fair one. This marked him as a man apart from the madness of his Nazi teammates. It didn't mean whatever wit and cunning the 'Desert Fox' had could match ours. Near the Tunisian coastal town of La Goulette, shortly before my dad sailed from Cap Bon for Italy, he watched thousands of captured Germans march into their prison camp. This they did in immaculate order, seemingly perfectly according to character. Then they fell into weird nights behind the wire, when their mood alternated between crazed merriment and near riot.

The British army's attitude to the enemy appeared to be as much a worry to the top brass, even after the Germans had been defeated in Africa and the Sicily landings completed. Maybe the official view was that the soldiers' achievements might go to their heads. My dad's company was called together in the almond grove where they were camped near Syracuse and, in line with a War Office directive, bawled out for their apparent misconceptions about Rommel. Not that they took a great deal of notice; there had to be some lone symbol of decency even in the worst of worlds.

All in all, my father said, he was lucky. His brother Reg was sent to Burma. At Kohima the British were besieged for weeks, separated by the width of the High Commissioner's tennis court from the Japanese screaming at them on the other side. My uncle had injured mates pleading with him to shoot them and put them out of their misery. He was lying wounded in a makeshift hospital himself when the Japanese stormed it at one door and caught up with him after he'd got out the other. Injured by a bayonet thrust, he feigned death in the long grass.

In comparison, the Royal Signals was a doddle. My father had to master Morse Code and spent much of the day tapping it out. He'd applied for the Royal Engineers, thinking it wanted people from the building industry. In relief, when that came to nothing, his dad explained he'd have been constructing Bailey bridges across rivers and repairing phone lines in no man's land, under what the army liked to refer to as 'hot fire'.

But events had a way of springing themselves upon you, pulling you suddenly in. You had to beware of the unguarded moment. The German attack on Bari harbour in December 1943 came when we had got 'too cocky' and confident of victory. Everyone saw the single German spotter plane circling very high and watched the anti-aircraft fire chase it away. They thought no more about it till at night the aerial assault came in. The harbour was floodlit; the twenty-boat convoy, recently arrived was being unloaded. Two ammunition carriers went up and took fourteen other ships with them. One explosion, like the crack of a large whip, threw my dad 15 feet across his room, door and windows with him; this was 6 miles away along the coast in Santo Spirito. 'A chance hit,' wrote Churchill, '30,000 tons of cargo lost.' He didn't mention the thousand killed among the Italian dockyard workers, merchant seamen and Allied military personnel. In the yard next morning victims, dead and alive, had turned yellow. The medics had no idea for days what they were dealing with, till word went around that General Eisenhower had ordered a consignment of mustard gas. Not that we'd have used it without cause, mind you. We just had it in case the Germans used it first.

During a plague of typhus in Caserta, north of Naples, my dad's unit was billeted in the abandoned royal palace, with its water cascades and hanging gardens, while for several weeks the Allied advance was held up by the battles for the monastery at Montecassino. Driving through the streets in a truck, he saw an old man fall over and die. Some soldiers who ventured out on the town in their free time suffered the same fate. Sometimes there was nothing to be done, except withdraw, observe and wonder what it was that made such things go on in the world. A degree of separation, if there was a choice, afforded a perspective that was lost on the unthinking crowd. On Piazzale Loretto in Milan, he saw the bodies of Mussolini and his mistress hanging from their heels and urinated on by an angry mob. Weeks before, the same crowd might have been cheering them.

After the war, soldiers rarely volunteered their recollections. They only came out over the years. Experiences had either been too awful, mundane or similar to those of many others to merit earlier mention. Besides, the cities at home had had the bombs. Even Sandy High Street was machine-gunned by a German fighter, my nan having to launch herself into a shop doorway with baby and pram. Anyone who went on about moments they had endured abroad in face of the enemy, or how many of them they'd injured or killed, would have been a suspect personality. Few, too, were asked. Until prompted, my dad said little more than he had seen the eruption of Vesuvius, from Caserta, filling the sky with black smoke for three weeks in March 1944. As in the time of Pompeii, the prior impression had been that it was extinct. Further north in Siena he began to learn Italian by walking out from the city's fort and reciting door numbers. He came home speaking the language well, one among very few of the quarter of a million Allied soldiers in Italy to do so.

Talking about the football, rather than the war, was easier. Games were played between stages of the Allied advance up the Italian leg. My father played in goal for 15th Army Group HQ and was nicknamed 'Flash', though only, he insisted, after his white blond hair. You changed in barracks or tents and, if playing away, went by army truck. Match locations ranged from the landing strip in Syracuse, to Rome's Dei Marmi stadium, encircled by statues of emperors and gods. In the Comunale stadium in Florence, England were to draw 1–1 some seven years later and maintain their unbeaten record against Italy. In Bologna, my dad occupied the goal where David Platt volleyed the last-minute winner past Preud'homme of Belgium in the 1990 World Cup. His reports of the games he played in suggest he'd have probably saved it.

As for the spectacular moments, the most memorable was reserved for when the army had moved far north to the Yugoslav border to fend off Tito's claim to Trieste. It was made in the small stadium in Monfalcone, on a baked-earth goalmouth full of large stones. A brisk advance by the opposition down the right-wing forced him to cover his front post. But the ball swung over to the fast-advancing centre-forward, who volleyed it hard towards the far corner. A Liverpudlian, naturally vocal, the centre-forward was shouting for a goal from the moment he hit it. My dad made it across the full 8 yards of his goal, diving to push the ball away with his right hand. The save was unique in anyone's recollection, though others may have emulated it since.

Immediate thoughts of self-congratulation were tempered by the impact of the goalmouth surface on his knees. As my dad pulled himself up in pain, his opponent – driven by a fit of frustrated expectation and Adriatic sun – rushed in, yelling and hammering him with his fists around the shoulders and head. This incident was 'comical', which left me with the impression goalkeepers were not averse to gaining pleasure from the annoyance of others. But they also performed an important public service. Contrary to a common prejudice that it was keepers who, by virtue of their role and isolation, were insane, they showed that it was out there, in the wider, collective world, where madness was to be found.

o o o

At the start of the war, Frank Swift had signed up as a special constable in Manchester. He was put to directing city traffic, an ill-advised move, since his presence was more likely to attract a crowd than clear it. One congested day on Market Street, with his efforts achieving nothing, he waved a cheery 'bugger this' and went home. Like many top footballers, he became a trainer to younger soldiers who were about to be shipped abroad. My dad was trained by Roy Goodall, the Huddersfield Town and England half-back, and passed out as a PT instructor. This qualified him for a comfortable home assignment in one military gym or another but before one arose he was *en route* for Africa. Again, he said, he was fortunate. Many of the younger trainers who were at first kept back from service abroad, found themselves later pitched on to the beaches at Normandy.

Football at home ticked over, with teams raised from whoever was on hand on any given Saturday. Sam Bartram played in two successive wartime Cup Finals, one for Charlton, the other as a guest for Millwall. As the war moved towards conclusion, opportunity arose to put on exhibition matches for the troops abroad. Victory in Europe was on the point of being declared as my dad's unit progressed to Florence, when it was announced Frank Swift was due in town. He was to play for a team led by Joe Mercer, the Everton half-back, against that of Wolves captain, Stan Cullis. It was to be an occasion for great celebration, till on the morning of the game, my dad and fellow signalmen were told to pack their kit and advance up country to Bologna. VE Day was an anti-climax. Each soldier was issued two bottles of beer, which he and his mates poured over their heads: 'Bloody stupid, really.'

Full international games were under way at home more than a year later. It was obvious to many that the choice for the England keeper lay between Swift and Bartram. In conversation their names were mentioned in the same breath. Yet, in an era when the average forty-year-old didn't have a tooth to talk of, at thirty-two they weren't young. The England selectors had dallied with the idea of jumping a goalkeeping generation. Ted Ditchburn of Tottenham Hotspur, ten years younger, was the object of their attention. He had played well in big wartime games against Scotland and Wales, which suggested he was in for a promising international career. Unfortunately for Ditchburn, the Royal Air

Force thought so as well. When he was posted to the Far East for two years, the selectors' hand was forced. By default as much as instinct, they tossed the keeper's yellow jersey, undersized for the part, into the huge grasp of Frank Swift.

He played commandingly in the first seventeen internationals after the war. For two, he was selected as England's first goal-keeping captain. What he described as his own greatest day was when he led the team against Italy in May 1948. Originally England were to play Czechoslovakia but after February's communist coup in Prague, the fixture was rearranged. The team went by air from Northolt, a dozen journalists in tow, among them former players like Charles Buchan, ex-Scotland and Arsenal and then of the *News Chronicle*. The mode of transport, however, was sufficiently novel for the *Daily Herald*'s man to opt to go by boat and train. The weather deteriorated over Switzerland, where the captain felt it necessary to stop and change planes. Swift described the rest of the journey over the Alps in a twin-engined Dakota as a 'bit of a snorter' and said he wasn't the only passenger relieved to get off again.

The match was on Juventus's ground in Turin. World Cup holders from before the war and in front of their own 85,000 crowd, the Italians were expected to win. While England had given themselves three days to prepare, the home team had been under-going three weeks' intensive training. Continentals clearly took this kind of thing very seriously. Furthermore, where England's training in Stresa was open to view, recorded Swift, Italy's was 'at a mountain hideout'. In the England dressing room, there was no concealing the pre-match tension: 'We knew what we were up against and changed quietly.' Come the moment, Swift was unable to find the words for a captain's speech of encouragement. Instead, each member of the team filed past and shook his hand.

Outside all was turmoil: loudspeaker announcements, with adverts and exhortations to the crowd, aeroplanes promoting everything from newspapers to cordials, and others swooping low over the pitch with cameramen on board shooting the scene. Hordes more photographers joined Swift in the middle for the toss. 'Some standing on ladders, which they toted across the field, some lying on their stomachs,' he said, 'all of them arguing and gesticulating.'

England's response to the apparent anarchy was to score almost immediately. Stan Mortensen raced to the byline and beat the Italian keeper Bacigalupo from what seemed an impossible angle. This was to the 'astonishment and chagrin' of the crowd, said Swift, which prompted their team to storm back. 'For twenty minutes they threw everything at us with bewildering inter-passing and brilliant speed.' Shots, overhead kicks, headers, the lot 'flew at me from all directions'. Probably the most startling was from the Italian centre-forward, Gabetto. Eight yards out, he didn't turn or take aim but back-headed the ball. A British keeper couldn't have anticipated that kind of thing and the surprise and speed of it beat Swift. The ball hit his crossbar and bounced down just in front of the line, near enough to have the crowd screaming at the referee to give a goal. When play switched to the other end, Swift invited one of the photographers crowding behind the net to step around into the goalmouth so he could show him where the ball had landed. The fellow accepted the offer and quickly took a photo of the spot. His colleagues would have followed, said Swift, if the Italians hadn't been straight back on the attack.

The England captain stopped everything he had to, though handed the compliments to his team. His defence was 'rock-like', not least Jack Howe of Derby County in his first international, 'and incidentally the first man to play for England wearing contact lenses over his eyes'. By contrast he was sniffy about the Italian defenders, who sometimes 'indulged in acrobatic antics while clearing the ball'. England's forwards left the Italians dumbfounded with their simplicity of approach, namely the way they cracked the ball into the net with first-time volleys and after quick one-pass movements. But most of the honours won from England's near incredible 4–0 victory went to Swift. It was acknowledged as his finest game in the finest England performance ever. Hitherto there was no question that Britain had the finest keepers in the world. In Turin Swift proved to be the finest yet seen.

The England selectors may even have agreed at the time. But it didn't take them long to think again. The following season, little more than six months later, Swift was dropped. He competed for his place with Ted Ditchburn for a couple of games but, soon after, seemed to have been overcome by the affront to his pride. He stood down not only from the England line-up, but from football altogether.

The decision to drop him could have been put down to the passing years but it was not so much Swift's age, more his style that was cracking on. The selectors were an aged crew themselves, a panel of half a dozen or so club directors or other luminaries from the football establishment. There was a picture of one of them, Arthur Drewry, in my encyclopaedia. He had the brushed-back grey hair, nervous smile and starched collar look of a Neville Chamberlain. He and his colleagues sat in learned committees, their anxiously awaited, often haphazard and mysterious decisions worthy of a puff of smoke when finally revealed. But they did what they believed was for the good of the game and chose those whom they felt were the right type.

Before the war, Swift had never been considered ready for the England team, yet he was the national character for the moment. He had acknowledged that the pressures of life were enough to get anyone down but embodied the spirit of 'get up and get on with it'. He, as much as any popular figure, symbolised the people 'smiling through'. Swift waved and laughed to each member of the crowd. To those going off to Africa, Sicily, Normandy, or wherever, this said, 'It'll be all right, son'. They didn't know it would, but it was the best they had. With luck, and the right distance between them and the explosion when it came, they might even survive to get their medals from the king.

For my father and the other soldiers in Florence, Swift was to arrive almost at the very moment of victory. In person, not just in spirit, he was going to be on hand to begin the celebrations with them. Swift's team won 11–0, so no one would have seen him do much goalkeeping. But you could bet when the ball was up the other end, he'd have been turning to chat with the squaddies behind his goal. My dad said it took him several years to get over the disappointment of missing that game.

Still, Frank's elevation to the England team meant he was on hand for the party back home. As the returning soldiers ejected Churchill from Downing Street, so they went to be entertained by Swift between the posts. As a keeper able to put on a show, there was no one more perfect for the occasion. Long after Swift retired, my father and anyone who spoke about him continued to do so in terms which raised him to the status of a giant and friendly god, who made you hardly able to believe your luck that he was on your side.

By the time I heard about Swift, revision of the record had been going on for a while. My encyclopaedia made what sounded like noises of approval, yet didn't throw its compliments around. Swift was 'massive' and had 'exceptional height and reach', features which represented no great achievement on his part. Harry Hibbs, after all, had not enjoyed such natural advantages. Swift was also 'likeable'. There had been nothing to say whether Hibbs, Hardy and Scott had been likeable – or even whether to be likeable was a good thing. They were no doubt the soul of decency as people but their virtue as keepers was in their hardly being noticed. With Frank there was little chance of that and here lay the problem. 'Swift might have been the greatest goalkeeper of all time,' intoned the encyclopaedia, 'but for a tendency to showmanship.'

He had been great for the fleeting post-war moment of celebration but deemed inappropriate for the dour times which set in. People were expected to get back to where they'd been. Women from the Naafi or the Land Army – like my mum's sister, Olive, who'd driven a tractor, worked with the Italian prisoners in Sandy, and even had an Italian boyfriend – were wanted back in the home. Men were required in the jobs that would reconstruct the nation. Men and women were wanted back in stable relationships; *Brief Encounter* urged them to forget their little flings. Everyone had to knuckle down to austerity. With a large part of the harvest being sent to Germany, there was bread rationing, something that hadn't happened throughout the war.

Abroad it was all going haywire. India demanded and gained independence. This was serious, although in the popular mind explained by the usual muddle-mindedness of foreigners – the 'half-naked fakirs in loin-cloths' that Churchill referred to. Really threatening was that the Russians had the Bomb. When Moscow Dynamo had come to tour Britain a few months after the war it was amid great public excitement. They met Rangers in Glasgow, with demand to see them so high that tickets priced at three and sixpence were touted for as much as £1 outside the ground; 90,000 people crowded into Ibrox for the 2–2 draw. But the Russians' tour had transmitted early signals of suspicion. They said there weren't enough flags, flowers and music to greet them. In London they wouldn't sleep in the guards' barracks they were given saying the beds were too hard. (How soft had the feather mattresses been during the siege of Leningrad?) They decamped to the Soviet embassy. Churchill spoke of the Iron Curtain descending from the Baltic to 'Trieste on the Adriatic'. Churchill made his speech in the USA, among friends; his mother was American. But the USA wasn't on our side over the empire, not least when Palestine broke up and Israel emerged. They wanted us out, for the 'freedom' of others, and to slip in themselves. We were being pushed back again. These weren't Swiftian times to be bouncing around gleefully off your line.

When Swift was dropped from the England team, his response was, in character, more dramatic than it strictly needed to be. A little more than a year after his greatest international game, he retired. Manchester City could not believe he was giving up and kept him registered for another five years to ensure he didn't play for another team. But he sought more security than was possible in football. A giant of a keeper, he went off to be a sales rep, for Smallman's the Manchester confectioners.

He, at least, had relished his international career. His old rival, Sam Bartram, did not win the honour. The general view was that he was kept out of the England team by Swift's brilliance. Then, when Frank was being lined up for replacement, it was easy to pass over Sam as too old. But short of his one appearance for England Possibles, he had not been in with much of a chance. Near deified by the fortnightly 60,000 or so who turned up to enjoy his performances at the Valley, Bartram never overcame the objections of those who watched in judgement. He was condemned by them as too sensational and for playing to the gallery. His bravery in the way he threw himself at forwards' feet – normally a commendable feature of a keeper's game – earned him the criticism of being a 'danger to football'.

I heard my dad talking with his brother Reg about Bartram by the coal fire in the waiting room on Sandy station. My uncle was seeing us off after one of our monthly weekend visits – dismal night, the late Sunday train, with a probable change at Hitchin or Three Counties. Bartram was good for times like this. My uncle recalled a game against Birmingham City near the end of his career when he had left his goal to take a penalty. He ran non-stop from his own area to hit the ball, which struck the crossbar with such force that he had to chase hilariously back again after it. Sam was a great laugh like that, the shame being the selectors couldn't see the joke.

In Swift and Bartram the selectors may have noticed something like the unruly ghost of 'Fatty' Foulke looming from the grave. Swift they had gone along with as an exception to the desirable rule. To have sanctioned a second showman would have risked established tradition. Protective of the nation's sterner values, Bartram was where they drew the line. He had to get by with the unofficial title of 'England's greatest uncapped keeper'. He played till 1956, by when he was forty-two. At the Valley they named a set of gates after him. Seeking a living, like Swift, out of the English love of humbug and sherbet lemons, he ran a sweet shop and tried football management, without huge success.

I got his autograph on the platform forecourt of St Pancras station on a Saturday morning when he was manager of Luton Town. Had Luton been a big, as opposed to Fourth Division, club, this wouldn't have been possible. The station would have been alive with big kids who pursued the signatures of the stars and gave any younger kids present a hard time. Bartram was tall, with a big face, wrinkled forehead and wave of sandy hair. He signed my book in front of the cafeteria, as his team grabbed cheese rolls and cups of tea before taking a train somewhere north for their afternoon game. I was aware that here was the man who had been Frank Swift's chief rival, England's greatest uncapped keeper. Not so long ago, that had made him one of the finest in the world, and I was surprised more people in the St Pancras steam and grime didn't give some sign that they recognised him. He was the type who'd have happily called and waved back.

C h a p t e r 3

In Swift's Succession

The Swift succession played to an unprecedented audience. More than 41 million fans attended the stadiums of the nation in the 1948/9 season. Most of them were prepared to stand on exposed and crumbling terraces for the sake of an afternoon's entertainment and they established a record that would never be beaten. With so many potentially critical eyes on them, the England selectors replaced Frank Swift by stages. In discreet British fashion, they dropped a hint here and there to prepare the crowd.

Putting Ted Ditchburn of Tottenham Hotspur between the England posts represented a return to reality. He was in Swift's commanding physical mould at just under 6 feet 2 inches, but his style was different. Ditchburn, fearless and agile, generally did not embellish things. He was solid, consistent and, as such, more within the tradition.

A year and a bit younger than my father, he was of the generation that came to maturity in the war and had to become serious while still very young. There was no time for any of the old inter-war mood of trying to put the bad times behind you – they were on you before you knew it. Ditchburn came from Gillingham near the naval dockyards of the Medway and had volunteered for the Royal Air Force at the start of the war when he was eighteen. Younger keepers gave a new edge to the question of fitness. It was not something you had for the sake of your game or personal pride, but a matter of national necessity. Physical Training became such a high priority that it crossed the frontiers of fanaticism as PT boys were rolled off the wartime production line. Ted Ditchburn was the first of them to occupy the England goal.

Off the field at Spurs he was the players' representative, at a time when there was talk of a strike for wages higher than the going rate of about £10. The club board threatened to put amateurs in the team. But Ditchburn was not one for ill-discipline or unchannelled aggression. He had a talent for boxing. It went with being a PT boy. If you were expert on ropes and wall bars, likely as not you could handle yourself with your fists. When done properly, it was a fine individualist art – its rules had been laid down by the gentry – which stood you in good stead against the instincts of the mob. It had for my dad when cornered by a bunch of yobs by the Roman arena in Verona. They were yelling the usual stuff about 'British troops go home' and edging in. So he put up an orthodox guard, left paw well forward ready to jab the first to make a move, and shouted back in Italian that they should keep coming. Good-in-a-crowd types, they backed off. Ted Ditchburn could have been a boxer, like his father had been, but he chose football and played his first game for Spurs in 1941.

Ditchburn's military record contained an important element of sacrifice. On the verge of regular international selection, he'd been sent to India in 1944 when the call came for a dozen PTIs – physical training instructors, or so it was thought. He arrived to find the need was for Parachute Training Instructors. Once there he had to stay for two years, thus giving up the opportunity of individual honour and playing for his country for the relatively mundane duties which went with serving it. He returned to find someone else had his place in the team, but didn't sulk and went out and played well week after week for his club. Ditchburn was made of the right material.

Fog in north Islington meant his international debut against Switzerland at Highbury had to be postponed for a day. A 6–0 victory was duly recorded the following afternoon. My dad's youngest brother, Bim, who was eighteen and came down from

Sandy by train for all the internationals, said all the action was around the Swiss keeper's goalmouth. While the fans were fired by the moment, Ted Ditchburn had nothing to do.

It was logical to give him another run out in the side, a proper opportunity to show his international worth. For the time being, however, the selectors didn't feel they had another one available. The function of matches like that against the Swiss was to help plug the gaps between the truly important international games. These were the home championship contests, between ourselves, the British, playing our game. Scotland were the chief opponents, but Wales and Ireland could never be taken for granted. Their players, with few exceptions, played in the English league, the 'finest in the world'. Foreign international teams were brought over for the delectation of the masses, the fun part of a bread and circuses exercise. With the basics of daily sustenance now in such short supply, their role was all the more significant. Like Christians in the Colosseum, they provided a chance for the lions, without excessive exertion, to keep themselves in trim. No team from abroad had managed so much as a draw against England on home soil.

In the last ten games between England and Scotland either side of the war, each had won four, with two drawn. Swift was chosen, the selectors still not ready to forsake his experience and make his execution too blatant. That was largely taken care of in the match itself by the Scots keeper, Jimmy Cowan, of Greenock Morton. Few people in England had heard of him but, at Wembley and with a performance that was the highlight of his career, Scotland won 3–1. Swift, by comparison, looked jaded. He was at fault with one of the goals and injured a rib when one of the Scots forwards had the temerity to shoulder-charge him. The selectors felt more justified in replacing him.

On the 1949 post-season tour of Scandinavia, they chose Ditchburn for the reasonably stiff task of facing Sweden in Stockholm. Sweden were remembered as gold medallists at the London Olympics the year before. Nevertheless, most of them were still mainly amateurs. From undiscovered centres of foot-balling excellence like Norr- and Jönköping, Swedish players likely passed the their days as steambath masseurs and cross-country ski instructors. In four previous internationals they had not got within two goals of England.

Captain Billy Wright made the first mistake when, having won the toss, he elected to play into the setting sun. It dipped slowly below the Swedes' crossbar for much of the first half and into Ditchburn's eyes at the other end. On the high ball particularly he did not ooze confidence. Worse, as England lost 3–1, he was held to have abused that placed in him by the selectors. He had been invited into their high-risk strategy of toying with the public mood as they displaced Swift. Now they'd been embarrassed. Swift was brought back against Norway, for an easy final international of his career. Ditchburn the selectors sniffily dropped from the reckoning.

They knew they'd find support among the fans. Ditchburn's popularity on his home ground at White Hart Lane was unconditional but Swift's enormous national following would have had its fair number of sceptics whoever was replacing him. My dad's first reaction to mention of the Spurs' keeper's name was to scoff. If pressed, he would concede that Ditchburn was a 'good keeper', but given my understanding that British keepers were habitually brilliant, it followed that all of them were at least 'good'. To say so was hardly a compliment.

Spurs were top of the Second Division and the most exciting London team of the season. As well as Ditchburn, they had full-back Alf Ramsey and inside-forward Eddie Baily, both pushing for places in the national side. Ron Burgess was captain of Spurs and Wales and the year before had played left-half for Britain in their 6–1 win against the Rest of Europe. They pulled crowds of more than 50,000 to White Hart Lane fifteen times during the season. The attendance for the visit of Queens Park Rangers was 69,718. Your arms were pinned to your side, my dad said. Lift them to applaud or wave around and you wouldn't have got them down again.

The game in October was another one-sided contest in which Ditchburn had very little to do. On one occasion when he did – out of character and bored out of his mind – he jumped a little extravagantly at a shot which needed only a simple catch, and spilled the ball. Under no pressure, he retrieved it bobbling in his 6-yard area. He even put on a bit of a smile to the packed terraces. This worked well enough for the Tottenham faithful but my dad was near apoplectic. In his view, the Spurs' keeper was not only an unworthy pretender to Swift's national selection, but also a poor imitator of his style. 'He should have stuck to goalkeeping, not clowning around,' he said. 'He could never do it like Frank could.'

Spurs won but their constant attacks managed only a single goal – a lucky bounce off Baily's shin. QPR's keeper, Reg Allen, otherwise stopped everything: 'The finest display of goalkeeping seen by any man,' said my dad, adding that it finally got him over missing Swift in Florence three years earlier. Allen, a former commando, had spent four years in a harsh German prison camp, which later caused him bouts of heavy depression. He left the field at the end of the ninety minutes, to an enormous ovation from the crowd, with head bowed and an embarrassed, barely detectable smile. Manchester United bought him soon after for £10,000, the first five-figure fee paid for a keeper (inexplicably, centre-forwards were going for three times the price).

One of Allen's best moments in the match caused the crowd to surge forward for a better view. A steel barrier buckled and spectators fell in front of my father in a heap. If any more had gone down there'd have been injuries and quite possibly a disaster. But thanks to a bit of luck, and several years of army PT, he stayed on his feet. When he got back home, I'd been crying most of the afternoon and my mum had been left holding a three-month-old baby for the sake of a game of football. It was a natural enough moment to leave off watching it for a while.

o   o   o

After England's defeat in Sweden the selectors went for Bert Williams of Wolverhampton Wanderers. He had played in one wartime international while still on the books of Walsall, a Midlands club of limited ability and such uncertain geography that in the 1930s it bounced between the Third Divisions South and North. Walsall's greatest moment had distracted focus from Hitler's ascent to power. In the winter of early 1933, and within the shadow of the laundry chimney at the side of their ground, they'd taken Arsenal to the cleaners, 2–0, in the Cup. The two seasons before the war, as Williams was finding his feet in the team, Walsall had been on more familiar form and at risk of dropping out of the football league altogether.

Walsall's manager in the late 1940s was none other than Harry Hibbs. If old Harry saw something in Williams, the selectors reckoned they might, too. In his wartime international against France in 1945, he'd made a mistake in the first couple of minutes and the French had scored. But he had retained his nerve, recovered from the setback and played well in the rest of the game. Stan Cullis, returning from his role as a wartime entertainer of the troops to become manager of Wolves, bought him for £3,500 and Williams was elevated to football's top flight, the English First Division.

Blond-haired and of the same age and frame, Williams looked like my father in his army photo wearing uniform and shorts in Algiers in 1943. At the age of fifteen Williams had been only 5 feet 2 inches tall and built himself up with exercises, which included dangling by his arms from door frames. He grew 8 inches in two years. He was another PT boy, a former instructor at the same RAF camp as Ted Ditchburn. A high-class sprinter, he could speed off his goalline for crosses, or to get down at the feet of onrushing forwards. His saves were often dramatic; he covered huge distances with his dives. These midair gyrotechnics were certain to raise the spirits of a crowd, and have a similar effect on the eyebrows of the selectors. But if he wasn't their automatic choice, he had an undeniable quality. There was no doubting his seriousness.

Williams was shy and quietly spoken. In no picture I saw of him was he smiling, but since he looked like my dad I imagined he did. From Staffordshire, he lived several miles from the Wolves ground, a distance he would walk each training and match day on his toes and the balls of his feet. His reckoned that to rest back on your heels left you ill-prepared for sudden attack. He had a tortured look and masochistic edge. His training programme comprised a tireless stream of handstands and somersaults into mud. He'd round things off with a full-length dive on concrete.

Williams was the ideal compromise for the England goalkeeper's job. He had enough of what, from their varying perspectives, the selectors and fans wanted. The sharp shift from Swift to Ditchburn – triumph to reality – had been too much. Williams borrowed from both styles and was perfect for the transitional times. He mixed drama with dour necessity. He was the first keeper I heard my dad describe as 'spectacular but safe'.

The term could have applied to the country's view of itself. It was obvious to anyone with a brain that by standing alone from the fall of France to Pearl Harbor we'd saved the world but, as obviously, that Britain was no longer the dominant player. As the Russians and Americans carved up the world between them, it wasn't certain how we fitted in. But we could still lead by principled example and were still able to show the world 'a thing or two', even give the enemy 'a bloody nose'. Alert on our feet, we could get out there, sharply off our line if necessary, to save this new world from the dangers it was creating.

Bert Williams played his first full international as the Soviet Union was being persuaded to lift its siege of Berlin. For nearly a year the US air force and the new England keeper's own RAF had airlifted in water and other basic supplies in defiance of the Soviet blockade of the west of the old German capital. The Soviets had tried to strangle the place. In taking them on, we dared them to shoot us down. They didn't have the nerve, and we held ours. This was what we were like. We did the spectacular when we had to, to keep the world safe.

At the same time, the *Amethyst*, a British boat sailing up the Yangtze river in China, was fired upon and besieged for weeks by communist troops. Why it was calmly steaming through a country in midst of revolution was unclear; it was also beside the point, as the Royal Navy made repeated attempts to rescue it. Finally, it just slipped away and, under cover of darkness, got back to safety, brilliantly, as you'd expect and to rapturous cheers at home. The enemy were 'caught napping', resting back on their heels. Like Bert Williams, we wouldn't have been. We were the types prepared to dive on concrete – piece o' cake these Chinese.

Just a few days after the flop against the Swedes, Williams was drafted into the team for the season's last international. Three weeks earlier he had played in Wolves' FA Cup Final success against Leicester City. A nerveless performance in the 3–1 victory over France in Paris secured his place in the England team. It also tidily completed the otherwise messy process of the Swift succession.

The new era got off to a shaky start, however, early the following season. As with Williams's old club Walsall, the uncertainty owed something to geography. In September 1949 the Republic of Ireland came to play an international at Goodison Park, which posed the question 'Who are they?' England played Ireland every year but that was the north of the island. This team were more rarely taken on and went under the title 'Eire'. Few people knew how to pronounce it: was it 'Air', or 'Air-rer'? As it turned out, it rhymed with Eamon de Valera. Even few Irish people used the term, preferring simply 'the Republic'.

Still it was convenient in a way because it emphasised to us the foreignness of the place. For reasons best known to themselves, they had gone their own way and wanted to be different. In the war, for example, they stayed neutral even though Irish regiments fought with the British army. De Valera refused to give Churchill guarantees, my mum would recall, that German U-boats wouldn't be allowed to use Cork harbour. You never really knew where you were with them. They weren't people who stuck to clear-cut lines; the edges were always slightly blurred.

Some of their players had played for both 'Ireland' and 'Eire'. Johnny Carey, their captain, was a case in point. In the Protestant north of the island, football was played on Saturday, Sundays kept sombrely free. In the south they went about things in the chaotic-but-fun, Catholic–continental way of lumping church and football all into the Lord's day. Some Irish footballers had played for both the island's national teams in the same weekend.

Not that Eire's team was cracked up to be much. Most of them played in British league teams but back at home football came a poor third in popularity after Gaelic football and hurling. Their 1949 team was a suitably makeshift outfit. It had three goalkeepers. Tommy Godwin of Shamrock Rovers was to play between the posts on this occasion, but Con Martin upfront had also won international honours in goal, and Carey had played a league match for Manchester United when the regular keeper had cried off late before the game.

The fact that they won the match, therefore, was cause enough for English disillusion. But it went further than seeking reasons and scapegoats for the 2–0 scoreline. If this Ireland was the alien 'Eire', then England had lost their proud record of never having succumbed at home to a foreign side. Hadn't they?

The problem was deftly solved in a Celtic rather than Anglo-Saxon way. The edges were blurred and the lines made less clear-cut. Sure, weren't we all a bit Irish anyway? In my family there had been Great-great Granny Smith, with her one eye and caravan in Sandy around the turn of the century. But, fundamentally, it was noted that nine of the winning team played in the English or Scottish leagues, including both the goalscorers: Martin of Aston Villa and Peter Farrell of Everton. At Goodison Park Farrell was on his 'home' pitch. Keeper Godwin was an exception, but he soon won a transfer to Bournemouth in the Third Division South, and you could hardly get more English than that. No, whatever they were – and forget the signs in landlords' windows saying 'No dogs, Blacks or Irish' – they were not foreign. After a nasty scare, England, it was decided, had kept their home record intact.

Two months later against Italy at White Hart Lane, there were no ambiguities about the opposition's national status, but many nasty scares. In front of a 70,000 crowd – Ditchburn, ruefully, among them – it was Bert Williams's finest game. Despite the cold, misty afternoon, the Italians tiptoed through the England defence and pounded his goal. The spectators watched in amazement, the Italian players with their heads in their hands, as Williams saw them off. One shot he diverted with his legs, while diving in the opposite direction. England managed a couple of effective breakaways near the end to win 2–0, but Williams took the credit. Italian newspapers nicknamed him 'Il Gattone', 'the cat' (to be exact, 'the big cat', such had been his presence).

The performance placed Williams second only to Swift in the ratings of post-war English, and arguably British, goalkeepers for much of the next two decades. But in a key sense, it was almost immediately forgotten. Although Italy had made England look inept for most of the game, the final score encouraged the thought that we were ready to advance off our lines, at least with a quick dash to take on the newly emerging threats caused by upstarts, the lot of them, who needed to be put in their place.

Before the World Cup arranged for Brazil in 1950, the tournament had been staged twice in the 1930s, then war intervened. British teams had shunned it; as a notion dreamed up by a Frenchman, Jules Rimet, it was a bit of a cheek. Foreigners had created a competition which presumed to anoint the champions of 'our game'. Sensible analysts knew who the world's champions were. They were the annual winners of Britain's home international championship, the toughest international competition in the world.

The World Cup illustrated just how like foreigners it was to go organising fancy events with fancy titles. They always had to show off. When you played them, before kick-off they presented things like elaborately tasselled pennants. Even when Moscow Dynamo came in 1945, they had taken the field with great bouquets of flowers for each of their opponents. The British players looked lost, the crowd laughed. What was the point? All insincere gestures and flashing smiles (well, in this case, maybe not the Russians), foreign teams tried to wheedle their way into your affections, then turned on you and got nasty once the game started. They were people who weren't what they appeared to be. Play them on their grounds and, like as not, they'd fix not only the match ball, but also the referee.

England went to Brazil in keeping with the new spirit of international cooperation and comradeship. Having fought with, or against, each other we had to live together, rather than, as after the First World War, retiring to our respective corners, in effect to prepare for the next conflict. Something else had also begun to gnaw away at us. There was no need to announce it to everyone, but perhaps we had something to prove. The World Cup was creating an alternative pole of development which others might come to regard (wrong though they would be) as the true yardstick of greatness. We wouldn't have been wrong to stay away, but would not have wished our actions to be misinterpreted as shirking a challenge.

When England turned up in Rio de Janeiro in June 1950 they were greeted as the 'kings of football'. The arrival of the inventors of the game was an endorsement of the competition. The England party regarded it less seriously. Most arrived ten days before the competition's start, allowing little time for the players to acclimatise. Their first game was to be with Chile in the coastal humidity of Rio, the next against the United States in the rarefied mountain air of Belo Horizonte. Four players, leading lights like Stanley Matthews among them, came via a post-season tour of Canada and arrived just three days before the opening match.

Conditions confirmed the party's suspicions of what living abroad must be like. From a country blessed with the Broadstairs and Blackpool B&B, the players were scathing of their hotel on Rio's Copacabana beachfront. Egg and bacon breakfasts were obtainable, but served in black oil, not wholesome melted lard.

Players survived on bananas, risky in itself. When the first bananas, not seen since the 1930s, arrived in Britain after the war, there had been reports that a young girl of three had overdosed and died eating four of them. Alf Ramsey was the first to go down with a bad stomach, a bilious episode that was to colour Anglo-Latin American relations on and off for the next thirty or forty years. English pressmen on the trip also warned against whom, not just what, you could trust. The players were urged not to give autographs. Some Brazilians had, only to find they'd signed subversive 'communist' petitions.

The first game before a thin crowd of 40,000 at the Maracana stadium (capacity 110,000) saw England players suffer from the surprisingly thick air. They gulped from a cylinder of oxygen at half-time. Surprisingly, in a foreign land, rain then fell to make conditions a little more familiar and a 2–0 win was scratched out of a patchy performance. The manager, Walter Winterbottom, and captain, Billy Wright, thought there should be changes for the second game against the USA, but the decision was in the hands of the one selector on the trip, the Neville Chamberlain look-alike Arthur Drewry. He chose to change nothing. The USA was a small footballing nation about which we knew and cared little. Thus, he waved his sheet of paper with the England line-up before an expectant world. There were to be no changes; a case of peace in our team.

Other factors were also blamed for England's subsequent performance. The stadium at Belo Horizonte had been built for the World Cup but was a rickety structure. With a capacity of only 20,000, it summed up the players' feelings that this was not a serious competition. The surface, recently laid, was a scrubby desert of tufts of tall grass, interspersed with bare earth. Any of the 111 pitches just created from the east London rubbish dump at Hackney Marshes – with so many posts and crossbars it had caused a national shortage of white paint – might have been better.

Neither could the USA be regarded as serious combatants. One of their better players was a Scot named McIllveney, who'd played in Wales but, after seven games for Wrexham in the Third Division North, had been given a free transfer and emigrated. Keeper Borghi's first sporting love was baseball. The centre-forward Joe Gaetjens was from Haiti, a place few had heard of except in lurid discussions about voodoo. Several of the US team took the field in a zombified state. Imagining they would have little to celebrate after the match, they'd stayed up to party through the night before.

Surreal forces, whether brought to bear by Haitian Gaetjens or not, played no minor part. When England's forwards prepared to shoot, the ball stood up on the long tufts of grass, to be scooped, with uncanny regularity, high over Borghi's bar. No one was quite certain what magic fashioned the USA's winning goal. Bert Williams appeared to have a shot from the left covered but Gaetjens somehow got to it with the faintest of headed deflections. People wondered, had he touched it at all?

The British press hit upon the analogy of the defeat at Gallipoli in the First World War to convey how England had been routed in distant parts. When a loss to Spain meant ejection from the tournament, Dunkirk was the obvious parallel. Britain's first expeditionary force to a World Cup rapidly evacuated hostile territory, the instinct of the England team, officials and the press to get away as quickly as possible, back to the safety of home. They didn't stay to study the form of those who remained in the competition and missed the eventual final between Brazil and Uruguay. The view was that there was nothing to be learned from places where the conditions for football were never right, nor from the teams which played there. If they weren't out-and-out cheats (the Football Association toyed for a while with the idea of protesting that the US team had contained ineligible non-Americans), then they were as good as. An official report darkly pointed to how the Brazilians had cancelled all league matches for months before the competition. The Uruguayans had been together for no less than two years. This was typical of such people. They got together in darkened rooms to concoct their plans. If that won them games, well, it showed what a state the world was in. Doubtless in the estimation of Monsieur Rimet, Uruguay's victory in the final was *magnifique*, but it wasn't football.

What did the World Cup mean, anyway? 'Even if we'd have won it,' said Stanley Matthews, 'the public would have said it was "just another cup".' What had happened was in a remote part of the globe. Unlikely defeats had happened before in those sorts of places, where climatic and other quirks allowed Johnny Foreigner his occasional day. Losing to the USA at football was as humiliating as Gordon going down to the 'mad Mahdi' and his whirling dervishes at Khartoum. That had been in the desert. The pitch at Belo Horizonte was much the same and the Americans had played like a team possessed. But it was also distantly forgettable. It wouldn't happen at home. England turned back on itself from its failed beachhead in Brazil, bruised and ready to draw its line in the sand.

The assault began almost immediately, in the irregular shape of Marshall Tito's 'partizans', with Yugoslavia's visit in the late autumn. Yugo-, or Jugoslavia as it was often written, had beaten England 2–1 in Belgrade before the war, one of their players rugby-tackling an England forward in the penalty area to prevent an equaliser. The war had confirmed Tito and his mountain men as a belligerent bunch. The British soldiers called them the 'Jugs', which rhymed with 'mugs' and sounded funny. But the Jugs were definitely no mugs. When the British forces were based there during the stand-off over Trieste, anyone tempted to go looking for wine and women in the hills behind Gorizia was in serious danger of never coming back. Partizans came down into Trieste, marched off groups of Italians and shot them. A stealthy band paddled across from their Slovenian haven to my dad's camp around the bay one night and removed and made off with the tyres of seventeen jeeps. Now the Yugoslavs came from the depths of Serbia and Montenegro to the dim hinterland of Hornsey Road to snatch a 2–2 result at Highbury. Thus, Islington, and a site but a mile up Upper Street, and through Highbury Fields from our street, took its place in history: it saw the first draw by a foreign team on English soil.

Just under a year later the venue and the score were the same, only this time the French were the opposition. It was more perplexing. France had regularly played against England since 1923 but usually in Paris when the English selectors felt like a jaunt across the Channel. Taken with the game against Yugoslavia, it suggested a pattern was developing. Foreign teams need no longer be fodder for the cannons of the England forward line. The two drawn games also meant England were only one slip or stroke of ill-luck away from losing their home record. Control of events was ominously slipping out of our hands.

This was clear in the war in Korea, where the Americans and

Russians were dictating events. In addition to 40,000 British troops, the Labour government under Clement Attlee sent along twenty-five warships, but they were under American command. Thanks to my dad's extra year facing the partizans, he was spared the call-up. His younger brother, Bim, was bound for Korea, till at the last moment India was persuaded to join in by sending some medics. My uncle's ambulance division went to sweat it out in Hong Kong. The Chinese were a range of hills or so away from his base at Sek-kong and assumed to be ready, on an order from Moscow, to sweep down in their millions. Many soldiers had to be treated for depression and some committed suicide. All you could do was wait. The tension, he said, was awful.

I came downstairs and heard a report on the wireless one morning that British troops in Korea had been attacked on somewhere called the Imjin river. This sounded like my dad's name, Jim, and a funny thing to call a river. They'd fought off the attack, which was to be expected. But what was alarming was that the assault had been carried out, the broadcaster said, by 'communist gorillas'. My parents were at work, so I asked my grandparents what this meant and picked up the impression that communists got up to all sorts of tricks. Thereafter, gorillas kept cropping up everywhere.

In Malaya they killed someone called the British High Commissioner. In Kenya, they'd been stealing from white people's houses in Nairobi. Here they'd formed an armed band with the frightening sounding name of 'Mau Mau'. It was said they got together in the jungle in secret to 'swear oaths'. This wouldn't have done round our way. With the exception of people much further down the street, you didn't go around swearing oaths. Why were they like this? It was said they wanted the white man out of Africa, yet it was we who did things honestly and openly, wasn't it? The British police and army, for example, were doing their straightforward best to deal with them. The gorillas, on the other hand, in Asia, Africa or wherever, did things in an unreasonable and underhand way. Reports of their activities suggested that now everything was against us, even the animal kingdom.

Soon after the France match, Bert Williams suffered a shoulder injury which threatened to end his career. Given the gravity of the global situation, there could have been few worse times for it.

Chapter 4

End *of* Empire

For a small village, Great Marfold had a good team and could call on players from a much wider area. The uncle married to my dad's oldest sister, Laura, played centre-forward. She went to watch when they'd advanced to the late stages of one of the Bedfordshire cups. It was a Saturday afternoon game, quite sunny, at the Victoria Works ground in Bedford. Their keeper, Bill Farrell, was twenty-one and due for a trial at Luton Town the following Monday.

In the style of the day, their opponents had a hard centre-forward, a curly-haired fellow called Red Venner. 'Dirtiest man ever walked on a football field,' said my aunt. 'I heard him shout out during the game, "Get that big bugger!", pointing at Bill.' When a cross came over, Farrell took it arms outstretched, body taut. Venner came in, studs raised, and caught him hard in the chest and stomach. 'Well, you said you'd get him,' my aunt shouted at him, as they carried the keeper off. My uncle took over in goal.

In the dressing room they gave Farrell a cup of hot sweet tea. When they took him to hospital and he was waiting to be seen, he kept doubling over to ease the pain. The proper sister wasn't on that evening. Something had perforated in his stomach and he died next afternoon. 'The day his banns were called,' said my aunt. 'And he'd have got in the Luton team easily.' Venner's son was apprenticed to my uncle as a toolmaker. He said his father had hung up his boots, would never play again, and didn't sleep for a month after the incident.

Bert Williams had been injured before. It may have had something to do with the way he played, taut and, like a compressed spring, waiting to bounce. But there were always good stand-ins available. We had the greatest goalkeepers in the world and any one of them could be drafted in to do a perfectly adequate job by our standards. By anyone else's, it would be superb.

Bernard Streten, Luton's veteran keeper and favourite of my Bedfordshire uncles, had deputised for Williams once in 1949. He came in, did all that was required in a match in which he had very little to do, and never played for England again. His only international cap was a reward for long-standing service to the cause, bestowed by the selectors in the spirit of 'they also serve who stand and wait'.

The same sentiment guided them as they brought in Gil Merrick of Birmingham City now late in 1951. Williams wasn't expected to be gone long. Though two years younger, Merrick was already thirty. He'd been overlooked as a contender in the Swift succession. At that time Birmingham had been promoted from the Second Division to the First, thanks to his conceding only twenty goals in forty matches. But next season his team's form was so bad that two of their players started arguing on the field on a visit to Highbury, and almost came to blows. Team captain Merrick ran upfield and told them to 'turn it in'. A selector was in the stands and concluded that a keeper had no business out there getting involved. An army man in the war, Merrick soldiered on as his team was dispatched back to the lower division. Eventually he was deemed worthy of reward and proved a decent stop-gap for Williams.

For the spring-to-autumn months up to Merrick's selection, Clement Attlee's Labour government had tried to lift the nation's spirits with a celebration of its new British way. The Festival of Britain was held down by the Thames on bombed wasteground by Waterloo Bridge. There was a steam train, and big iron wheels standing there for people to look at. My parents said there would be a firework display and some kind of dome. They took me along and told me it was good. The festival made no impression on me, other than the strangeness of its slogan: 'A Tonic for the Nation'.

A tonic was something my grandparents had when they were ill. They'd get it from Dr Dadachanji's surgery at the end of Colebrooke Row, opposite the gardens, the last house before Goswell Road. His waiting room in the front parlour was cold and dim, with a few wooden chairs, and his surgery was at the back. Dr Dadachanji was small and quiet and, to me, mysterious. He probably was to everybody. I'd gone to see him when my nose bled badly and people didn't know what to tell me but to put my head back. The blood ran down my throat and came back later in livery globs. Dr Dadachanji sent me to the children's hospital in Hackney Road, where they plugged my nose with cotton wool soaked in snake venom. Mysteriously, it worked.

Millions were spent on the festival and millions came. It was pronounced a great success. An uplifted people should have gone to the polls in the general election the month after the festival closed and swept Attlee back into power. He was running against Winston Churchill, who had lost in the 1945 election because he was considered yesterday's man. Many people, however, had picked up the idea that the nation was a bit poorly. A large part of the electorate did certainly vote Labour, even though many of them were in places much too far from London to have gone to the festival. They were in the big industrial constituencies, with enormous Labour majorities, but they only counted for one seat. Many in the lesser populated areas – strangely, a lot of them nearer London, so they may have visited the festival – voted Conservative. Labour got more votes, the Conservatives more constituencies, and Churchill returned to office.

I'd never realised he'd been away. With his solemn presence in the wings – his pronouncements on the 'noble cause' of the Korean War, and the like – he'd been awaiting his call, available when the country took stock of the seriousness of the situation. Enough people felt it was not the time for 'tonics' but for harder stuff to raise the spirit. A few more finest hours, that's what was needed. Churchill came back with memories stirred of resolute wartime leadership and the glories of unflappable defence. Gil Merrick made his international debut three weeks later.

The selectors found the man they'd been looking for. They could have invented him. Merrick was from Birmingham City, the club of Harry Hibbs himself. Where Harry had been safe rather than spectacular, and Williams had modified the goalkeeping standard to spectacular but safe, so under Merrick it took a step back into history; he was referred to as 'never unnecessarily spectacular'.

Merrick was in the image of Birmingham itself, capital of the English Midlands, the industrial heartland. It was just up the road from Coventry. Birmingham people didn't say much, not that we'd have understood them when they did, but were quietly engaged in the job of rebuilding. They made hammers and drills, anchors and chains, gear boxes and other bits for cars, which was all pretty dull, really, but they 'got on with it'. Gil Merrick played with the sleeves of his jersey neatly rolled to the elbow.

He was the model of post-war man. With a dark, neatly trimmed moustache, he looked like one of my scoutmasters and anyone's gym teacher; apart from the rolled sleeves, it was his only hint of affectation. The programme my dad brought back from Wembley when he saw him in the Belgium game the following year said: 'One of the few goalkeepers in the football league with a moustache.' In the 1930s my mum used to write away to film stars in Hollywood and they'd send back autographs. To a generation brought up on Clark Gable, moustaches had an element of dash and made men 'handsome'. Unfortunately, Hitler and, with his periodic returns to the country to save us, Sir Oswald Mosley had intervened and done nothing for them as far as I was concerned. But that wasn't Gil Merrick's fault.

Merrick was a PT expert and fitness fanatic. You could imagine him in white singlet and long trousers, crease finely pressed, standing calmly at ease as he awaited the order to vault the wooden horse or cartwheel across the rough coconut matting (if it chafed the skin, you just took no notice). When I later saw photos of him, his face was entirely placid. As far as I knew, he never smiled or looked as if he was about to. His hair, dark and receding at the temples, was brilliantined back and flat. As a goalkeeper, he was unflappable. He said it himself, he was 'born to the defensive position'.

His debut was in his home city, at Villa Park, and a comfortable 2–0 win against Northern Ireland. It was an uncomplicated game in the manner of the home international championship, where football was played in the right way. Nippy wingers jinked down their right and left touchlines and inside-forwards were artful schemers. Respectively, they were marked by the full-backs – unsung, decent men with neatly greased and parted hair – and the half-backs who matched their opponents by being muscular and wily. In the vanguard of each attack was the centre-forward, a physical, thrusting player, much of whose game was reduced to single combat with a strong and unyielding centre-half. The goalkeeper stood detached and beyond, awaiting the outcome of the set-piece battles in front of him. This was how things were and were meant to be.

My dad, instinctively a Williams man, was a rapid convert. The Belgium game ended as a comfortable 5–0 win but the Belgians had put a few good shots in on goal. The day was November damp, the ball becoming heavier with each revolution across the Wembley surface and with each yard travelled through the afternoon murk. But every Belgian effort Merrick handled with absolute ease. He caught the ball 'like he didn't have a care, just picked it out of the air,' my father said. 'That wasn't easy with those leather balls, they'd weigh pounds on a day like that.' Actually, in the second half a white ball was used. It looked like the new plastic continental type that didn't absorb water. Merrick later wrote that he didn't like them because they swung around unpredictably, though this one proved to be the only one he came across that didn't. Maybe it was a normal leather one which somebody had slapped a bit of white paint over.

In any event, Merrick's handling was impeccable. Someone in the newspapers called him 'the Clutch' and the terraces picked up on it. From Bert Williams, 'the Cat', with its overtones of continental panache, England goalkeeping passed into the clutch of Merrick. It spoke again of the industrial Midlands, with its car factories and things. Very solid, reliable and British.

Just as well, because his first game in London, two weeks after his debut, brought home the nature of the outside threat. My father went again. In our role as founders of football, 'everyone wanted to beat us', he said. The latest to try were the Austrians, who came armed with the concept of 'tactics'. These weren't entirely new. Austria's pre-war 'Wunderteam' had employed 'tactics' when they beat England 2–1 in Vienna. This was in 1936 shortly before Hitler had annexed Austria. The war had come and we'd largely forgotten about 'tactics', trusting the world might have the sense to do the same.

The Austrians were held in such high regard they were invited to play at Wembley. By contrast, France had never been afforded this full international honour, inferior footballers and poor ally in war that they were. Austria had flourished as a playing nation till overrun by the Nazis. Though on the wrong side in the war, this could largely be attributed in people's minds to German belligerence. Austrians had about them underdog qualities. They might even rate as plucky. They still had the unwelcome occupying force of the Russians on their soil and it was touch and go in these grave times whether they'd leave. We instinctively liked the Austrians. They showed their gratitude by turning up at the headquarters of world football with a devious plan to overthrow us.

Against all natural law, they played with an attacking centre-half: Ernst Ocwirk, *ernst* in German meaning 'serious'. He performed in a manner that made the conventions of the centre-half position a joke. He took the field with a number 5 on his back, as he should, but then showed this was a deliberate attempt to deceive. Instead of holding back to await the thrusts of the England centre-forward, he advanced to occupy something more like his own team's central attacking position. Had he any decency, he'd have worn number 9 on his back. Then, just when the English team had noted where he was, he'd be gone, and back in his own team's defence. Up and down the field in flowing fashion he and the Austrians played. The terraces, according to Fleet Street, nicknamed him 'Clockwork' Ocwirk. The Austrians ran into open spaces where they weren't expected to run. They passed the ball to each other there and held it, while thinking next what to do. They kept it from the England players for lengthy periods of the game.

England couldn't get a handle on them. The Austrians wouldn't attack in conventional, civilised combat form. Nor would they stand up to be attacked. Characters you'd least expect would pop up and attack you. As suddenly they'd be gone. From the dark heart of the European continent, they were like those gorillas in the

Malayan and Kenyan jungle. They, too, got together to concoct plans and tactics. They also probably sat in the dressing room swearing oaths. But everyone agreed they were damned tricky. (A few years later when one of my comics started giving away small photos of foreign players, Ocwirk's was the first I collected.) With a minimum of effort they scored two goals. England did most of the running, often fruitlessly chasing the ball. But we had more muscle. Through physical endeavour, England scrambled a draw.

The menace of tactics was obvious but it was difficult to know what to do about it. In the absence of clear thinking, it was decided to ignore it. Resolve and character would have to do. An empire had been built on them. Britain lost 'every battle but the last'. There were no defeats, merely setbacks 'on the road to eventual victory'. Actually, it was Karl Marx who said something like that, the fellow who had claimed that by bringing the railways to India, Britain had only laid down the iron path of Indian revolution. Off the rails though he was, he'd done his best work in Bloomsbury, in the British Museum, a few streets from where my nan had been born off Theobald's Road. Lenin had lived in Finsbury for a while, just north past the end of Exmouth Market. He'd have walked along it, as my grandad and great-grandma served up carved roasts to the poor and workers of the area, and around the streets of Clerkenwell *en route* to his own eventual victory. Marx and he would have picked up some of the grit and mood in the air.

It wasn't that foreigners like them, or any other, were not clever people. Tactics, whatever you felt about the morality of them, showed they could be. But could their keepers calmly catch a ball? Would they take a cross, with the pressure really on? They were form rather than content, capable of something thrillingly dangerous or elaborate but impossible to sustain. Foreigners couldn't 'hold the line'; they couldn't see things through.

Churchill saw through the Labour Party as soon as he was back in Downing Street. Our position slipping, they'd tried to stop anything that might be construed as our retreat from greatness by quietly taking us down the nuclear path. Churchill didn't mind, he just wished he'd been told. He soon visited the USA to push his arguments for the alliance of English-speaking peoples, our special relationship. It was the alternative to dealing with the chaotic Europeans. The USA had always liked the cut of the old boy's jib more than that Attlee fellow, with his pink ideas. In return for aid, Churchill said they could use our military bases for the two countries' 'common defence'. That'd hold the line.

On the customary end-of-season tour, in May 1952, England went to Italy. In the goalmouths of Florence stadium where my father had played before him, Merrick did his bit maintaining the score at 1–1. They travelled on to meet the Austrians again, in occupied Vienna. The game was played at the Prater Stadium in the Russian zone, but British troops packed the crowd. The forward line was led by Nat Lofthouse of Bolton Wanderers, a centre-forward in the old physical mould. Ocwirk's mechanism failed to tick for the occasion, while Lofthouse so intimidated the Austrian keeper, Walter Zeman, that he scored two of England's goals in a 3–2 victory.

Unintimidatable, Merrick had his best England game. He made the winning goal, rising to pluck a swirling corner kick from the angle of bar and post and clearing, via Tom Finney, to Lofthouse on the chase. Zeman came at him boots first – as Merrick noted, this was 'the wrong way of going down at a man's feet'. We went down with head and hands, bravely, either to smother the shot or pluck the ball from the rampaging opponent's toe. Zeman's feet laid out Lofthouse, but not before he slipped in the winner. The troops carried him off on their shoulders at the end, Lofthouse the 'Lion of Vienna'. Merrick, however, quietly claimed a greater prize than a mere title. England field players kept their shirts from each game, but the keeper was never able to have his jersey. He had to hand it back to an FA checker perched over the kit basket; something about them being more difficult to obtain, thought Merrick. The feel of this one was like wearing 'a special and expensive suit for the first time'. The mood in the dressing room was so jubilant that he asked if he could keep it and the ecstatic Winterbottom was happy to comply. 'Do you wonder,' said Merrick, still moved by the memory years later, 'I treasure that jersey more than anything in football?'

For reasons I could never grasp, my parents were moved to take holidays on the continent – about once every four years, with a week at a holiday camp between times, while they saved the money. This was my mum's doing. My dad – country boy, big family – would as happily have stayed at home. Before the war she'd taken a couple of day-trips to Ostend from Margate and a boat trip down the Seine for her fourteenth birthday. At work, Waterlows had organised a football tour to a small town near Ypres and she went as a spectator. That was Easter 1939; a member of the ship's staff counting them off at the Ostend quayside said: 'There's more than ever now. Everyone thinks there'll be a war.' Then the civilian traffic stopped and my dad went in khaki. He wrote romantic letters back with sketches of happy soldiers jumping off landing craft on to beaches. The censor would let those through. My mum felt she'd missed out on the fun and dragged him back as soon as he was home. Much of Italy was destroyed. They hitched army trucks to get from Florence to Siena, wangled special visas to get to Trieste. This was thought very strange round our street.

When I went abroad at the age of three, the Channel was very rough. It always was. My parents said they'd been on one crossing when even the crew was sick. We stayed with my father's friends in Siena in a small street behind the cathedral. It all seemed extremely poor. Aunts, nieces and grandmas competed to scrub my face at night and parade me back in front of the applauding family. It was very embarrassing. Trains were always late. There was a huge mob on Florence station, which my dad said would all leap through the open windows when the train came in to grab a seat. So, clever move, we stood on the platform behind a priest, our seating arrangements thus assured. When the train came in, he threw his suitcase through the window like the rest of them and, habit ascending, dived dramatically after it.

If it hadn't been for the last game on the next summer tour – this time stretching itself to the newer frontiers of South America – England would have stayed unbeaten. Uruguay, the World Cup holders, won 2–1 in Montevideo. It was a pity but much too far away to matter. Of more immediate importance was the fact that the spring and summer of 1953 proved that reward came to those who stayed the course. Stanley Matthews received his winner's medal at Wembley, with his last chance to appear in an FA Cup Final. His runs down the Blackpool right were defined as the thrilling difference in a 4–3 victory against Bolton Wanderers. That much of the score resulted from errors which would have disqualified either goalkeeper from appearing in the South East Counties League, was a detail laid aside in celebration of a long and distinguished career. A month later, Gordon Richards, unable to win a Derby in three brilliant decades in the saddle, did so at his final attempt. 'It felt like it all came right,' said my dad. There was a sense of justice and harmony to the world. Master the fundamentals and eventually the glorious moments would follow.

No one did either like we did. In June, who else could have staged a coronation in all that rain? Look at Queen Salote of Tonga, the only royal guest to ride with her carriage hood down, soaking Haile Selassie in the process. God bless her, people thought, for being such a good sort and showing why the empire was necessary in the first place. My fourteen-year-old Uncle Keith and I squelched around to the special school in Colebrooke Row, near the Manchester Union of Oddfellows, for our red jelly and pink blancmange. They were served in the hall, not the playground where the kids' party was meant to be. It didn't detract from the day. The national spirit had been buoyed that morning by the news we had conquered Everest. At least, that was as I understood it.

There was some confusion over the men who had reached the summit. Neither was British. As a New Zealander, Edmund Hillary was almost, but not quite. Our butter came from New Zealand and had a picture of a kiwi stamped on the wrapping. New Zealanders were called 'kiwis'. The fellow who went to the top with him clearly wasn't British. He was Sherpa Tensing. 'Sherpa' was the name of the group, like a tribe, he belonged to; his name was Tensing Norgay. The BBC and everyone called him 'Sherpa Tensing'. They could, by the same token, have referred to his partner at the summit as 'Kiwi Edmund'.

The Sherpas were loyal and trusty, a bit like the Gurkhas who fought with the British army. My dad had a kukhri, one of the Gurkhas' curved knives, in a leather sheath on a shelf in the sitting room. This one was blunt but a frightening-looking thing. You were glad these people were on your side. The Gurkhas were from a similar part of the world, but the Sherpas lived at the foot of Everest itself and were mountain guides. Amazingly, they were guides who hadn't been to the top of the mountain themselves. Their god had forbidden them to do so, we learned. Only on our authority, it followed, had they been happy to ignore his ruling. It was a mark of how loyal and trusty they were. They'd just been waiting for us to come along and lead them to the conquering heights.

There lay the answer to my early confusion. Two non-British types had reached the summit but the conquest was ours. It was a British expedition. A little down the mountain was its British leader, John Hunt, who had selected the two to go to the top. He could have chosen himself but it was to others we allowed such honours. We took quiet satisfaction from knowing that without us it wouldn't have been possible. As on Everest, we led by rock-like example, uninterested in public glory. Britain's role was naturally that of the man at the back.

There was no one more natural in the role than Gil Merrick. He had been born to the position upon which everything depended. He was the sort of person who exemplified our response to a threatening world. He faced it as we would, quietly and calmly, and if not to win every title on offer abroad, then at least to stay unbeaten at home.

The first challenge of the autumn was to be the game staged for the FA's ninetieth anniversary. The team sent along in October by Fifa as the 'Rest of the World' wasn't exactly that. The Latin Americans found it too difficult to travel half the globe in boats and planes for this one game alone. But with a collection of mainly Austrians and Yugoslavs, plus a Swede, German, Italian and a Hungarian-born Spaniard to make up the number, it would represent a good test of our renewed confidence in our game and the forces of the universe.

An Austrian, Willy Meisl, a journalist whose brother Hugo had been the goalkeeper of the 1930s' 'Wunderteam', was given the honour of writing an introductory note in the Wembley programme. True to the character of such people, he abused it. It had long been recognised in other countries, he said, that 'there was little hope of defeating a British national team by orthodox tactics on its home ground'. The Rest of the World would employ Austria's methods of an attacking centre-half and 'charmingly precise, short-passing game'.

This was boastful of him, as well as mischievous to suggest that the 'orthodox' way was itself a form of 'tactics'. Right-minded people knew it was the right way to play. He showed further bad grace in suggesting that although England might be getting used to such 'tricks' as tactics (he used quote marks to suggest he didn't really think they were tricks), its teams were 'so stereotyped' that they were 'still prone to be baffled when unusual methods are introduced'. In response, they could only play a hard physical game and get 'stuck in'. It was 'why the true craft of soccer has experienced a decline in the game's homeland' he claimed, concluding that the Rest of the World would prove superior on the day. But England's fighting power might achieve a 2–2 or 3–3 draw.

Shoddy though his intentions were, his forecast proved almost correct. The Rest of the World were 4–3 up with one minute to play when England fortunately won a penalty. Some said the referee's decision was dubious. But Mr B. W. Griffiths was a transparently neutral Welshman who had served in the RAF during the war. He'd been a sergeant-instructor and was now a schoolteacher, a stickler for doing it by the book. In 1950 he'd been among the first British referees to officiate at a World Cup and seen at close hand the tricks foreign defenders got up to. They needed watching. Besides, there was an order to be upheld here. England and Tottenham full-back Alf Ramsey, a man with a stomach for the occasion, strode up to take the penalty kick and drove the equaliser home from the spot.

The crowd had been in such a state of cliff-hanging excitement that they'd probably forgotten the advertisements in the programme for Wembley's forthcoming attractions. England's next opponents at the ground in one month's time were to be the Olympic gold medallists, Hungary. They figured modestly on the page of events on offer. At the top was an ice hockey match between Wembley Lions and Harringay Racers in the Empire Pool (seat prices from half a crown to twelve and sixpence); next, tournaments of amateur boxing and 'indoor lawn tennis'. The Hungary game – for 25th November, kick-off 2.15 p.m. – was then mentioned, but in far less space than the ad for the imminent start of the year's pantomime season. Understandable, really, since as a spectacle it would surely not rate with 'Humpty Dumpty on Ice'.

On the day itself, the programme notes did anticipate a significant contest. At the Helsinki Olympics the year before, the Hungarians had beaten Yugoslavia 1–0 in the final. They were, of course, among the communist countries making a mockery of what should have been the thoroughly amateur Olympics. Their players claimed to have jobs outside football. Hungary's captain, Ferenc Puskas, was an army officer, the 'galloping major'. He would be marked in one of the day's crucial battles by England's captain and 'human dynamo' Billy Wright. Centre-forward Nandor Hidegkuti and goalkeeper Gyula Grosics were 'clerical workers'. Centre-half Jozsef Bozsik was to set a Wembley record as 'the first Member of Parliament ever to play in an International match upon the famous pitch'. He was member for one of the Budapest constituencies, whatever that meant in a totalitarian state. No one was fooled. They were full-time footballers.

Their beautiful football in Helsinki, said the programme, had made them famous the world over. They were unbeaten in the past two seasons. One note, which had a 1066-and-all-that ring to it, went so far as to say that this was the day 'England faces perhaps the greatest challenge yet to her island supremacy'. To meet it, Gil Merrick was cast in a classical role; he was Horatius facing the Etruscan hordes across the Tiber: 'It may well be his duty this afternoon to show that unspectacular anticipation is the best weapon of all to hold a heavily attacked bridge.'

But this was to get things out of proportion. Others had been and gone before this lot, the cherry-shirted Hungarians, all continental short shorts and short passing game. The privilege of writing in the programme on how the match might go was not given this time to any cheeky foreigner but to the football correspondent of the London *Evening Standard*, Harold Palmer. In a half-century or so, he noted, fourteen foreign international sides had been seen off. Hungary had been among them, losing 6–2 at Highbury in 1936. It wasn't that they hadn't been a clever team, Palmer conceded with magnanimity, and they had even been superior in midfield. They'd just lacked that component of seeing things through. Having got so far, they 'let themselves down by their weakness in front of goal'.

Theirs was a style fairly common to central Europeans. Like their neighbours, Austria, they moved away from their adversaries to find open space and retain possession: 'they reason that while they hold the ball the opposition can do nothing.' But they couldn't run away for ever. Today they would also find conditions not to their liking. Heavy fog had threatened to have the game postponed and the novel concession was being made, in their honour, of using a white ball for the whole game. But they were not accustomed to playing on 'heavy grounds like ours in mid-season' and the hard tackling of a team of 'superior stamina'. They were, in short, about to discover it was a man's game. There was not so much wrong with our football, the *Standard* man concluded, as the 'jaundiced jeremiahs' made out. This set of opponents would no doubt come with their schemes and plans. We had no need, however, to worry unduly about tactics. Honesty would triumph above deviousness: 'The English game is all right.'

Elsewhere, the programme noted the Hungarians' tactics would differ from the Austrians, but not greatly. Rather than an attacking centre-half they came with a retreating centre-forward, Hidegkuti, the Budapest clerical worker, filed away mischievously in the wrong shirt. It had number 9 on its back, but he 'usually lays well behind his inside-forwards'. From here he was apt to feed them with through passes, or run through himself on to passes they supplied him. It wasn't, therefore, that England didn't know about this. As Palmer had recommended, they chose not to worry unduly about it. In the event, the words of Meisl came back to haunt: faced with unusual methods, England teams were 'prone to be baffled'.

The England defence retained control of their faculties for all of fifty seconds. In as many years, no foreign team had been able to storm the citadel. A sign that things might be otherwise came with the Hungarians' first attack. Advancing from behind his midfield line, Hidegkuti collected the ball and hit a hard shot from the penalty area's edge into the top right corner of Merrick's net. A 'stunned hush from the packed Wembley terraces' greeted it, said a Hungarian report. It took their players several seconds to dance at the sight of the 'white English ball in the net'. Geoffrey Greene, *The Times* reporter, also had his eyes on it: 'it was meant to be a dove of peace. Instead it was the angel of doom'.

Within fifteen minutes the same player had scored twice more, one of them charitably disallowed by the referee. The appearance of a retreat that the deep-lying centre-forward gave, suddenly revealed itself as attack. Not only had the match programme given warning, history had seen it all before. In the last such challenge to England's 'island supremacy', the nifty Normans had pretended to run away, then turned with the home team caught unprepared. First Hastings then, 900 less a few years on, Hidegkuti worked the same trick. The victim was a Harold, now as then. Harry Johnston, the Blackpool centre-half, couldn't fathom whether to follow Hidegkuti and be caught out of position, or leave him to cause havoc at will. Mind befuddled, he looked through the mist for help, calling out across the pitch to his captain, Billy Wright: 'What do I do, Billy?' Wright's reply was succinct and honest: 'I don't know, Harry!'

The score was 4–1 by half-time. In the second half England dug into their reserves of resilience and scored twice. So did Hungary. A combination of their easing up – a lack of 'superior stamina', possibly – and a first-rate performance by Merrick, kept the score to 6–3.

At five o'clock, a little over an hour after the end of the game, my dad walked the couple of minutes to Gloucester Road tube from the Natural History Museum, where building works were going on around a new air-conditioning system to fan the dinosaur bones and drawers of dead beetles. The papers were on the streets, the placards and men at the newsstands screaming the match outcome. He had to walk up and down the pavement by Baileys Hotel with the *Evening News* for a while to take it all in. 'We thought foreign teams were nothing,' he said. 'The big games, the ones you were frightened about, were with the Scots.' He'd had the chance to see the match but hadn't taken up the offer for the sake of a lost afternoon at work. He was glad he had. He didn't want to face the journey home: 'If I felt like this, I wondered how bad it was for those who were in the stadium?'

As for all internationals, his youngest brother, Bim, was there. In his early twenties he had no worries about missing a half-day's pay and no regrets that he had. It was an incredible occasion, breathtaking – actually, the very opposite of that. It made you realise how long you'd been holding your breath and didn't have to any more. You'd felt it coming for so long, that the waiting was the problem. The tension was off. The hordes had finally stormed down from the hills. 'To those who had seen the shadows of recent years creeping closer and closer, there was perhaps no real surprise,' said Green of *The Times*. England must 'awake to a new future'.

For the Wembley crowd the true shock had been Hidegkuti's goal in the opening minute. It was one of four in the afternoon hit with such power as to make the dusky continental 'weak in front of goal' ghost look more pallid than old Harry Johnston. The second following within a few minutes of Hidegkuti's initial strike made the spectators realise this was to be no flash in the pan. By the third, they were fully disposed to savour what was served before them.

That goal came after a sharply hit diagonal pass from the wing found Puskas on the gallop a few yards out from the right edge of Merrick's area. Severely left-footed, Puskas easily controlled the ball but, skidding to a halt, found himself with his back half turned towards the goal. He may have appeared off-balance to those near him. He rocked back on his right foot, as if he might even fall and let the ball go beyond reach in front of him. Billy Wright, driven to new heights of dynamism at having been caught out by Puskas's move into a dangerous position, ran and threw himself at the ball in a sliding tackle. He aimed to sweep it out of play for a corner kick and on the damp turf his momentum carried him into the crouched row of photographers across the touchline. The problem was he didn't have the ball with him.

Puskas was the 'tubby brains' of the Hungarian attack. In addition to his plastered-down, centre-parted hair, he was short and of square frame. In technically polite terms he had a low centre of gravity. He hadn't been unbalanced at all, and placed the studs of his left boot on the ball to drag it back swiftly out of Wright's path. In a continuation of the same movement, he pirouetted on his right foot, drew his leg back and hit an unstoppable shot. Merrick, knees buckling, hardly had time to lift his hand.

Billy Wright witnessed this as he detached himself from the sprawl of grey-coated cameramen and dislodged trilby hats. Stanley Matthews was off in the fog on the right-wing but four decades later could still clearly see Puskas's goal in his mind's eye. The Hungarian report observed how the crowd 'applauded for a very long time'. What they'd seen had been so simple that anyone in British football would have been proud to have done it. The footwork was perfectly no-nonsense, and effective enough to dump the England captain on his backside. It was rounded off with an example of shooting to equal anything England's own forwards could have provided. It was brilliant, might even have been very British, yet was a million miles beyond us.

Puskas's 'drag-back' captured the imagination sufficiently to be given the name. In scarcely a second, it fused elements of the game – deftness and directness, skill and shooting power, the scurrilous tactical stuff of foreigners and the straightforward decency of home – thought unfusable. It was a moment of football creation and for England the moment of much wider defeat. We had to acknowledge we were beaten. What the crowd witnessed wasn't some overseas reverse, explained by the quirky things that went on abroad and distant enough to be forgotten. It had happened here, on our turf and before our own eyes.

Allowing for a few thousand neutrals at the game, a bare minimum of Magyar émigrés and a scattering of communist diplomats, some, say, 95,000 people went back to the workplaces, pubs and working-men's clubs of an England approaching full employment and spoke about it. According to the old marketing principle that everyone knew 250 people – or, even if the number were pared to a conservative 100 – it meant that somewhere between nearly a quarter and over half of the population of England heard of the moment from someone they knew who had been there. This was in addition to what they discovered through the papers and radio. TV had missed the moment; only the second half was broadcast, because the FA didn't want people staying away from several afternoon replays between lower division and non-league clubs in the second round of the Cup. But all channels of communication reflected on this matter of wide national concern. Scots, Welsh and Irish joined in, in appreciation as much as glee.

Puskas's achievement was of mythical proportions. My dad talked about it with his brother and many other people. When he told me about it, I understood it to have been performed by someone from somewhere called 'Hungry'. This put it in the same funny-country category as 'Turkey' and 'Grease', though it turned out to be not some old gag but a stroke of magic. Puskas, I gathered, rolled the ball beneath his foot backwards and forwards several times. This had cast a kind of spell on the England defence, as if they were under the influence of an old Indian snake-charmer like Dr Dadachanji. They had swayed back and forth with it, till Puskas's final dispatch of the ball snapped them out of their trance.

I practised rolling an old tennis ball under my foot in the backyard and tried it on the other kids in the infants' playground. Far from mesmerised, they shouted at me to get on with it. It occurred to me this might not be my skill; also, that foreigners could do very impressive things.

The Hungary defeat was not Merrick's fault. He'd had to be necessarily spectacular to stop any number of Hungarian attacks. My encyclopaedia showed one, the England keeper springing left with rolled sleeves and black wool-gloved hand to push the ball around the post. A strand of dark brilliantined hair out of place confirmed the pressure he was under. Puskas said that if Merrick hadn't played so well the score would have been 12.

By the time a quarter of that figure had been reached, the outcome was certain. We had been out-performed and the most implacable last line we could muster was unable to stop the foreign tide. As Puskas's shot flashed by, Merrick's raised hand clutched only a gloveful of November gloom. Half turning his head to watch the ball on its way into the net, his eyes were unmoved as ever, staring at the end of empire.

Neck *on the* Block

We learned at school that the tree which best survived on the streets of London was the plane tree. For several years I assumed there was no other tree around, failing to register the chestnuts on the steep embankment of the canal and evidence from Sunday visits my mum organised to leafier places like Kensington and Hyde Park. The plane tree's visible trick was to shed its bark regularly to shake off the effects of the London smog. But its secret lay in its name. It was the 'good old' plane tree, plain and straightforward as we were, a tree for the common man. It was strong and it survived.

Crossing Danbury Street on my way back home from school, about a week into 1954, it started to rain. The taps in the playground had been frozen, so I leaned my head back and for about twenty seconds drank from the sky. A few days later I was sent home from school early with a head like death. My stomach came out in sympathy. No one quite knew what it was as I was put in bed, but when my dad arrived back in the evening he recognised what was wrong from his time in Italy and Africa. He carried me to my grandad's car and they took me to the children's hospital in Hackney Road, which confirmed the problem as dysentery. I was kept in for three weeks and treated as if victim of a tropical disease.

My grandad generally had a ton of coal delivered just before winter started. The coalman, who wore a flat cap, trousers held up by braces and looked like he'd climbed out of the chimney, shot the 20 hundredweight sacks of the stuff down the coalhole in the pavement and into the basement area cellar. It shone in large, tar-laden chunks. After its dust was swept into the gutter, the stain in the paving stones remained for at least a day of rain. A month later the smog came down, from about the third week of November, and hung around on and off into February. You wore it as a badge of honour, a mark of living in the largest city in the world. The newspapers said that thousands of people with bronchitis and other illnesses died from it. When you put a handkerchief over your mouth, by the time you'd walked down the street and back, a wet, black mark had appeared. Many football matches would be abandoned, the ref finally giving up hope of an improvement some good way into the game. Every year there'd be one when, with the teams back in the dressing room, it would be realised a goalkeeper was missing. The trainer or a policeman would be sent out to find him, at the edge of his penalty area, peering into the smog, unaware everyone else had left the field. This happened to Ted Ditchburn, Sam Bartram and any number of them until the smog as an annual event finally disappeared.

Ours was the black ash variety, particles of the stuff floating before your eyes. The Americans came up with a new one. They carried out an H-bomb test on the Pacific island of Bikini. Japanese fishermen heard the explosion and saw the mushroom cloud rise from 80 miles away. An hour and a half later, it started to rain, or rather snow on them, a kind of white-ash smog – probably pieces of Bikini, as well as whatever else comprised such a phenomenon. Fortunately, the Americans were on our side (the Russians only had the A-bomb). My dad said the GIs he'd met abroad were as friendly as anyone you could come across. But despite the fact they spoke English, you couldn't say they were exactly like us. Johnny Ray began a tour of Britain, smiled a lot and collapsed into tears at the end of his songs – nice, but funny people.

It was just as well that this time the USA were not among

the teams in the summer's World Cup finals. Neither England, nor Scotland (who turned up for the first time) needed the embarrassment. In an act of self-punishment that would have done Bert Williams proud, England chose to go for one of their warm-up games to meet the Hungarians, in the Nep, or People's stadium in Budapest. A local reflecting on the occasion with British writer John Moynihan said he was amazed when England took the field: 'We had always thought of them as gods. But they looked so old and jaded, and their kit was laughable. We felt sorry for you.' That was before the kick-off. His sorrow had surely turned to Johnny Ray-like sobs by the final whistle. Hungary won 7–1.

In the World Cup in Switzerland, Merrick was blamed for three of the four goals Uruguay scored when eliminating England in the quarter-finals. Out of touch with home newspapers during the competition, he was surprised when a reporter asked him on his return whether he had any comment on having 'let the country down'. He replied it was a 'poor show' if people had said that, that only the last Uruguay goal was his fault in a 4–2 defeat and that none of his teammates had blamed him.

Actually, Stanley Matthews – often cast as one of football's ambassadors – commented that Merrick 'disappointed' us 'when we were playing well and had a chance'. This in itself showed a new feeling towards the tournament. In Brazil four years earlier the players had given the impression they couldn't have cared less. Suddenly they wanted to win. After the years of suspicion towards a 'foreign' trophy, it was at least a tentative advance from the line into territory mapped out by others.

There was obviously something to be learned from the wider world. As well as dispatching England, Uruguay scored seven against Scotland. The British teams' performance helped start a debate about training methods. Merrick noted that before a match, teams like Hungary and Brazil did stretching exercises in the middle of the field. British teams tended to stand around stiffly, rubbing their hands from the cold and having a few desultory shots at their keeper. It was suggested that back home British clubs might put less emphasis on dogged cross-country runs and encourage the more refined, if slightly prissy, practice of training with a football. Not any old football, naturally. Officialdom remained sceptical about the new white one, rejecting it as contrary to our natural game.

The absorbent leather ball was an important test of how men met the sport's varying challenge. It was designed to be played in the rain. It was just like the sunny continentals to run up the white flag in the event of a downpour.

The selectors, anyway, had enough experimenting on their hands with a new generation of keepers. Ray Wood had come into the Manchester United team; Reg Allen had been part of United's championship-winning side in 1952 but, as a result of his war experiences, had suffered a nervous breakdown. Wood appeared modest enough to satisfy national requirements: a degree of shyness meant, in his photographs, he tended to incline his head down and look guardedly at the camera. He also had elements of a greasy quiff, an unnecessary bit of styling when compared with the plastered-back fashion of the wartime generation. Did this place him in the ranks of surly youth? He played in two games, did his bit to register two victories, and was promptly left out of the team.

The next overseas visitors to Wembley were the new world champions, West Germany. Hungary had hammered them 8–3 in an early World Cup round in Switzerland but somehow the Germans contrived to keep going through the competition and met the Hungarians again in the final. Puskas was injured, the Germans triumphed. This showed characteristics not associated with them. They were the types who went on to an early offensive – Schlieffen Plans, Blitzkriegs and Operations Barbarossa – then collapsed when things got tough. The World Cup had showed ominous signs of an ability to claw their way back.

The selectors reverted to the tried and trusted. Wolverhampton Wanderers were the reigning league champions and Bert Williams had proved he was back to fitness. He made a reassuring return in England's 3–1 win. One thing mentioned in the programme notes, and otherwise largely missed, was that the Germans were building for the future. Their players were part-timers, their team experimental. Uwe Seeler, for example, their centre-forward, was apprenticed to a Hamburg firm of furniture removers and now in the van for his country at only eighteen. It made him the youngest player to appear in a full Wembley international.

Chelsea won the league in 1955 and were invited to take part in the newly constituted European Cup for national champions. The

London club wanted to enter, the Football Association said no. Unnecessary games on the continent would clog up the fixture list at home. And could teams going abroad for what amounted to little more than an exhibition match on, say, a Wednesday, guarantee they could have their players back fit and well for the proper stuff of life on the Saturday? We should maintain our distance.

In Downing Street, Churchill had had a stroke and decided to retire. He convalesced by bricklaying in his garden. What with the renovation of our house, there were bricks around and so, using sand instead of cement I put up a few temporary walls in our backyard. My dad said they were better than Churchill's, which were more 'serpentine' than straight. Clearly the old boy could have benefited from a seven-year apprenticeship. But building walls seemed a thoroughly good thing to do.

The new prime minister, Sir Anthony Eden, agreed in that there was too much of this modish European integration stuff floating around. Germany and France, enemies for most of the last hundred years, were getting together, combining their coal and steel industries. Britain should block this and anything like it. It would only lead to the kind of imbalance in Europe that in the past we'd had to go in and sort out. Eden had previously been foreign secretary and knew about these overseas places. He said himself, he understood the affairs of the continent inside out. He'd studied Persian at Oxford.

In Persia, no less, we were under attack. British people had been forced to leave our oil refinery at Abadan. Things were worse in Egypt where types like General Nasser had taken over the Suez Canal. 'Their canal', they said. Really? Who built it? England's football season got under way with its first international but showed that roughneck forces were infiltrating our borders, too. England played Wales in Cardiff and lost 2–1. The by now venerable veteran Bert Williams was harshly treated by some of the young Welsh forwards out to show off their muscle. They used shoulder barges, as the law said they could. But wasn't there a spirit of the law they were offending? In the opposite goal, Jack Kelsey of Arsenal, whose display was key to the Welsh victory, thought so. He agreed a keeper was there to be hit, within reasonable limits. The way Williams had been targeted was unnecessary. That said, he quickly added that the rule book should not be changed. Take away the right to barge keepers and they'd end up like those on the continent – allowed to flap around when they had the ball and, as Kelsey said, 'do just as they like'.

James Dean died as *Rebel Without a Cause* came out in London. More worrying to people than Johnny Ray, he didn't cry but looked sullen, like the Teddy Boys on the streets, with their long Edwardian-style jackets, sideburns down to their necks, drainpipe trousers and thick rubber-soled shoes. A week later the 'King of the Teds', who lived around the Walworth Road in south London, was arrested for throwing a firework at a policeman; with intent to do him grievous bodily harm, said the police. Five years, said the judge.

Eden took the boat from Southampton to the USA for talks on the Middle East, where Russia was supporting Nasser's seizure of the Suez Canal. Three weeks later he reported back to Parliament that the Americans fully supported the British position. The Russian leader Mr Khrushchev was booed as his train arrived in London at Victoria station. He had come by sea from Russia to Portsmouth and during his stay a Royal Navy frogman, Commander Lionel 'Buster' Crabb, disappeared in the harbour. The crew on Khrushchev's boat complained they saw him surface and dive back underwater. No one else saw him again alive. There was nothing these people wouldn't do. On the wireless I heard the Russians went in for things like 'brainwashing' and assumed Crabb's body was back in Moscow, his brain extracted and being washed right now. Yet it was the Russians who protested. He was a spy, they said, and, incredibly, it was Eden who had to apologise.

Crabb had been awarded the George Medal in 1944 for searching the bottom of British ships for limpet mines. Of the wartime generation, there were pictures of him with lined face and wearing a black roll-neck jersey under his frogman's suit. The passing of Bert Williams from the England team saw the goalkeepers' roll-neck all but disappear. It had been creeping down towards and below the Adam's apple for years. Keepers now appeared less wrapped up against the cold and, in a dangerous world, went bare-necked into the fray.

Manchester City reached the 1955 and 1956 Cup Finals with Bert Trautmann in goal. It had seemed a crazy decision by them to have a German keeper. Badly bombed in the war and with a large Jewish population, Manchester was not likely to feel well disposed towards him. Then, someone had to follow Frank Swift and, as England had found with Ditchburn, anything like a 'normal' goalkeeper would have had a tough job. No one would have been able to 'do it like Frank could'. Manchester City's first choice had been Alex Thurlow, who was taken ill and died of tuberculosis. Trautmann was drafted in, his one advantage that his nationality lowered the level of the crowd's expectations. Anything good from a German was bound to be better than the fans had anticipated.

When he was a boy in Bremen in north Germany, Trautmann had joined the Hitler Youth. This was shocking to learn but, when you thought about it, not much different from my joining the 31st North London cubs over the canal bridge in Vincent Terrace. You went for the games, suffered the church parade every fourth Sunday, and tolerated the rigmarole of learning to fold the flag and not to fly it upside down. From our get-togethers, there was little or no grasp of any underlying mission.

Trautmann had been a paratrooper, my dad said, which was 'very important'. Paratroopers were an elite force on either side, floating above the dirtiness of war. My dad's brother Cecil was at Arnhem. Under fire and moving from house to house, he and a mate had stopped to shelter in a doorway. He heard a gurgling sound and turned to see the throat of his friend had been cut by shrapnel. I thought paratroopers were small men: my uncle was 5 feet 5 inches and, as a signwriter by trade, often found himself working at the extent of his ladder. Trautmann was tall, at 6 feet 2 inches. Short or long, you knew they were tough.

Trautmann was blown up in retreat from the Russian front, then later buried in rubble and injured in a bombing raid in France. Captured by the Americans when the Allies invaded Europe, he assumed he was going to be shot; armies on the move didn't always want the bother of prisoners. Instead he was allowed to slip away, picked up almost immediately by the British and shipped to England in 1945. The prospect of seeing Germany again, he said, was only a dream: '*es war ein Traum*'. Yet he stayed on when the war finished. My mum had told me German prisoners had to be kept in captivity because they wanted to escape and get back and fight. Only one ever managed to get free and off the island. The Italians, in contrast, weren't bothered. Those in Sandy were allowed to roam more or less free. They hadn't wanted to go to war like the Germans. The fact Trautmann didn't want to go home, I assumed, meant he must have been different.

He was blond like Bert Williams, though altogether more outgoing. In his photos he invariably smiled. My dad said he was a 'good bloke', like Rommel, one among the enemy who gave you hope. The Chief Rabbi of Manchester came out in support of him. As a keeper, he didn't court acclaim and got down to the job. He was no showman, but he had an important element which was familiar. He engaged the crowd, waved and chatted to them from his goalmouth at the start of the game and even between opposition attacks. It was a direct echo of his predecessor Swift, who before the war had assured the crowd it'd be all right. Now after it, Trautmann seemed to be saying the same. He liked us and people liked him. Just before the 1956 Cup Final he became the first goalkeeper – leave aside the first foreigner, the first German – to be made footballer of the year.

When my dad got back from work on Saturday afternoons he sometimes took me to the cinema. On Cup Final day *Moby Dick* was on at the Carlton, beyond the Essex Road library by the tube near New North Road. By the time he was ready and we had passed by at my grandparents to say hello, the match was not far away from starting. Birmingham City and its veteran keeper Gil Merrick with his dark moustache were firm favourites. A German smiling cheerily at the future was cast as underdog. Arthur Caiger, the small man in a baggy suit who stood on the high wooden platform wheeled out on the pitch for the communal Wembley singing, was saying: 'Now, Birmingham City fans don't have a song of their own, so I've chosen one for them.' He asked everyone to join in with 'Keep Right on to the End of the Road'. The band in bearskins and red tunics struck up what sounded like the Funeral March. Televised Cup Finals were no substitute for something to go out for; I was happy to leave for the pictures.

Moby Dick kept just the right side of very frightening. Captain Ahab was the brooding, isolated type, fixed in his goal. He suffered a kind of death on the cross. His arms were out, strapped to the side of the whale by the harpoons and ropes. As it smashed in and out of the waves, its eye kept staring at the camera. My father liked the whirlpool the whale made at the end, which sucked everything into it, except the one person who survived to tell the story. It was clever how they achieved that effect, my dad said, with what was actually a large piece of concrete.

When we got back home Manchester City and Bert Trautmann had won 3–1, which was good. Trautmann had been injured quite badly near the end, but had played on, which was even better. There were the photos in the *Evening News* and in the papers my grandad brought back from Fleet Street next morning. Trautmann was being led from the field at the end, head down, hand clasped to the left side of his face. The front of his jersey was soaked from the water splashed over him by the trainer with his sponge and bucket. Another showed Trautmann diving at the feet of Birmingham inside-left, Peter Murphy. His hands were gripping the ball on the ground but his bare neck was close to Murphy's outstretched left leg and his right, about to follow through. It must have been that one that had caught him. The clash had happened fifteen minutes from the end and Trautmann spent the rest of the game staggering around his goalmouth in agony. One newspaper was amazed how he came through 'this alarming situation'. We heard he had been taken for X-rays; later, that he had broken his neck and nearly died.

If Trautmann was well-regarded before the match, there was no measuring his popularity after it. There could be no clearer example of a keeper who 'took it', which was precisely what the best British keepers were meant to do. Yet this one was a German and people loved him for it. He hardly seemed foreign at all and was really 'one of us'. Also, it only added to his attraction that he wasn't. He could have had a British passport if he'd asked and would have certainly played for England. For some reason obviously not connected with the quality of their keepers, Germany failed to select him. But Trautmann didn't seek to become a British citizen. As he said, that wasn't what he was. My dad told me this with approval and it met with national acclaim. Had he applied to become British, he'd have been seen as toadying up. His only reward in terms of international honours was that he was chosen to captain the English Football League in a couple of matches. His lasting achievement was to inspire a national change of mood. In the future we might have to get along with these people and Trautmann showed it was possible. He did more than any other person for post-war reconciliation between Britain and Germany. In passing, he also performed the almost unbelievable trick of remaining an outsider while winning the acceptance of the crowd.

o   o   o

The Brazilians had been in the stadium watching the Cup Final. They were in town for the first game between Brazil and England the following Wednesday. I spent a long time over reports of the match in the papers. They were the first team of top standard England had played that had a number of black players. They came from somewhere that was almost of another world, yet at the same time quite familiar. If you looked at an atlas, Brazil was on the border of British Guyana, one of the outlying pink bits of the British Empire. In a sense, the Brazilians were our next-door neighbours The way we went about things, however, didn't bear a great deal of resemblance. You couldn't tell exactly from the pictures in the papers that their team was in yellow shirts and light blue shorts, but their outfits were obviously much trimmer than ours. The shirts had collars. These weren't limp and floppy but looked like they might have been ironed, as if the shirt could double for use on a summer Sunday School outing. The goalkeeper Gilmar had a collar poking out from under his top and wore an all light-grey outfit that must have been specially tailored for him. His wasn't a jersey he gave back at the end of games, with a view to it being baggily handed down through the keeping generations. On it was the globe, dotted with stars, of the Brazilian flag. It was all a bit pretty-pretty compared with what we were used to.

The reports said the Brazilians were 'maestros', with a 'special relish for flexibility' and a 'lovely patterned approach'. The star of their forward line, Didi, was a 'black panther' of a player. This didn't mean they had what it took. They lacked the 'depth, teamwork and creativity that shaped great sides'. They were subject to peculiar things like 'gyrations'. This put them on a level with the whirling dervishes I'd heard my nan refer to, those who had beaten Gordon at Khartoum. Once you overcame the shock of them, and confronted them firmly – preferably on your own turf where you could make them behave – they could be quelled.

There was no doubt they were brought to Wembley for a lesson. Brazil's 'sudden spasms' ran up against the 'solid oak of England'. Like the resilient plane tree battling the London smog, so we were constructed of other stuff, too, that saw off the threat of flimsier foreigners. Our 4–2 victory was described as a triumph of old over new worlds. Then again, it couldn't be said they were without their bit of plain, old-fashioned resistance at the back. England would have won much more comfortably but for Gilmar saving two penalties.

In our goal the selectors had felt compelled again to experiment with a younger type. Wood had recently had another game, and Ron Baynham of Luton Town was brought in for three. All were victories but neither keeper was given the job permanently. Next the selectors awarded it to Coventry's Reg Matthews, and it was he who played against the Brazilians. He was blamed for one of Brazil's goals, though given another chance. With it, he proceeded to play brilliantly in Berlin a fortnight later.

My family went to Italy again. I didn't want to go and the Channel was as rough as the first time. After twenty-four hours on the international train, we stayed two days in a hotel near Milan station. We visited the Italian friend who been a prisoner in Sandy in the war and my aunt Olive's boyfriend. He was now married to a woman who was pale, quite square and solid-looking and came from Trieste, like he did. His family did not approve because hers was from across the border in Yugoslavia. They'd have preferred him to have married my aunt. We ate red peppers, cooked in the oven. They were like nothing on earth, smelt and tasted like they were going to be sweet but that someone might have mixed in something bitter with them, maybe gunpowder. I ate them and, in the end, thought it was worth it.

For the three- or four-hour journey to Siena, the old train from Milan was very hot, with the sun blazing in on to the wooden-slatted seats. Fortunately we didn't have to change in the pandemonium of Florence. We stayed with the family again behind the cathedral. At the communal meals I mastered spaghetti and was allowed to drink red wine mixed with water. Italian water was unsafe – liable to give you dysentery, we were told – but was miraculously all right if you put wine with it. I was expansively praised for eating and drinking everything. We had breakfast alone – as my parents explained, Italians didn't really eat it – but Luciano, the boy of the family who was about my age, joined us. My parents had brought tea. When Luciano finished his cup, he scooped up the leaves with his roll and ate them. My sister and I gasped, though he didn't notice.

He took part in the marches for the Palio. Horses representing the districts of Siena raced each other round the main square, like Islington might have against Finsbury or Stoke Newington. Members of the family were born in different areas and were rivals on the day. We had the best seats, wooden tiers put up at the base of the buildings of the square. We sat for three hours as the procession of the Siennese boroughs went around. We didn't see or hear a British person anywhere. The race was over in a minute, many horses crashing into mattresses on the sharp corners. Jockeys who fell off were immediately suspected by their supporters of having been bribed and, if caught, were kicked and beaten up. The winning horse was from the area of the porcupine, *Istrice*. The jockey was feted, the horse the guest of honour at a banquet in the victorious part of town. But it didn't matter if a particular area won the race, just as long as they'd beaten their neighbours. Victors of these tribal battles would walk around their vanquished rivals' streets shouting and taunting. Everyone did this twice a year.

When Luciano practised throwing high and catching his heavy lead-ended flag, a smaller one was bought for me and I practised with him. In cultural exchange, I brought my cricket bat to Italy. It was the right season and not the weather for football. We played for several hours each day between the small bleached-ochre houses of the tiny Via del Poggio. He lost his patience once and threw his bat on the ground when, too triumphantly, in the compact medieval conditions, I caught him out one-hand-off-wall. It was a rule he never quite grasped.

When we came back to England, Jim Laker restored the natural world order by taking nineteen out of twenty wickets against the Australians in the Manchester mud. In Cyprus Archbishop Makarios, in his black hat and garments, was proving a sinister figure. We found letters between him and General Grivas, the head of Eoka, the terrorists who wanted to unite Cyprus with

Greece. Without our bases in Cyprus it would mean more insecurity in Egypt and other parts of the Middle East. Who knew what the Russians would get up to if we didn't have our watching stations?

You could guess. Their athletics team came for a two-day international at the White City but went home before it could be held, when their champion discus thrower, Nina Ponomoreva, was caught stealing hats – five in all, worth one pound, twelve shillings and eleven pence – from C & A in Oxford Street. Moscow protested that her arrest was 'wanton provocation'. These people defied belief. They snatched our frogmen from our harbours, our hats from the West End and said *we* were to blame. Ponomoreva was whisked away into the Russian embassy, the Soviets refusing to let her stand trial. After a couple of months a judge said that, as guilty as she was, she should be allowed home, and discharged her at three guineas costs. The Russians hurried her straight to London docks and one of their ships, which sailed the same night.

If these were the kind who were in charge behind the iron curtain, it was little wonder the Hungarians went into revolt against them. When Hungary demanded to leave the Warsaw Pact and that the Russians get out of their country, the Soviet army did appear to leave for a while. Then their tanks came back. The staggering thing was, the Russians announced to the rest of the world that they had been 'invited' to return. What did they take us for? We'd heard the Hungarian leader, Imry Nagy, make an SOS call on the radio. We couldn't answer it, of course. Against the Russians we wouldn't have had a chance. But at least we could land a blow elsewhere. The day after the Soviets recaptured Budapest, British paratroops, flown from Cyprus, were dropped into Egypt. It was the strike back against the forces closing in on us. They'd had us pinned back on our line for too long.

The England selectors rallied to the cause. Our younger keepers had done reasonably well – Wood, Baynham, Matthews, eleven games, no losses – but had they established reliability and trust? The selectors looked to history to find what they wanted and turned to the keeper they'd have been happy to have seen in the goalmouth since the end of the war. While Eden sought to conjure imperial glories, from a puff of smoke the selectors produced Ted Ditchburn.

I detected an intake of breath in the reports of his selection – a kind of hushed 'the old man's back', and the sense that it was the right thing to do. Ditchburn had played well for Spurs for as long as anyone could remember, from roll- to round-neck, from war to far less disciplined Teds chucking fireworks in the Walworth Road. He'd re-emerged before, not convincingly, in a 6–3 win against the USA in New York, but went back to his club and did all that was required. With developing age, Ted Ditchburn was a true exponent of the long game.

He returned as British paratroopers marched on Port Said. He played in three games – Wales, Yugoslavia and Denmark – and three victories. He performed well, the way the selectors knew he could. In their minds, they'd been right all along. Britain was similarly confident. As the tricky high ball floated over, we made our decision to leave our line and come for it. Others wouldn't, nor were quite able to as we were, but someone had to be. We jumped, rose to the ball and, above the rest, took it cleanly. There was only one problem. As we landed, the lines of the penalty area had been redrawn. We were beyond them, with the ball in our hands, and the world – the Russians, the Americans, more or less the lot of them – cried 'Foul!'

My grandad spent a long time running around the garages of the City and Goswell Roads to find a gallon of petrol and a few shots of oil for his Ford Popular. On 'The Archers' Tom Forrest had to chase off a thief siphoning petrol from a car. There were fights on Tower Hill, protests among students at Oxford and Cambridge and other signs of a 'nation divided'. But this was not in and around our street. The conversation down at the Polish newsagents was that Nasser had a 'ruddy cheek'. The Suez Canal belonged to us, no less than the Regent's. If the world failed to understand this, it was a sign that it, not us, had gone mad. Hungary proved the point. The newspapers pictured Soviet tanks in the streets of Budapest and people fleeing into Austria across snowy fields. I heard Puskas had fled and pictured him galloping with them.

At six each morning my dad came in before he left for work with a cup of tea for my mum and the overnight results from the Melbourne Olympics. Britain won six gold medals. We thought we'd got another one when Ron Delany won the 1,500 metres, a bit less than the mile. My dad came back in to correct that, because

Delany came from Eire. Why the Irish should be separate from us
– my father was just off to spend the day working with them –
made no sense and was a disappointment.

Nina Ponomoreva lost her discus title, which was fair enough.
Given that she'd presumably had to practise for weeks throwing
ladies' hats around the grounds of the Russian embassy, it was also
no surprise. But the Hungarian football team hadn't enough top
players left to defend their title and it was the Soviet Union which
took the gold medal. Their goalkeeper, Lev Yashin, was said to
have played well but it only showed how unfair things could now
be in the world. It confirmed there was a need to stand up and
hold the line against them, and how right we had been to try.

Ted Ditchburn's performances were a display of our way of
doing things and evidence of how it was best. His last game was
shortly before our withdrawal from Egypt and with it the selectors
were content to have made their point. He did not reappear for
England's next match the following spring. Suez drew a line under
the old generation of goalkeepers, as straight as our canal across
the road.

Chapter 6

Into *the* Fire

The Gold Coast became the first black African country to be granted independence. Why it wanted independence was difficult to understand. Why it changed a perfectly good name like Gold Coast to 'Ghana' was incomprehensible. The same month the Germans, the French and others on the continent signed up to the European common market. We kept well away.

Alan Hodgkinson of Sheffield United came straight in for the big game at Wembley against Scotland. There was no easing into the job against small countries from the continent, no comfortable 6–0 wins over Switzerland. The Scots scored within a few minutes. The wireless in our kitchen came to the match at half-time. The first thing 'young Hodgkinson had to do in his international career,' the commentator noted in a sober tone, 'was pick the ball out of the back of his net'. He might have added on behalf of the selectors: 'Welcome to the world, *son.*' These young fellows presumed to take on the job; now they'd find out what it was like.

Hodgkinson and his rival for the position, Eddie Hopkinson of Bolton Wanderers, a year older at twenty-one, were small, 5 feet 9 or 10, with greasy forelocks, 'all mouth and trousers'. Hopkinson smiled cheekily at the camera, Hodgkinson looked at it chin up, with a sort of cocky defiance. The selectors were said to have got their names mixed up, sometimes choosing one when they meant the other.

After the Scots' goal had gone in, Hodgkinson waved away the offers of some of the older players to retrieve the ball for him. But as he stooped to pick it up – 'in front of 100,000 people, about 95,000 of them Scotsmen' – he said he had to wonder what he was doing there. In the second half, England soon equalised. Manchester United's Duncan Edwards scored the winner. Such had been the anticipation in the commentator's voice when the ball reached Edwards running in hard to the edge of the Scot's penalty area, you could hear the explosion when he hit it. After his performance in England's victory in Berlin the year before, the Germans – so our press said – nicknamed him 'Boom, Boom'. At home it was goals like that against Scotland that confirmed him as the universal hero: cheery, muscular, short-back-and-sides, the image of acceptable youth. When Bill Haley's *Rock Around the Clock* had been shown the autumn before, police had been called to cinemas to throw out people who were clapping to the music, chanting and jiving in the aisles; as Haley made his first tour of Britain, the Teds ripped up seats at his venues. But far more kids wanted to be like Edwards. Parents would have been happy if they had. He seemed the perfect combination of skill and strength. My dad, very aware of legs since his childhood paralysis, said mine would be strong. To have 'thighs like Duncan Edwards' became something to aspire to.

In my case they failed to deliver when my cubpack had a game with another group on Highbury Fields by the open-air swimming pool. My mum took me to buy boots in a shop at the Angel, near White Lion Street, cut low in black and with a white stripe along each side. No rough brown leather rose to cover the ankle and there was no hard toe-cap. Why had there ever been? The first thing, surely, everyone learned was that power and direction came from hitting the ball with the instep. Though I knew this, there were no Edwards-like explosions from his vaguely half-back position that I occupied. Near the end of our defeat, though, the cubmaster became animated with our keeper, yelling 'Come out, son, come *out*!', as he waited for a ball rolling towards him. It wasn't obvious to everyone, apparently, but the trick to goalkeeping seemed fairly straightforward – a matter of when to leave or stay on your line.

Everyone cheered the progress of Manchester United in Europe. Matt Busby, their manager, a Scot, persuaded the English FA we should advance into the unknown. The Scots were like this – it was how much of the empire came about, the railway track laid, the distant outposts established. Busby insisted this was the future. There was no need for the FA to worry about its fixture list because, what with modern air travel, games would be played midweek and everyone would be back in time for their league match on Saturday.

Manchester United travelled to play Bilbao and lost 3–1. I saw a picture of the Spanish team's keeper lying on his side, stretching his left arm to put his hand on the ball before the Manchester forwards reached it. The surprising thing was that he looked as comfortable on the ground as a British keeper would. This was Spain, yet it wasn't hard and rough baked earth he was on, more a mixture of snow and mud. When United were at the airport ready to fly back, they had to disembark from their plane to help clear snow off the wings. All good fun and they sewed up the tie by winning with three clear goals at home. The match was at Manchester City's ground, Maine Road. Old Trafford wasn't up to this level of competition and Busby called on the club he'd been a player for to help out. In the next round, however, they were eliminated by Real Madrid, who, as we saw, were brilliant. Still, United got a creditable draw in their home match and we all agreed this was a good effort. Everyone supported them when they played teams from abroad.

Domestically things were different. My dad and the Bedfordshire uncles followed either Luton Town or non-league Peterborough United, who were only a little up and along the railway line from Sandy, past the stretch where the Mallard had worked up steam to break the world record. In our London street, it being Islington, you supported Arsenal, if anyone. My grandad supported Spurs – like Oxford in the boat race – just to be different. By the time Manchester United reached the Cup Final they had already won the league. People were talking, endlessly, about Edwards and their other young players, the wonders of the 'Busby babes'. They were great, and were bidding for this century's first league and Cup double.

Why was it people went on like this? Why did they feel the need to go for the favourite, the big guy? If he always won, where would people like us have been? In the war Hitler was the favourite, the big guy. Brilliant organisation, storming bit of offensive play, he'd done several doubles: Czechoslovakia and Poland, Denmark and Norway, Holland and Belgium, France and . . . With the continent gone, you'd have put your money on him. But it wouldn't have done for the rest of the world to say, 'Oh well, let's support the Germans, then'. Fortunately, as we stood alone, it won time for the Russians and Americans to see sense.

I was in Sandy the weekend of the Cup Final and watched it with my uncle Bim. Aston Villa hadn't got a chance. Their name sounded nice and I hadn't the vaguest idea they were from Birmingham. They looked more cheery than the 'keep right on to the end of the road' types, who were turning up to have a go and see where it got them. It was only fair to give them a shout.

After six minutes a header from the Villa left-winger, Peter McParland, was comfortably collected by Ray Wood. McParland kept running towards the keeper and smashed into him with his shoulder. Wood was knocked out, cheekbone broken and he never fully regained his confidence as a player. In this match centre-half Jackie Blanchflower deputised in goal. McParland scored the two goals past him that won the game. My uncle said this was all wrong, I said that it was a 'fair barge'. I didn't believe it was but, aside from backing Villa, knew that a British keeper took whatever he had to. The year before a German had played with a broken neck. What demands of spirit did this require of us? Yet, well after the game the feeling lingered that what had happened was unfair. There had been the onslaught on Bert Williams about eighteen months earlier, and now this. There was also a different mood hovering in the air. The keeper symbolised the holding of the line; this was at a time when the line itself was beginning to move, to smudge at least, as its whitewashed sharp edges ran into the sand and mud of the goalmouth. We might not have understood why such things had to happen, but both Britain and its goalkeepers, it appeared, were suddenly susceptible to new ideas of what was fair and what wasn't.

At school the marches in the playground on Empire Day stopped. The flag over the BDH had not flown stiffly for some while. The view down the canal from our first-floor classroom window to the City Road bridge was less populated by brightly painted canal barges. If you looked harder, those you did see were dirtier than you'd thought. Police turned up at the locks, amid rumours of kids missing in the canal, trapped by the weeds building up below the waterline. Nets and wooden poles were produced to drag the depths and we saw frogmen go down.

The body of Buster Crabb was found in the sea near Chichester, not far from Portsmouth harbour. There was no surprise that its head was missing. The Russians needed our brains. Sputnik was launched to orbit the earth a few months later. We went in the garden at Sandy and watched it go over at night – actually it could have been a shooting star but it put the Russians in a better light. The 'bleep, bleep' signal was kind of sweet. Laika, the dog whom they put up next, was sweeter. You didn't have to like them much but perhaps we did all have to live together. It was a shame the Russians let Laika burn up in space.

Our area's annual bonfire on one of the corner bombsites of Gerrard Road usually lingered till about midnight. Firemen would then put it out with a few pumpfuls of effluent from the 'tank', – their practice run for the much larger fire down on the corner of St Peter's and Frome Streets. Grown men, scrap metal dealers, ex-boxers, market boys, built and protected that one on the days before November 5. The fire brigade would approach it only at about 4 a.m. – maybe a little earlier if it threatened nearby houses – for fear of sparking public riot.

Most of the kids at school came from that end of the street and others nearby. Teams in the playground were chosen by Kenny Bell, whose mum and dad had a sweet shop. His uncle ran the informal bookies at the back of it. Kenny was small, of Italian background on his mum's side. The 'cheeky chappie' type, he laughed and chattered like a monkey. He was not especially likeable but he commanded a following.

Kenny was the only kid who could afford a steady supply of balls. They came from his parents' shop, rust-red rubber ones, tennis-ball size without the hair but with sufficient bounce to send them over the canal wall and high wire fencing. Anyone who lost them could slip out the school gates and round the quarter of a mile to the lock-keeper's gate. Here they might enter, under threat of having the police called, and try their luck fishing them out of the bilge by the sluice gates without falling in. When they got back, there was the fear of the cane from the headmaster. The alternative was somehow finding the money to pay Kenny for the ball, the replacement for which he got free. Anyone silly enough to bring in their own ball, risked having it lost by him or his friends. They'd be sillier to imagine they'd be compensated. Balls were best left to Kenny.

And so he always had first choice in picking teams. Top selection was Teddy Merryman, who looked and played in the style of Fulham's Johnny Haynes – a lot of pointing and directing, a lot of skill. Others, in Fulham's case like Jimmy Hill, did most of the running. Kenny chose Teddy even if he didn't win the toss. His opposing captain would know to seek other options. On one occasion someone did choose Teddy. Kenny felt restrained from saying 'my game, my ball' but went into a miserable, distracted mood. Teddy did likewise, as did everyone else when play got under way. It petered out after a few minutes, with no one able to concentrate.

Kenny's second choice, whom again everyone else knew to avoid, was a big kid – on the fat side, to be honest – who played in goal. He was in the year above Kenny, and two years older than me. When he left school he wasn't easy to replace. There were no volunteers. Kenny chose one of his mates from Frome Street, Peter Lithgoe, who was big. But Peter was lumbering rather than athletic, with thick National Health glasses on the end of his nose. He played with his mouth open, unable to see the ball in flight and in danger of swallowing it. He didn't want to play, either in goal or at all, but Kenny forced him to under penalty of expulsion from his crowd. Kenny's team was a closed circle and very nearly always won.

A national shock came on the afternoon after bonfire night 1957, when England lost to an Irish national side for the first time in thirty years. The north's 3–2 victory was their first ever in London. Harry Gregg of Doncaster Rovers put on 'one of the greatest displays of goalkeeping ever seen at Wembley', said the programme for one of England's later games, recalling the momentous occasion. 'Here Gregg is seen cutting out an England corner kick,' it said under a picture of him leaping high and beyond the edge of his 6-yard box. He was transferred straightaway to Manchester United to replace Wood, for a record £23,000.

When Gregg and the United team came to Highbury the following February, it was a waste of time asking my parents to let me go. After my dad's White Hart Lane experience in 1948, they wouldn't entertain my joining a crowd of over 60,000. I took the bus along Upper Street with a friend from across the street to kick a ball around on Highbury Fields. We took it in turns in goal. Manchester fans walking through from Highbury Corner joined in, shouted encouragement and went on to the stadium. I turned on the wireless for the score when I got home, as a formality. A Manchester United win was inevitable. The first thing the results man said after he'd solemnly intoned 'League Division One', however, was 'Arsenal 4 . . .' This was unbelievable, not only to win against the Busby babes, but with such an impressive score. Then he added '. . . Manchester United 5'. It was as if they'd been playing around with you. Nothing nasty, but, rather similar to their supporters walking through Highbury Fields, just joining in the fun, a friendly kickabout, after which they were on their way.

They flew to Yugoslavia for their European Cup match, which was played the following Wednesday. Thursday was a freezing day, dark as soon as I'd got home from school. My mum came in a little later to say she'd heard the plane carrying them back had crashed. In the evening we heard several players were dead, Edwards seriously injured, Busby on something called the danger list. Then it came out that Harry Gregg, the goalkeeper, had gone back into the burning wreckage several times to rescue people. He'd saved fellow players, like his roommate in Belgrade, Johnny Berry. He really became frightened, he said, when he saw Berry's head covered in blood. Berry had such severe injuries that he didn't know for three months he'd been in a crash and didn't play again. The United keeper also helped Busby and pulled out a Yugoslav mother and baby.

Gregg was only there because of his display of goalkeeping at Wembley three months earlier. The night before the crash he'd been having a drink with Frank Swift, who was on the trip and now working as a journalist. 'Don't be a keeper who stays on his line,' Swift had advised him. It was not that Gregg was that way inclined, but he was apt to be criticised as a result. Busby had defended him against the Old Trafford crowd. He often came to the edge of his penalty area, sometimes beyond. If he was wearing a cap, he might remove it at the last moment to head a ball clear. I was sure once

I'd seen him do it with his cap on. He had been discussing what gloves a goalkeeper should wear. Swift said he'd had his made for him, a special type. He was going to tell Gregg about them when they got home. Swift no doubt would have done if he hadn't been killed in the crash.

The aircraft ran into trees and houses at the end of a runway at Munich, where it had made a brief stopover. A build-up of snow was responsible. Before the team had left their hotel in Belgrade, they were told to hand over their passports. Gregg went for his and offered to get that of Johnny Berry, from his bag in the room. A Yugoslav visa was with the passport but no one had asked for visas, so Gregg dropped it back in Berry's suitcase for safe-keeping. At the airport customs officials demanded to see Berry's visa, which was in his bag and already in the hold of the plane. It was hardly likely he didn't have one: how else would they have let him into the country? Maybe they were just acting like officials the world over. They were certainly acting like those on the chilly frontiers of eastern Europe. The delay meant the flight landed about an hour late for its stop in Munich. It had just started snowing.

Duncan Edwards died twelve days later. My dad said it was only his strength that had kept him alive so long, by which I assumed he meant the girth of his thighs. Harry Gregg was the hero of Munich. But whenever people put it to him that he was, he wouldn't have anything to do with the idea.

Manchester United bought and and borrowed players to rebuild. They beat West Bromwich Albion in the quarter-finals of the FA Cup to a countrywide gasp of amazement, if the reports I read were anything to go by. I wasn't that surprised. They still had Gregg, after all. Bill Foulkes, their right-back, had been uninjured and Bobby Charlton had survived, though shaken. The players they bought were very good. But a picture of their winning goal against West Brom bothered me. It was taken from below, presumably by a photographer crouched behind or to the side of the net. The effect was of the floodlights framing the scorer's head like a halo. What had happened at Munich was awful, yet not the fault of the teams United played. But there was a kind of clamour for sacrifices to the spirit of mourning.

The next in line were a relative bunch of minnows. Fulham had good players – Johnny Haynes, Jimmy Hill, Bobby Robson

– but the team as a whole was modest. Craven Cottage, their home ground by the river, was small and quaint, not Maine Road or Old Trafford. Their chairman, Tommy Trinder, a comedian, made jokes about them when he introduced 'Sunday Night at the London Palladium'.

In the game the performance of Fulham's goalkeeper, Tony Macedo, almost managed to swing the result and the mood the other way. Even a depleted Manchester United should have been able to see off Fulham and the way he played – under continual pressure – adjusted people's sympathies from unbridled support for United to recognition that here was a hard-pressed small guy battling away. My parents let me stay up to watch the news highlights of the game. Just twenty, Macedo was younger than even the new keepers who had come to the fore. He was dark-haired and with distinctly continental features, not least his style of play. It was one of the most exciting exhibitions of goalkeeping imaginable. He sprang rather than jumped, and spent much of the game twisting dramatically in midair. One shot in particular was heading with great power for the top left of his net, but he soared to it, clawed it back as it had virtually crossed the line. He kept this up throughout the match to earn Fulham a 2–2 draw, and a replay at Highbury.

The response to Macedo's display included firm statements that here was a really exciting prospect for the future. He didn't look like some sullen or cocky rebel against the short-back-and-sides. He seemed separate from that and was, because he was different. But there also lay a worry. Macedo's dad was Spanish. He was a goal-keeper, too, good enough to have had a trial for Barcelona. Nothing came of that and he eventually ended up in London, just north of Islington in Tufnell Park. His son obviously had brilliant qualities but with a background and name like that, could he really hold the line in the solid and unshaking way required of British keepers?

A newspaper came up with the answer. Macedo wasn't from any old place on the continent. His family had got out of Spain a little after the civil war and they had moved to Britain via Gibraltar, where Tony was born. You couldn't get more solid and unshakingly British than that. Thanks to his performance in the first semi-final against Manchester United, Tony Macedo was nicknamed the 'Rock of Gibraltar'. There was a sigh of relief. We could all love him now.

The big game of the day in the Hanover playground was staged in the midday break after we'd finished school dinner. On the Monday, I borrowed a pair of my mum's gloves which she used to wear for best but were too old for that now and stood with the rest as Kenny ran through the routine of choosing his team. Peter Lithgoe had gone missing, either off at the clinic in Popham Row having his eyes tested or lingering over his spotted dick in the dinner hall hoping his absence wouldn't be noticed. When I volunteered after Kenny had won the toss and chosen Teddy Merryman, he looked astounded. I was a year younger than any of the team he usually compiled and no one since the last school year had willingly offered to go in goal.

I was put to defend that at the school, as opposed to the BDH, end of the playground. This was roughly bounded by the boys' toilets, or piss'ole, to the right, and drinking taps on the school wall behind me to the left. I knew exactly what would happen. From 12 yards, over by the entrance to the piss'ole, a kid swung his right leg at Kenny's red rubber ball and it flew to the top-left corner of my goal. I started my jump the moment it left his foot, sure to the half-inch of its rising path, and leapt – Macedo-like – above the drinking taps. The ball slapped into the palm of my upraised hand; I was watching as it did so and clawed it back from the angle between left post and crossbar chalked on the school wall. Easy . . .

Others weren't to know this and it took a moment for it to sink in, whereafter Kenny took leave of his senses. ''E's saved it!' he shouted, and with a scream sufficient to grind playground activity to a halt, added, ''e's fuckin' *saved* it!' He bounced up and down like Rumpelstiltskin, with his loyal crowd yelling their approval. I shrugged away this nonsense like Harry Gregg or Reg Matthews would have done, and was picked first when the teams were chosen next day.

o   o   o

Kenny went on about it too long. He loudly retold and replayed the story to the gathered mass, throwing the ball up in the air, jumping, arching his back after it. This was nice at first but by the time we resumed playing, I felt distinctly uncomfortable. It was great to get in the team but I wasn't sure I wanted to be Kenny's performing seal. Not least, it applied a degree of pressure which hadn't been there before. I was under its influence as a similar sort of shot came in during the day's match. I felt unable to jump and it sailed above and past me. The circumstances of it weren't exactly the same; the ball was an inch or so higher, and when it was hit I was a foot or more towards the other side of the goal. But I stayed – as I read goalkeepers did sometimes – 'rooted to the spot'.

'Jump!' Kenny yelled, in confusion rather than anger. 'Fuckin' jump, like you did yesterday.' I called back an explanation somewhere between 'too high for me, Ken' and 'fort it was going over'. He wasn't any more convinced than I was and looked at me awkwardly, trying to work out if I was having him on, letting him down in front of his mates, flouting the honour of being made part of them. Such was the capital stock of credibility I'd accumulated the day before, however, it was soon forgotten as we played on to his team's customary victory.

Clear from all this was that a miracle one day was the next regarded by the crowd as routine. They took it for granted, came to expect it. In our assembly or, if it couldn't be avoided, at Sunday school at St Peter's round the corner (just past the Polish church) in Devonia Road, there was more a less a story a day of miracles Jesus had performed. But he was no fool and knew to move on once he'd done them. Had he lingered too long having raised Lazurus from his palliasse, he'd have no doubt heard the matter-of-fact call of 'Another one over here, Jesus'. The football crowd might rise to their feet in shock and amazement at the wonders they had seen the goalkeeper perform, only then to subject him to the tyranny of mass expectation. Their presumption, and failure to appreciate the difficulty and weight of responsibility that went with the task, was annoying. It was liable to encourage only more of the bloodymindedness the position required in the first place.

Tony Macedo dismantled his reputation as an international keeper-in-the-making the following afternoon. Fulham scored three against Manchester United in the Cup semi-final replay at Highbury; at the opposite end, Macedo conceded five, most of them attributed to his mistakes. On a wet day he had opted to play without gloves. Later on in the game he put a pair on but not before several shots had slipped through. Keepers didn't play without gloves in the wet. So what possessed Macedo? When asked about the match, and his disappointment, the impression was he didn't feel any. He seemed 'relieved' to have played badly. He'd only recently come into the team and the pressure on him had been building up as he played well week after week. He had worried about having a bad game and knew it would have to come some time. Now it had, he was suggesting, some of the tension was off.

Fulham supporters forgave him because they knew that without him they would not have reached this stage of the competition. I thought it was a shame he'd had such a game but still liked him because of his flair. Other reaction beyond the Fulham Palace Road was of derisive condemnation. People were angry at his having lulled them into thinking that he might have been anything but a continental. 'Macedo!': the name spoke for itself.

I got together a scrapbook of goalkeepers' pictures cut from the newspapers, using glue and some stiff-papered pages left from ledgers my mum had bound together at Lowe's the printers. Some keepers were in flight across their goals, mouths open, eyes staring after the flight of the ball they'd put around the post. Several were standing and waiting, an arm raised or finger pointed, shouting and organising the team. In others they climbed, arms stretched to catch the ball above and just in front of their heads. These pictures were the most impressive. They portrayed the keeper high above the other players. Defenders and attackers alike jumped without hope or were left flat-footed on the ground. They looked up with expressions of awe and admiration as the keepers took the ball.

Pictures of continental keepers often showed them punching the ball. In the programme for the Rest of the World match five years before, there was a scene from England's pre-war game against the Rest of Europe. 'Goalie Olivieri', the Italian said to be one of the best in the world, was reaching to punch away 'a sharp header' from one of the England forwards. Why didn't he catch it? The only other person jumping remotely near him was his own centre-half, whom he should have told to get out the way. Compared to our commanding presence, alert and in waiting, even the better continentals flew, fretted and conveyed their nervousness to their team around them. It wasn't what keepers were for. As with the priest on Florence station, whom you'd have thought would surely impart some calm to the crowd, it was a shock when he launched himself through the incoming train window to grab a seat. He wasn't there to act like every-one else.

My dad reeled off the names of keepers he'd known at their best. There were the obvious ones, Swift, Bartram, Williams, Merrick, Streten. But there were others more unsung. George Swindin of Arsenal had an old and lined face and had not long retired. He'd played for many years in a team that had won both the Cup and league, yet, with too many other good keepers in his way, he'd never won an England cap. He was succeeded by Jack Kelsey at Arsenal, only after he'd dropped a corner kick against Chelsea. Sheffield United's Ted Burgin went as reserve to the World Cup in Switzerland, but didn't get an international game there or after. I had a picture of him in an old jersey, solemnly directing events from a very muddy, dark and, I assumed, northern goalmouth. Now replaced at Sheffied by Hodgkinson, he'd been transferred to York City in the Third Division North. He had moved from the brink of world competition to about as far down as you could get in ours. It was further evidence of our depth of talent. Wherever you looked, from Bramall Lane via Berne to Bootham Crescent, our keepers were all great.

Other positions had their own special characteristics and characters. Centre-forwards tended to be 'swashbucklers', making anarchic forays abroad like pirates on the Spanish Main. Drake (Ted of Arsenal, rather than Francis of Plymouth) had been one, some time before my day, and was now manager of Chelsea. They were all centre-partings and plastered hair. Apart from one or two new ones coming along, like Brian Clough at Middlesbrough – to whom I sent a photo and had it returned in forty-eight hours signed 'Best Wishes' – they were of a bygone time. We weren't swashbuckling abroad like we used to. The keeper was the vital position and the one to be revered.

No greater evidence was necessary than the picture in the paper of Bolton's Nat Lofthouse playing against Wolves. His keeper was injured during the game and Lofthouse substituted for him. Wolves got a penalty, Lofthouse saved it. His team's fans went wild and I read he described it as one of his proudest moments in football. As the 'Lion of Vienna', he'd had a few moments in his time.

I glued the picture in my book. I was glad for Lofthouse but even with a limited experience of goalmouth scrambles around the piss'ole, I could see it was a poor penalty. It had been hit straight at him. A proper keeper might have anticipated it going towards a corner of the net and moved, inadvertently, out of the ball's way. Lofthouse, with not much of an idea what to do, just stood there and it slammed into his chest. The crowd's acclamation, therefore, was excessive, but it showed one thing: as hard as keeping could be, it had its compensations. Facing penalties was potentially easy. Any goalkeeper knew it, unlike players from lesser positions and the mass of fans watching. It underlined the keeper as an all-wise character, and the crowd as a little dim.

In the 1958 Cup Final, Manchester United came up against Lofthouse and Bolton. Most people wanted United to win. But Lofthouse generated competing emotions. As with Matthews in 1953, this was probably his last chance to crown a distinguished career with a Cup medal. Over the course of the ninety minutes, Bolton's keeper, quiffy Eddie Hopkinson, smiled and dived around into several important saves and was really the man of the match. The scorer of the game's only two goals, Lofthouse, would have been, if it hadn't have been for the nature of his second.

Harry Gregg had parried a shot high into the air by his goalpost and turned to jump for it. Lofthouse leapt, too, and slammed into the goalkeeper's back with his elbow. Knocked out as Ray Wood had been a year earlier, Gregg ended up in the net, the ball alongside him. In terms of the rules, everything about the ref's decision to give the goal was wrong. Lofthouse hit Gregg in the back, not the shoulder. Gregg did not have his feet firmly on the ground as was required in a shoulder-charging duel; he was in midair.

In a sense, however, the rules were irrelevant. The keeper was a character required to perform above them, a symbol of endurance no matter what. People needed such a thing. The father of my mate Eric, the best friend I had among the crowd beyond Danbury Street, had been at the fall of Singapore – virtually walked off the boat on his arrival and, with one or two hundred thousand others, ushered by his commanders straight into three years in a Japanese prisoner-of-war camp. Eric's mum, who had been at school with mine, didn't know whether he was dead or alive. He walked back into their house when it was all over, with a stick and minus a leg. Amid the years of mistreatment it wouldn't have done him any good going on about the rules. No, to go screaming for support from a lot of words on paper was for softer people than the keeper.

But there were flaws with the argument. Harry Gregg was not the remotest bit soft. We had the evidence. The Lion of Vienna had not taken on some young keeper in need of a few lessons in life but the Hero of Munich. Also, it could not be claimed Lofthouse was typical of some cocky new bunch in society trying their muscular luck with the good and traditional way. The actions of the old swashbuckling lot were as wanting as the new. Two successive Cup Finals in which Manchester United's keeper had got the worst of things, demanded the rules be changed. The keeper had to be protected.

I didn't accept this for one minute, nor for many years afterwards. Protection meant being embraced by the warmth of the communal law: 'Come on in, we'll look after you.' It was an early sign that the keeper was drifting towards becoming just another member of the team.

o   o   o

England embarked on their summer tour and with Hopkinson in goal were hammered 5–0 in Belgrade. Their next destination threatened worse. For the first time England were to play the Soviet Union, and in Moscow, too. This was an outfit prepared to resort to any means – kidnapping, brainwashing, hat theft, invasion – to win, added to which they were nuclear-equipped. They would surely blast us out of sight. The thought of us facing them was as frightening as anything I could remember. Colin McDonald, Burnley's keeper, was chosen to play his first international. I couldn't imagine how he'd stand the strain.

The papers next morning reported back an incredible 1–1 draw. McDonald made a commanding debut. We were unlucky not to win. My surprise was tempered by the picture of the England goal. Derek Kevan of West Brom was nodding the ball down and in by the near post. The Russian keeper, Yashin, was hopelessly out of position by the other upright. Dressed all in black, he had the trappings of a sinister Russian. His name had that ring to it, and rhymed with assassin. But this bloke, whom they called the 'Black Octopus', looked more like a spider, with spindly arms and legs flapping to no useful effect.

Days later, England, Northern Ireland, Scotland and Wales went on to the World Cup in Sweden. The BBC and, for the first time, ITV went to cover their progress. Since Switzerland, television had been refining the art of the outside broadcast. A camera rigged up on the bridge of the boat, for example, would present the gripping manoeuvres of a trip across the Channel. In order not to disorientate people too much, it would be in the homeward direction, the navy guiding ship and viewer alike from Calais to safe refuge beneath the white cliffs and into Dover harbour.

The opening match saw the hosts play Mexico. The Mexicans' goalkeeper, Antonio Carbajal, had created a record by appearing in three World Cups. Kenneth Wolstenholme lingered over the syllables, 'Car-var-hal'. True to form, he was the slick-hair moustachioed type – Pancho in the 'Cisco Kid', all bar the sombrero. I thought Wolstenholme chuckled at his antics in a manner which said, 'Well, you know what these Mexicans are like'. The Swedish captain Nils Liedholm sent him the wrong way for a penalty kick but was ordered to retake it. Carbajal jinked and beamed about his goalline, as if we should be in no doubt this time he'd save it. Any proper keeper knew it was unwise to celebrate at all, let alone too soon. Liedholm sent him flying the wrong way again. I laughed.

I couldn't take to the overawed tones that the commentary lapsed into when a distant land's keeper smiled or jittered into view. When Gilmar took to the field – 'There he is, Geel-marr' – it was as if a god had deigned to descend among us. He was good, but not that good, very much of this world rather than any other, despite the globe and stars on his jersey. When we saw the black Russian emerge, it was 'the *great* Yashin'. On what basis was such a claim made? The commentator said it breathlessly, cautiously, implying he was wary of not having sought the Kremlin's permission.

The Soviet Union met England again and Yashin disgraced himself. After the referee awarded the penalty with which England drew the game, the Russian grabbed his arm and threw his cap at him. We had thought the penalty was a bit doubtful but this was no way to carry on. It was their way, of course. And having had their keeper assault the referee, next, no doubt, the Russians would be demanding an apology. One thing, though, you couldn't help but notice Yashin. He had a presence. With his antics and black kit, he was set apart from the paler Ivan Ivanovs (well, there were at least two Ivanovs) who constituted the rest of the team. They were more like the faceless machines who'd have driven their 'invited' tanks into Budapest. Maybe, just maybe, Yashin might have been the type to wonder what that was all about. And in the play-off – the two countries' third meeting in a month – he did play reasonably well. Russia won by the only goal.

True to form, the foreign keepers generally had a nattier strip. They all wore the number 1 on their back. I made the mistake of telling my dad I thought this looked good and wondered why it wasn't the practice for British keepers. I was surprised how angry this made him. 'Daft!' he responded. The gist of his argument, succinctly put, was that everyone knew what a keeper's number was, so why wear one? It was unnecessary, somehow typical. A British goalkeeper was judged by what he did, not this numeric symbol which said what he was *meant* to do. A '1' on a keeper's back was form not substance and, likely as not, substitute for a backbone. 'Daft!'

Brazil won the competition. In the two years since Wembley they'd transformed themselves from a new world team of spasmodic gyrators into one which could beat anyone, ancient or modern. At seventeen, Pele arrived to prowl and flash alongside Didi and other panthers. There were enough tight games for Gilmar to be called upon to display solidity at the back. He kept a clean sheet in four of Brazil's six games.

But it was Harry Gregg who was voted goalkeeper of the tournament. And among the British keepers the 'all great' tag applied. When Gregg wasn't fit for a game against Czechoslovakia, Portsmouth's Norman Uprichard took over and played well as Northern Ireland advanced to the quarter-finals. Colin McDonald was superb in England's games against the Soviet Union and in a 0–0 draw with Brazil. Scotland's Bill Brown, of Dundee, impressed everyone with his performance against eventual semi-finalists, France. The finest individual display, however, was Kelsey's when Wales took on the Brazilians in the quarter-finals. In a swirling wind in Jönköping he caught everything, including a succession of crosses lofted over from the wings. Brazil won by the game's only goal – Pele's first in an international – but with a shot Kelsey had covered till it deflected off a defender's leg. Pele ran around crazily, hardly able to believe it. The Brazilian press denounced him and his teammates, saying they should have been ashamed to have scored such a goal. When asked how he'd managed to handle the ball so well in the game, Kelsey claimed he hadn't had a lot to do with it. It was the chewing gum, he said, that he habitually rubbed into his hands.

In the summer, an army revolt in Iraq led to the burning of the British embassy and the collapse of the Baghdad Pact. The BBC pronounced it in staccato rhythm and as if it was all one word: rat-tat-tat, the 'Bag-dad-pact'. Its end put nails in the coffin of Britain's bid to lead a counterforce to the Russians in the Middle East. But such an effort – we whistled up Turkey and Pakistan, as well as Iraq to help us – was out in a distant midfield over which we had no firm influence. Duncan Sandys, our defence secretary, was left with a pact rendered headquarterless. Soon, too, he was the object of suspicions he'd been the 'headless man' in photographs with the kneeling, and naked but for three strings of pearls, Duchess of Argyll. The Russians were behind it, of course – not the headless man, in this case, and the duchess's unfortunate divorce – but the summary dispatch of the Bag-dad-pact, and the shocking blow it represented.

It was alarming enough that young men in Britain strongly objected to their two years' National Service. It was said they had to salute everything that moved and paint whatever didn't. What recently had been nothing less than the 'finest army in the world', was suddenly subject to headlines urging 'Cut out the Bull!' My young uncle Keith was one of the last, reluctantly, to be called. Friendly local doctors – there was a good one off the Essex Road just past Packington Street – could be counted on for sickness certificates. But it would surely never have come to such a thing as an uprising in Aldershot or Brize Norton. In Baghdad, on the other hand, someone had killed young King Feisal II, aged twenty-three. From the way people talked, we took this personally. Feisal's coronation had taken place in the same year as the Queen's. He'd been educated at a British 'prep school' and at Harrow. Prince Charles was being educated at 'prep school', whatever that was. He played cricket there, like any other schoolboy, as the press suggested, even though the photos of him made it clear that he couldn't bowl overarm. But in the same month the Queen struck back in the cause of legitimacy. In Cardiff, where 'and Commonwealth' was inserted within the title 'Empire Games' for the first time, she decreed Charles to be Prince of Wales. I thought the stadium's cheers were a bit orchestrated as she made the announcement but, if the stirring response of the massed bands of Welsh Guards was anything to go by, she'd held the line against any threat of army revolt.

My parents finally let me go to see a first-team game when the new season got under way. A friend of my mum's who also worked at Lowe's went regularly to Highbury. This and the fact Bert Trautmann was coming to town won me permission to go. We arrived an hour and a half before the start to guarantee a place at the front of the Clock End terraces. When Trautmann came out and ran to our end, the people around me, all home supporters, cheered and applauded. He smiled, shouted back 'thank you' and waved. But he and Manchester City quickly went two goals down.

Jack Kelsey trotted towards us in the second half, without looking up at the crowd banked behind the goal. He continued reflectively chewing and sniffing a small length of cotton wool. Someone said this was soaked in ammonia and to clear his head. Manchester City won a corner on the left a minute after the restart. Kelsey retired to his backpost, spat his patented mix of saliva and gum juice on his hands and rubbed it in. My position at the lowest level of the terraces, straight behind the goal, gave an unobscured view and the impression of being virtually under his crossbar. As the ball came over, Kelsey advanced across his goal and called to his defence that he was coming for it. When he'd made the eight yards to his front post, he took off, hands moving aloft. At the apex of his jump, his arms were stretched to their full extent and just in front of a line with his head. His legs were raised back at right angles from the knee, leaving him clear of the ground by between four and five feet. Eyes fixed on the ball, he smiled as it slapped into and stuck in his hands.

I had seen pictures of him doing this, so it was not unexpected. What was, was that there was very little applause, no spontaneous cries of loud acclamation. People around me relaxed and shuffled their feet as the tension passed. They murmured, reventially, 'Good old Jack', or '*That's* it, Jack', in relief at a responsibility assumed. On the face of it, all Kelsey had done was leapt and caught a ball. In fact, what he had achieved was to bring an immediate end to the danger. Only the goalkeeper had the wherewithal to restore calm and balance like this and put matters at rest. Others played their part but tended to add to the chaos. Applause, however, was apparently not called for. Taking the cross was something the crowd expected and keepers just did.

○   ○   ○

Our schoolteacher, the sternly bespectacled Miss Carter, staged class quizzes. These were getting me into trouble, particularly in geography. The weirdness of our holidays meant I was the only one who answered questions on the world's capitals. Our trains had either passed through several of them, or within a few hundred miles of others. A brief glance on any map revealed their names next to the larger black spots, and maybe the rivers they stood on. A bad mistake was to have guessed that the largest river in Russia was the Volga. It was the only one in that part of the world I'd heard of, when someone requested its boatman's song on 'Desert Island Discs'.

On awkward days this won me the title 'teacher's pet', but it wasn't forced – or punched – home with conviction. This was partly thanks to an intuitive grasp in the playground of the fact that no such character would play in goal, partly because no one could really imagine Miss Carter having a 'pet'. In brown laced shoes and with her grey hair tied back, while she chalked at the blackboard she'd catch people talking from the reflections in her glasses. She claimed to have eyes in the back of her head. Members of the class doubted this was true but never felt fully confident that it wasn't. I got the impression she'd been to other countries, to France at least. She spoke with some assurance about Marseilles, which, I assumed for our benefit, she pronounced Mar-sails.

'Has anyone else been abroad?' she would periodically ask, in resigned tones. 'I have, miss,' came the answer, though from a different person every time: 'Isle o' Wight!' The class collapsed into laughter, briefly, till she shut them up. It was always easier when I could report back that we'd been to Butlins at Clacton. The years we went to Ostend were OK because it sounded like Southend. Jill Tatley and her cousins, the Mancinis and Nicholls, might go to places like Seasalter, on the north Kent coast near Herne Bay. Jean Black next to me went hop-picking in Kent, which sounded nice.

But she looked embarrassed when she told me and it turned out to be a working holiday. Many went to caravans on Canvey Island, a popular location for working people seeking a few days' leisure and where a caring government did its bit to improve the Thames estuary view by building an oil refinery. One of the two kids of half-Italian background in our class was proud to announce he had never been to Italy, nor had any wish to go. The other terrorised my sister, who was five years behind us and had scarcely started school. I must have let it slip that we had eaten spaghetti – he went around telling her friends how we lived on a diet of worms.

Staring at the map on the classroom wall was, therefore, something of a curse. But it was an alternative to dismal views over the windswept canal, while we listened to schools' radio broadcasts on the grain fields of Saskatchewan and the rustic lifestyles of the Basques, as well as which it revealed one clear truth: Britain stood alone and in its own area. This was a little away from a much larger mass of land, the 'continent'. We belonged to the continent – it was our team. Then again, we learned it wasn't really. We were of, rather than in it. Britain's position and boundaries were also quite clear. Those of the countries in front of us were uncertain, haphazard lines on a map, which could change at any moment.

Ours had changed but at some time back in the distant past. We understood that Britain had once been joined to France. It gave the impression of cavemen strolling between Calais and Dover. Thanks to an intervening ice age and the English Channel, we had then been left on our own. It was sad in a way, lucky in another. Our knowledge of fairly recent history was that the continent in front of us periodically got itself into a lot of bother. The boundaries between its members in the last war, and others before it, disappeared as some of the countries merged with one another. Such events drew us in, dangerously, but only as long as it took to restore order, at which time we'd be off again to our own area.

Even a wartime defeat like Dunkirk we had turned into a victory. We'd been badly caught off our line. But 300,000 troops were rescued and the triumph lay in their getting back. A London newspaper cartoon showed a soldier waving a fist at the blazing continent. 'Very well, alone,' said the caption. Britain emerged from the map and history as the world's goalkeeper. We were naturals and it was no wonder we played the position so well.

There was no one who played it better than Jack Kelsey. On one occasion he took part in two big games in a day. During an early winter's afternoon he played in Wales's 2–2 draw against England at Villa Park and at the final whistle was rushed to Birmingham station. In the three hours available, it was doubted he'd get to London by rail and car for Arsenal's evening friendly with Juventus, but the novelty of playing a club from abroad was not one Kelsey wanted to let pass. He arrived at the stadium in his kit and made it on to the pitch during the five minute kickabout before the start of the game. The crowd loudly cheered his arrival, as Jim Standen, his stand-in, left the field trying not to look as fed up as he felt.

It was noticeable, however, that Kelsey did pick up quite frequent injuries, which gave other keepers the occasional look-in for club and country. Several goalmouth occupants in the league just played on and on, game after game, season after season. Blackpool's George Farm went back to the ark. When I saw him he looked withered and much too old to be in shorts. In the 1953 'Matthews final' his errors – if you read between the lines of the effusive reports of the match – had nearly handed the cup to Bolton. But these were passed over as a lapse in a career of noble consistency. Harry Leyland of Blackburn Rovers, short and chubby, rolled up in every goalmouth action shot or team picture of Blackburn I'd ever seen. When he materialised in person a few yards from me in one game, he got into a slanging match with his centre-half over whose should have been the ball both of them had just missed. 'Oi!' reacted the crowd around my mum's friend and me: 'There are women and children here!' I hadn't caught what was said, but it was a little shocking, whatever it was, as if I'd heard one of my uncles swearing. Leyland and teammate looked round at us sharply, shut up and went back to the game.

Bobby Charlton, air crash survivor, clean-cut, quiet and unassuming, eased into the acceptable youth vacuum vacated by Duncan Edwards, when he appeared for several weeks on 'Double Your Money'. No one begrudged him his £1,000 prize, which about doubled his income for the year. He gave his chosen subject, 'pop music' a new respectability, certainly more than the Teds had. Gangs of them had been confronting blacks on the streets of Notting Hill for another of Sir Oswald Mosley's comebacks.

The first foreigner in our class arrived in the shape of Cassandra, thin and very pale, whose family had moved away from the crisis in Cyprus. Her clothes were too frail for the weather. Taken with the fact she was from abroad, we assumed this meant she was poor. She didn't seem to know English, which may have been because she was just shy. Apart from one or two girls who took her under their wing as if she were an abandoned waif and stray, no one had much to do with her. When the nurse came to check everyone's hair, with no evidence one way or the other, the word went around she had fleas.

My friend Eric announced that when he left Hanover he wanted to go to Highbury, the school his brother had recently started at. This sounded good enough to me and I mentioned it to my mum. She had a word with our headmaster, who spoke to his Highbury counterpart. After I'd had an interview, I was lined up for a Governors' Place, in the event of my failing the 11-plus. I brought the matter up again with Eric, about how we'd be going to the same school. He said he'd changed his mind. There was too much homework at grammar school. He'd be going to Barnsbury instead, with the other kids.

They wished me luck when I took the exam, a week later than everyone else, as I'd just come out of hospital. While walking across the desk tops when we were confined to class during a rainswept dinner time, I'd crashed forward and broken my nose, my inadvertent dive impressing the crowd. The 11-plus, the rest of the class assured me, was easy. In the event, I only just finished it in time, answering the last clue in the English crossword as the teacher collected the papers: four-letter word for the hole in a net, 'mesh'. When Miss Carter received the results she sounded disapproving. She wouldn't go through everyone's. It'd be far quicker to read out the names of those who had passed. There were only five, she added, which made me breathe easily. If I had passed, I wouldn't be alone. Then she said: 'Four girls, and one boy.' The bell tolled for the end of the day as soon as she'd listed the fortunate five. She left mine till last. My speed proved enough to get me from my desk near the front of the class to the door at the back. Through the school gates and up the road, the mob was still in pursuit. It was safe to slow down once I'd crossed the Danbury Street divide.

My friend Eric had moved into flats near the clinic in Clephane Road. Long lines formed when Jeff Hall, the Birmingham City left-back, was taken ill with polio. He died two weeks later. He'd played seventeen games for England, including those with Reg Matthews against Brazil and Germany, not once on the losing side. My mother had already taken me to have my injections but there were many who hadn't had theirs. For the last six months of primary school, Eric came and went on the bus the mile or so along Essex Road. His small road off St Peter's Street had been demolished and replaced by two large blocks of flats. The council could have knocked down any number of other streets – Burgh, Allingham, Frome – for the harm it would have done the area. But it was as if it was an experiment, and they stopped there.

After months of subtle pressure from us, our teachers arranged a game with William Tyndale, the school which turned out on Friday mornings next to us on the cinder pitches by the old clock tower at Highbury Barn. They played in yellow shirts, we in whatever we could get our hands on. Mainly kids from the back of Barnsbury, between Caledonian and Liverpool Roads, all of them were as tough as anyone from St Peter's Street and most of them more so. They easily beat us, 4–2.

Other journeys out of school had been confined to destinations like the Tower of London, with teachers happy to let us play for an hour or so afterwards on the beach at Traitor's Gate. In our last couple of years, horizons were gently expanded. We went on daytrips along the Thames on the *Daffodil*, which sailed from near Tower pier to the estuary, looked across its brown expanse to the southern reaches of the North Sea and swung back. Between there and London Bridge, boats lined both banks more or less all the way. We learned London was the largest port and city in the world. There were disturbing hints others were catching up – insignificant places, like Antwerp. It was perhaps unsurprising that New York should rival London in size, but Los Angeles? Tokyo? When our class went on its two-week trip to the Isle of Wight, as we waited on the ferry at Portsmouth for the trip to Ryde, the SS *United States* sailed past. Sadly, it now did the trip to New York faster than the *Queen Mary* or *Queen Elizabeth*.

While we were away at least some of the best traditions and decencies were upheld. When Nottingham Forest beat Luton in the Cup Final, I won a football for predicting the 2–1 result. It had been on show for several weeks in a TV rental shop in Upper Street near

St Mary's church – twelve stitched panels of best absorbent brown leather, this was none of your gleaming white continental rubbish. Actually, if it had been, the competition would have attracted more entrants and probable winners. Six days later George Marwood, who'd shot a policeman, was hanged in Pentonville. 'Hysterical' protests, according to some reports, were staged outside the prison. Rab Butler, the anguished home secretary, was said to be on the point of intervention. He'd have won no bouquets in our boarding house, where the final days of the case were followed closely. 'Why doesn't this Butler bloke just get out the way?' said a member of our St Peter's Street number, whose family had an ambiguous relationship with the law. On the day of execution, Marwood went to the gallows before we had breakfast. 'He'll be rotting in lime now,' said one of the kids across our cornflakes, rack of cold toast and view of the ornamental gardens of Ventnor. 'That's what they do to them, after.'

o   o   o

Most of the kids at my new school came from the area around Highbury, the north and east of the borough. Groups of them knew each other from their previous schools. The boy who sat next to me in class had had polio when much younger and had a withered left arm and leg. He made every effort to be friendly but I failed to reciprocate in anything like equal measure. One boy's parents were divorced. His mum was German and had met his dad while he was in northern Germany with the British army after the war. His dad had custody over him.

There were two black kids in the year, from Jamaica, and two Greek Cypriots. Of the two Jewish kids, Martin Klein, was no good at gym, though withstood our early laughing at him and the more persistent jeers from our gym teachers. He was brilliant at French. Both of these aspects of his make-up were put down to his being Jewish. He was probably more brainy than we were and had something about his background that would have given him the advantage when it came to learning other languages. Whatever that was, we didn't need it. Besides, our French teacher shone no guiding light on to the outside world. After a bright start in our first forty minute lesson – 'Levez vous! Asseyez vous!' – he fell into morose silences, scowling at us to get on quietly with irregular verb exercises in our books, while he sat at his desk at the front doing his football pools.

By custom, speech night was held in St Pancras town hall in Euston Road. After the last chords of 'Jerusalem', the headmaster, a small man in a black cape and thinning grey hair, rose to give his speech from the stage in a powerful voice. It centred on his efforts over the several years he had been at Highbury – a step up from Holloway school, where he had taught earlier – to persuade the authorities, national and local, to provide us with a new building. The one we occupied dated back a hundred years. Classes crammed into the narrow spaces of what had once been, according to unconfirmed rumour, a reform school or a mental hospital. He proclaimed the urgent need to build a modern school, for us the educational cream of the area.

History was taught by the headmaster himself, sitting on the edge of his desk, hands clasping one knee reflectively, his other leg swinging a few inches above the floor. King John was the worst king we'd had. We all knew this from the adventures of Robin Hood, but the best was relatively new to us, Edward I, who had united Britain. 'Hammer of the Scots', he was also a wit, as he'd shown the Welsh. 'Give us a prince who doesn't speak a word of English,' they'd demanded, thinking they'd got him on that one. So he presented his baby son who didn't speak a word of anything. All of our class thought: 'Very clever, we English.'

Discipline and firm rule from the top was also one of the elements which set us apart as a school. First years were instructed to be in bed by 8.30 p.m. and any seen yawning by the headmaster would be challenged. Transgressors rarely had the nerve to deny they'd missed the deadline, albeit they might lie by a half hour or so. For every fifteen minutes they admitted to having gone to bed late, their soft-skinned faces would be given one scrape from the headmaster's ever-present five o'clock shadow. Holding their heads at the forehead and chin, he'd rub his beard across their cheeks. More or less everyone liked or respected him. No one admitted to thinking such punishment strange.

Most masters gave the slipper, one of the gym teachers to boys in bathing trunks at the side of the small, chlorine-steeped swimming bath (freezing-clear on Monday mornings, pea-soup by Wednesday afternoons). He was given to violent swings of mood and would also lash out at your face with the flat of his hand, twice before he controlled himself. This was for crimes like forgetting to bring in your gym stuff. Terry Hexham, the small kid who sat near the front of the class, was badly knocked about like this for chirping a little more loudly than normal one afternoon, when the weather was too bad for games and the master was convening one of his sports quizzes (same questions and jokes every time). Only senior teachers, in their fifties or sixties, and the headmaster used the cane. Members of the small group of smokers, who gathered under a tree at the distant reaches of the senior playground bordering a large bombsite, routinely felt it. I was given two strokes for not attending an after-school choir practice, an act unlikely to have pinpointed anyone as a potential Public Enemy Number One. At Risinghill, the large and rowdy secondary school at the end of Chapel Market, the headmaster had banned the cane altogether. His picture was in the papers, smiling benignly at his school gates, behind him a bunch of his cheering flock. You could tell from their faces they were from the market locality, and what they were thinking: 'This geezer's a wanker.'

Games were staged at Walthamstow, near the Crooked Billet. This was about eight miles away at the greener extremes of the East End, yet somehow the nearest available set of pitches and dressing rooms to north London. We went by hired school bus one afternoon a week and were handed sixpence each to get back by public transport afterwards. The fare was invariably more than sixpence.

All who had played for their primary school team were put with a coach, Pat Welton, who had played in goal for Leyton Orient. No one else seemed especially impressed by this, less when he put them through a few sprints and routines like dribbling around a line of traffic cones. They wanted to go straight into a game. There was nothing specifically assigned for goalkeepers – not being a spoon-fed bunch, whatever keepers learned, they picked up themselves – but this was the first time I'd had anything like formal training. We played for half an hour at the end. In one of our earlier sessions I dived to the left to palm a shot around the post. Amid the usual shouts of anguish or joy from the other players, I caught the much quieter, 'That's a good save, son'. From an ex-professional goalkeeper, one of the 'all great', it was a moment to savour.

Of the school's four houses, ours had the worst team – no bad thing since I got plenty of practice. Near the end of the season's final débâcle, the ref awarded the first penalty I'd had to face. As far as I could gauge, this was meant to be a moment of tremendous tension. From one perspective, it dramatically reduced a team match to one-to-one combat, with the odds stacked in favour of the penalty-taking gladiator against the keeper as hapless Christian. From another I couldn't figure what there was to get so tense about. The keeper hadn't much of a chance and all was as good as lost. It was others who had buggered things up to create this situation and left you to sort it out. With only your own resources to rely on, not the variable qualities of others, you could perform. It was an entirely familiar moment: 'Very well, alone!'

The penalty-taker, older by a year, strode confidently to place the ball on the spot. He flashed a glance towards the left of my goal. He did the same thing on his run up. What did he expect me to do? I pushed his shot away, diving to my right. He and his team gasped, the masters on the line applauded. My team cheered in amazement. It was surprising what these people didn't know.

Most of the school goalkeepers were of foreign background. The First XI keeper, in the sixteen to eighteen age bracket, had an unspellable Polish name. He spoke English more correctly, bordering posh, than anyone else in the school. Two years above me in the third year, both keepers were Greek Cypriot. One dressed entirely in black, which matched his Makarios beard in the making. Wiry and agile, he wore padded kneeguards. The other, whose name was Peter, was bigger, less athletic, but played well when called on. He had other interests and was thought more academically inclined than a regular football boy.

I had only one rival for our year's school side. He had come from a primary school in the Barnsbury area which had won cups and medals and was regularly watched by those who selected the London Schools' XI. I assumed he would walk straight into the team. But when I spoke to him about it he said he was fed up with playing in goal. He wanted to play on the field, where all his mates were, and where there was less hanging around.

There was something in what he said. You were either in the

thick of it, or standing actionless trying to concentrate, getting cold. The Greek Cypriot kid had his kneeguards but for others bare knees and thighs were a cultural obligation. A professional keeper whose team, in the first round of the FA Cup in November, were 2–0 up at half-time, had had nothing to do and was so frozen he put on a pair of tracksuit bottoms for the second half. His opponents came back to draw the game. His manager blamed him for the goals, saying the leggings had slowed him down. The report I read didn't query the manager's view, presenting it as kind of self-evident truth. The weather was immaterial. If it was freezing you could 'run on the spot, son!', get your mind off it and the blood moving. So what if it flowed from grazed knees? When we had house matches in the senior playground, if you wanted to make saves you had to adopt the Williams option and dive on concrete. The keeper made sacrifices. Tracksuit bottoms – in the unlikely event of having a pair available – showed unwillingness to do so, weakness of resolve. 'Splash on the Dettol, son. It'll do you good.'

Caps were more acceptable, on the rare occasion of sun. The old flat cap was from the age of custodians, a link between the keeper as 'ordinary bloke' and the crowds, who to a man and boy had all once worn them. One might last a keeper his whole career, its subdued grey or brown tweed becoming greasier by the season from being either warn or chucked in the back of the net with his gloves. It was now giving way to more dashing jockey-style items, in reds and blues. Apart from the fashion statement, I couldn't see these were of much use. Their peaks were as inadequate as any other when you lifted your head in an attempt to focus on that ball descending out of the sun at angels eleven.

The big problem was hands. In the cold they warmed up after a few minutes but only stayed so with constant action. Mine never felt big enough. I was thankful for the many days when I could wear gloves and would have liked always to wear them but an unwritten law said you couldn't – only in the wet. For other occasions, Jack Kelsey had claimed chewing gum was the answer. This wasn't true. He was just being modest about his abilities to command the cross. I tried gum – Beech Nut or Wrigley's, no matter – as well as mud, dust and spit, but they were all apt to dry by the time the ball next flew at them. If anything, this made the palms and fingers shinier than they had been and the ball more likely to elude their grip.

There was little attention paid to gloves. Maybe Frank Swift had had the answer but he'd died with his secret. Gil Merrick's book promised a debate on the subject but when I turned to the page it said something like, 'Oh, you can always pick up a pair of gloves', and moved to the next business. Some keepers, like Sam Bartram in his book, insisted on wool, which was thick and made your hands feel bigger. I found it absorbed too much rain and mud stuck to it in lumps. The pair of my mum's old dress gloves that I tried, I rolled down so they didn't stretch too fetchingly up my arms. The ball remained slippery. String gloves, my dad said, were better for grip. They were made from oiled-cotton, a beige pair of which he might wear on Sundays. He gave me an ancient set, and they did the job, not perfectly, but as well as any. Importantly, they stood for the right mood of resolution. In the freezing damp they provided none of the warmth of wool and you could see your skin through their wider mesh. They were appropriate for a British keeper, a minimalist hero reliant on his own resources to face whatever was thrown at him by enemy and elements alike – the man in the oiled-cotton gloves.

In our area a spate of fires had occurred, generally in chimneys as unswept soot erupted into flame. My grandad had the sweep in every spring, a sombre day when all the furniture was covered in dust cloths and we were required to go out in the street and shout when the brushes broke cover from the top of each chimney. But most landlords called for the service once a decade, if at all, for houses occupied by families on basement, ground, first and second floors, with at least one burning grate at each level. Other accidents were caused by oil fires falling over, or the encroaching wonders of the deep-frying chip pan. Matters were compounded by the fact that, around our way, the fire brigade had to search for new sources of water. The 'tank' had been pumped out, cleared of rusty prams and piping and replaced by work on a low-level block of flats. Nearby, at the bottom of Gerrard Road, I watched a family carried out one by one on the backs of firemen and down ladders from a window beneath the roof, virtually as the flames reached them.

A fire in St Peter's Street, just along past the first couple of shops from the corner of Burgh Street, had burnt the house out by the time the firemen arrived. Ronnie Minto lived there. He had first gone to St John's, the Catholic school at the top of our street, then moved to Hanover for our final primary year. It was that few hundred yards nearer his home. One of the friendliest kids in the school, he'd call out and wave from half a street away if he saw you, though never quite made it to full acceptance by the time we all left.

He had helped get most of his family out of the fire but, in the chaos, no one could find his disabled sister. Ronnie ran back, helped to get her moving and on her way to safety but he was overcome and killed by smoke. His picture, smiling, was on the front page of the *Mirror* the next morning. It was very sad, and very strange that someone from our area should be the focus of national attention. Next to his photo was the paper's report, of the twelve-year-old boy in a little known part of inner London, who had gone back into the fire alone.

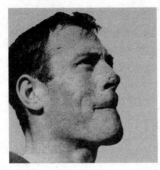

Booked

A big black car, a Bentley, had been standing for a while on the corner outside Lowe's the printers. Among the half dozen vehicles that usually parked in the street, its like in size had never been seen, save the grimy lorries with tarpaulined loads from places like Runcorn, whose drivers lodged down at Mrs Fox's. In terms of grandeur, it was as if the street corner had been inappropriately cast as a film set. This impression was not dispelled as a crowd formed and began its approach. The woman on the back seat with long curling blonde hair and red-painted lips was soon identified as Jayne Mansfield, lately of Hollywood.

Her husband, Mickey Hargitay, an ex-Mr Universe and Hungarian bodybuilder, had somehow arrived here along Mr Lowe's arcane chain of east European contacts. Over the following months, amid a chaos of old, clanking machinery and battered glue-pots bubbling on gas burners, my mother and fellow workers were to compile glossy 'keep-fit' brochures of Hargitay projecting his muscles and Jayne her bust. But, while he was now inside negotiating the deal, she sat for at least two hours, signing scraps of paper pushed in through the car window. As the amazed kids and headscarfed housewives thronged the top end of the street, she smiled and waved benevolently.

A few weeks later, men, lorries and a bulldozer arrived to level the waste ground where the barrage balloon had flown. The council planted willow trees, rocks and winding pathways along it in front of the Catholic church. Benches were installed to encourage people to linger, and gates and wire perimeter fencing erected to keep them out at night. In Cape Town, Harold Macmillan, the British prime minister, shocked the South African Parliament with his speech, in early 1960, on the 'winds of change'. Gusts had been detected along the canal side of our street as, attracted by the view and unaware of the rats, new people started to move in.

The first was a major, in the house next to the bombsite of numbers 6–8, and his younger wife. She had long black hair and glasses and spoke, as was said, 'very well', as if she came from somewhere like Putney. Quite soon, a baby arrived. The major had been injured badly in the leg and captured in a wartime effort to kidnap Rommel. Grey-haired, he walked with a stick and appeared to be gruff but responded positively to a uniformed call during Bob-a-Job week, when he'd put you to work polishing the chrome and silver.

One of the next to join us was a dancer, or 'choreographer', as we learned he was called. Thin-faced, billiard-ball-bald but for hair hanging stringily at his ears, he held his pointed nose some degrees above the horizontal. He did make some effort to meet the locals, his misfortune being that he chose to do so in pubs frequented by the Brays. This was not a cheap option. He'd buy all of them and their friends a drink, while relatively few of their number would reciprocate before the landlord's call for time. But it was occasionally enough to get him drunk. One afternoon he wove up the street in his car and pin-balled off several others to his left and right. Such a display of public drunkenness was regarded with quiet contempt.

Our team from the evening play centre at Hanover went for a cup match to Moreland Street, a half mile away over the Finsbury frontier at City Road. Staged in their basement-level playground, the game was so one-sided I had little to do but stare at the Gordon's brewery looming over us. Teddy Merryman was the toast of the night from our perspective, and scored several of our many goals.

The game almost over, a hefty kick from behind was inflicted on him. We were prepared to overlook this as the act of a desperate and defeated opposition. Their referee, however, chose to make a moral example. So indignant was he at his side's poor sportsmanship and so concerned that, perish the thought, we might take back to Islington the impression that Finsbury was populated by tosspots and roughnecks, that he sent the errant player off and abandoned the game as a victory in our favour. We were, thus, through to the next round of the play-centre cup, but in the league of goodwill gestures the ref's proved useless. An already dicey situation became worse. The Moreland Street team's big brothers ambushed us as we walked home. Ted, a creator and director of events rather than a runner, proved too slow on his feet. We turned to see him go down in a barrage of fists and boots by the Gent's at the junction with City Road, as we sped back over the borough line.

Real Madrid came to Hampden Park to play Eintracht Frankfurt in the European Cup Final. The Germans' keeper wore a quaintly flat cap; at school we'd all noted they had a half-back named Stinka. They scored first but any whiff of an old-fashioned upset was dispelled within minutes. Real Madrid won 7–3, in as brilliant a display of football as anyone had seen. At the centre of it was Puskas – barrel-stomached, centre-parting plastered in place – galloping to score four.

We heard one Saturday that, just across Colebrooke Row and up Charlton Place, some stalls were being put up in Camden Passage to sell things, old things. Someone said antiques. A fellow named Michael Medwin, who'd played a Cockney corporal in the 'Army Game' on TV, was brought along to open it. People were surprised to hear how posh he spoke. There was a rumour Princess Margaret would be around on its first day, though she certainly wasn't by the time I arrived with a group of friends. We all agreed, in candid fashion, that the stuff on sale was a load of junk. Though Tommy Mancini did pick up an old nude painting and loudly announce: 'Now this I *would* buy.'

The dancer had had something to do with setting up the place. It was possibly there he found the old coaching lamp that he shined up and stuck on the wall by his front door – a beacon leading us along a new and better way. As he strode off ahead, however, he soon managed to get himself on the wrong side of the Brays. Maybe he'd caught on to the regularity with which, in the pub, it was his round. On a drunken return from the York, one member of the clan with more mouth than the family average stormed the dancer's doorstep and, with two hands, wrenched the lamp from the wall. Hurling abuse at its unseen owner, who was presumably cowering behind a curtain, he smashed it into the basement area.

Archbishop Makarios was miraculously transformed from a terrorist into someone we could speak to. Cyprus became independent after Britain persuaded him to see things its way. He didn't want to be a mere member of a team run by the Greeks when he could – give or take a British base or two – have an island of his own.

My parents came up with the idea of a holiday half on the continent and half at home. We took the boat for a week in Ostend, then came straight back for another at Butlins, Clacton. My mother and I bumped into one of the Bray wives, who was very pleasant and talked for a while. Her husband wasn't with her. On occasions when I'd noticed his absence in the street and asked, say, my grandad where he was, the reply was usually that he was 'away', or 'on his holidays'. My grandad would laugh at this. It certainly seemed peculiar, given that it could happen at such times of year as February. Now the fellow was away again, though at a more usual time for an annual break. As a family they obviously just didn't take their holidays together.

The football competition of the Rome Olympics was on in the Butlins TV room. Great Britain had Mike Pinner in goal. An amateur, he had played for several of England's best professional teams, such as Aston Villa and Sheffield Wednesday when their regular keepers had been injured. He played very well. We drew with Italy but went out against the Brazilians. One of the goals they scored, a bending, long-distance shot, which had him at full stretch, though with no chance of a save, brought a gasp from the television audience that fairly cleared the clouds of smoke in the room. We only won two gold medals. At the last stages of the Games, however, I had hopes for the marathon. It was staged after dark, in order to miss the worst heat of the Roman day, and was the type of event in which we did well. Then, against a backdrop of the Colosseum, a black face trotted out of the night. The shock was felt by the BBC commentators, who had to scrabble among their papers to discover whose it was and from where; someone called Abebe Bikila of

Ethiopia. At school next day one of the Jamaican kids, Billy Lake, who was brilliant over the 100 and 220 yards, was as shocked as we were, though, in his case, ecstatic. Black people could sprint and spring – Jesse Owens, panther-like Brazilians – but weren't known as exponents of the long game.

Thirty-five million Nigerians soon won the right to play it, halving the population of the colonies and doubling that of independent black Africa. Touchingly, a competition to compose Nigeria's national anthem was won by Miss Lillian Williams, a British employee of the ministry of labour and welfare in Lagos. Her entry was chosen from 3,693 'submitted from all parts of the world' – a clearly global endorsement of our enlightenment. The Home Service primed us with the name of the new state's leader. In class or playground, it rolled off the tongue: Sir Abubakar Tafawa Balewa. Only three years before, Jack de Manio, when reading the BBC radio news, had pronounced the country's main river, the Niger, as if spelt with a double 'g'. They moved him quietly aside to present the early morning 'Today' programme, the graveyard shift no one else wanted.

The scaffold poles and boards were removed from the gap at number 25. A new structure arose, in a lighter brick but in a style to blend in with the houses around. It was divided into four flats, about £2,000 each, said my grandad. An elderly couple with two dogs moved into one of the lower floors. The man, who looked beyond retirement age, went out in large polished boots and a commissionaire's uniform. A younger duo took residence in the top flat. They always left the house together, walking side by side, their gaze trained on the pavement a yard in front of them. One, who walked with slightly splayed feet and the type of satchel kids carried their books in, wore a short navy-blue coat, like a builder's donkey jacket – if a little finer and with leather patches at the elbows – and a leather cap, slightly askew. The other usually had a duffle bag. If they approached as I was kicking a ball around against Lowe's wall, I'd stop to let them pass and they'd do so quickly, without acknowledgement. I didn't expect them to say anything. As far as I knew or had seen, they didn't speak to anyone, or to each other. More novel was that they were both men. While noted, subliminally by most, this drew no expansive public comment. The street and they upheld the principle of keeping themselves to themselves.

In the US election, vice-president Richard Nixon was up against John Kennedy. Nixon appeared as a reliable sort, who had stayed the course in Eisenhower's shadow. Kennedy was some fly-by-night I'd never heard of. My mum mentioned his father had been ambassador to Britain, and was never much in favour of the USA coming in at all to help us in the war. On the radio, they wondered whether his being a Catholic would tell against him. The biggest concern was his age, forty-three. No manager in an office or company, let alone in charge of the western world, could be expected to have the right experience at anything less than forty-five to fifty. Kennedy was altogether too fresh-faced for the job. Then again, that won him the election. His narrow victory was put down to a marginally vital group of voters being put off on polling day by Richard Nixon appearing on TV with a five o'clock shadow.

The headmaster had abandoned his as a form of punishment now that we'd reached the maturity of the second year. It was the first time we were allowed to choose between subjects: languages, Latin and German. Latin, whose roots were inherited by a people I had seen were incapable of keeping quiet for more than a second or talking on the phone without the expansive use of their hands, might have been fun enough had it not been the subject of the rigid, arch-disciplinarian deputy head. In one exam he had set, a fourth year had scored 100 per cent. The deputy head said no one could ever be allowed full marks and, thus, he was reducing them to 90. Never let it be said he wasn't a fair man, however, he added, everyone else would have 10 per cent lopped off, too. About five kids in the class were left with zero and minus scores and would have done as well not turning up on the day. German, as a subject, could only be breezily relaxed and modern by comparison. I went for this Trautmann alternative.

Disturbingly, when I wrote to the Manchester City keeper and sent pictures to be signed, they were never returned. I put this down to greediness on my part. I'd imagined he was such a good bloke I sent almost every picture of him and his Maine Road teammates I had, between thirty and forty in all. Shame as this was, cracking the Manchester United problem was bigger. You could write to their players confident several hundred kids a week would be doing the same and that chances were limited of hearing back. They attracted crowds and 'crowd' people. Wait for them outside a stadium on their visits to London and you were part of a mob, not only of kids but also their dads, smiling, getting in the way. The only good thing about it was there were so many of them that as the players dashed from the door of the ground, down the steps and on to their coach revving up to make the 5.55 from Euston, they denied their signatures to everyone, dad-accompanied kids included.

You could try getting on the pitch. I'd seen one or two older kids do it. At Highbury, they'd jump the yard-high railings and dodge the police and commissionaires patrolling the narrow cinder track between terrace and turf, and run on as teams came out for their five-minute, pre-match kickabout. I did when Rangers came down from Glasgow to Arsenal for the teams' seasonal friendly. I wandered around among them as they hit shots at goal and generally warmed up. Of the players I wanted – some of the top men in Scotland, Ralph Brand, Eric Caldow, George Niven in goal – none refused to sign. I forgot to approach centre-half Harry Davis, and ran on again as the teams came out after the interval. The ref delayed the start of the second half.

For Manchester United I assumed there'd be a dozen others taking their chances. That'd be a lot better than the 200 outside the ground, and at least their grinning fathers would have too much shame to come gleefully sprinting on. Since it was pouring with rain I put myself at the covered north end of the ground and, as the teams came out, leapt the barrier. I was over the cinder track in one step and, head down in the deluge, had my eyes on my left shoe as it made contact with the grass. I watched it sink beneath two inches of water and mud. When my right foot joined it, I was in up to my ankles and easy prey for the police, but none of them was ready to get his boots dirty. I was the only kid who had made it on the field and could not be held to constitute a mass breach of the peace. My bad luck was that the Manchester team were peeling away from the tunnel by the halfway line towards the goal at the far end.

I skated precariously into the vicinity of the last of their players out. He was straggling some way behind the rest and, absorbed with the view of the packed stand opposite, looked new to all this. His wasn't a face I'd seen on any photograph. Vaseline stood out from his eyebrows and he smelt like he'd taken a bath in horse oils to keep out the cold. As I shouted at him through the rain, 'Can yer sign, please?', he started, shaken out of his concentration. He slowed down to a walk and even looked as if he might back off.

'Go away!' He snarled it, out of the corner of his mouth and looking shiftily to his side, as if someone might see and think he was willingly joining me in conversation. But I knew he must have only recently been promoted from the reserves. With the likes of Bobby Charlton and Harry Gregg on the pitch, he was lucky I was asking him at all. 'Oh, please . . .', I followed up, whining, if barely restrained from adding, 'Whatever your name is'. He grabbed the pencil I was thrusting at him and, to get rid of me, scrawled illegibly on my piece of paper.

Harry Gregg was my major objective and only other realistic target. In a team known to the London autograph fraternity as containing its share of prima donnas, his reputation was one of being receptive to kids. I had no evidence to suggest Bobby Charlton, for example, would sign under these or many other circumstances. Gregg, I was certain, would. Sliding through the cordon of forwards shooting in from the edge of the penalty area, I gained the steadier ground of the goalkeeper's box. Across its levelled mud and sand, Gregg had just caught a ball in front of his face and was drop-kicking it back out again. He glared and frowned as he saw me approaching from his left. This could have passed as a scowl but I knew he was a decent bloke. What else would someone who'd walked back into a blazing aeroplane be? He signed with a large gloved hand, sloping loops and flourishes, and took time to do so. Charlton and Co carried on banging the ball in hard at the goal and around our heads. Upwards of 50,000 people watched.

The teams changed ends as I returned down the pitch, side-stepped a policeman and jumped back into my place at the front of the crowd near Gregg's left post. Arsenal scored two quick goals, pleasing enough in terms of the score, but people around me said they were his fault. I wanted to disagree but they were right. One shot along the ground crept inside his post as he watched, 'rooted to the spot'. Maybe since the air crash and his performance at the World Cup in Sweden, I expected too much of him. At half-time I looked in the programme at the photos and potted biographies to see whose was the other autograph I'd managed to get. He had written 'N', then stabbed a full stop. It narrowed down to being one of the two players in the team with the strange, northern-sounding name of 'Norbert'. Close study of the hieroglyphic surname showed, unfortunately, that it wasn't the better known of them, Lawton, but the other one, Stiles; he'd only made his first-team debut three weeks before. Hero of Munich aside, I had the signature of the one member of the Manchester team no one south of the Ship Canal had heard of.

They came back strongly in the second half of the game, scored once and with a few minutes remaining matters fell at the feet of Bobby Charlton, the hardest shot in British football. A throw in from the left bobbled in front of him some 10 yards outside the penalty area and, on the run, he hit a half-volley at full power. It caught Kelsey out, 3 or 4 yards off his line and not, under the circumstances, where he might have been. The nature of the shot was that it would beat him for height at the point he was standing, then dip viciously to pass under the crossbar. He took to the air, therefore, I imagined, as a formality, the ball far beyond reach as it flew above him. When he jumped, however, he didn't attempt to stretch straight up. He arched his body in imitation of the ball's flight, flinging himself backwards with the suppleness of spine of an Olympic gymnast. He reached it with his fingertips on its hard downward swerve, deflecting it the inches necessary over the bar. My attention flicked back to the players at the edge of the penalty area. Most noticeable was the new boy, Stiles, who threw his hands up in open-mouthed anguish and brought them to his thighs with a slap I heard through the din. Whether he'd ever achieve anything in football, he'd clearly been handed an early lesson in its disappointments. Raising himself to his knees in the floodlights and mud, Kelsey turned intently to confirm the ball had cleared his goal, saw the terraces cheering back at him and laughed.

Owner of a well-used Jaguar, Kelsey was one of the few members of the team to have a car. Some brought them on match days to park out of view on the cinder training pitch behind the Clock End. Only the most senior players arrived in their own set of wheels for training. A young reserve, Johnny Petts, a short, ginger-headed half-back, did one day. He had a second-hand Triumph Herald. A group of about ten of us gathered round him, standing off slightly, as he got out and locked it. He thought we were going to ask him to sign our books, motioning as if to receive the first pen offered him, while on the point of offering the customary footballer's comment at this stage of the day: 'Com'n lads, not before training, in a bit of a rush . . .' But most of us had long since had his autograph and there weren't enough pictures around of him in the papers and magazines to create much further demand. 'Flash bastard', was the consensus when he'd gone in. The other players may have got at him as well. More often than not, he turned up on foot.

Most of the players came by underground, walking the last few hundred yards from Gillespie Road. Even George Eastham did. He'd gone on strike at Newcastle to break the feudal rule which forbade players the right to transfer. He was quiet, quite frail, walked stiffly to the stadium, ran no less awkwardly on the pitch but split defences wide open with his passes. Apart from him, Kelsey, Tommy Docherty when he arrived from Preston, Vic Groves when he reverted from inside-forward to half-back and Joe Haverty the Irish left-winger who was usually consigned to the reserves, there was very little to cheer at Highbury for years. Eastham arrived and came towards us each morning from the tube as a national personality. A lot of older people called him a 'troublemaker'.

Kelsey would emerge from the marble hallway and walk swiftly down the steps gruffly protesting he'd sign no one's book. But he'd often relent. I argued with him one match day, when I was the only kid around, as he slipped into the Clock End car park. He was with Mel Charles and another young first-team player who'd cadged a lift from him. Kelsey may have been trying to impress them as he swept by me and through the crowd making its way to the terraces. 'Come on, Jack, you're the only one I need to complete this team photo.'

'Well, count yourself lucky, then,' he said, which surprised me because I hadn't expected him to reply. So I kept alongside him, somewhere about the level of his elbow, waving my biro under his nose. When he'd let the two younger players pass first through the small side entrance to the east stand, he swung around, stuffed his cigarette in his mouth and signed, before disappearing to change for the game.

On training days he might sit signing a few books and pictures at the wheel of his car, before whipping up the window when he'd had enough or decided he was running late for his dinner. He drove off, presumably to a meal cooked by his wife at home. Many of the younger players ambled down to nearby Finsbury Park station and ate exotically in the Wimpy bar on Seven Sisters Road. Most went on to hang about during the afternoon and evening at the snooker hall above Burton's at Southgate, the area where the club housed them. You could stick around at the top of the stairs waiting for them, though this was no less dull than a considerable part of their lives seemed to be.

When it came to relations with kids, the players of most teams were obliging, some friendly. Some were neither. At Spurs, Danny Blanchflower was football's first TV personality but rarely as accessible to his younger fans. Bill Brown, transferred from Dundee after a superb performance for Scotland at Wembley a year earlier, stood signing one morning when I was at White Hart Lane, to the amazement of local kids. 'Miserable so-and-so', was the general view. He was keeper to the 'double' team and a highly rated international – it was difficult to know what it took to cheer some people up. Tony Macedo at Fulham was continentally friendly, dealing with whatever number of kids grouped around him. Johnny Haynes – the first £100-a-week footballer – celebrated by lining everyone up and counting them with the deliberation he might have reserved for checking whether Tommy Trinder had fiddled his wages. He'd sign one each – maybe twenty in all – for which you said thank you but didn't warm to him. Jimmy Hill, Bobby Robson, et al. were friendlier. Reserve players were the easiest. They'd linger outside the ground to give the impression of waiting for someone, hoping you'd ask. Geoff Hurst, West Ham's reserve wing-half, I eventually approached to sign when he stood around for several minutes before going in to train at Upton Park one morning. It put us all out of our misery. Pending arrival of the big players, like centre-forward Johnny Dick, I had nothing better to do.

One of our school team was already lined up to join West Ham. Fulham were about to approach another kid and both of them had been selected for London. Our results were mixed but whatever the variable qualities of our team, when the mood took them they could all excel in their ability to blame the goalkeeper. It'd come in waves, not always but often independent of the facts, and something you just had to take. They all knew it was wrong, that it was too easy to find fault with the nearest witness to the crime. They just found it difficult to resist the temptation. The keeper of the team one year up from me, who got on my bus in the morning at Sutton Dwellings opposite the grey presence of Islington town hall, told me he shouted 'good goal' whenever there was the remotest chance of him being blamed. 'That throws 'em for a moment, then by the time they've thought about it, the game has started again.'

It did him no good when the headmaster turned up to watch a cup match against his old school, Holloway, expecting great things. With Charlie George, already on Arsenal's books, playing for Holloway, they were favourites, but the Highbury keeper kept them at bay till a late winner. It could have been blamed on several members of the defence. Headmaster and teachers alike, however, chorused their disapproval of the goalkeeper. For all their accumulated education, they hadn't the wit to know better.

When the Scots came to play at Wembley and lost 9–3, friends of mine who saw it came back speechless with the magnificence of the scoreline. The pictures next day were of the England team chairing captain Haynes off the pitch, full of themselves, laughing at the ease of it all. I couldn't see where the satisfaction of it was. Scots' keeper Frank Haffey of Celtic was blamed for as many as six of the goals. He was their third choice, only playing because Brown of Spurs and Lawrie Leslie of West Ham were injured. And the Scottish selectors were as batty as their counterparts south of the border. For years they'd overlooked, for example, a keeper like Ronnie Simpson, who played for Britain in the 1948 London Olympics, Newcastle in their Cup Final victories of 1952 and 1955 and was still performing well. We had won, but why the revelling in the fact that a substitute keeper had been beaten nine times and was at fault with so many of them? It made you wonder whether civilisation had developed since the time when people lined the fences of Bedlam to laugh at the inmates. The mob was funny like that. They might know it was wrong, unfair or wouldn't like such sentiments if ever they were turned in their direction, but just couldn't help themselves.

In the same week as Haffey's and Scotland's goalkeeping reputation was shot to Kingdom Come, the Russians fired Yuri Gagarin into space. Especially impressive was the way the Russians, as compared with the Americans, appeared to do things the right way around. They put satellites, dogs and men up into space and said, 'There, we've done it'. The Americans would announce what they were going to do and we'd all watch as their rockets blew up. When they got a man up there briefly a few weeks later, they were merely trying to keep up, turning to the crowd and saying, 'Please applaud us, too'. The response was, 'So, what?' They were our friends but, like continental keepers, showed off with little to back it up. The Russians were our enemies but sometimes more like us, doing it quietly and effectively at the back.

As my mum said, we'd never know, of course, how many men and animals they'd launched unsuccessfully. Then again, it soon materialised that the Americans weren't above messing up a secret operation either. Within a week of the Russians putting a man in space, the USA launched its Bay of Pigs invasion of Cuba. What were they trying to do, wrest back some of the attention for themselves, or take advantage of it being focused elsewhere? Probably both; anyway, it failed. Billy Lake walked around chanting in the school playground and corridors and chalking on the black-board, 'Cuba Si, Yanqui No!' Few of us knew what he was going on about.

The third years went on an Easter school journey to Portsmouth. While the others were engaged in patriotic exploration of HMS *Victory*, three were caught shoplifting in Woolworth's. Theirs wasn't random thievery, furthermore, but guided by shopping lists from their classmates. Matters were kept from the attentions of the *Islington Gazette* and public scandal was avoided only when the police agreed to hand the Pompey Three back to the headmaster for punishment. On the third years' return he convened a special late-morning assembly. At the eleventh hour, he announced, we would gather in the hall at the sound of one bell (there were normally three). All 500 boys of the school and every teacher, including the new convent-trained French mistress from Ireland and the young French assistant Mademoiselle Boulée, would attend. Word had not yet spread around the school of what exactly had happened, nor who the guilty parties were. But in the subdued mass shuffling along the corridors towards the hall, you could have guessed because they were the only ones laughing and talking, trying to keep up their spirits.

The headmaster's five o'clock shadow, already well in advance of itself, seemed to have turned thunder-grey. He held the lectern to control himself as he gave a brief preamble about the crime and the benevolence of the police force, and commanded the three to the stage. Each was told to take their trousers down. The ringleader, who I had some vague recollection had once been a member of the school choir, wore old off-white underpants which looked as if they'd been cut, thigh length, from his dad's long johns. The headmaster delivered the cane off a run-up of some two to three yards. At six strokes, hitherto the maximum punishment, the ringleader made to get up but was shouted at to get back down again, and was given two more. The accomplices, who looked about to faint, were happy to get six.

With this, the headmaster felt he had brought matters under control. The Teds, the decline of National Service, off-key music and a breakdown of discipline in the suburbs of Nairobi – he was one man against the historical tide, and felt he might have stemmed it with a wave of the cane. It was as a person drowning, however, that he announced weeks later the main story of the summer term. Two fourth years had gone missing after a nighttime burglary of a cigarette warehouse in Highbury Barn. They'd been seen selling cigarettes on the wasteground behind the smokers' tree in the main playground, then disappeared. The police were seeking information, the headmaster comprehension. The rumour, he said to the school in strained, almost pleading tones, was that the two had 'fled abroad'. This was almost true. The Irish police picked them up off the ferry at Dun Laoghaire.

o   o   o

The East Germans started to build the Berlin Wall. The news showed bricklayers with trowels and cement boards laying masonry blocks. This wasn't what walls were for. They were to keep out the cold and the attacking forces, not for people to erect their own prison before their eyes. At the start of our third year our class teacher issued us a stern warning. Last year's fleeing fourth formers grew out of the third years, who had defiled the high streets of Portsmouth. 'This is the year when the trouble starts,' he said darkly. He doubled as our biology teacher. He'd have explained it as hormonal.

A new geography master came to the school, an aged Welshman who wore a gown and commanded us to 'stan-nd!' when he walked in the classroom. He'd taught in the school years before and had been away to the empire. In Cyprus and Egypt, he said, you couldn't rouse the locals from their dossing under a tree. This raised much mirth in the class. At his best in front of maps, he spoke with poetic force, and sweeping arm, of the course of the Arctic convoys to Russia, enduring the harshest conditions of the war at sea and trying to dodge the *Tirpitz*, as they ploughed past the north Norwegian coast: '*Hammer*-fest! *Trom*-so! Lo-*fo*-ten!'

Our PT lessons were taken by the teacher who was subject to violent mood swings. No one could be said to have liked or trusted him. He'd be affable much of the time but it just seemed like a cover. We got back at him at the start of a class when Billy Lake, the black kid, customarily at the front and talking more than most, was brought to order. 'Calm down, Lake,' said the gym master, jocularly, 'you're not in the jungle now.' It brought silence from all of us, suddenly fully aware this wasn't quite the thing any more. When Billy came back at him, quietly, that he didn't think this very funny, the master spluttered that he'd been 'only joking'. We glared, happy to see him on the hook.

The fourth years maintained the reputation they'd established for themselves in the third year, venting their collective spleen on a new games master named Charlie Jeffries. He had a small, well-trimmed moustache, and a superior and testy manner to match. The sixth form, in the emergingly liberal spirit, had written a letter to the headmaster, signed by all of them and at pains to be polite, complaining that Jeffries 'took umbrage' at the slightest provocation. The head was impressed by their surprisingly erudite language, but did nothing. The fourth years approached the problem in their way, on a dark evening after a day of snow. 'Fuck Charlie' was found daubed in large frozen letters on the playground wall opposite his office window the next morning. The headmaster himself tried painful reason. Hinting heavily at assembly that he knew who the culprits were, he said he'd cane them, if they had the decency to own up, and expel them if they didn't. They called his bluff and nothing happened to anyone.

If anything, it was Jeffries who tried to build bridges. After school matches, if he spotted kids walking to the Crooked Billet bus stop, he might give them lifts back to Islington in his Wolseley. He nabbed me passing his office one morning break and gave me what he implied was a fascinating job. He handed over a large collection of local press cuttings from his youth and National Service days, with reports on his prowess as an amateur boxer, and had me sellotape them over his walls.

When the police cruised around to our street and called on the two men in the top flat of number 25 they found an even more fascinating collection of clippings. Islington borough council had quietly observed the fate of many of the books from its main library, the one a little beyond Highbury Corner in Holloway Road. They'd been smuggled out by the satchel load, so it was said, to find their way back to the shelves in scandalously less than original form. A large collection of photographs from them was found arranged on the two fellows' walls, stuck not haphazardly with sellotape but in the form of a fetching collage – quite enough to fetch down the force of the municipal and juridical authorities.

My mum told me about it as I was heading off for school. I hadn't caught the story on the front of the *Mirror*. Copies at the Polish newsagent's had been in unusually short supply. Policemen who later arose in court were almost too embarrassed to speak of what things had been done to the books: lewd inscriptions in place of authors' biographical notes, heads of sinister monkeys superimposed on blissful beds of English roses. Men in uniform, who endured the risk of being gunned down by the likes of a George Marwood and were daily engaged in maintaining an increasingly uneasy urban peace, had to be gently coaxed into giving evidence by sympathetic counsel for the prosecution. The contents list of a collected works of the eminent playwright Emlyn Williams suggested the volume included his previously unknown masterpieces 'Up the Front' and 'Up the Back'. A picture of Dame Sybil Thorndike, acting the role of First World War heroine Nurse Edith Cavell, in her cell awaiting execution by the Germans, had her staring into the groin of a superimposed Greek statue. The caption said: 'During the Second World War, I was working from dawn to dusk to serve the many thousands of sailors, soldiers and airmen.'

The presiding Old Street magistrate was so outraged on behalf of the authorities, as well as our own, that he sentenced the bibliophobic malcontents to six months. You had to hand it to them. Beyond returning books late and falling asleep over the newspapers, it was amazing anyone could dream up an offence to commit in a public library, let alone an arrestable one to get banged up in jail for. The street pondered this soberly and, having availed itself of such details of the case as appeared in the public prints, said no more about it.

One of my schoolmates from the Essex Road area went to watch games and hang around for autographs at Leyton Orient, distant eastern territory. In theory, the East End started a couple of miles away from the Angel; in practice, as many light years. I hadn't voluntarily been there except for school games at Walthamstow and a summer collecting bus numbers, which took me to obscure places like Poplar garage. This had been located amid terraces of small back-to-back houses, doubtless to give the characteristic and cheery people of this part of London – dockers, costermongers and whistling baker's roundsmen – a handy early morning call. Orient were managed by Johnny Carey, ex-centre-half for both Ireland and Eire, Rest of Europe captain and one-time goalkeeper for his former club Manchester United. He had Brisbane Road afire with promotion fever, attendances at capacity. A black Rolls-Royce eased through the crowd on the Saturday I went, though through the dark glass it was difficult to see whose it was: chairman Harry Zussman's? Maybe it belonged to one of the other directors, Lew Grade or Bernard Delfont. These were the types who went from Saturday afternoon at Brisbane Road, to Sunday night at the London Palladium. Orient went down, 3–2, to mediocre Bristol Rovers. They still clambered into the First Division, behind Second Division champions Liverpool, but I had the impression they'd use some extra goalkeeping.

Brazil was of the same mind when it invited Wales to play a couple of warm-up matches after the 1962 season and just before the Chile World Cup. Kelsey's efforts four years earlier had won Wales the invitation and the Brazilians' rating of being the type of hard-to-beat British outfit they needed to practise on. In the second of the two friendly games in São Paulo, Kelsey went down to save a ball at the feet of Vava and was kicked in the back. He managed to get up but then couldn't move and had to be carried off.

With an old team, Pele injured early in the competition and Gilmar calmly efficient in goal, Brazil retained the World Cup without undue stress. When they beat England 3–1 in the quarter-finals, clamorous and successful attempts were made to attach the blame to keeper Ron Springett. He was short-sighted, it was claimed, and couldn't spot a ball hit at him from a distance. Detached analysis observed that two of Brazil's goals resulted from vicious shots – one a swerver, the other a dipper – by winger Garrincha that would have eluded anyone. The third came when the same player, bandy-legged and born a cripple, outjumped Spurs centre-half Maurice Norman, who was the taller by seven inches.

If you wanted disappointments, you had no further to look than the Europeans. Czechoslovakia were entirely unfancied as their bald keeper Schroiff's performances won them through to the final. Thus far, he'd been the revelation of the competition. Then, when he was expected to play well, he dropped every ball Brazil punted in his direction. He did no worse than the Black Octopus. The Russians came to Chile as holders of the European Nations' Cup, introduced two years earlier and ignored by most of the continent. With few eyes watching, Yashin had played brilliantly as the Soviet Union won it. Victory was enough to make them joint World Cup favourites with Brazil. But with the pressure now turned up during the finals, Yashin played poorly. One foreign newspaper pronounced his career dead.

My parents had bought a car and with it we were able to avoid the vagaries of the continental rail network as we went on holiday. The Channel seemed relatively calm, though my mum wanted us to drive down and see Naples. My father said we wouldn't want to, really. In Rome we stayed the night with relatives of our Siennese friends. 'Ahh, bella Napoli,' they affirmed. My dad told us they were just being Italian. 'See Naples and die,' they sighed.

'Quite right,' he said.

On the *Autostrada del Sole*, we passed the monastery at Monte-cassino, where the army's advance had been held up for so many weeks in the war. Rebuilt now, it stood high above the road, shining in the sun. We arrived in Naples in the early evening and parked outside a mid-range hotel in Via Roma. We got the bags from the car, having to leave everything else, tin cans, chairs, the collapsible table we had our roadside lunch on, and other bits, in the boot. A crowd of at least twenty people formed to assess its resale value.

My dad and I went out to find some bread and he asked an old man in a straw trilby on a street leading from Via Roma where we might buy it. He lifted his chin an inch or so in mystification: '*Pane?*' Morning was when you bought bread, he said. But he indicated to follow him and shuffled off, speaking a few words in an accent which came from the back of the throat and my father found difficult to understand. We went into echoing streets where laundry hung high on lines between tenement balconies. People called over their bedsheets and underwear to each other. They peered down through them at us. A combination of the night and city closing in meant the circle of visibility around us was soon barely greater than in a London smog, and that it was the moment to advance no further. My dad made profuse apologies to the old man and agreed evenings were not when you looked for bread. We retraced our steps, taking double the time it had to make them and, in the dark, beat an uncertain retreat from the Spaccanapoli.

We left early in the morning, in as much haste as the England team fleeing Brazil in 1950. We viewed an unperturbed Vesuvius from afar and were through Pompeii by lunchtime. The fountains of the hanging gardens at the palace at Caserta where my father had been billeted were turned off. We saw the streets on which the old man had dropped dead from typhus. I thought they couldn't have been any worse then than they appeared now immediately in front of us. We drove back to Siena without an overnight stop. Having briefly witnessed Naples, northern Italy never looked poor again.

o   o   o

Back home, the main London stations were run by three big kids: Reggie Duke, Tom Smithson and Paul Viollet: Reggie, Smiffy and Viollet. They were around seventeen or eighteen, four to five years older than most of the rest of us. A scattering of would-be hard nuts were at their coat tails and aged somewhere in between. Two were from Islington, Reggie from somewhere near Hackney and the Balls Pond Road, where he worked in one menial job or another. Viollet lived between the Essex and New North Roads. He carried his books in a kind of builder's tool bag but had recently gone 'white collar' as a messenger down at the Bank of England.

My schoolfriend who went to the Orient came from the same vicinity as he did. This seemed a potential 'in' and I turned up a couple of times at the stations with him. Viollet saw this as 'taking liberties'. Stoke City left late one night from Euston, coming through London after a game on the south coast, and I made the mistake of imagining a Second Division club wouldn't attract the big kids. I didn't bother to sort through my photos for those only of Stoke, and brought my entire scrapbook. Alas, the club had just re-signed Stanley Matthews from Blackpool, which meant the heavy brigade was in attendance. I slipped away just before the train left but Viollet sent one of his aspirants to put me right: 'Oi, mate!' He caught up with me by the ticket barrier. Looking embarrassed, not quite knowing yet what he should do, he rapped me on the chin with his knuckle. It was like he was knocking on a door and only jarred my head a bit. 'Don't come back,' he said, trying to induce menace. They had a go at him later for not relieving me of the contents of my book.

I reappeared next Saturday on the stairs of the small underground entrance into St Pancras. They led up to near the door of the station bar opposite platform 7, where Peter Grummitt, Flip Le Flem, David Pleat and fellow travellers of Nottingham Forest were having a light ale before boarding the 6.40. Viollet, Reggie and a few privileged others – I saw Teddy Merryman's face but he moved away quickly – were leaning over the handrail, peering down at the steps for unwanted arrivals. Viollet saw me before I him. 'I've told you before,' he said quietly, if technically incorrectly, from above and behind me. 'Now, fuck off.' I turned with a 'who, me?' expression on my face but could see from his that there was no alternative. I fucked off.

Only really little kids wrote away for players' autographs, while stadium entrances on match days were too crowded. The stations, and the hotels where the teams stayed, therefore, were the only feasible options. Players wandered from their hotels on Friday nights and Saturday mornings. Manchester United stayed in Lancaster Gate, by Hyde Park; Manchester City at Baileys, opposite Gloucester Road tube. Blackburn Rovers rested in Mayfair, a small hotel in Half Moon Street, 100 yards from leafily clean Green Park. They ambled the other way towards the narrow lanes of Shepherd Market, with its restaurants, few shop windows and highish-class women of the night. Married men, internationals of repute among them, they only went to window shop.

Players had to be confronted in the flesh and their scowls withstood as they took the air in, say, the small park in front of the Russell Hotel on Russell Square. On Friday nights Sheffield Wednesday players might make off from here for Soho. Some walked back around midnight after the last bus, maybe kicking a few empty bottles along Old Compton and New Oxford Streets to get matchfit for a few hours later.

If a picture was half decent you requested, in a demanding sort of way, they write 'Best Wishes' above their signature. Most were willing (lower division players without being asked), some didn't seem to be but did anyway, and others weren't. They might scribble something roughly akin to their name around their ankles or forehead, or walk through you. I heard Jimmy Armfield, Blackpool and England right-back, after bundling, hands in pockets, down the steps of the Russell, tell a taxi driver he was going to the Royalty cinema near Aldwych. I jumped on a bus and beat him to it. He saw me – I was the only one there – looked no more impressed than the first time, and pushed by, moodily, to see Brando in *Mutiny on the Bounty*.

The chief problem was how to handle the ruling troika. Reggie, square-built, 5 feet 6 inches, was the acknowledged madman, head-butting his favoured art-form. Given his height he might have to jump, which provided extra force. Instances where he'd felt driven to violence were relatively few, due mainly to others spotting the signs. No one liked him but the crowd processed its views to have him come out as somehow lovable. One Saturday night he robbed a kid called Haffman, who was presumed to be Jewish. He was quiet, arrived, went home, stammered when he spoke, and was sufficiently un-station-wise to bring his scrapbook with him, all the pictures he'd collected, not just those he needed at the time. One night Reggie had the lot. The crowd laughed in the story's retelling: 'Shouldn't have brought his fuckin' book.'

Smiffy was a *Buchan's* man. He couldn't be bothered with pictures cut out of the *Evening News* or *Standard*, from the weekly *Soccer Star* or the team photos in experimental colour from the Sunday *Reynolds News* (shirts, especially stripes, often transposed to players' faces). *Charles Buchan's Football Monthly* magazine had black-and-white and colour pictures, but Smiffy streamlined everything down to the *Buchan's* annual. It was A4 sized, hard-covered. The *Topical Times* was a comparable album, but the *Buchan's* the most popular, comprising about 150 pages of head-and-shoulders portraits, action shots – mainly goalmouth mêlées – and players' stories. Everton's Gordon West was on page 14 of the 1962–63 edition, talking of being Britain's most expensive keeper after his £25,000 transfer from Blackpool.

A story on Kelsey was allotted two whole pages. There was no telling what value you'd have put on him. It was strangely titled 'Ignore Aeroplanes if You Want to be a Successful Goalkeeper'; when as a schoolboy he'd been playing in a game in Swansea, the rare sight of a plane caused him to concede a soft goal. The piece was mainly devoted to diagrams showing how he advanced from his line against onrushing forwards, thus, to obscure their view of the goal, or 'narrow the angle'. It was a reasonable effort by the *Buchan's* to get into the goalkeeper's brain, though it was probably of more use to players of other positions. Anyone who didn't have an instinctive grasp of what was being said wouldn't have been a keeper in the first place.

The *Buchan's* was handy for stuffing under your coat or in a bag. It was easy to conceal from ticket inspectors keen to stop kids getting on platforms (St Pancras was bad for this) or to dash with, either between signing players or away from danger. Smiffy liked it because it didn't look like a scrapbook and detract from what he thought of as his impressive appearance. He had Brylcreemed hair – a bit quiffy, was Smiffy – and wore suit, tie and polished shoes. In process of being left stranded by the 1960s' turn, he was more Elvis than John, Paul, Ringo and George. Still, he wore warehouse overalls most of the week, so getting dolled up like this made a change for him.

From west London, he supported Chelsea. You might have a laugh with him about it, in a good mood. As Jimmy Greaves had headed for Italy, so Chelsea had gone down to the Second Division. They were coming up again, with Tommy Docherty as manager. They didn't want to be nicknamed the Pensioners any more, but to convey a zippier image of Chelsea. They had a young team – George Graham, Terry Venables, Peter Bonetti in goal. Bonetti had made his first-team debut two years before. Kids with no interest in goalkeeping came back talking about it. Not especially tall, he was slim, very agile and exciting. Someone called him 'the Cat' – this was funny, because the *Buchan's* I was given and pored over on Christmas Day had a picture of his Chelsea predecessor, Reg Matthews, now with Derby County, in a midair twist on page 139 and saying he was 'the Cat'. What with Bert Williams before them, that made three Cats a'keeping in less than a decade. As for Bonetti, it went with the name. What was he, Italian? It turned out that he was of Swiss background, which was still a bit flash, a bit continental. The word was, though, he could also take a cross.

Buoyed by Chelsea's changing fortune, Smiffy was also subject to changes himself. Till he arrived one evening, at the Mount Royal Hotel near Selfridges, I'd been the only kid claiming the rare prize of Rangers, on one of their periodic visits from Glasgow. Handing my pen to Willy Henderson, I saw Smiffy running from the Marble Arch direction. He was hastening, I imagined, not to miss the signature of the diminutive Scottish international left-winger. I nodded an insincerely cheery 'hello' to him, then thought there was something about his face and Dunn's mac flowing in the wind that suggested Dracula descending. I withdrew my pen as he launched into something related to a wrestler's drop-kick, or possibly a bit of kung-fu about twenty years before its time. His left leg whistled past Henderson at about eye level and where I would have been, had I not already been around the corner in Oxford Street hailing the nearest 73.

Smiffy took a pride in getting more signatures in his *Buchan's* than anyone else. Enjoying the unfair advantage of always being at the front of the queue, he was in the lead at all stages of any season. Finally, a fat kid, about fifteen, named Hunt (he didn't have a first name and was always Unt); took up the challenge. There was only a finite number of faces to get signed in the book, so he explored new terrain and took to asking players depicted in action shots who they thought that teammate or opponent was standing behind them – the player of whom you could only see his elbow or knee. Armed with this informed guesswork, he would get these bodily extremities signed and soon overtook his older rival.

'How many in yer *Buchan's* now denn, Smiffy?' rang out the impertinent crowd's question one morning at the Russell Hotel.

'Dunno,' he answered nonchalantly, as if he hadn't been counting them on the tube from West Brompton. 'About 237.'

'Unt's got two-fifty!' came the cry, from a suitably safe distance.

'Fuck Unt!' said Smiffy, apparently laughing but stuffing his *Buchan's* under his mac in disgust. 'Fuck 'im, wiv 'is elbows an' knees.'

It was outside the Russell he eventually cornered him. Sheffield

Wednesday's Ron Springett, who still lived in Shepherd's Bush since his transfer from Queen's Park Rangers and only joined up with his teammates on match mornings, had just gone in. He signed the full-page, black-and-white picture of him leaping to the right to catch a battered old practice ball in Smiffy's *Buchan's*, and also that in Unt's. Smiffy got moody and demanded 'subs' from everyone. This was a favoured measure of extortion by the big kids, especially if their Thursday wage packets had been spent by the weekend. The rate was usually sixpence if kids wanted to stay; not having the money to spare I'd either absent myself when such demands were made, or withdraw to maintain guerrilla operations from a side-street. This day, Smiffy demanded a shilling, well above the surplus cash in most schoolkids' pockets. It showed he was out of touch with reality, his mind clearly disturbed, but Unt was either too dumb to gauge the moment's gravity, or simply a kid of principle. He always refused to pay, he said, and saw no reason why he should leave. Smiffy, not of the Brains Trust persuasion himself, posed his argument in terms of a right to the chin. Unt was laid out and had to be helped from the foot of the hotel steps, before Wednesday's players could come out for their Saturday stroll.

It was safer to go for the small clubs. Bradford City had come to play Arsenal in a third round Cup-tie in the middle of a typhoid epidemic. The question was publicly raised whether they should be allowed beyond the satanic mills of the north to put southerners at risk. The finger of blame was pointed at Bradford's rising Asian community. I was the only kid seeing their train off as they went back home from King's Cross and, for that time on a Saturday night, the station was strangely empty. Centre-forward 'Bronco' Layne told me they were still feeling dosed up from the injections.

Small London clubs often travelled early on Saturday mornings, management saving the expense of hotels. The players were half asleep as you mingled with them in the station cafeteria. They had friendly keepers with quaint names: Gerry Cakebread of Brentford, Ray Drinkwater of QPR. Crystal Palace's man in the frame was Bill Glazier. South coast teams passed through London *en route* to the north. I spent half an hour with Portsmouth on their train at King's Cross, Dick Beattie, their Scottish Under-23 keeper chatting away in Glaswegian. When he'd dealt with my pictures he opened a brown envelope that he'd brought along, sent to him by a fan and containing a Porstmouth team photo; would he kindly sign it and get his teammates to do likewise? This was a perfect opportunity, since they were all in the compartment with him. Instead, Beattie autographed his picture and started to sign the names of the other players across theirs. 'Nae problem,' he winked cheerily in my direction, when he saw me gawping. 'Och, come on, son,' he followed up, laughing. 'Who's going to know?'

Some teams you never saw. They made their way to their fixtures not by rail but coach. There was the M1, although in the absence of many other long and wide roads, this mode of travel wasn't easy. Gillingham got lost trying to find Barrow. Notts County were another team to arrive and depart along mysterious routes. For some reason the *Soccer Star* regularly had pictures of them – their clerically-groomed keeper George Smith, Bert Loxley, Jeff Astle – which if you wanted signed required catching them at the stadiums. Still, it got you around. As a north Londoner, going south of the river to places like New Cross felt like a clandestine mission into alien territory. After County had beaten Millwall 3–2 at the Den, I waited at the corrugated entrance to the dressing rooms, the Coldblow Lane mob gathered in force. They spat fury and bits of offal at their team. 'Not worth this fuckin' meat pie,' shouted one gap-toothed aficionado, at pains not to throw its remains at home keeper Reg Davies. His thoughtful analysis of the game's winning goal was that Davies should have caught, not punched, the cross which led to it.

Later in the season I got Kelsey to sign the black-and-white, head-and-shoulders of him by the article in the *Buchan's*. It pictured him looking up pensively as if at the featured aeroplane that caused him to let in the soft goal near the start of his career, or conceivably at his future. He said nothing, which was unusual, not even anything gruff. He didn't argue when I asked him to write 'Best Wishes' and took more time doing so than might have been the case a couple of years earlier. X-rays after his injury in Brazil showed he had a congenital spine deformity and had been lucky to have played at all. He soon had to give up hope of doing so again.

I was bawled out in the school's First XI trial for not taking a cross early enough. I'd grown 4 inches since the previous season but, not realising I had the height, waited to catch the ball and ran the risk of the forwards reaching it first. The unpopular games master, Charlie

Jeffries, selected me anyway, then backed down as other masters and senior school team members argued fourth years were too young to play in goal for the First XI. The place was retained by the Greek Cypriot guy with kneepads. When my year played a cup match on fields out near the Robin Hood roundabout and a high ball came over in the first few minutes, it still took me some part of a second to realise I was required to move out and rescue the situation on behalf of my distressed defence. I did so casually, pretending it didn't matter if I caught it or not. It miraculously stuck. I expected the crowd to rise in wonderment. My teammates didn't say a word. Our sub on the touchline mentioned that our teacher who had come along for the trip murmured approval.

On our way back we passed Dolphin Square where John Vassall, who was standing trial accused of spying for Russia, had lived. The driver had most of the coach in stitches going on about bum-boys and benders and other aspects of the case. The teacher was embarrassed but inhibited from telling anyone to shut up, since it would have meant telling the driver, too. Speech night was held in the middle of the Cuban missile crisis. The aged and cheery Bishop of Stepney, guest of honour, tried to lift spirits by recalling how he'd gone to his headmaster many years before, lost for what to do in life and seeking some note of guidance. 'His words were precise and to the point, . . . "bend over!"' The hall erupted. The headmaster's speech followed and he announced that, in these grievous times, he had heartening news. The governors had informed him we were to get a new school, 'unless the world is about to go entirely mad'.

Reggie was the first of the big kids to stop appearing. Smiffy and Viollet followed him. At eighteen they'd found better things to do of a Friday or Saturday evening. In their absence, others stepped in. A large lumpy kid, at least seventeen, from the East End, named Jackson, had long been turning up, though keeping out of the fray while the Big Three were around. His size and the remains of a harelip gave him an innocent look at first. He proved surprisingly nimble in creeping up on people. 'Oi, come 'ere!' I heard him grunt nasally from the shadows of the Euston arches one evening when we were seeing off Everton. The two points attained from their visit to the capital had kept them on course for the championship, and Albert Dunlop, who was in the squad for the injured Gordon West, had just dismounted from the coach smoking a 6-inch cigar.

I abandoned heading with him towards the platform and was into my stride out of the station before Jackson shifted his bulk into second gear.

He habitually came with a mate of a similar age, named Brindle, and a small kid called Scobie, after Breasley, the jockey of the same nickname. Nearly as old as the other two, Scobie had suffered the kind of growth deficiency which prompted worthy theses on the sociology of areas east of the Tower. He had a pointed nose and spoke in a high-pitched ferret's voice appropriate to the part. Jackson and Brindle cornered likely candidates for theft and extortion, Scobie moved in with the abusing and stealing.

One of the worst things about this trio was that they were in the habit of turning up for the smaller teams. Previously, you might get time off from the tension by lolling around outside a Third Division team's hotel, or attending some lowly outfit's departure for the sticks. Now the threat was as likely to be present for Bury as for Burnley, for Millwall as for Manchester United. The previous troika had also had a readily understood system. If kids paid, they stayed. Once they'd greased the appropriate palms, they and their books were largely safe. There'd been a sense of honour to it, which, with the advent of the new lot, began to look like it belonged to a golden age. They took money, books, pushed people around. The members of the old regime had also been separate operators, who tolerated rather than worked with each other in a sort of balance of terror. Jackson and his crew – East Enders, group people – operated together. They dotted around and cropped up you'd never know where.

I found they could be outmanoeuvred at St Pancras. Most stations had a benevolent policy towards kids looking for autographs. You went to the stationmaster's office on a Thursday and asked what reservations they had for teams leaving at the weekend. A railway-man in a waistcoat and with dark-rimmed glasses at the end of his nose, put down his mug of tea to look through the sheaf of papers on a bulldog clip where the information was typed up. St Pancras, however, had a stationmaster from the tradition of scoutmasters and colour sergeants, who wasn't going to have unaccompanied children crawling over his station. You might find a friendly type in charge of the reservations sheet for the sake of your prior research, but the blokes at the ticket barrier had been told to see off anyone who remotely looked like a kid out to pester the country's finest young athletes, *en route* from public bar to smoke-filled, second-class railway carriage. Even if you'd invested twopence in a platform ticket, they'd stop you getting on.

Jackson, Brindle and Scobie never overcame this problem. They looked what they were, kids from the east with their *Buchan's* under their arms and alien to the cultural mecca of north London. I'd get on the platform half an hour early, when there was another train waiting at the platform and the ticket barrier wasn't yet on the red stage of kid-alert. If you buttoned your book under your overcoat, looked kempt, and waved your platform ticket under the inspectors' noses as they clipped that of an old lady, you were through. This way I spent a comfortable half hour with both Eddie Hopkinson and Bolton, and Leicester and Gordon Banks.

You had to take care to jump off quickly when the whistle went, or you ended up at first-stop Luton. On one occasion I had to outrun them off the station forecourt and on to the first bus up Pentonville Hill. On another, I imagined a similar escape might be required but saw, when I left the platform, they were fully occupied with a small kid. He came to the stations about one week in three, from somewhere suburban like Shirley, and spoke as if he went to a school that made a point of playing rugby. Were Reggie still regularly present, maybe he'd have got around to him as he had to Haffman, but till now the kid had been left alone. Jackson, Brindle and Scobie took his money and every signed picture. They were smiling, ripping through his book and had him in tears as I walked past them.

This may well have touched a sentimental nerve. Either that, or the word went out that the situation down the stations was simply 'out of order'. Smiffy was distantly out west, while off the Essex Road Viollet had found more post-pubescent pursuits to occupy him. The news passed on towards the Hackney borders and the Balls Pond Road. Reggie, to be sure, had ruled with an iron hand but a greater terror had followed. There was no one else equipped to take on the responsibility of restoring balance to a chaotic situation. Reggie was urged to come off his line, and to come back.

He appeared on a wet and dark night from the Cromwell Road entrance to Gloucester Road tube. Manchester City – Bert Trautmann and all – were staying at Baileys hotel. The others spied

Reggie coming – sooner or later they had expected he would – but Jackson did so too late. Reggie grabbed him two-handed by the lapels of his coat and yanked him towards him as he brought his forehead smashing into his nose. Jackson went down before Reggie could hit him again in an upright position and landed, beyond the narrow width of pavement from the hotel, in the gutter. In view of the startled Friday night crowd at the tube entrance opposite, Reggie screamed down at him, 'And – don't – you – fucking – come – back – mate', kicking his head in staccato rhythm against the granite kerb: 'Don't – you – fucking – come – back!'

It lacked the embroidery, perhaps, of one of Shakespeare's set-pieces. Yet, as a rallying cry to the spirit, Reggie's oration at the gates of Baileys hotel did its bit. Word went quickly around the rest of the hotels and stations that evening and the following morning: Reggie had returned, Jackson was finished and things would be back to what they were. The blessings were mixed, as far as I was concerned, but the consensus view was one of scarcely qualified glee.

It lasted about twenty-four hours. Jackson was back with his henchmen at Euston next evening, keeping a black and swollen eye out, wary should Reggie be there. He didn't bother us, but he was there. 'Gotta 'and it to de bastard,' said one kid. ''E's 'ad de nerve to show.'

In the first week of December, the smog came down. I walked home from school because it was quicker than the bus. One evening I went through the empty, paved lanes of the antique market and past Pierrepoint Row, which shared its name with the hangman and looked a likely location for Jack the Ripper. A tall, old tramp with white beard and coat tied with string at the waist stood up in the doorway near the single streetlamp and made me leap as if I'd seen Magwitch in the graveyard. The worst of the London smogs for nearly ten years, and also the last, it merged into the Big Freeze of 1963. When it lifted, warmed up and football started again about three months later, Reggie was nowhere to be seen.

The Distant Orient

When General Charles de Gaulle refused Britain's request to join the common market, few could fathom what had possessed us to apply in the first place. Yet it was the cheek of the man that got you. If it hadn't been for the likes of us liberating France from the Germans, he'd not have had a country to rule. He said we had nothing in common with the continent, that we valued our links with the Commonwealth and the USA more. You couldn't argue with him on that. But really he was still angry at how Churchill had patronised him during the war, when he was here in exile. He might also have let us into 'Europe' if we'd shared our nuclear secrets with him.

Alf Ramsey took control of England in the middle of the Big Freeze. He arose out of it, imperturbably cool. He had managed Ipswich, of all clubs, to the league title. Whenever we'd seen them off from Liverpool Street, to my knowledge, he'd never been so stand-offish as to refuse an autograph but he was always slightly aloof. There also something different about his voice. He was a Cockney boy (well, from Dagenham) who, after he'd spent his career at Spurs, sounded like he'd been taking speech lessons. He said 'shootin', as in 'huntin and fishin'.

He took a gun to the England selectors straightaway. He would choose the team, not cabinets of elderly men in starched collars. Ramsey was of the lower ranks, and knew how to mess with them, as opposed to mess them about. He was liable to introduce a dour and, for some, disturbing element of professionalism into management. Whether it would amount to anything was another matter. Ipswich had probably been just a flash in the pan.

France hammered England 5–2 in his first game. Hot on the heels of de Gaulle's rebuff, the European Nations Cup qualifier was played in Paris, relatively unaffected by the cold. But England's team was out of practice, and Ron Springett in a bit of a fog. He was faulted with several of the goals. The alarm in Kenneth Wolstenholme's voice was tangible – 'Oh, Springett's *dropped* it' – as crosses eluded the keeper's grasp. Ramsey seemed no less out of touch. In three years' time when England hosted the World Cup, he said, we would win. It took a while to realise he meant it, that he wouldn't suddenly crack a smile, nudge his interviewer and say, 'Only kiddin'. But he didn't, and prompted near universal ridicule with one of the more brilliantly calculated statements made by a public figure.

I was caught by the Jackson gang early on a Sunday morning at King's Cross. Sunderland were in the habit of staying an extra night at the Great Northern Hotel at the back of the station. Their journey back to the north-east, via Newcastle, on a Saturday would not have got them home till well after midnight, if at all. I was surprised by the gang's arrival because to get here for a train leaving a little after eight, they'd have had to crawl out of their eastern habitat at some hour before dawn. Then again, the sun rose that bit earlier there. They began by scrawling their signatures – they had trouble writing – over the book I'd brought with me, which didn't much matter, because it was an old one in which I'd temporarily stuck my Sunderland photos for the purpose of this trip. 'Getew after, mate', they promised, when at this point the players came out of the hotel.

Reserve goalkeeper Jimmy Montgomery – just down for the experience of a trip to London – was signing my *Reynolds News* team photo with the wayward red stripes, as Brian Clough slipped behind us and headed for the station. Detouring fatefully via Stan Anderson, Len Ashurst and Cec Irwin, I caught him up at the train. Good with kids, he'd sign the several pictures I had of him, I knew, whereupon I'd slip away while the Jacksonians were occupied with the rest of the players. The timing of my retreat was wrong. The guard was blowing his whistle as I made to leave the train and they were already off it waiting for me. They took only about half the photos I had with me, restrained by the niggling thought I might be able to whistle Reggie up again from the dead. But it was upsetting enough to prompt a reassessment of life's priorities.

Our last school match of the season was a victory out at the lavish grounds of Leyton County. Our Religious Instruction master was deputed by the staffroom to make the early Saturday morning trip to watch it. Of vicarish tendencies and knowing nothing of the conventions of football, he complimented me profusely throughout and afterwards. Nearby, Leyton Orient lost at home the same day and confirmed, after only one season in the First Division, their return to the Second. Their need for goalkeeping help was now obvious.

Northern Ireland was not short of such talent. They came to Wembley to play England in the final of the World Youth Cup and lost 4–0, but Pat Jennings, their keeper, played well enough to make my grandad say he hoped Spurs signed him. It was an ex-Spurs player, Ron Burgess, who'd played with Ramsey and captained Wales, who snapped him up for Watford. Jennings described Burgess as a 'real gentleman', if anything too gentle to be a football manager, a job which needed a 'tough approach'. He offered Jennings £15 a week, three times his wage in a Newry timber yard. Jennings was tempted to say no. He had heard Jimmy Hill at Coventry was interested. But then Hill wondered if, at seventeen, Jennings wasn't on the small side. Instead, he bought Crystal Palace's Glazier the next year for £35,000, a keeper's new world record fee.

In April, at the end of the 1962–63 season, I had one more run with my books, phoning the Scottish League to ask what hotel Scotland would be staying at when they came for that year's big game at Wembley. The friendly man at the other end – it wouldn't have happened in London – said they were having a reception after the game at St Ermin's hotel in Westminster, next to Caxton Hall. I was the only kid there and joined them in the hotel bar as they celebrated their 2–1 victory. John White and Dave Mackay of Spurs, Denis Law of Manchester United and Ian St John of Liverpool were friendly and joking around. Keeper Bill Brown was morose. He scrawled on a glossy colour photo of him kneeling and smiling by his post in my *Topical Times*, as if a spider with blue ink on its feet had staggered across it. He didn't so much sign as disfigure it, so I later cut the picture out and discarded it. Rangers left-half Jim Baxter was the only other one who acted out of keeping with the occasion. When I spoke to him he looked down, as if he was crippled by shyness, unable to say anything.

You would have thought these two had had an awful day, not taken part in the biggest victory in Scotland's sporting calendar. Yet when I saw the highlights on TV, Baxter was running the Wembley turf juggling the ball from his knee to instep, making England look silly. He waddled off at the end with the ball under his shirt, scorer of both of Scotland's goals. The first was gifted to him by Jimmy Armfield, the second a penalty when he sent Gordon Banks the wrong way. Of the two keepers on the field, it wasn't Brown but Banks who had greater cause to worry. It was his international debut, an ignominious home defeat to the Scots. He wondered if his England career was over, no sooner than it had started.

One of our school's Greek Cypriot goalkeepers (not the one with the kneepads) was arrested in central London during the visit of Greece's Queen Frederika, Prince Philip's sister. A thinking person, he had joined a demonstration over the poor state of Greek human rights. While here the abuse of library tickets had recently sparked a judicial clampdown, in Greece it was the possession of a union card that could lead you to jail. The police charged him with possessing an offensive weapon. It was a piece of brick, not cleanly cut by a bricklayer's trowel but jagged at one of its edges. The Conservative government hastened a grovelling apology to Athens. One of our Sunday papers ran a report – the boy's father was keen to take matters further – on how strange it was there was no brickdust on him or in his pocket. How coincidental, too, that two other kids arrested by the police, though unknown to our Greek Cypriot keeper, were charged with carrying remarkably similar bits of brick. The newspaper had the picture of the pieces. They fitted together perfectly, without quite making the perfect fit-up. For the first time many people, apart from the always dissident few, began to wonder how fine was the 'finest police force in the world'.

There were more British cars on the boat going over the Channel – not a great number but too many to think of waving at on the other side. The car meant continental travel was possible in a closed space of your own, requiring only minimum engagement with the forces around. They couldn't be entirely evaded, and on the passage back people sat in groups comparing their experiences. One man told how, having covered the length of France in two directions, his family had found it impossible to get a decent meal. They arrived back in Calais famished, in need of nothing more complex, garlic-laced or steeped in rich sauce than a piece of bread. There wasn't anything like a sliced Wonderloaf in the boulangerie, so they gestured towards a half dozen rolls, more pastry-like, less crispy than we were used to. 'And do you know what we found inside them?' said the man, still in shock, and whose family had been perched ready to insert pieces of fortnight-old Cheddar between the rolls' flaky folds: 'Chocolate!' The crowd gasped its sympathy. His wife looked on the point of tears.

Gordon Banks had a disappointing game when Manchester United beat Leicester City 3–1 in the Cup Final. The defence was notoriously leaky but, by some, he was faulted with two of the goals. He returned to Wembley four days later to face Brazil, the first foreign international side he had played. Alf Ramsey was insistent in warning him how the Brazilians could bend a ball from free kicks. Brazil were given a first-half free kick and bent it around him. Ramsey was fumin'.

The Profumo affair was twisting the establishment out of shape. Britain's war minister had an expressionless face but a peculiarly continental name: 'Che profumo!' I'd heard my father exclaim as we'd driven past the manured fields of Lombardy, or sought out what was loosely classified as a public convenience on hot days anywhere from Pisa to Pescara. John Profumo raised an odour of no small magnitude in denying he'd had anything to do with Christine Keeler. He had, as had a Russian military attaché. Kids at school said she was a 'slag', the common view of their dads, when discovered reading the *News of the World*'s accounts of the affair by their mums. A photo showed her pouting and, presumably with nothing on, legs either side of a high-backed chair. One paper claimed she went about the streets of Notting Hill picking up tramps. It made you want to don a dishevelled overcoat and go shuffling down Ladbroke Grove. Mandy Rice Davies, incredibly, was only eighteen, almost within our age-range but worlds away. When told Lord Astor denied he'd been 'intimate' with her, she half-winked into the cameras and said the old dog 'would, wouldn't he?'

Lord Denning struck back on behalf of the establishment team. In his official report of the scandal, he said Lord Astor may have had 'frolicsome' parties in his swimming pool at Cliveden, but no bathing suits were removed. After all, Lord Astor was a staunch supporter of charities. Everything could be laid at the door of Stephen Ward, the sinister osteopath, who'd manipulate anyone, no matter their patronage of Oxfam or Guide Dogs for the Blind, into compromising positions with call girls and Russian spies. The case 'started and ended' with Ward. With gaping holes in the establishment's defence, it predictably turned to blame the lone guy at the back. Prime minister Macmillan escaped for an afternoon to swear in the vice-chancellor at Sussex University, one of the new centres of high-learning set up by the Tories, and said 'Isn't politics fun?' A dour Profumo went off to devote himself quietly to saving the poor in London's East End.

Engaged in a comparable mission, I caught the single-decker bus which stopped at the back door of school, with the vague assurance from kids who took it to Dalston that it went on from there to Leyton. The Orient had a pre-season friendly with Morton, from Scotland. As the bus wound past Ridley Road, the haul from the day before's mail train robbery had reached over £2 million, a figure that was exciting just to see daubed on the placards. Once the gang had added up all the old banknotes and ten-shilling postal orders, they'd have been able to buy every house in our street, whether north or south of the Danbury Street divide. At Brisbane Road, no one objected to my wandering in the front doors after the game and around the concrete corridors to the dressing rooms. I wrote off to the club next day. Its letter offering me a trial was back by return, and in about as little time as it took the police to extend a similar invitation to the first of the arrested train robbers. Some, like Ronnie Biggs, had left their fingerprints on a sauce bottle.

Little clubs had trials. Big ones like Spurs and Arsenal didn't. They had scouts roaming the country, men in trilbys and long dark overcoats, a length of hand-rolled Old Holborn and Rizla stuck to their bottom lips as they watched school and club games from behind trees near the touchline. Like glorified flashers, they'd reveal themselves at the final whistle to say, 'We want you, son', and be round to see your dad with the £10 signing-on fee. No one watched Hanover when we played William Tyndale, nor did they, as far as anyone knew, turn up to see Highbury.

The Orient trial was to be played at the London Transport ground in Walthamstow, near the Crooked Billet. It was fixed for the same hour and morning as our inaugural First XI match of the season, 200 yards up the road. I announced I'd be crying off from the school game, certain they wouldn't mind. There were keepers available in the senior years above me and it would, obviously, be an honour for the school to have one of its players vying for a place on the books of a team in the football league. But the school captain, a kid of some German descent, and Charlie Jeffries, our sports master, were outraged, appalled that, in these days of the £100-a-week footballer, youngsters were losing all sense of values. Possessed by the Corinthian spirit, they stated firmly there was no honour to compete with that of playing for the school.

The night before the match, a swirling mob of fifty kids from Barnsbury school turned up at our school gates. They subjected us and teachers alike to their withering stare as we left and had to walk through them. It turned out that it wasn't a mass bundle they were looking for, but our centre-forward, who had in some way offended a few of them at a rhythm-and-blues club they went to near the Waste, the street market in Kingsland Road. He got on my 38 at Dalston Junction the next morning, with black eyes and broken teeth. He'd rarely been popular even among us and, spiritually, he was no worse for his ordeal. He scored a hat-trick in our 3–0 win over Hackney Downs.

While he was doing so, over eighty trialists at the London Transport ground down the road were being given ten minutes apiece to catch the eye. Only a couple were chosen, no keepers among them. My father had phoned Brisbane Road to say the school wouldn't release me for the occasion. 'He must be all right, then,' said the voice at the other end. 'Where does he go to school?' When he said Highbury it made things sound even better. Under the impression they'd snatched one from under the nose of Arsenal, the men in long overcoats and trilbys dispensed with the formality of trials and straightaway sent a letter telling me to report for training.

Limbering up exercises were conducted on the concrete beneath the rattling main Brisbane Road stand. This was where on match days the fee-paying public, with their meat pies and cups of tea, lingered between halves and siphoned through the Gents. Among the thirty or so Junior and Colt squad members, I was slowest to find a space and did my press-ups and leg-lifts stuck in its doorway. The club's apprentices, employed on £7 a week to clean the stadium and the senior players' boots, and play a bit themselves when they'd finished, had skipped this area with their mops. We then set off through the small streets towards a cinder pitch to the west of the stadium, where the serious training would take place. Curtains twitched in the dark as we jogged past the small terraced houses. I imagined the locals set their mantelpiece clocks by us, sighing, 'There go the Orient boys', as they settled in their armchairs. We were all part of the tribal framework. To seal this common bond, several of our number unloaded mouthfuls of saliva on to their tiny pathways and front gardens.

Everyone else came from east London, or from places further out into Essex like Rainham. But by extension, this was still the East End. From Islington, I was the only real foreigner. We ran a few circuits of the cinder, did some more exercises and a sprint or two before setting up a couple of games. The older kids, the Colts, played on one half of the available terrain, we on the other. The floodlighting was scant and it was difficult to spot an old, worn ball coming out of the black sky. As much light emanated from the railway marshalling yards at the edge of Hackney Marshes. Shunting engines and their couplings clanged and screeched throughout. In an unfavourable wind, the smell from the large plastics factory half a mile away towards Lea Bridge Road hung overall.

In charge of the Juniors was Harry Weaver, tall, oldish, with a lined faced and a gammy leg incurred in the Malayan emergency. Tommy Collier, a younger bloke, smaller, with blond hair and a hook nose, trained the Colts. When their positional sense was lacking, he'd yell: 'You're on top of that ball like flies round a lump of shit!' The youth manager, Eddie Park, we saw only briefly before and after training. The club manager, Benny Fenton, I saw only once. His predecessor Johnny Carey had moved on to manage Blackburn. Fenton stepped a yard into the dressing room one evening, put a comb through his hair in front of the mirror and disappeared again into his office. In a post-relegation season, morale wasn't high and he had a lot on his mind.

The Rest of the World came to play England at Wembley in October 1963 to mark the Football Association's centenary. Law, Baxter, Puskas, the West German Uwe Seeler were selected to play for them, as well as Eusebio, Portugal's new star from Mozambique, who could hit a ball as hard as Bobby Charlton. Lev Yashin was to play in goal for the Rest of the World and was received by all as the obvious first choice. He, a Russian no less, had recently become the first goalkeeper to be named Europe's Footballer of the Year.

In the seven years since anyone west of the Oder–Dnieper line had heard of him, Yashin had transformed into the keeper regarded as the best in the world. His name no longer had a sinister ring to it, more that of a magician's spell. Uttered by the mouths of boys or men, it left a momentary hush. At school, in the Orient dressing room, on TV, it was self-evident that, in his black outfit and at 6 feet 2 inches, he was magnificent, a supremely commanding presence. This was not confined to the 18-yard box: 'does not hesitate to leave the penalty area if he can cut off a pass,' noted my encyclopaedia Even in dour modern England manager-speak, he came out rhyming with dashin'. 'The great Yashin,' the commentator had oozed, as long ago as Sweden 1958. Everyone now agreed. It was remarkable.

The Russians were certainly from a goalkeeping tradition. It went back to the 1920s and '30s. In the war the Russians had performed a similar role to our own, under siege – Leningrad, Stalingrad – relieved only occasionally by the arrival of the battered Arctic convoy. This contrasted with the involvement of the United States. By dint of geography and debating whether or not Europe was worth saving from itself, the USA's role was more of an incursion into distant conflicts. Many thousands of US lives were lost, personal tragedies all, but the national psyche absorbed them without undue trouble. They were in far-flung places, while at home the economy flourished. For the USA, the war fostered no great sense of struggle. By contrast, the Russians, like the British, viewed themselves as having 'stuck it out', the shambles all around them.

Yet as far as the popular perception of Yashin the goalkeeper was concerned, something was going on that went far beyond football. His best performances – the Melbourne Olympics in 1956 and the European Nations Cup in 1960 – had either been in far-off time zones and difficult to witness, or failed to rouse much public interest. Only a year earlier at the 1962 Chile World Cup, he'd been a great disappointment. It was said that he'd returned home to rebuild his morale with Moscow Dynamo, and they had gone on to win the Soviet Championship. But few people in the rest of Europe would have known or cared.

The Cuban missile crisis of the previous late autumn had seen relations between East and West reach their lowest. After it ended, quite the opposite happened. In the relief of the moment, optimism soared. The 'hot line' between Washington and Moscow was established for the sides to talk more readily amid the atmosphere of 'never again'; the Test Ban treaty, whereby the USA, USSR and Britain agreed to ban nuclear tests, was quickly negotiated and signed in the summer of 1963. Relations had never been better.

Where, though, were the figures to celebrate the fact, the personalities to symbolise the new era? There were very few Russians we knew. Khrushchev was a reformed man since he'd seen what he thought was the glint of steel in Jack Kennedy's eye (blank confusion, possibly) but was symbolic of nothing new. Rudolph Nureyev was well-known to a cultured minority because two years earlier he'd leapt the departures gate at Le Bourget airport, but he had expressed no vote of confidence in those on the other side of the great iron barrier. Yuri Gagarin was smilingly pleasant, if seen only briefly on his world tour. Laika would have had the popular appeal for a sequel and her premature cremation in orbit was doubly unfortunate.

It was the special ability of the goalkeeper to construct necessary myths in people's minds which, at this point, came to the fore. Frank Swift had done it before and after the war. Bert Trautmann had followed him. Now Yashin emerged in a similar guise to that of Trautmann. His was the human face of the enemy, somehow separate from the untrustworthy mass.

There was no doubt Yashin was one of the enemy team. Just as Trautmann had been in the Hitler Youth, Yashin was a member of the Soviet secret service, the KGB. Moscow Dynamo were run by the KGB. Lev wasn't about to defect to the West any more than Bert had been interested in converting from being German. This was good. If they'd come over wholly to us, we'd have had no one to place our hopes in over there. Nevertheless, neither was wholly *in* their respective teams. Signing up for the Hitler Youth at a tender age was not tantamount to a career as camp commandant of Belsen. Similarly, Lev was not in the KGB for a life in torture and brainwashing. He was a sportsman and never rose above the rank of non-commissioned officer. He was no more a coolly inhuman 'Ivanov', than Trautmann was a square-headed 'Fritz'. As a keeper, it was entirely in keeping that he wasn't a fixed-face systems' man, but a singular character in a singular position, which was something we were quite able to like and recognise. If there were Yashins, then there were characters with whom we could get on, and maybe eventually come to 'do business' with.

At Wembley, Yashin appeared not in his black outfit but in a rather nondescript grey jersey. At least it detracted from any sinister spideryness. Otherwise he performed precisely to cue. Not always at his best when the weight of expectation was heaviest, in this exhibition match the tension was off. Yashin dived, swooped and saved pretty much everything thrown at him. His final save was a boxer's right jab to a shot by Jimmy Greaves which sent the ball high, and back half the length of the pitch as the whistle went for half-time. He and Greaves collided and fell in a heap, slapping each other on the back. Yashin ran off, leaving the encore to his second-half substitute, the crowd enraptured.

Gordon Banks could hardly believe he was on the pitch in such elevated company. At the banquet after the match, he mingled with the likes of Yashin and Puskas feeling like a young kid, he said, as he happily collected their autographs. There were no big kids around, of course, to tell him to 'fuck off, mate' and nick his *Buchan's*.

Having personally graduated from all that, I made my way to training the next evening at Brisbane Road, amid the whisper from the flowerbeds of Coronation Gardens that our Junior team keeper was in no fit state for Saturday. He was down with Asian flu. We'd been drawn at home to eastern arch-rivals West Ham in the first round of the Winchester Cup. Orient as a club were grappling with post-relegation trauma, while West Ham were in top division-winning mode. Bobby Moore was first-team captain, reserve wing-half Geoff Hurst had been drafted as stand-in centre-forward and found himself a natural in the position. Kelsey's former understudy, Jim Standen, was in goal. Optimism permeated to their Juniors, five teams below. They were fancied to beat us comfortably.

I took the same bus from the Angel to the Crooked Billet as for Saturday school games, except this was the afternoon and felt serious. The dressing room at the London Transport ground was on the first floor up a narrow staircase, above the bar. A dozen or so coat hooks on its wooden walls, it was no bigger than 10 feet by 10. A table, covered when I arrived in half-laced boots, jockstraps, bandages and rolls of elastoplast, took up much of the space in the middle. A sash-cord window looked on to sodden fields and a dismal October afternoon. It wasn't the occasion when the Cup Final commentator viewed the green-baize pitch mowed in perfect stripes beat down upon by the May sun to announce: 'The conditions are absolutely perfect for football.' These truly *were* the perfect conditions for football.

The dressing-room mood moved quickly from friendly and animated, to keyed up and tense. A glass bottle of heavy-smelling liquid – horse oils, one of my teammates said – was passed around, but I wouldn't have known what to do with it. Several of the players plastered their faces with vaseline. All of them wore jockstraps. Only one or two boys in our school team did. They were those who'd developed first and had a longer-standing grasp of scrotal protection. I made do with an old pair of swimming trunks or, if I forgot them, the St Michaels I arrived in. The rest of the Orient team had been at work for at least a year, apprentice welders, capstan turners, bricklayers' labourers. At school, our vicarish RI teacher thought our class right for an early shot at the 'O'-Level. I'd spent much of the week mugging up Amos, Luke and the Acts of the Apostles.

The West Ham team was shooting into the nearest goal as we went out on the pitch. This *was* West Ham, in their claret and sky blue. We were in Orient's shirts of Royal blue. I had one on, too, which helped fill out my green jersey, which was several sizes too baggy for me. I started to jog to the far end in the affectedly stiff, professional-footballer-just-getting-into-motion way, wondering how long I could keep this up. I expected someone to jump out, the groundsman from behind his shed, perhaps, and say, 'Oi! what yew doin' 'ere?'; or benevolently, 'Son, I think you've come to the wrong place.' In the kickabout, I rubbed my muddied gloves studiously on the ball when I fielded it, and drop-kicked it back out again looking nonchalantly away from the player I was passing to – disengaged, like I did this, at this level, every week.

I reasoned I might as well endure the first few seconds. If a shot trickled through my hands or legs, there was always the bus stop at the Crooked Billet which I could sprint to before they'd got the ball back to the middle for the restart. The first minute or so would be important, to get a feel of the match ball. It was a new and polished light brown one. If I called for a back pass, I'd get an early opportunity to make a mark on the game. The nervous defence would be happy to release it in my direction: 'Good call, keep!', the captain would shout. He might throw in a couple of claps of the hand, looking around at the team urging them to get on with it, like the goalkeeper was.

What you didn't need early on in any game was the high cross and accompanying challenge from the attack. The centre-forward would hit you in midair, quite happy to give away a free kick for the destabilising effect it would have on you. Thankfully, I didn't get such a ball. But I wasn't sure I wanted what came in its place: a low centre, hit hard from the long grass on the right wing, to skim across the goalmouth mire. It passed every flailing defender's leg which tried to make contact and arrived at the feet of the West Ham centre-forward. He stood with his back to me, at the right of my goal, on a line with the post, 6 yards away at the edge of the keeper's area.

This was an intriguing moment which I observed as I had the pre-match goings-on in the dressing room. Not really part of it, I found it interesting to watch. I could make out the ball on the ground and between the stripes of the centre-forward's socks. He'd brought it under control, very deftly in the slippery circumstances. He started to turn on his left foot to tee the ball up for a shot with his right. Halfway through his turn it occurred to me that possibly I had to do something about this. No one else was going to. A mere ninety seconds into the game and the team were already down and out of it. The centre-half and others were on the floor struggling to regain their feet and position. They were all very anxious; I wasn't at all. In the first two steps I made from my line, I'd covered most of the distance between me and the centre-forward, whose foot was making contact with the ball.

I launched myself at it, not in Trautmann's head-first sacrificial fashion, but that of the loyally unthinking presidential bodyguard throwing himself on a grenade. The ball travelled, perhaps, 2 feet at full power before connecting with me at diaphragm level. I was aware of a thud, and momentary oblivion. On the ground, I heard appreciation at the glory of my exit. There were some cheers of the 'Oh, yes! for the youngster' variety from the defence and a bit of applause. I pulled myself to my knees and from there was hauled up at the midriff by our right-back. Theatrically passing his hand in front of my eyes to check for signs of life, he shouted 'Y'awright!?' into my face. My answer was overruled and Harry was summoned to limp on with his aluminium bucket. A slap round the face with his wet sponge, and the ref waved for play to resume from a throw in, the ball having bounced off me into touch 30 yards away. Dazed, and having achieved more than could have been reasonably asked of him, the valiant keeper played on.

The speed and quality of the game was as nothing I'd been in. I cleared the ball in a long punt towards our inside-left, who was running away with his back to me as I kicked it. At the instant it reached him, he half turned, took off into the air to flick the ball on with his chest and hared after it to goal. This was only the South East Counties League, Division Two.

We were 2–0 down at half-time. I blamed myself for the goals, a couple of floaters into my left corner which had me feeling 'rooted'. Harry, in charge of the sweet tea in the large metal pot, chastised the team for their lack of support. Staring into their steaming chipped cups the team said nothing about it. In the second half we scored three each. A save I made near the end, diving on the ball in a mêlée of boots, brought a gasp of frustration and appreciation even from the West Ham centre-forward.

On Tuesday evening, there was a full house in the Brisbane Road dressing room. Eddie Park was sitting on the white wooden treatment bench in the middle of it, conducting a post-mortem on Saturday's defeat. No one was saying anything when I walked in but as I hung my coat up, he said quietly, 'Went well, then'. Several of the others nodded or grunted agreement in my direction. I tried to fend this off – 'It was just those wankers in front of me, Ed' – more brutally than I meant to. 'They made it look good.' The others, though, had already accepted this as the official version of the truth. We'd lost badly to our East End rivals, and only the keeper had staved off total humiliation.

The mood of congratulation continued through training. By Thursday, it was getting difficult to bear. If I was selected again, what would they now expect? Others more elevated than me knew the problem. Gordon West, I'd heard, threw up before games. After training I slipped away from the stadium before the Saturday team sheet went up. The other keeper was certainly well again and bound to be on it.

Death *on the* Cross

'WWW here were you?' said Eddie Park, when I got back to
the ground the following week. They knew I lived in a
far-flung part of north London. No one was sure exactly where and
like most others at the club I was assumed not to be on the phone.
They'd raised the other keeper out of bed. It didn't matter, they
said. The game had only been a friendly. My disappearance without
checking if I was in the team was put down to modesty.

Harry Gregg played his last international when Northern Ireland
were beaten 8–3 at Wembley. In their wisdom, his management
assigned three people to mark Bobby Charlton. They forgot Jimmy
Greaves, who scored four. Gregg took the blame, though he had
stopped much of what was thrown at him.

President Kennedy was killed two days later in Texas. The
BBC suspended its radio programmes and played soothing music.
As awful as the whole thing was, this seemed unnecessary, the
BBC's way of doing what Soviet radio had when Stalin died,
with its message to the poor and ignorant masses of 'don't panic'.
Fortunately, we had no need to. The news soon came through
that the Dallas police had arrested the likely culprit. He was a US

citizen, who had at one time gone to live in the Soviet Union. The rest of the tale had a more familiar ring: he was a lone operator, a maverick, and possibly mad.

At training I was put with Mike Pinner. He'd finally turned professional for Orient last season when they'd been in the First Division. He remained a solicitor by day, training at night. We practised throws and crosses, calling for the ball as we jumped to take it. His 'keeper's ball!' was perfectly clipped and almost too polite. In the dimly illuminated mist, resonance of the marshalling yards and pervasive hum from the plastics factory, it helped raise the tone.

During his career, he said, distribution was the feature of the keeper's game that had most changed: 'No longer the last line of defence but the first line of attack.' When he'd started to play he hardly had to throw a ball at all. This was in spite of Frank Swift being so well known for it before and after the war. England's winner in Vienna in 1952 had been launched by a Merrick throw, but, in film of the Hungary game a year later, the commentator was stirred to remark on the regularity with which the Magyar keeper, Grosics, threw the ball. Harry Gregg said he'd get yelled at by his home spectators back in Belfast for doing so. The crowd wanted its value for money in the long and hopeful kick or punt upfield. Kicking was the physical and, as such, relatively easy option. I'd have rather left it to a beefy centre-half. It was always a lottery, too. Accuracy wasn't easy and even when a kick went straight to one of your ream, it took such a while in the air getting there that the defence was usually able to cover. Your player had to bring it under control, often with difficulty as it came from height, and opponents were promptly on him. Kicking represented passing the buck to someone else: 'Here's me getting rid of the ball, let's see what luck you, far away upfield there, have with it.'

The throw was different. Not only was it with the hands and something only the keeper could do, but also another example of how the keeper took responsibility. With it he could direct events well beyond the penalty area. He could surprise and split the opposition's defences with a hard and well-placed ball. It had to be accurate – from distance, straight to the man, either directly to his feet for him to trap beneath his studs, or one bounce, a yard in front of him. Very much more than a yard and by the time it reached the player it would be rising too high to make control easy. From there, an attack was on, not occasionally or with a bit of luck, but virtually every time. Keepers like Jim Standen at West Ham hurled the ball 60–70 yards. He played cricket in the summer for Worcestershire and topped the county bowling averages. I bowled for the school, so throwing was fine. With it having become so much part of the game, said Pinner, he couldn't envisage how goalkeeping could develop further.

ITV couldn't really compete with the BBC on Saturday nights so it started to show football on Sunday afternoons, with highlights from one of the previous day's London, or local games. They often needed things to talk about, so studio analysis became a feature. One week someone noticed, as if spotting an unannounced appearance of Haley's Comet, that keepers were often standing a few yards off their goallines. This was not solely as a forward bore down on them. They were positioning themselves, therefore, more or less permanently to 'narrow the angle' and block the opposition's view of its target. Presented as revolutionary, it was more a case of others not having noticed it before. For as long as I'd been playing, keepers had been in the habit of being at least a couple of yards off their lines. Kelsey had been, when he'd bent himself back to make that save from Charlton three years before. That was what they didn't mention – it was the great historical lesson, that if you were off your line, you'd better make sure you could get back. There was no sense in thinking those out on the field would be covering for you.

The comment on TV had immediate effect. Whether at school or the Orient, suddenly outfield players knew that little bit more of the mysteries of goalkeeping, and availed you of their knowledge. 'Come out, keeper, come out!' they offered, with useless waves of the hand. Maybe they were right, maybe they weren't. In the end the goalkeeper decided. Their interference hampered your thinking and was an invasion. If you came out and made a save, they said, 'There we are, then'. If you didn't and a goal came to pass, their observation amounted to the same, if more strongly put. It also meant a subtle shift in the balance of power between keeper and defence. The nearer you were to your line, the more power of decision you had. The nearer you got to their territory, the more they professed to know what you should be doing. It suited them to have an extra person to help them with their job. Team players were responsibility sharers – shedders – when things got difficult, not responsibility takers. Given half a chance, they'd have you out playing there with them. And should, then, the ball fly beyond and behind you: 'Keeper, where were you?'

Kenya became independent and after the years of Mau Mau surprised us with its moderation. It didn't do anything as unwarranted as a Gold-Coast-to-Ghana transformation, yet both changed its name and kept it at the same time. We'd known it as 'Keen – ee - er'. Now it was 'Ken-yah'. As for that old terrorist Kenyatta, he'd become president and, like Makarios before him, suddenly someone we talked to. Funny, piggy-eyed people called Empire Loyalists jumped up to complain at Conservative Party conferences. Stewards ushered them out and Tory chins quivered with embarrassed laughter. Most would have instinctively agreed with them, namely that it was a 'sell-out', but the party line had changed. Anyway, we were having to confront more sinister changes. The friendly Sultan of Zanzibar fled from the dripping heat of his perfumed island to Britain in January. Julius Nyerere unsmilingly said Tanganyika and Zanzibar would be joined. He appeared in shirts with a half roll-neck. Neither coveted nor hallowed, they were less Merrick than Mao Tse-tung.

Rumours had circulated about our new school building, and indeed the possibly revised circumstances of the school itself. In the interests of economy, we heard, it would have to be shared with another school. The suggestion was Holloway, which was galling to the headmaster. As a humble teacher, he'd been a Holloway man and, since he'd left it, claimed we were much the superior. Further, it was Highbury that had fought for years for the new building, only for another school to reap some of the benefit. The rumours proved groundless. Shockingly, the truth was worse. It wasn't to be Holloway that we would share with, after all, but Barnsbury. Any of the Barnsbury crowd who wanted to beat up members of our first XI wouldn't have to take a bus from Holloway Road any more, but merely stroll to a neighbouring gate. In this, the headmaster clutched at some final straw of hope. He tried to take solace from the fact that the building would be shared. That was to say, the elevated grammar and lowly secondary modern elements of it would be separated by a form of partition wall. Except for an annual joint assembly, perhaps, the two would officially mingle only on rare occasions.

Terry Hexham, the little kid I sat next to, was the class's first mod. He had mates with Lambrettas, front panels covered in headlights. His mum spoiled him and he appeared at school in smartly-cut trousers and a thin overcoat of dark blue nylon. When he went out at nights he wore, on average, a different coloured pair of trousers each week, lime green to salmon pink, or so he said. He claimed he'd lost his virginity to an older woman who lived along the balcony of his block of flats in Clissold Park. He and a few others in the year frequented the R & B club by the Waste in Kingsland Road. Its owner was named Dave. Situated east of the Balls Pond Road and south of Dalston Junction, he was out to give his establishment a touch of class. It was called the 'Chez Dave': a bit flash, a bit continental.

Terry got his purple hearts there. I cut a cartoon out of the *Daily Mirror* of the North Vietnamese leader, Ho Chi Minh – 'Uncle Ho'. It made him sound friendly, though as a communist you assumed he wasn't. He'd been a pastrycook in London, at the Carlton hotel in the Haymarket, before taking to the guerrilla warpath. Perhaps he'd been driven to it, frustrated that his chocolate-riddled French delicacies found few willing takers over our side of the Channel. Clearly there was more to the fellow than your average flaky pastry, since he was now giving the US troops who were up against him a very hard time. When ever they got one back on him, the American soldiers, we read, were awarded the 'Purple Heart' for acts of bravery. In our class this raised great mirth, at the quite absurd notion of a modern western army being doped up to the eyeballs. Martin Klein purchased a spare purple heart before a PT lesson. Martin was the only one of our number who couldn't yet climb the rope, to the extent that he'd never got off the gymnasium floor. He now pulled himself up in four powerful hauls. We applauded as he sat at the top holding on with one hand like a trapeze artist. Till ordered twice by an amazed gym master, he wouldn't come down.

Chelsea had climbed back to the First Division under the ebullient Docherty and were representative of the rising glamour of King's Road. When I went to see them at Highbury they coasted the game 4–1. Peter Bonetti gave as composed an exhibition of goalkeeping as could be imagined. When he took off for the high ball, I thought I heard the zip of him leaving the turf. He brought a flavour to goalkeeping not seen since the enthusiasm that, at first, had greeted Tony Macedo six years before. Coincidentally, the following Wednesday, I was playing against Acland Burghley school from Kentish Town, who were coached by Macedo. Fulham's keeper stood on the touchline as we won 2–0.

Coupled with his name, Bonetti's agility caused people to say he was flasher than he was. He had made enough mistakes to prompt scepticism at Stamford Bridge in his early days but had ironed them out and won critics round. John Moynihan, writer and old Chelsea supporter, compared him to Bert Williams, spectacular in the same way 'with a phenomenal leap and split-second anticipation'. Moynihan added that Bonetti was a 'self-critical lad who is always ready to admit his mistakes'. With this he developed a reliability which made him a realistic contender for the international jersey.

Its holder, Leicester keeper Gordon Banks, was proving by no means flawless. On one occasion when he came to Highbury, I saw him dive high to his left to a free kick from outside the penalty area, when he should have moved his feet to the ball more before take-off. There was also no need for him to have made quite such a flourish of his heels in midair. The ball brushed through his hands and bounced weakly over the goalline by his head as he came down to earth. Later I heard him complain about playing behind Leicester's porous defence, yet England's new keeper was not obviously less spectacular than Bonetti, nor safer. In the 1964 international against Scotland, he misjudged a corner. As he was at pains to point out in his book, the ball hung in the Hampden Park wind, 'stopped as if it had brakes on it'. The fact that the elements in the Scots' national stadium played tricks like this, however, was even better known than the Brazilians' ability to bend a ball around a free-kick wall. The misjudgement led to the game's only goal, and the first occasion in eighty years that the Scots had beaten England three years in succession.

Next day, the *Sunday People* ran the story that three Sheffield Wednesday players, Bronco Layne, Tony Kay and Peter Swan, had bet against their team. This was the first time in its series of 'bribes ring' stories that the *People* had found First Division involvement, albeit the idea that the players had actually thrown the game concerned wasn't backed by evidence. The following week the *People* exposed Dick Beattie as one who'd developed the goalkeeper's art of 'throwing' to a new and sophisticated degree. He was so adept at it, he'd been complimented for his brilliance in games that it was later discovered he'd thrown. Clubs had offered to buy the former Scottish Under-23 on the strength of what they'd witnessed. I thought this all was a shame because he was a nice bloke, if wayward: 'Och, come on, son,' echoed his words as the Portsmouth forger. 'Who's going to know?'

I turned up at Brisbane Road to find training had been cancelled for the night and another trial scheduled instead. Anyone who was already part of the club was allowed to watch the eighty-odd aspirants make what they could of their few minutes of exposure. We loafed around the dug-out, making it clear we were part of the established structure and regarding all before us with critical expressions. Looking up into the stands at those awaiting their turn I noticed the tiny form of Scobie, his nose twitching nervously. He was at least eighteen and over the limit for Juniors or Colts but had obviously lied about his age. I pondered whether to bring this to Eddie Park's attention as Scobie took to the field and began to play well. I got the better of myself when he saw little more of the ball and faded. He left the pitch unchosen and, stationed at the tunnel as he passed, I made a genuine effort not to gloat.

Many leading players in the top division had been given a rise to between £50 and £80 per week. Manchester City offered Bert Trautmann £35, not a sum he thought worth risking his neck for, and he announced his retirement for the end of the season. Shortly before it, I was promoted to train with the Colts. These were older kids. Several, like David Webb, were already apprentices and comprised a friendly East End fraternity. I was the one from elsewhere and the youngest. They were all very encouraging: 'Well played, keeper,' shouted Webb; 'How did you save that, keeper?' they went on. Afterwards I was told I'd been selected in place of the normal goalkeeper, to play in a six-a-side competition at Eton Manor. This was a sports club with huge grounds, enclosed as if within castle walls to keep out the great unwashed, on the edge of Hackney Marsh.

A regular end-of-season event, Orient were traditionally the only professional club invited and favourites to win.

None of this augured well, nor did it that someone on the sartorial side of the Orient set-up had decided our appearance should be as prominent as our reputation. When the brown wicker skip was opened it contained the regulation Orient blue shirts and my green jersey, but not our ordinary white shorts. Today's issue was in catchy blue stripes. None of us had seen any team in striped shorts before. Nor had people outside the dressing room, where they were taken within the context of the day. 'Bunch o' fuckin' mods', was one comment, as we walked to the pitch through hundreds of players and supporters from lesser clubs. There was an obvious swagger to our stride, however. A league team, we reminded ourselves, we were of a rarer stripe.

We went out of the tournament in the first round to an amorphously-named team from Walthamstow and District. This meant the dubious honour of entering the competition for early losers. Eton Manor's B team knocked us straight out of that. We were the first team back into the very echoing dressing rooms, where we dumped the blue-striped shorts in the skip. Their like was never seen again and we slunk away through the castle walls unnoticed by the crowds.

Nothing was said of the débâcle back at Brisbane Road. What rankled personally was that when we'd been ahead 2–1 in our first game, with just a few minutes left, our opponents had equalised with a shot hit hard and close to my legs. I dived and it slipped fast under my body. A player out on the field would have stuck a foot out and stopped it. Had I done so, we'd have won the match. But a keeper was required to use his hands and with them execute not the makeshift but perfect save. Technique was what was called for, not ungainly improvisation.

John White, Scotland and Tottenham Hotspur's inside-right, was struck by lightning on an Enfield golf course, sheltering under a tree. Tottenham had just bought Pat Jennings from Watford and the first thing he had to do when he joined the team was attend White's funeral. Initially he didn't fit in too well at White Hart Lane. He'd been brought in to replace Bill Brown but it took time before Spurs had much confidence in him.

The first black kid appeared at our evening training and in his first practice match scored with an overhead kick. After four weeks I thought he was doing pretty well, but then he was called to Eddie Park's office and told he didn't have what it took. Labour won the general election by four seats to the near general disapproval of the members of my school's sixth form. Martin Klein, our class's only Liberal, was allowed to bring in a transistor radio to hear the results. The west country Liberals did well using US-style razzamatazz – not a great deal more than a few lines of cars ('cavalcades') through Paignton and Newton Abbot. For Labour, Harold Wilson brandished his pipe and pulled up the collar of his overcoat so you could see the tartan-like pattern of its interior. It was a kind of poor-man's Burberry and meant to round him off as the ordinary bloke with that little bit of extra style. Patrick Gordon Walker was packed off from Smethwick where someone (the Tories denied it was them) had put about the slogan, 'Nigger for a neighbour, vote Labour'. Wilson wanted him as his foreign minister and put him up for a by-election at Leyton, a safe Labour seat. He lost again, the locals objecting to having him foisted on them.

I'd assumed I'd be Leyton's automatic first choice for the Juniors in the new season but the memory of Eton Manor silently lingered on. I lost my confidence, chipped a bone in my thumb and had to sit out the first weeks as new keepers were tried. One let in ten against Portsmouth, another six in two successive weeks to Bexley, the only South East Counties League team not part of a professional club. These weren't permissible numbers. A keeper could sometimes concede, say, five goals and be regarded as having had an inspired day behind an awful defence. Six, however, had the mark of the devil about it. Some, or several, must have been your fault. Above that, and things, strangely, could revert for a while back to the keeper's favour. He'd win sympathy, maybe, for obviously having been sacrificed by his teammates. But should the number reach ten, then that really was beyond the pale. The results were in the stop-press of the *Evening News* and I told myself I shouldn't have been so pleased to read them. Keepers didn't glory in misfortunes of their own kind. I demanded to know of Eddie Park whether it wasn't time now that I was given another run. He said it probably was. It should have made me happy, therefore, when my name appeared near the top of the next team sheet. Only, just above it was the bit that said we were playing Tottenham Hotspur.

Spurs were the phenomenon of the age, the 'double' team, the first to win league and FA Cup in the same season this century. They'd done it three years earlier, then won the Cup again the season after. They were now holders of the European Cup Winners' Cup, having trounced Atlético Madrid 5–1, the first British club to seize continental glory. When Jimmy Greaves wanted to come back from Milan after a few months – he'd scored virtually every time he'd walked on to an Italian pitch but he and his wife couldn't take to the absence of old mates and a decent cup of tea – he could have gone anywhere. He came to Tottenham and scored a celebratory hat-trick past Blackpool and England's Tony Waiters in his first game.

The Spurs team we'd be facing would, in as little as three or four seasons' time, be expected to match this peerless standard. They were so far ahead of our division at even this stage of the season that it sounded wrong saying the words 'Tottenham Hotspur' and 'South East Counties League' in the same breath (and that was forgetting the 'Division Two' bit). It was one thing to be up against the hot favourites to win – usually something to relish – but when I reported the news of being selected to my Spurs'-supporting grandad, I felt rather sick.

Our minibus left Brisbane Road at a watery November's dawn. There was nothing which passed for a conversation on the trip. The driver tried to cheer things along but drew as much response from us as an undertaker telling jokes on the way to a funeral. Had the game been scheduled at home, we'd have been bound for the familiar long grass and clodded mud of the LT ground in Walthamstow. As it was, we were making for Spurs' own luxury training grounds at Cheshunt, in exotically rural Hertfordshire, where it borders Essex at the River Lee.

We arrived a little after nine o'clock. When we'd changed and were ready to leave the dressing room, a crowd of about a hundred Spurs' team relatives and camp followers had gathered on the touchlines. Some, judging by their accents, had travelled overnight from distant parts of the country. Our sole support was Harry and his magic sponge. We edged from the warmth of the embrocation cloud into the morning chill, scarcely daring to look at the opposition. They were in Spurs' usual white V-neck, short-sleeved shirts with cockerel emblem and navy-blue shorts. I wished they'd have worn something different, to help us forget who they were and what they could do to us. Their outfit was intimidatingly simple, almost black and white – more or less what we anticipated would be the outcome of the game.

The pitch was prepared as near to perfection as was possible ten weeks into the season. The grass down the wings was clipped, the lines marked in a thick, shining whitewash which looked as if it had been applied since our arrival. The goalmouth mud had been groomed to a condition far superior to anything I'd played on. It was rolled flat and so firm that my studs refused to sink in. Sand was sprinkled over it, rather than strewn in irregular lumps as it was at the LT ground. The chief groundsman might have been another frustrated pastrycook, trained to dust icing sugar on delicate gateaux. Thousands of small holes had been made with garden forks by teams of junior groundsmen, to remove any semblance of surface water. This was against all nature. Mud was the 'great leveller', especially for a keeper. It bogged the others down, evened out the odds. This pitch had been levelled to aid the silky skills of the home team.

Within five minutes of the off, however, two shots of ours had left filthy imprints on the Spurs' keeper's once gleaming right post. A minute later our centre-forward sent in a 30-yard screamer which hit the underside of the crossbar. It went fast over the head of the keeper, who was standing the normal couple of yards in front of his line. His defence was in such a panic, that his right-back had rushed in behind him and was jumping, head dramatically thrown back, though he was also well beaten. Shots which hit the bar's underside like this could generally be trusted to ricochet into the net. This wasn't one of them. It came straight back down towards the goalline, its plunge synchronised with the right-back's descent from his leap. The ball hit the ground and he landed on it, hard, in a sitting position. Our forwards closed in and could have kicked the ball in the net but would have ruined him for life in the process. He was in agony, a lump of inflated leather wedged in his crotch, but his keeper was able to turn, pick it up and clear. For us it was painful confirmation that this was not a match we were meant to win.

The Spurs crowd started to get at their own side, and cheer us in frustration. On a steep grassbank behind me stood Eddie Baily, their trainer, ex-teammate of Alf Ramsey's and possessor of nine England caps, including one from the victory against Austria alongside Nat Lofthouse. Not to put too fine a shine on it, Baily was doing his nut. Then Spurs broke away and one of their number slipped on the surface on the right-hand angle of my penalty area. As the crow flew, this was over 20 yards from me and a far from threatening position. Who saw the alleged incident? No one but the referee. He was war generation, knobbly knees, regulation black satiny top and shorts, the latter pressed with a crease to cut your hand on, and he promptly whistled up to award a penalty kick to Tottenham.

We'd been so completely on top I hadn't been in the match before that moment. It stopped the flow of the game and gave the Spurs' players and fans time to regain their habitual composure. The forces of the universe, quirkily haywire for a brief spell, were about to be put back on course. The penalty-taker, their captain, strode up to place the ball on the spot 10 yards from me in the fashion of one who, on big match days, walked acknowledged by commissionaires through the iron gates of White Hart Lane. They wouldn't have known who he was – some 'cocky little tosser' with razor-cut hair from the boys' team – but they'd have given him a nod. This was his chance to make amends for what till now had been a poor show. 'Can't beat the Orient . . .', you could hear him having to withstand when he later got back to White Hart Lane. 'Bottom club in the Second Division. What are you?'

By popular reckoning, he should have no trouble now. He was a mere five Spurs' captains and penalty-takers down from Danny Blanchflower. To my knowledge Spurs never missed penalties. Blanchflower didn't. He'd sent Burnley's Adam Blacklaw the wrong way – uselessly slumped on to his right knee, the ball in the net to his left – when Spurs retained the FA Cup two years ago. How would this fellow try to do it? At our enhanced level of football, he wasn't going to do anything so obvious as a half-disguised look to one side of the goal before hitting it towards the other. But probably he hadn't yet become such a master of the art as Blanchflower. The easiest option for the right-footed player, with the natural follow-through of his boot, would be to curl it to his left and my right. Frankly, I had no idea what was he going to do but that guess was as good as any.

The ref pipped primly on his whistle for the kick to be taken. The Spurs' captain ran up, oozing apparent superiority in this one-to-one duel but knowing as well as I did the pressure was bearing down on him: Eddie Baily was on the grassbank, the home crowd on the touchline, the 'double' team on his shoulders. He fluffed it. He sidefooted the ball in what should have been a carefree Greaves-like pass to the right corner of my net. I fell sideways on to my knee – a full-blooded dive unnecessary – and took it first bounce into my chest. An acceptable measure of drama was added by my toppling shoulder-first into the mud.

It was a workaday keeper's save, competently professional and under normal circumstances scarcely worth comment; 'piece o'piss', in the argot of the post-match communal bath. But a penalty – and a penalty against Spurs – was not normal circumstances.

Their captain clasped both hands to his eyes and forehead and moaned 'Oh, no!' at his vision of a career disappearing. The angry crowd let out an ill-defined groan, some of its members waving dismissively in the direction of the field as they turned and pretended they were about to stomp off. 'Serves you fucking right!' screamed Baily, voicing their contempt. Several of our players jumped and threw their arms up. When they took word of this back to Brisbane Road the possibilities were without limit. I'd heard players talk in awe of other keepers' penalty saves, no matter how good they really were, or against whom they were made. Saving one of Tottenham's would make my career. At training on Tuesday, they'd offer me the best apprentice terms: that £7 a week and a proper brush to scrub out the Gents' below the main stand.

But, 'Get a grip, son', said a voice in my head. There was a game going on here. I could hear Harry thinking it on the touchline. 'No time for any patting ourselves on the backs when facing those communist guerrillas at the arse-end of Johore Bahru, co'blimey, yus!' I was on my feet running before you knew it, bouncing the ball each four steps at speed towards the edge of my area. The team took the cue and sprinted away in anticipation of my upfield clearance. I hared past the penalty spot in no time at all, then wondered why the referee had not moved from his position just to the right of it. He was looking at me, glaring in such a way as to make me stop and look at him. 'You moved!' he barked, as if I had caused him personal offence. 'You moved before the kick was taken.' And to the Spurs' captain, who was beginning to peer out from behind his hands, he added quite benevolently: 'Take it again.'

He was right, of course. Rules were rules and where would we have been without them? All whistling 'Colonel Bogie' on the railway of death, no doubt, trying to keep our spirits up. But keepers always moved before penalty kicks. There was an unequal law which said they couldn't, and this was its unwritten counterpart which redressed the balance. It favoured the underprivileged, the small guy against whom the odds were stacked. As long as he didn't flout it – jump and prance, or dive an absurd amount of time in advance of a kick – it was OK. But this ref looked like he was of the 'RAF sergeant trainers' category and believed there was an order to be upheld. Spurs, at home to humble Orient, were decreed to win. No bending of the rules should be permitted to challenge such a near holy ordinance, or defy the divine right of things to be done in the proper way.

They chose someone else for the retake who just blasted it past me. A couple of minutes later the ref gave them another penalty in circumstances similar to the first. My attention was drawn to the fact that something might have happened by Eddy Baily, shouting again: 'Cahr-mon, ref, that was *never* a penalty.' They scored again and as I tangled with the net to retrieve the ball, Baily shouted out to me for all Cheshunt to hear: 'Bad luck, keeper, that referee's a total pillock.'

After that, we'd have had as much chance turning back the River Lee at Picketts Lock gates with our bare hands as stemming the Tottenham tide. Maybe my gloves should have stopped a couple of the five more goals that went past me at intervals of about four minutes apiece. Every attack they constructed resulted in a goal. Back in the dressing room none of us had been in a team 7–0 down at half-time before. Harry should have been as lost for words but rattled his bucket and said if they could score seven in the first half, 'then we can get back out there and do the same in the second'. It made me laugh – hysteria, more than anything – till I realised he was serious.

Both teams scored two each. Tottenham hardly slowed their pace and the last twenty minutes became a personal battle to keep out the tenth goal. A game in which a saved penalty might have made my career, threatened the double figures that would have certainly ended it. Back at the ground for the afternoon's first-team game, senior players bound for the dressing room asked how we'd got on. 'Drew 2–2 . . .' we responded, as they passed us with looks of pleasant surprise, '. . . in the second half', we muttered, once they'd moved beyond earshot.

Eddie Park and Harry decided that if they'd made any changes to the team they'd have had to unravel it completely. The result was put down to the fact that we'd been up against Spurs. At the LT ground the next Saturday we comfortably beat Queens Park Rangers. Just before Christmas we played Chelsea on their training grounds at Honeypot Lane, which were the equal in manicured and whitewashed luxury to those of Tottenham. We drew 2–2, then beat them when they graced the Crooked Billet with their presence for the return match in the new year.

We even stole some of their glamour. Dave Sexton, Docherty's assistant at Chelsea, decamped from SW6 to manage us in E10. We worked on things called 'set pieces'. David Webb he put into the first team to come charging up late from defence to add the final touches. Training generally became much harder. We had to do 'doggies', a series of full-out 40-yard sprints, which the Chelsea team had so named because they did them by the side of the Stamford Bridge greyhound track; first four sprints, with a 5-second break, another four, 5-second break, then another. Curtains twitched violently in the streets by the stadium as kids on their way back from training threw up their tea. But Orient beat top team Newcastle and started to stir at the bottom of the division.

Our junior squad clawed the same upwards path. Having beaten Watford in the league, we scored our greatest triumph in easily winning against West Ham on their training ground at Chadwell Heath. This was well received at base. Not only was it revenge for the previous year, but Messrs Moore and Co. had put the FA Cup in the West Ham trophy cabinet and cast Orient even more into their east London shadows. Our victory took us to the semi-finals of the Winchester Cup. Someone reckoned we could go on and win it. It was a shame, therefore, that when the names came out of the hat we were drawn to play away to Spurs again but, never mind, this time we'd face them with our morale higher.

Harry was stood down for the match and Tommy Collier, the Colts' trainer, drafted in. He didn't only carry a bucket but also a substantial medicine box, filled with bandages, liniments and general emergency supplies normally reserved for our seniors. Its wooden exterior was daubed, painstakingly in red, with the sign of the cross. This was serious business.

The box was soon called into action. Tommy was summoned to my goalmouth after only the first couple of Spurs' assaults. As I moved out and up into the air for a cross from the right, the centre-forward slammed into my chest with his shoulder and elbow. My upper body went back, the bottom half kept going forward, and I assumed a state of yogic levitation some few feet off the ground. Here I stayed till physics reasserted control over philosophy and I pancaked back to earth. The Spurs mud, being firmly rolled, failed to absorb the fall. All wind took flight from my body and the noise of my efforts to regain a lungful, I was told, caused some alarm on the touchline. The referee ticked the centre-forward off. You couldn't do this to a keeper any more, he would have said half-heartedly. Tommy cracked a cotton wool stick of ammonia under my nose, nearly blew my head off and the crowd applauded my Lazarus-like recovery.

Spurs scored a goal either side of half-time but, when we pulled one back, the crowd became impatient with them again and got behind us. Their left-winger drove a hard shot to my right-hand corner which I had to dive to and parry around the post; it was a 'much easier than it looks to those who don't know' save which greatly impressed the touchline. Young kids stood behind my goal, cheering, asking in amazement how I'd done it. With such miracles being performed, it was only a matter of time before our forwards scored the equaliser that would get Spurs back for the replay at the LT ground. Then we'd see how their style of play fared amid conditions suited to the real man's game.

With ten minutes left, they got a free kick in what was, undoubtedly, a dangerous position, on the left a little beyond the penalty area. A neat cross from here would put the ball in the path of the advancing forwards. The left-winger himself, the fellow who had not long since hit the hard shot at me, shaped up to take it. My edginess subsided as soon as he kicked it. He overdid the weight he put on the ball and as it ballooned over our wall of defenders, it was clear it was going to be too far in front of his attack. The centre-forward was charging in, as usual, but before he was near the ball I'd easily reach it.

I found it difficult to credit this as a free kick from a team so elevated as Spurs. Such wasted 'set pieces' at Brisbane Road these days would have meant an hour's extra training to get them right. I thought 'what a useless cross' as I moved to the edge of the keeper's area to catch it, without need to hurry or jump.

That was the problem. Adversity would have been better. Had the ball been a yard nearer the Spurs' players, I'd have had to come for it hard. This one was such a doddle that real action would only resume once I'd caught and cleared it and got our team back on the attack. I must have been half looking to see which one of them I'd throw the ball to, when I felt it escape my grip like a wet piece of Lifebuoy in the bath. For a half second I didn't know where it had gone. Looping off my fingers, it had dropped a few feet to my left and the centre-forward was on to it. I still felt hope. He would have been no less surprised than I was and could yet fluff it. Besides, what was in it for him? He had done nothing special to create this situation. He couldn't really get any satisfaction from a simple tap in from a basic error by the keeper, could he? Maybe he'd knock it back to me, saying, 'Have another go, mate, I'd rather beat you when you're at your best.'

I'd forgotten players on the field didn't think in this way. Like dogs they latched on to weakness, pursued it once they'd spotted it. The upper hand gained, they revelled in grinding your face in the mud. Keepers were not of the same mind. That was why only they of all positions made sure, if they had the chance, to shake hands with their counterpart before the start of a match. Perversely really, keepers didn't wish upon each other a poor game. Field players did. They were obvious, unsubtle characters like that. The centre-forward proved it, by eagerly booting the ball into the empty net. He wheeled away – looking peculiarly at me, it was true – and rushed back to receive the congratulations of his team, as if he'd done something marvellous. They were social primitives, the lot of them.

My team looked at me, mouths wide open. I wondered whether the ground might be persuaded to follow suit and sunk to my knees to contemplate it. An earthquake would have done nicely. But here on the Herts/Essex frontier there were no fault-lines to pass such a biblical judgement on my error. Giving up on the game, Tommy Collier, with his treatment box, walked back behind my goal towards the dressing room. I mumbled a feeble, 'Sorry'. He continued slowly with his head down and and murmured, 'Sawrite'. It was nice of him. A keeper who couldn't take the cross was really no keeper at all. What he meant to say was, 'You're dead, son.'

o o o

My dad and I joined the reverent shuffle to see Churchill lying in state at about ten o'clock on the evening before his funeral. My mum had taken my sister. The line went back from Westminster, across Lambeth Bridge to the Archbishop of Canterbury's palace and towards St Thomas's hospital. It moved over the river slowly, the wind freezing your right ear. At the Salvation Army's tea-wagons, people flapped their arms about themselves. When they got their cups they grimaced, as if to say, 'This tastes like boiled cat's piss', then smiled. One said: 'At least it's wet and warm.' With 200 yards to go, the line stopped. When someone finally thought it might not be disrespectful to inquire, we were told the soldiers were having a dress rehearsal. My dad and I gave up at four in the morning.

The symbol of an old world passing when the new one was showing obvious moral weakness did little to reduce the stiffness of punishments in the football bribes trial. Dick Beattie was sentenced to nine months and, like all the others charged, banned from football for life. At Brisbane Road, Orient scraped out of the Second Division relegation zone. Liverpool went out of the European Cup in the semi-final to Inter-Milan. Keeper Tommy Lawrence was criticised for not getting to grips with the ever more outlandish balls bouncing around on the continent. White, with black diamonds, they spun patterns which seemed designed to deceive. However, some tenacious investigative reporting suggested it wasn't the ball, but the Spanish ref who was bent, and who'd enjoyed lavish gifts from his Italian hosts. Bobby Moore lifted the Cup Winners' Cup trophy for West Ham at Wembley and, as he did so, Kenneth Wolstenholme wondered if he'd do the same with the World Cup next year. He was in television, by extension show business, and could be forgiven for saying things like this. Ramsey had no such excuse but muttered on in the same vein as madly as ever.

Our patch of Islington acquired its first fully-fledged celebrity, Paul Jones, the lead singer of Manfred Mann, whose face in close-up on 'Ready Steady Go' promised all boys a life after acne. He moved into a house with his wife and child, across the other side of what had been the stretch of waste ground, a couple of doors from the Catholic church. They put a rocking horse in the parlour window. My sister went to babysit for a designer and his wife just down the street from us and found them waiting for her with Paul McCartney and Jane Asher. She said hello and otherwise pretended not to notice. The wild cats and bombsite at 8 to 10 were replaced by a block of apartments. These were considerably more 'luxury' than those where the two guys lived with their library-book murals. The architect cheekily turned their backside on the street, and their 'front' to overlook the canal. Twiggy came to view, wrapped into a bulky, mini-length, brown-and-white fur coat, looked miserable and went. For a Hornchurch girl the area held no special fascination.

It did for people from such as Fulham and Chelsea looking for a bit of inner-city rough. The steel garage door of the luxury block was swung up one workday afternoon and a pavement party convened. Guests dressed as if for Ascot swilled champagne and looked in smiling, if awkward, wonder about them. 'Bloody interesting place,' their expressions said, 'but will it work?' Someone said they'd seen Anthony Armstrong-Jones at the do – possibly the same person who'd said Princess Margaret had turned up for the opening of Camden Passage. A breathless *Evening News* diarist reported on the occasion and the louche concept in modern living it heralded: 'I went today to the once-dingy backwater of Islington . . .' While even the Bray family knew better than to go chinking their glasses in public, the arrival of those who didn't somehow signalled that our lives had moved to a more vaunted plane.

Labour's election victory had sounded the death-knell for the headmaster's hopes for the school. The idea of sharing the new building with Barnsbury, while staying separate, was dropped. There was to be a fully fledged merger into a new 'comprehensive'. The head announced his resignation and broke down in front of the upper sixth, saying he'd 'failed the school'. They weren't without sympathy but, as grammar school boys, were disposed to regard such sentimentality with contempt. As I moved into my final year, we were called to a mass gathering of sixth formers in Central Hall, Westminster, to hear prime minister Wilson's education plans. Minutes into his speech, the PM was slipped a note by the chairman and said he regretted to inform us that 'Rhodesia has declared UDI'. I had no idea what this was, other than that I'd heard a few of the boys in gaps between our A-level lessons arguing with Bill Lake that they 'could see Ian Smith's point'. Billy got involved in issues like this and one day he'd yelled at me that the British empire was guilty of 'exploitation'. I'd looked the word up to find out what on earth he meant but was left none the wiser. The chairman called a vote: 'That this house condemns Rhodesia's Unilateral Declaration of Independence.' Thousands of us agreed, with only one vote against, and that from one of our lower sixth who said he felt as if he was at Nuremberg. Wilson put his pipe in his mouth, his mac with tartan-like interior on and apologised for having to end his speech abruptly. He rushed back to the Commons to effect the imminent end of the renegade white regime. It was as well he did, for how much longer than fifteen years would it have taken otherwise?

A boy who'd recently left our school, and who I'd been in the scouts with, was shot in the legs in Stoke Newington. A Jamaican was shot and killed as he walked through Camden Passage at pub closing time on Christmas Eve. We heard he'd wished a fellow coming out of the Camden Head a 'Happy Christmas', who took exception. Some MPs blamed the bill to abolish hanging. 'Life doesn't mean life,' they said, more like nine to fifteen years. The train robbers were serving thirty.

My mates moved on from the Chez Dave at the Waste to the Marquee in Wardour Street. I went along and we collected pass-outs at the door from people who had to be on the last district line to Upminster, and, thus, we got in free at half-time. The Who, looking to break into the big time, were the regular Tuesday night group. Eric Clapton appeared first for John Mayall's Bluesbreakers then graduated – to Cream. The police one night raided a club called the Scene off Little Windmill Street looking for purple hearts. Some of the club's patrons were on the 'Today' programme next morning denouncing the police as 'bastards'. A BBC producer, staggeringly, let the tape run uncut. Jack de Manio was so shocked to hear that the average copper wasn't universally regarded as Dixon of Dock Green that, departing from his standard practice, once or twice during the programme was heard to give the right time.

The week Orient cast me to the East End streets, Ronnie Kray walked into the Blind Beggar in the Whitechapel Road and killed George Cornell. The police had been restrained from moving against the rackets of Ron and twin brother Reg by their friendship with Lord Boothby. Boothby had enjoyed the close company of Harold Macmillan's wife over many years, and that of East End boys procured for him by Ronnie. Cornell called Ronnie a 'fat poof'. His biggest mistake was then to move off his home territory of south-east London one night and come looking for a drink in the East End. Ronnie held court near the Blind Beggar, his back to the wall and facing the door of the pub called the Grave Maurice (Maurice as in 'Chevalier', a bit flash, bit continental). Not expecting that Parliament's deliberations of the moment on homosexual law reform would satisfy his outrage, Ronnie took on the responsibility himself. He advanced from his backline position, strode the few yards necessary along Whitechapel Road, and shot Cornell in the head.

I went briefly to non-league Bedford Town. Club manager Ron Burgess, ex-Tottenham Hotspur, captain of Wales and left-half for the Rest of Europe, knew his goalkeepers. When manager at Watford, he'd discovered Pat Jennings for English football. Jennings described him as possibly not tough enough and too much of a gentleman to be a manager. Burgess broke it to me as nicely as he could that I wasn't going to be the next Pat Jennings.

Highways, Cemeteries, Cleansing *and* Baths

W e had trouble finding a boat home and came back from Dunkirk. This was on a cargo carrier, a small ship when compared with the usual ferry, and rapidly reassigned in the emergency to take passengers. Masts of the wrecks in the harbour stuck above the water as we left. Aside from the crew, only a few other people had made it aboard. Knots of Swiss and Germans passed the warm and quiet weekend evening playing cards at tables in the buffet area. The 1966 seamen's strike in the ports may, by and large, have left Europe cut off, though it had not deterred all on the continent from their efforts to get over for the World Cup.

On the Monday England kicked off the tournament against Uruguay with a dull 0–0 draw. At the final whistle, the Uruguayan keeper, Ladislao Mazurkiewicz, did a polka around his penalty area to celebrate. I failed to see why he was so excited. He couldn't surely have believed we were favourites to win?

Ramsey continued to say so with conviction and was no less isolated than his strike-bound sea-faring nation. Bobby Charlton's goal from 25 yards against Mexico on the Saturday lifted hopes that

England might be worth first-round survival. Then the 2–0 win against France the following week at least meant we'd qualified for the quarter-finals, but it wasn't till the next weekend's victory in the sun against Argentina that the national mood turned. The Argentines were one of the best teams in the world. Pele and Brazil had been clogged out of the competition by their cousins from Portugal. Vague hopes of victory transformed into an ominous sense of popular anticipation.

Ramsey had prepared for this. Since the snows of three years ago he had grimly dug in for victory, his predictions inviting universal derision. But by drawing the hostile fire and taking the flack himself, he provided a protective shield for the team. Tommy Docherty, Chelsea's voluble manager, was among those who suggested Ramsey was talking through his hat.

Just about anyone in the public eye who thought England didn't have a chance was encouraged to air their views by the newspapers and radio. Ramsey's squad went into the World Cup with very little expected of them, and, therefore, their earlier performances were no worse than foreseen. By the time anyone really thought England could win it was too late to matter – the team had built enough faith in itself to withstand the tyranny of mass expectation.

With such talent, Ramsey should have been a goalkeeper. He almost was, of course. Full-backs played just in front of the last line and tended to be characters as quiet and uncelebrated as the man behind them. At Tottenham he used to annoy his goalkeeper, Ted Ditchburn, by retreating to the goalline during the other team's attacks and shouting imperiously from the vicinity of the right post: 'I've got this area covered.' They called him 'the General'. He was also the penalty-taker whose job, at a moment when it was he who had everything to lose, was to outfox the opposition keeper. He'd take the responsibility, stride up from the back and sort out the problem. Ramsey had done that with a minute to go against the Rest of the World thirteen years earlier to keep England's home record intact. He'd converted another penalty a month later against Hungary. It did nothing to deter the afternoon's comprehensive defeat, and Ramsey understood the shock of losing that match as much as anyone.

It had ended his career as an international player, as rudely as the national sense of certainty that – since Hastings, really – we had always won at home. He knew the loss of confidence ran so deep that his saying England would win the World Cup was bound to prompt derision. For his players this offered not only cover, but also the chance to raise a glass to themselves and two fingers to the jeering mob. Where was the fun in winning when the crowd said you were going to, anyway? They took you for granted, undervalued the achievement. How much better to do it against the odds and prove them wrong. They would revel in the greater glory of a victory gained from such a disadvantaged position, the impression of which they'd helped create themselves. Ramsey showed not only that he had the right qualities himself, but also brought out that edge to the national character that said, 'We're all goalkeepers really'.

The international careers of various players, Nobby Stiles, Geoff Hurst and others, were built as a result. But few reputations were enhanced by the World Cup as much as that of Gordon Banks. From the back end of Sheffield, Banks had worked in a range of jobs from coalbagger to apprentice bricklayer. A Royal Signals man, he played for the regimental team while doing his National Service in Germany. As a league player he first appeared for Chesterfield, with no ambition higher than playing in the Third Division North. The club told him they were going to sell him when Leicester City offered £7,000 in 1959. He went, but had little idea which division Leicester was in. Two unsuccessful Cup Finals and several otherwise featureless club seasons later, Banks was back at Wembley to concede no goals in the World Cup's opening four games.

The first that got by him was from a semi-final penalty against Portugal. This itself showed he still wasn't faultless. The penalty came about after he'd flapped at a cross and Jack Charlton felt obliged to handle the ball to stop it going in. But such errors could no longer be interpreted as in character. He had become a solid, efficient and almost old-fashioned type of British goalkeeper, appearing to have restrained his 'spectacular' side, to the benefit of his 'safe'. This didn't make him entirely self-deprecating in the old mould. His favoured dressing-room tactic, when he sensed blame was to be apportioned, was to get in with his attack first: 'Goalkeeping is the loneliest job in football and you have to learn to stand up for yourself.' After the World Cup he was quite open in saying he felt disappointed at not being voted the keeper of the competition. The title went to Yashin. The veteran Russian, now thirty-seven, had had a good game in the semi-final, when the Soviet Union, down to nine men, the odds stacked against them, lost to the Germans. Yashin deserved his plaudits though they derived as much from the lingering Lev effect as from a dispassionate assessment of his play.

In the evening after the final I met up with a few mates outside the Marquee. We spent it either in the Intrepid Fox on Wardour Street or among the crowds wandering Piccadilly Circus and the Haymarket. Older people compared the celebrations to those on VE Day, the difference being that there may not have been so many Germans in the crowd then. Those we bumped into offered their congratulations and made no mention of the third goal. We were not of a mind to subject to detailed analysis whether Hurst's shot had really ricocheted from the bar and down over the German goalline, but agreed that the Russian linesman who said it had probably had vivid memories of the defence of Stalingrad. (When, more than twenty years later, the Cold War ended and everyone's geography of the old Soviet Union improved enormously, we discovered he hadn't been Russian at all, but from Azerbaijan.)

After the triumph of the World Cup, there had to be faced the disaster of A-level results. Orient's rejection weeks before the exams left me too little time to adjust priorities to any effective academic end. The weighty tomes on the reading list for European history were too dull. Whoever marked my answer to the annually certain question on the Austrian chancellor Metternich was obviously not impressed by my references to Barbara Cartland's biography of him. Quotes of the 'he entered her room a boy and left it a man' variety were a more apt analogy of Gordon Banks's rites of passage through the hotbed of the World Cup, than an insight into the diplomacy of the post-Napoleonic age. In German, Brecht never captured my imagination – his work had to be performed in an entirely sparse setting, our teacher said. This was more suited to the post-war generation of keepers than the mid-60s enlightenment. Kafka's *Metamorphosis* proved ominously prescient as far as the exams were concerned. It was about the kid who had a nightmare that he'd changed into an unworthy insect, then awoke to find it was true – *es war kein Traum* ('it was no dream').

○   ○   ○

Islington town hall, therefore, loomed like a dreadful apparition. It stood back from the main road, the Highbury Corner side of the fire station, and almost opposite the old Co-op, which had lost its glass front to the world when the borough turned it into the public health department. With its mock-classical columns the town hall had the grey solidity of some middling mausoleum to Mussolini – Milan station without the grandeur and sense of arrival, and certainly none of its opportunity for escape. Beyond the large front doors the grand stone staircase leading up to the council chamber was roped off. Employees passed to the side of it and along dark echoing corridors as cheerless as those in the kids' hospital in Hackney Road. I was shown into a high-ceilinged first-floor room, where a dozen people sat at six long desks arranged across it, working to the click of Lever-arch files. Bright rays of sunlight beamed through two tall windows, together with the sound of children laughing outside. Cruelly, this municipal tomb had a view over the playground of William Tyndale school. I was given a handful of bills from the London Electricity Board and told to transfer their details to white cards filed in a cardboard box, which recorded how much electricity had been expended in the urinals of the Hornsey and Holloway Roads. The amounts were so small I assumed someone, somewhere, was taking the piss. The impression heightened when I was told I'd joined the department of highways, cemeteries, cleansing and baths.

Once a month I was required to balance the books of the council's crematorium at Cockfosters, thus determining the ebb and flow of demand for such services provided by the borough as niches in the Columbarium and entries in the Book of Remembrance. The first time I did this a brochure passed across my desk which I'd never seen but had been sent to school-leavers like myself, advertising a town hall career as a 'real life job about real life problems'. Technically, death was a 'real life problem' but it still felt like liberties were being taken with the truth. The phone rang about twice an hour to break the room's eery stillness. On a morning when the sense of being buried alive was acute, the woman on the switchboard reported me for making two personal calls, which she'd listened in to on behalf of the residents of the borough. Our section head, an aged snuff-user, who rubbed the brown residue of each noseful on his lapel and could be smelt coming down the corridor on the breeze preceding him, gave me a stern lecture on wasting ratepayers' money.

Islington was run by old Labour councillors and aldermen who, at their evening meetings, had occupied all seats in the chamber for as long as anyone of my grandparents' age recalled. Councillor Butcher drove a number 4 bus between Tollington Park and St Paul's. If anyone he suspected of being staff boarded as it passed the town hall on the dot of five o'clock, he'd report them for obviously having left their desks early. Councillor Raymond, white-haired, kindly-spoken, had a stall up Chapel Market. Long lines formed at it as he heard out people's grievances. At plenary gatherings of the council, he could brilliantly reduce every discussion to marginal movements in the price of potatoes. Fiscal conservatives, the borough's elected representatives fought every ha'penny on the rates.

As such, they hadn't the vision of their counterparts in other inner boroughs of greater London, where old housing was being ripped down to build fashionably tall blocks of flats. These were thought thrusting and exciting, each building in its way an imitation of New York's Empire State. I had a Saturday job at the head office of the Tote in Ludgate Circus, where most of those working with me came from the East End and south London. A friend of the girl I started going out with had just been moved from a crouched row of cottages by the railway in Stratford, where to spit with a following wind risked execution on the live rail of the Central line. After twenty years on the housing list, her family was ecstatic at their new home, on the top of a block off Leytonstone High Road. Islington's ancient representatives remained stubbornly sceptical about such improvements in the quality of working-class life.

The borough treasurer did manage to twist their arm into buying a computer. I was confined to the dark room next to it on Fridays, when it was fed information on the hours clocked at every dustman's depot from Wedmore Street near Highgate, to Helmet Row at the northern fringe of the City. Filling a large, bright and air-conditioned room, it processed time-sheets into pay-slips in no time and throbbed promises of an improving future. I was in its presence as the news arrived at the end of October of the National Coal Board's ancient slag heap slipping and killing more than 140 people, most of them children, in Aberfan. But the computer was often accused of getting things wrong and being a waste of money. Dustmen stormed the wages office, getting abusive with young women at the counter. The one black guy in the town hall, mixed race and built like a Pacific island prop-forward, came out to bear over them.

The year saw Britain three states of the empire lighter. British Guiana became Guyana, which meant we could no longer count the Brazilians as neighbours. Basutoland's change to Lesotho suggested it was another place we'd been mispronouncing all these years. Barbados stayed as it was and went it alone. Relatively small states, they implied decolonisation was in its last stages. 'Europe', meanwhile, was back on the agenda. We'd previously been no less cool about joining it than de Gaulle had been about having us, but, all credit to it, the continent wasn't the mess it once was. As my family drove through it each year you could see how French farmers were gradually learning to use tractors more than horses to pull their ploughs. Everyone we saw or met from first landfall at the Pas de Calais to our destination at the main piazza of Siena had improved their living standard.

Britain's moves towards the continent remained ambiguous. The gravity of the nation's Balance of Payments led to curbs on foreign travel. From November the amount people could take abroad with them was restricted to a mere £50 a year. While Harold Wilson was leading the bid to get into Europe, cabinet members like his minister for trade, Douglas Jay, were avidly against it. Strangely, Jay, who looked the absent-minded professor type that slept in his suits, had twin daughters who had become icons of change. Few people knew what they did, apart from being mini-skirted students at Sussex University. They turned up regularly in the papers as representatives of modern Britain, one leggily free of the petticoats of empire.

Wilson was no less keen to indulge in a little contemporary image-making. Was there a hint of risqué, continental dash? With his pipe and the upturned collar of his mac, he became a kind of

Anglicised revamp of Inspector Maigret sniffing the air for clues on the night streets of Montmartre. Whatever it was, there was something on the wind. And the goalkeeper, the most British of positions, was quick to detect it. The English football team had beaten the world, Gordon Banks's efforts in goal as important as anyone's, so no one could doubt our substance. Why not, therefore, relax and pay a little more attention to matters of form. In line with Britain's bid to re-create itself as a more brashly European state, Banks appeared in an England sweater with the number 1 daubed on its back.

The modernist movement in our area was reflected in its migratory patterns. The traditional residents were being shipped out, either by their landlords or of their own accord, for their own three-up, two-down, with a patch of grass and garden at front and back, in outskirts like Enfield and Ponders End. They, the Arthurs and Dollys, were leaving, while others with names like Jasper and Crystal were moving in. Actors with supporting roles in *Dixon of Dock Green* and *Coronation Street* took over sole possession of houses. Multi-family occupancy faded as a social phenomenon, so fewer people could be seen, back windows of the houses raised in summer, washing at their kitchen sinks before having their evening tea. Bathrooms became warmer places to be and were used on a daily rather than weekly basis. Shower rooms came into existence, with string-operated bamboo curtains at the window. They were see-through when the light was behind them. Original residents were minded to look away, while the newer lot were not nearly so keen on keeping themselves to themselves.

'I see your neighbour's on TV tonight,' my colleague at the next desk in the computer room suddenly announced. I asked him who he was talking about. 'Joe Orton,' he said, surprised. 'He's got a play opening in the West End.' I thought he was talking about one of the street's recent arrivals but it turned out to be one of the guys in the top-floor flat at number 25. He probably wouldn't have thanked me for imagining him in the role of 'gentrifier'. The space he and his friend shared was not a great deal bigger than what newcomers converted into that extra shower room. His name still wasn't one I recognised. If I'd heard it at the time of the library books kerfuffle, I'd forgotten it as the street drew a veil over the matter in the four years since.

The first time I heard him speak was that night on TV in a short one-to-one interview at about six o'clock. I'd never seen him in any other pose but with his eyes fixed on the pavement, as I held up kicking a ball for a few moments to let him and his friend pass. I might have done, of course, had I run into him on the Angel tube's emergency stairs – a popular passage for bunking the fare, though in Orton's case used for the occasional fleeting tryst. The fellow was brilliant. He had had another play, *Entertaining Mr Sloan*, on stage a year or so before, again to no local comment that had ever reached my ear. He said the critics had denounced that as obscene. But how they'd heard anything of it, above the sound of people they claimed were leaving the theatre in disgusted droves, he wasn't sure. He was under no illusions that his new play, *Loot*, would draw a more favourable response. It touched on various themes, society's hypocrisy and things usually not being what they seemed, oh and such matters as corruption in the police. It was well before TV's evening watershed and the interviewer chuckled along but delved no further.

What the play's opening and such acceptable notoriety as appearing on friendly TV talk shows (rather than in the dock of Old Street Magistrates Court) meant in the street was that two largely unnoticed characters took on a little more of an identity. Orton's clearly older friend, Kenneth Halliwell, had been the one with the funds to buy the flat when they'd moved in and, as such, had done quite a bit to support him. They were both writers, though Halliwell hadn't had any comparable success. He carried their shopping, what little they did, in a duffle bag when they went on Wednesday to Sainsburys in Chapel Market. Some quiet references might be made to the 'pair of Nancy boys' but, despite the reform of the law on homosexuality, that still wasn't really a debate people wanted to get into. My grandma, whose fondness for Liberace would continue beyond his death from Aids twenty years hence, just referred to them as 'the boys'. More common, perhaps, was that two previously nameless people might now be referred to as 'Joe and Ken'.

Not that anyone was going to buttonhole them into regular pavement conversation. Orton had escaped his background, in Leicester apparently, shunning its mediocrity and was said to detest the lives of 'ordinary' people. Yet he'd lived reasonably comfortably for half a dozen years in a street which could not really have been described, for at least most of that time, as anything but an ordinary place. Maybe he was happy among people who, whatever they thought about him or he them, left him alone.

He found good material, too. The gist of his conversations on the stairs with his downstairs neighbour, Mrs Corden, and her commissionaire husband, often found their way into his plays. When I took my East End girlfriend to see *Loot* at the Criterion on Piccadilly Circus, its theme of police corruption and violence was relatively shocking to a West End audience. But 'Truscott of the Yard', the play's main character which now confirmed Orton's career as a playwright, was based on that of Detective Inspector Challoner. Orton had heard and read all he could about him at around the time he'd been in prison. Challoner had come to public attention with the case of the broken brick – the one he'd tried to fit up against the quieter of our school's two Greek Cypriot goalkeepers.

My girlfriend was pursuing her own moral code, meanwhile, one typically right and proper among young women of the East End working class. She didn't exactly claim that she would hang on to her virginity till getting married, but asserted she'd not depart with it before some ill-defined time in the future. This left me in firm possession of mine. A student of the arts and humanities, she tried to divert my mind to higher thoughts. She put me on to Sartre. Iron in the Soul was what I needed, Nausea what I felt. I understood neither, and gave up both after a few chapters. Camus' *The Outsider* was easier to get an instinctive grip on. He was from Algeria, a goalkeeper, and had written the book from exile in Paris at the time when my father was landing with the British army in Algiers. My girlfriend also directed me towards painters of the late nineteenth and early twentieth centuries. Cézanne, Lautrec, all were exiles, rejected in their way. On nights when we weren't seeing each other, I wandered the Soho demi-monde, worthy works about them under my arm, convinced I was the only kid of my age denied the experience of manhood.

Jimi Hendrix lurched out of a taxi in mockery of my condition, as I waited with a few others for pass-outs outside the Marquee. Cast as an idol since he'd been discovered in Greenwich

Village the previous summer, he'd featured in many a groupie's pre-coital plaster cast since. We chatted with him for a few minutes, as much as anyone could chat with Hendrix. He stood in military cape and with brass-topped cane, beaming an abstracted smile. Now Clapton had left to form Cream, we were all there to run the rule over John Mayall's new lead guitarist, Pete Green. By the time I'd engineered my way in, Hendrix had disappeared, probably to assist another clay-modelling nightclass.

The Macabre was a good venue to head for, a dimly lit coffee bar with Ortonesque coffin-shaped tables in nearby Meard Street. My reckoning was that if I sat there reading my learned works, it would stimulate conversation with the liberal-minded female students of St Martin's art school who frequented the place. I struck lucky while perched in the pitch dark over a life of Cézanne. A fine-artist from the counties, familiar with the ways of horses and things, invited me back to her flat in a terraced crescent out near Chiswick, on the District line. In increasingly heavy foreplaying conditions, however, I fumbled my way into her affections no more deftly than the man in oiled-cotton gloves. I had no definite idea what was meant to happen, which clearly contributed to the fact that nothing was. Mumbling ambiguously this had 'never happened to me before', I ran into her kitchen, overlooking a small park and darkened houses opposite, to seek a solution in cold water. I splashed it straight from the tap to the offending area, though finally gave up this effort to turn 'em blue in Turnham Green when a light came on and a face peered out from a house across the way. The keeper was not up to the standard requirement of stiffened resolve, stayed rooted to the spot and consummately failed to rise to the cross. But I let matters lie, relieved there was at least someone who cared.

Billy Lake, ex of Jamaica, had been the only one in our arts part of the sixth form to get the necessary 'A'-levels and go to university. He was at Sussex and a friend and I went to visit him. Billy bounced down the arts block steps proclaiming he'd 'told everyone' about us. In the floaty, sylvan atmosphere of the campus, we were evidence of his rougher and, therefore, credible past. He left us with a girlfriend in his room in a low block of student houses on a grassy slope and rushed off to a lecture. Lost for anything deeper to say, I asked if she'd known him long. She answered that she felt she had, yet wondered whether she knew him at all. In fact, to what extent could Billy say he knew himself? This sounded OK to me. You could get a government grant to think and talk like this.

o   o   o

The Scots stuffed the genie of England's post-World Cup exuberance back in the bottle in April 1967 by winning again at Wembley and declaring themselves 'world champions'. England scored twice but the Scots put three past Banks. He couldn't be blamed but, equally, it showed that donning the number 1 jersey wasn't going to work miracles.

In the other goal, Ronnie Simpson made his debut for Scotland at the tender age of thirty-eight. The Scots' selectors had finally noticed he was there. When he had appeared for Britain in the 1948 London Olympics, Matt Busby had managed the team and had wanted to buy him for Manchester United. Modestly, Simpson went to Third Lanark. He moved on to Newcastle and, it could only be presumed, the selectors failed to register his two winners medals in the 1950s. He was dark, smallish at 5 feet 10 inches and maybe just too much for his own good in the old mould of keepers who went unseen. With Simpson *in situ*, the Scots could have had their goalkeeping spot sewn up for the better part of two decades. They'd never have landed themselves with laying the troubled ghost of Frank Haffey, or the jokes about Scottish keepers it stirred south of the border. A month after the Wembley victory, Simpson played in Lisbon, as Celtic outflanked Inter-Milan's mean defence and magnificent treatment of match officials, to become the first British team to win the European Cup. His presence was again quiet confirmation of the virtues of the long game.

Spurs won the 1967 FA Cup with Pat Jennings in goal. At 6 feet, he was a good height for a keeper but his really exceptional attribute was a huge pair of hands. Were he to misjudge a cross and find himself unable to take it two-handed, he could reach and catch it with one. He improvised in a way which wasn't within the tradition. He'd been brought up playing Gaelic football, which meant he was good with his feet. When Spurs, as Cup winners, played league champions Manchester United in the annual Charity

Shield at the start of the following season, Jennings scored a goal from his own penalty area. His kick caught the wind and bounced embarrassingly over Alex Stepney's head as the United keeper advanced a few yards too far. But in other ways Jennings was straight down the classical keepers' line. As a Catholic in Northern Ireland, his upbringing to some extent naturally borrowed from southern Irish culture. But there was no hint of his having been within many miles of the Blarney Stone. He was phlegmatic to the point of barely saying an unsolicited word on or off the field. In his early playing days he'd become used to the barracking from the predominantly Protestant-populated terraces behind his goal, which he withstood in a dignified silence.

I went to see England play out a comfortable 2–0 win over Spain at Wembley, having no idea that Ramsey was going to give Peter Bonetti a game. A late change in any other position causing one of the nucleus of the World Cup side to be stood down might have raised popular concern. But this didn't apply to the keeper. With someone like Bonetti coming in as substitute for Banks, you knew there was no need for alarm. Thus, half the goalkeeper's job, whether in the minds of the spectators or the defence playing in front of him, was done before he even took the field. England again enjoyed an embarrassment of goalkeeping riches.

If the reports from the heart of the country were anything to go by, so did Leicester City. Nothing necessarily strange in that, because this, after all, was Gordon Banks's club. Likely as not, Leicester had a young reserve on the up-and-up, who'd keep Banks on his toes till another club realised the junior keeper's potential and snapped him up. The word from Filbert Street, however, was that it was Banks who was surplus to requirements. Although he hadn't known where Leicester stood in the football league when he'd joined them, since then he was what stood between Leicester and obscurity. Without him, the city's football supporters might just as well have got behind its rugby team if they'd wanted anything to cheer about.

The fact was, nevertheless, that a club so previously untroubled by ambition now felt it could get rid of someone who wasn't far off being the best goalkeeper in the world. Matt Gillies, the club's manager, told Banks he had, in the keeper's words, 'given as much as he could to Leicester'; which was to say that the keeper who a year earlier had seen England to the World Cup had nothing further to offer the tranquil flatlands of the English east Midlands. There was a young reserve in the wings. Peter Shilton, seventeen, who was champing at the bit and needed to be given his chance. Any reasonable price for Banks, a geriatric twenty-eight, would be accepted. Pictures in the paper showed the two shaking hands with each other. Shilton looked youthfully determined, Banks as if he was having to force a smile.

If, as a kid, you ever met him on a station platform and asked for his autograph, Matt Gillies was a courteously obliging Scotsman. In the often feudal parlance of football, a reasonable description of him was 'one of the game's gentlemen'. But he'd had his moments. Before the Cup Final six years earlier, when Spurs were confidently crowing for the double, Leicester's chances depended on their free-scoring centre-forward, Ken Leek. On the eve of Wembley, Gillies dropped him. Reports said this was for an act of indiscipline. I certainly heard nothing of the errant striker's name being linked romantically with the wife of the club chairman. Surely, only such an awful transgression as that could have justified a managerial decision which, in effect, gift-wrapped the Cup and delivered it straight to the trophy cabinet at White Hart Lane. By contrast it was suggested it had been something to do with the player having enjoyed a late-night drink.

Among the station fraternity, Leek was thought of as a nice enough bloke, if a bit aware of how good he was. At a stretch the description might have applied, too, to Banks, which, if anything, was more provocative. Centre-forwards were expected to swashbuckle, keepers weren't. Hadn't Banks said after the World Cup that he thought he was the best goalkeeper around? Could it have been like the old Scottish football writer had said: a flash keeper was as welcome to some as a bank clerk in a sports jacket? In any case, Gillies, manager of a club without a trophy worthy of the name, showed that no one was too important to be cut down a notch or two. Alf Ramsey refused to accept Banks had given as much as he could and kept him as his number 1. Leicester sold Banks to Stoke City for £56,000. At about the same time, West Ham created a new keeper's fee record in paying £67,000 to Kilmarnock for Bobby Ferguson. It bordered on madness.

The bounds of sanity were crossed in our street, within weeks, as

Leicester lost another star. Ambulances and police cars were outside number 25 and people on their doorsteps when I came home from work. In the early hours of that day, Ken Halliwell had hammered a sizeable portion of Joe Orton's brains out as he slept in the stifling claustrophobia of their top-floor flat, then killed himself with an overdose of pills. The August weather was hot and exceptionally humid, which made sleep difficult. Everyone's bedroom windows were open, but no one was aware of the murder a few yards away. Elena, Orton and Halliwell's next-door neighbour, came home from her work at a West End restaurant at 2 a.m. and saw their light on, which was unusual but not anything to cause concern. Her brother, Mario, raised the alarm next morning. He'd peered through the letter box after a driver, who had come to take Orton to an early appointment, could get no answer from the flat.

Orton had finished his latest play, *What the Butler Saw*, a month earlier. In it, an explosion within the domain of the North Thames Gas Board destroyed a statue of Winston Churchill, whereupon someone made off with its excessively large private parts. 'How much more inspiring if, in those dark days, we'd seen what we see now,' said a character when dogged police work tracked down the war hero's replica stray items. 'Instead, we had to be content with a cigar.' It had been a wayward incendiary 'in those dark days' that eventually brought Orton and Halliwell to the street. This had led to their brush with the Islington libraries department and the law, Orton's fame and the death of both of them. Halliwell had rapidly found himself unable to keep up, and in growing paranoia about his partner walking out on him. One street rumour linked Orton's name with Brian Epstein, the Beatles' manager, who died a few days later from a drug overdose. That death was later thought to have been an accident. Anyway, when Orton had met Epstein to discuss a possible joint project with the Beatles, he'd described him as the 'weak, flaccid type'.

While on holiday in Tangier shortly before his death, Orton had noted how well he and Halliwell were getting on. That, and his having just finished what was sure to be another successful West End play, were obviously welcome but also disconcerting. At such moments the fates had a way of turning. Things had been, he wrote, 'too good to last'.

The script for Orton's funeral he could have written himself.

When his cortège arrived at Golders Green crematorium (though Orton would have opted for that at Cockfosters), a chapel attendant asked, 'Are you the 2.15 or 2.45?' Someone had suggested playing one of his favourite pieces of music, Lennon and McCartney's 'A Day in the Life', but the quality of the tape was so poor it could hardly be heard. From his diaries I later discovered he'd tried quietly to compensate the borough's ratepayers for the defaced library books, by helping make savings in other council expenditures. The low demand for electricity in the urinals of the Holloway and Hornsey Roads had been, in small but considered measure, because he and others removed the lightbulbs to disport themselves unobtrusively in the dark.

○   ○   ○

I played for a team mainly made up of fellows who had gone to our school – stock jobbers and brokers, one of the first money-dealers the City had employed when it decided it needed more native wit than could be provided by the public schools, a window cleaner and, occasionally, one of our younger former maths teachers. On Sunday mornings on Hackney Marshes, the price of a pitch included posts and crossbar, which you erected yourselves, but no nets. The sense of having a yawning expanse to defend, rather than a finite space, was more difficult and less fun – perhaps another reason why the British were goalkeepers and the continentals weren't. The Marshes had the added attraction that once the winter rains had fully set in, the average penalty area was transformed into a sump. When compelled to stand in the ankle-deep water in the middle of the goal, you could smell the rising evidence of the pitches' rubbish dump origins.

The 'four-steps' rule came in with the 1967/8 season, designed to stop 'timewasting'. Since barging had been clamped down upon, the untroubled keeper was alleged to have aimlessly wandered his penalty area, taking care to bounce the ball every four steps, till it eventually occurred to him to make his way to the edge of the 18-yard box and punt the ball away. With the new rule, when the keeper fielded a ball he was allowed only four steps in total before he had to kick or throw it out. The risky alternative was to avoid touching the ball with his hands as a shot or defensive pass-back came at him. Controlling it with whatever other part of the body he could, he was at liberty to dribble it with his feet to the edge of the penalty area, or beyond, if he wished, and then release it upfield.

This scandalous restriction could be traced back to keepers allowing themselves to go soft with the change in the law on shoulder barging. Once you became subject to the collective's rules of fairness – 'We'll look after you, keeper; we won't let anyone touch you' – you were subject to their calling in their favours. They'd start to tell you what to do. It was like joining the mafia, or any secret service, official or not: very easy to slip into, and near impossible to get out. The dictatorial four-steps rule was an obvious move towards sucking the keeper out of his unique role, namely the 'footballer' who played with his hands. He'd become just another foot-soldier – no longer the best, merely one of the rest. It would be the ruin of great keepers. I took it out on opponents by saving five penalties out of six in the season. The other one was taken by a fellow with hair like it had been razored for some ancient battle of Mods versus Rockers on the Margate waterfront and with slits for eyes. Whether he did look in the opposite direction to where he kicked it I couldn't tell. He hoofed it over the bar.

We met early one Sunday morning at Highbury Corner for the away trip to an East End team who played within the fall-out zone of Beckton gasworks. The talk was, as usual, of affairs of the night before, though the subject matter was out of the ordinary. Like an artful penalty-taker, Harold Wilson had deceived people by saying he wouldn't devalue the pound. He did so, on a Saturday, when he thought we'd be looking the other way. People slept on the news expecting to find their pockets and purses had been rifled for change by morning.

Our former maths teacher also knew his economics and explained that devaluation – Wilson used the word, as he did others like 'inflation' and 're-deployment', as if everyone understood what he was talking about – would hit the ordinary person only when they travelled abroad. They'd get less foreign money for their pound and find their time in alien parts more costly. Otherwise devaluation meant that imports would be more expensive and our exports cheaper for foreigners to buy. Therefore, what the government told us was the dire matter of the Balance of Payments would be squarely confronted.

Wilson bit on his pipe and turned his coat to the stiffening breeze. Britain 'was on its own' in facing this crisis, he said, and assured everyone that the 'pound in your pocket' was not under threat. In calling for the nation to draw deeply on its reserves of 'Dunkirk spirit', however, he only strengthened the belief that it was. West Germany, by contrast, was being urged to 're-value' its currency, because it was so strong. Germans would be able, thereby, to bring their marks over here and get more pounds for them than before. They'd lord it over us. 'All very well to talk about Dunkirk spirit,' was the response to Wilson. 'But who won the bloody war?'

The other little official announcement that slipped in was that the £50 limit on what people could spend abroad would stay, rather than be removed now its first year was up. This would be no problem, jollied Jim Callaghan, chancellor of the exchequer: 'Take your holidays at home.' He assumed he was on to a winner because that was where most people wanted to spend their holidays, if they had such a thing. As an advertisement for how bracing they could be, we saw Mr and Mrs Wilson pictured each summer in windswept deckchairs on the Isles of Scilly.

If anyone got the message of devaluation it was General de Gaulle. Those relatively few British people inclined to come out and off their lines for a continental sojourn were being told to desist from doing so. Furthermore, the pound's cut in value meant it was worth $2.40. Each penny in the pound, thus, was valued at one US cent. This was, clearly, just a matter of monetary convenience not to be misconstrued, even by lofty French nationalists as indicating the British pound was strung tightly to the mast of the dollar. But, loftier than most, de Gaulle again rejected Britain's application to join the common market. We were not kidding ourselves or anyone else that we were part of the continental team, he suggested, insisting we were happier with our more distant attachments to the USA and the Commonwealth.

The shock was greater than in 1963. Wilson felt he'd made the right gestures. Despite looking in deadly earnest on President Johnson's toilet-stops in Britain, he had refused to send even as little as a ceremonial goat to back the USA in Vietnam. At one stage he'd said the British army might be employed to put out brush fires in the world wherever they might occur, a kind of re-run of the Gloucesters holding the line at the Imjin river. This just didn't fit, though, with our divestment of imperial dependencies. When Wilson said we were pulling out 'east of Suez', it included places that hadn't even asked to go it alone. Not that they were distraught about it when told they would be. Lee Kwan Yew turned up on the steps of Downing Street, saying the prospect of Britain leaving Singapore left him neither 'euphoric nor manic depressive'. People rushed for their dictionaries marvelling at how well 'Chinamen' spoke these days. His tiny island was doing nicely, thank you, he added, and would continue to, whether we were around or not. What with de Gaulle on the one hand, the fading empire on the other, we were in danger of being left uncomfortably alone.

o   o   o

A portly character with a limp, well into middle age, in dark suit and heavy-rimmed glasses arrived in the street on Friday nights swinging armfuls of French bread and bottles of wine. Parking space was scarce these days but he shoved his car in wherever he found one, no matter outside whose house it was and whether or not they had a vehicle to park as well. First come, first catered for, so weren't you the unlucky one. He shunted into the cars in front and back of him if he felt the need, responded dismissively to anyone who complained, and disappeared till Monday, or even Tuesday, morning. He had a girlfriend, and a baby, a little down the street on the canal side. She looked much younger than he was, Jay-twin era, with long, straight brown hair and centre parting. He'd done well for himself; it was said his name was Joe Kagan and that he made Harold Wilson's overcoats. Every time the prime minister raised his collar to the cameras, Kagan got an extra cut – even Mao Tse-tung was inspired to wear one over his half roll-necked shirt. He had a factory somewhere in Yorkshire, where he left his wife over the shop. His girlfriend worked as a journalist on one of the Fleet Street dailies. It was a mark of the people who were moving in among us. They were the types who gave us guidance on how to conduct our lives.

My grandma told me she'd got highly fed up when a man with a loud voice knocked at her door and, as she looked out from the first floor, bellowed: 'I've come about yer rats.' In all innocence, she told him he should look to the other side of the street. The council's services to stem the verminous tide rising from the canal were in increasing demand. The day of the local elections was shortly after, and it was traditional for borough employees to staff the polling stations. It provided a day off work, £4 for the privilege and a chance to meet people from other departments. I was sent down the road, where voting booths had been set up in my old classroom overlooking the BDH, accompanied for the day by a fellow with the pudgy face of an ex-boxer who'd never quite mastered the defensive arts of the game. He said he worked in 'environmental health'.

As he sat ticking names off the electoral list, his excitement grew as people he recognised lined up for their ballot papers. Finally he couldn't contain himself any longer and, with a leer, barked in their faces: 'Still got them old rats, then?' One woman with long, fair hair, who looked and sounded only recently removed from the environs of Holbein Place, nearly dropped the baby she was clutching with one arm. She was gone so quickly she probably went down as a spoilt paper. He told me he had an interest in a stall up Camden Passage. Specialising in eighteenth- and early nineteenth-century pieces, he'd become something of an expert on the epoch of George III, Britain's 'longest reigning monarch'. I asked whether this wasn't Queen Victoria, but he said no, George III. He was doing rather well selling to the Jaspers and Crystals now entrenched on the electoral register.

Labour had enjoyed such dominance on the council that the Tories had struggled to find candidates. They roped in all-in wrestler 'Judo Al' Hayes to fill one space on the ballot paper, their hope to win a few seats and form an opposition. Yet, at the reckoning, they'd swept the ring: two falls, a Labour submission and a knockout all in one. Even 'Judo Al' made the council chamber (when it came to evening meetings of the cleansing committee, however, he was rarely able to break his public engagements at the Albert Hall or Caledonian Road baths). Before I went to bed I looked out my first-floor window at the empty street wondering if the election would mean momentous change. But to what? The result was a reaction against the Wilson government and, while the area was conservative with a small 'c', it was never Conservative. Still, the old Labour councillors retired to make way for a younger breed. If you searched for their monument, you had only to look around you. Days later in the East End, Ronan Point collapsed after a gas explosion to show they'd been right all along about tower blocks.

Islington had lurched right as much of the world went the other way. Students at the London School of Economics revolted, conveniently close to Fleet Street, which was able to decamp and stumble up the road after a decent lunch to get its photos and stories. De Gaulle was forced to flee from the sight of the barricades in Paris to, of all places, Germany. He came back from exile and rallied his supporters for a while but it was now clearly all up for him and, quite feasibly, for his visions of a Britain-less Europe.

On the day of de Gaulle's return to Paris in 1968, an English team had its first real chance to win the European Cup. One year on from Celtic's victory for Scotland, Manchester United had reached the final. Surely, this time they'd do it. Then again, who could be certain? Two years before, United had done the really hard work when, in the quarter-finals, they'd gone to the Stadium of Light in Lisbon to face Benfica. With no great expectation of victory they had won 5–1. George Best was the match-winner, whereafter proceedings developed into a punch-up. Harry Gregg, substitute on the night, soon ran on to sort out the brawling continentals as the United players struggled to leave the pitch. A much more comfortable path to the trophy now lay before them. They fell at the next hurdle against unfancied (but determined, if history was anything to go by) Partizan Belgrade. Matt Busby mumbled something about football being a game of tomorrows and putting our yesterdays behind us, yet looked as drawn as after the Munich air crash a decade earlier.

This year, against the odds, they'd progressed through the semi-final by eliminating Real-Madrid. They had everything in their favour as Benfica emerged as their opponents again. The Portuguese were unlikely to be as much a walkover as two years earlier, but their star player was Eusebio and United probably had the measure of him. Nobby Stiles had blocked him out of the game when England beat Portugal *en route* to winning the World

Cup. Like that one, this game was to be staged at Wembley, for an English team effectively at home.

Manchester United drifted through most of the game as if engaged in a Central League warm-up against Oldham reserves. By the second half they were 1–0 in front, when it might have been three. Even Benfica's equaliser with about fifteen minutes left didn't seem to inject much urgency into them. They seemed to believe their superiority would out in the end, as the game headed towards the likelihood of a half hour's extra time. Then, just before the regulation ninety minutes were up, the United defence, messing around with nothing much better to do of a Wednesday evening, offered the Benfica forward line the ball. It was played diagonally towards the penalty area, perfectly for one of the Portuguese to run on to and have a good crack at goal. It wasn't given to any old opposition player either, but placed right in the path of Eusebio, the Mozambican 'black ghost' with the hardest shot in world football.

We'd seen Eusebio score his goals against Brazil and North Korea in the World Cup. Nearly all of them were powerfully struck, some threatened to break the net. Gifting him a clear run to goal was one of the sillier things for a team to do at any time during any game – forget three minutes to go, scores equal, in the European Cup Final. As Eusebio left Stiles in his tracks, the prospects were very slim of any more 'tomorrows' for the ageing Matt Busby in the competition he'd pioneered as far as British participation was concerned, and involvement in which had seen the deaths of so many at Munich. There, right in front of him, his team had thrown it away. On the touchline, Busby turned his back on the moment in disgust. I closed my eyes, unable to believe what they'd done.

All that stood in the path of Eusebio, formerly of Lourenço Marques, was United's keeper, Alex Stepney, ex-Tooting and Mitcham. I'd come across him five years before at the end of my autograph-hunting career when he was with Millwall. Early on a Saturday morning Millwall were on a train at Paddington, bound for somewhere distantly west, possibly Wales, to play the likes of Newport. The players – Joe Broadfoot, Harry Cripps, Ray Brady et al. – sat six to a compartment on two bench seats facing each other. Stepney, with a short-back-and-sides that accentuated his flapping ears, was the most junior and sitting by the window reading his *Daily Mirror*. He wasn't initially popular with some senior players who thought his greenness lost them too many a match bonus. But while Millwall dropped into the Fourth Division, Stepney was tipped to breeze on to other arenas than Coldblow Lane.

On a whim Tommy Docherty brought him to Chelsea in 1966. Docherty had been the subject of great mirth as a result of his predictions that England wouldn't win the World Cup. In this, of course, he had only reflected a more widely held view, but his signing Stepney really put him out on a limb. There was little chance the Chelsea fans would be persuaded he could compete with Peter Bonetti and he was quickly moved on to Manchester United. In other countries Stepney would have played regularly at international level. With Gordon Banks and Bonetti his contemporaries, he wasn't going to get many England games, yet Alf Ramsey did select him for a match against Sweden four days before the European Cup Final. It proved to be his only cap and he played well, though the suggestion was Ramsey chose him mainly to give him practice playing at Wembley.

Not much could have prepared him for this, other than the keeper's instinctive knowledge that it was just the way of his team to consign their fate to others. The mob always believed in some other force beyond them that would lift and 'save' them. They created such a force to explain things they couldn't understand or to bale them out of tight situations. The crowd had faith, it didn't know in what exactly, it just believed. The goalkeeper's assumed powers were just such a creation. In fact, he usefully played a dual role: not only that of saving them from dire difficulties but also of causing others; God and the devil rolled into one. Only the goalkeeper knew this was all nonsense, that there was no one to turn to. The keeper understood what it was like to be alone, that in the end we had no one but ourselves.

The point had been made before, of course. 'The only philosophical issue is suicide,' Camus suggested. Why, knowing we were alone, that there was no more point to it than that, didn't we chuck it all in? He'd also said something to the effect that all there was to be learned from life came from goalkeeping – that there was no pattern, and that every ball came at you in a different way. He'd possibly just said this to get up the haughty noses of Jean

Paul Sartre and Simone de Beauvoir, neither of whom would have had much to do with a ball in their lives, and who excluded him from their Parisian café circle. A *pied noir*, he'd played in Algeria for his university team. He was a smallish keeper who, without the Gauloise at the corner of his mouth, might have been a ringer for Ronnie Simpson.

But here it was the team, not the solitary individual, who had gone for the suicide option. Stepney's practical, rather than philosophical, problem was deciding whether to go forward or back. His knowledge of the Wembley turf gained from facing the Swedes the previous Saturday was insufficient to prevent him being deceived by it. He thought the diagonally played ball was going to reach him without much trouble and came to meet it, then saw it slowed by the turf and latched on to by Eusebio. Nearly 10 yards off his line now, he believed he'd come too far and started to retreat in case Eusebio chipped the ball over him into the net. But then he noticed that the Portuguese striker had, on the gallop, nudged the ball forward as if teeing it up for one of his blasted efforts. So Stepney changed plan, and advanced to attack again.

He could have thrown himself blindly forward in the heroic 'do or die' style of the best British goalkeeping martyrs. Instead, he kept his wits and stayed on his feet as long as possible. Eusebio hit the ball full pelt, as Stepney had foreseen, from just a few yards away. After I'd unblinked my eyes – Busby was still looking aghast at the crowd – Stepney was falling to his left. He'd got his body behind the ball but had not only stopped it, he'd also held it. If he hadn't, Eusebio might easily have scored on the rebound. Probably realising that Benfica's best chance for victory had gone, Eusebio came up to congratulate Stepney, who waved him away brusquely, telling him to 'get on with the so-and-so game instead of yapping'.

He also waved away the compliments later. They were very kind, he said, but victory was won 'by the lads' as United survived into extra time and scored three more goals for what went into the record books as a comfortable 4–1 victory – along with Real-Madrid's hammering of Eintracht at Hampden Park eight years before, it appeared one of the easiest in European Cup history. 'I felt it was a bad mistake by Eusebio rather than brilliant goalkeeping on my part,' Stepney said, citing the Portuguese's failure to go for the delicate chip and not the artless blast.

It was his prerogative, within the traditions of goalkeeping modesty, to say this. I never felt it was that of his teammates, however, to agree with him. Several I heard comment on the incident – Bobby Charlton, Denis Law, who was injured and watching the game from the stands – spoke not in a dismissive way towards Stepney but with the focus an Eusebio's blunder. To my mind this detracted from a full recognition of what the save meant: England wouldn't have had its first European champions till Liverpool nine years hence; Matt Busby, the Scot who put English club football on the international map, would not have had the reward he deserved. What tended to come over from the 'yes it was a great save, but . . .' argument was that by extension Stepney was lucky. Left by his team to face the hardest shot in world football, undoubtedly he was.

Then, all such comment could be put down to the communal guilt of field players, with their habit of routinely making mistakes others were left to sort out. Every one of the United players should have been on his knees thanking Stepney for one of the most important saves ever by a British keeper. As they jigged around Wembley with their medals, you could see they were already oblivious to the fact there would have been no celebrations, had it not been for the one player who knew that, in the end, he was on his own.

Chapter 11

The Demise *of* Old Industrial Britain

England played West Germany three days later on the Saturday, June 1, in provincial Hanover. Kicking a ball about between the piss'ole and the BDH in the playground of my old junior school would have been as important within the global scheme of things. The absence of resting Manchester United players, and the approach of England's first game in the European Championships the following week in Italy, led Ramsey to field a weakened team. Franz Beckenbauer scored the only goal eight minutes from time, a deflection past Banks off centre-half Brian Labone's upraised left knee. Beckenbauer jumped and bounced back to his half as if this all signified something tremendously crucial. OK, we couldn't say we'd still never lost to the Germans but it wasn't run-of-the-mill friendly matches like this that counted any longer. We'd get back at them when it came to a real competition like the World Cup.

My girlfriend's older brother strode back into their family's flat from holiday tanned, fit and smiling. He'd been for two weeks with a group of mates from their meat-packing factory in Stratford to Spain. 'Great place,' he announced, as he settled into his dad's armchair. 'The sun, the food, marvellous. And you know what?'

he expanded, left thumb and first finger at full stretch. 'For a shilling you can get a glass of Bacardi that big.' The following week I went to pay the dustmen's wages at Wedmore Street, where the foreman had also just returned from Spain with his wife and another couple. They'd already booked the same trip for next year. It was a package deal. *Great* idea. You paid your big expenses like travel and hotel at home and so skirted, by and large, the official limit of £50. Most of that was left for Bacardi and chips when you got there. Wilson, Callaghan and Co. had asked the British people to stay at home. Their response was, for the first time out of uniform, to travel abroad in droves.

I'd assumed travel an isolated, often troublesome affair. Was enjoyment, an all-round 'great time', the point? You didn't expect it, as you looked for affordable pensions that weren't full on arrival in late evening in Rheims, searched for bread up the backstreets of Naples, or sat down to meals with people who ate and spoke differently and had a general propensity to be weird. You came back sometimes far from sure why you'd gone, though with some sense you'd had an experience. The idea, perhaps, was to confirm you were better off at home.

I'd intended to take my first holiday alone seeing the Prague Spring. Russian tanks – 'invited' again – invaded the morning I was to collect my visa from the Czechoslovakian embassy. I adjusted my plans to Hungary. First down the plank at Ostend, I was at the head of the hitchhiking line on the road out of town with my overweight rucksack and holdall, and sleeping bag. A Mercedes-full of Flems, who'd collected their daughter off the boat, took me to Brussels, gave me dinner, showed me around the city and insisted I stay the night with them at Waterloo. The battle, they said, had been fought virtually outside the window. My first lift in the morning was provided by two Belgian soldiers who took me for lunch to their base in Germany (I had no idea Belgium provided part of the occupying forces), talked about football, insisted I give them my address and drove me alongside the Rhine, almost as far as the Lorelei rock, because they'd nothing better to do with their Sunday. I reached Munich three days earlier than planned.

The beer festival meant I could find nowhere to stay, other than spend two nights in the station café. If you gave any sign of nodding off at the table bouncers grabbed your collar and threw you out. If there was collective German guilt about the war, these characters weren't part of it. I saw a bouncer at the Hofbräuhaus hit a dissident drinker double his size with a left hook, the slap of which quite buggered the *Gemütlichkeit*. In the café I spent one night half slumped at my table with an elderly couple, much of whose life had been spent in prison. An old lady next to me tried to protect me from having to listen. At 5 a.m. when the crowd was dismissed to wander the station forecourt, a young woman rushed up shouting '*Haben Sie die Zeit?*' did I have the time. I read it off the station clock above our heads, not registering she could have done so as easily. This caused her to burst into tears, yell that she needed the money because her husband was mentally ill and rush off saying she was going to get him to fix me (or Bavarian words and gestures to that effect).

A British student whom I'd let in front of me in the hitching line at Salzburg because he had to get to his university in Vienna, said he'd put me up if I met him at the west station in the evening. As I went into the Gents' on arrival I was grabbed in the groin by a guy who, walking on, turned and winked like Kenneth Williams in theatrical mode. I sat waiting on a bench on the mezzanine level looking down on him seeking clients around the station entrance hall, when a plainclothes policeman in an old mac flashed his badge and pondered whether to arrest me for vagrancy. Next day I took a tram to the Prater stadium, the driver pointing out in deepest Viennese that, or so I had to imagine, there was no game for a while. My vocabulary didn't reach to discussing Clockwork Ocwirk's role in the guerrilla assault on British imperial dominance, or explaining that I'd just wander around the stadium perimeter for a while anyway.

On the train to Budapest, a compartment full of Hungarians, though strangers to each other, jabbered throughout the journey. Their language, I read, bore no relation to anything much except Finnish. 'Forint', their currency, was a word often mentioned. Someone told me the first question Magyars were likely to ask each other was: 'How much do you earn?' They liked money but the Russians wouldn't let them enjoy it. At the border – as the guard eyed my visa from several angles – I imagined Puskas running across its ploughed fields in the snow and how risky it must have been under fire and given that they were almost certainly mined (several years later I read that he'd been on tour with his club Honved at the time of the revolution and had simply elected to stay abroad).

Outside the main station in Pest an elderly man in blue overalls, one among many who was hanging around, approached me, told me in German which tram to take to Buda and said straight out: 'Give me four forints.' Many trams were driven by women, the masonry of buildings *en route* to my hostel scarred by gunfire. I shared a large dormitory with snoring lorry drivers in a hostel on a high hill over the Danube, by a monument to the Russian army. A smart restaurant nearby had gypsy violinists, goulash and steak dinners with wine and extravagant tip at less than £2. I imagined this was a good deal, even by Spanish standards, but didn't inquire after the price of Bacardi. I took a city tour which included the empty Nep stadium, a bowl of a place which had deep concrete terracing where spectators sat, but which looked as decrepit as the standing areas at Brisbane Road. With only posts and no nets up, it was difficult to get excited. I caught a cold looking at the night view of the Danube from the hostel, swapped addresses with an East German woman over tea and aspirin in the lobby area and after another night of truckers' snores left in the morning feeling a long way from home.

Hitching from Vienna to Amsterdam took a day and a half. In the Paradiso near Leidseplein young people sat around in the afternoon on cushioned seats, the air heavy with what I understood to be 'hash'. I didn't smoke, merely inhaled. Everyone smiled and waved when the police walked in. They were looking for a young girl missing from home, asked if she wouldn't mind coming with them, to which she had no objection, and everyone smiled and waved again as they left. The Amstel brewery gave tours and all you could drink for free in the bar afterwards. Some American guys in a van, looking for contributors to their petrol costs, drove me to London, dropped me at Piccadilly Circus at 2 a.m. and I walked back to the Angel. Overall, it was like coming off the pitch after one of the better Orient games. You assessed the experience as good but, at the moment you'd been living it, would have not been entirely aware of having a great time.

On Boxing Day my father and I went to see Manchester United play at Highbury. Given the White Hart Lane incident more than twenty years earlier, he'd had to be asked. Some 55,000 were in the ground, a good part of them singing 'Jingle Bells' as Arsenal took a 3–0 lead: 'Oh what fun, it is to see, United lose away.' Two-thirds of the way up the Clock End terraces, the crowd surged from behind and the legs of a man in front of me buckled. Three others went down with him, a gap suddenly yawning which I was due next to pitch into. I stood for what felt like at least half a minute, striking the pose of Ahab roped to the side of Moby Dick. Someone to my right fell over my outstretched leg and I sensed it was about to be broken at the knee. In what was actually probably no more than five seconds, enough people made it to their feet to fill the gap. As a bit of lone defence by a keeper holding his line, it was the best I'd been involved in. My shoes had come off and I stood in my socks over the next few minutes until, by some tidal process, they found their way back to me on the terraces. Everyone got on with watching the game.

I got some games with the team a guy at work played for. Its members came from the other side of the Caledonian Road. Several had moved out to places in Hertfordshire, or were about to. Their motor-mouthed centre-half sold cheap frocks up Chapel Market, I assumed in great number. His generous goalkeeping advice came entirely without charge: 'Look alive, keeper'; 'Your ball, keeper!' Uncannily, you always felt he was in a better position to be dealing with the situation himself. Highlight of the season came on the Sunday I was marking out my goalmouth before the start of the second half.

I'd done this at the beginning and midway through every game I'd played since I'd seen Reg Matthews on a Chelsea visit to Highbury in 1959. He had fixed the crossbar with his eyes from the penalty spot and drew a line with his studs to the centre of the goal. In theory, it was to help a keeper get his angles and bearings right. If he found himself off his line, he could look at the mark to see where he was in relation to his goal. In practice, it wasn't always of much use – for a high ball a keeper couldn't wallow around looking down to see where he was and had to have his concentration squarely on the ball. But predominantly it was a way of the keeper staking a claim, marking out territory. When

I'd completed the operation, I noticed the referee pacing half the length of the pitch towards me.

'Name?' he demanded.

'What for?'

'I saw you doing it the first half as well,' he said. 'Defacing the pitch.'

This left me spluttering like a retired Wiltshire colonel on learning the Beatles had been awarded the MBE. There must have been a mistake. The penalty area was a war zone, not a landscaped garden. This was something goalkeepers just did. I didn't impress him and he pencilled my name in a small black book. The rules had changed, another unwarranted interference into the keeper's sovereignty over his own area of operation by a faceless authority that didn't understand. At this time of year there was scarcely a blade of grass in the goalmouth, so what was there for the law to protect? I got a letter warning me about my conduct from the FA. It ignored mine back in complaint.

o   o   o

I watched the moon landing with an American girl, a student from Maryland University I'd met while she was over working as a summer temp. She was living among a group of US expats in Maida Vale. Amid the general whooping, some aspects of their pleasantly uninhibited ways were newer to me. One of the guys asked me, as Neil Armstrong stepped down from his ladder, what the 'British reaction' to this was. Didn't we, too, think it a marvellous achievement by the United States? I mumbled I supposed we did, really, thrown by having someone English-speaking come out and say, 'Don't you think we're great?' When we went outside to look at it, my friend declared it 'our moon'. I didn't detect romance or philanthropy in her voice, to imply either hers and mine, or civilisation's as a whole. The suggestion was of an imperial US moon. She laughed and added she didn't mean it but I reckoned she was only half joking.

Late in the year I took up the invitation to visit the Cold War's front line in Berlin. The East German woman I had swapped addresses with in Budapest wrote to me and said she and some friends would be happy to put me up. I arrived in the middle of the western sector of the city at Tempelhof airport, which felt very enclosed and as if the plane had landed within the confines of White City stadium. It was where most of the city's supplies had been flown in during the Berlin airlift. After one night of the bright lights of the Kurfürstendamm, I took the U-Bahn to the swirling mist of the Potsdamer Platz near the Berlin Wall at Checkpoint Charlie. I thought this was where everyone crossed the frontier but it turned out it was really for people with their own transport. Even the bloke gunned down at the start of *The Spy Who Came in from the Cold* had had a bike. I wandered up with my suitcase, seeing no sign of buses or anything on the other side but was spared further research of the subject by the East German guards. They sent me back saying I didn't have the right visa.

I got one the next day at the more pedestrian crossing point of Friedrichstrasse. You couldn't get there by underground, which had only two or three stations in the East and these were closed and dimly lit. The train slowed as it went through them, the eyes of East German guards staring from slits in observation boxes by the edge of the platform, studying the passengers passing before them. You had to use the city's overground system, the S-bahn. At the crossing point they scrutinised a copy of *The Times* I'd brought along and took me to a tiny whitewashed room, where an officer came in to question me over some history magazines containing pictures of Hitler and Churchill. This was all very dramatic and a let-down when he didn't confiscate them, only making me promise not to give them to my hosts. The first people I stayed with laughed when I told them and insisted on having them.

For a week I was shown around and put up in flats heated by coal stoves, in old apartment blocks with echoing courtyards. At gloomy stations like Ostkreuz, old steam trains went past as in scenes from *Brief Encounter*. A small grocery shop at the end of one of the streets where I stayed near the Schönhauser Allee had received a consignment of washing powder to celebrate the recent twentieth anniversary of the republic. It had long sold out by the time we got there. 'You'll have to wait till Lenin's birthday for the next lot,' the shopkeeper said. Big-city humour helped lighten the burden, yet overall it was so depressing I felt guilty at wanting to get back to the West.

Life among the free wasn't without its peculiarities. Old ladies,

Prussian surely, who looked as if they remembered not only Hindenburg but also Bismarck in his prime, felt at liberty to let their dogs foul the pavements the length of the Ku'damm. When it came to crossing it, on the other hand, everyone waited obediently for the green man to flash at the traffic lights, regardless of whether or not anything was coming. A higher state authority spoke with a force people listened to. A crowd had gathered, for example, around an illegally parked Volkswagen, and was considering the 'For Sale' notice promptly stuck on its windscreen by the police. When I went to the freezing expanse of the Olympic stadium to see Berlin play Kaiserslautern, quite happy to commune with the ghost of Jesse Owens from 1936, and those of Reg Matthews and Duncan Edwards from twenty years later, a character a few rows from me broke the spell when he threw a bottle. My attention was drawn to this by the sudden anger that swept the crowd. Quite right, too. I'd lobbed an apple core during a reserve match at Highbury once, which hit the back of the sock of the Birmingham City goalkeeper, and had a commissionaire's finger waved at me for a few minutes. A bottle was an outrage. But as those near the culprit grabbed him and others dashed off, as if under orders, shouting *Polizei!*, I started to feel sorry for the bloke.

Confined again to Islington town hall I filled in time escaping to the vaults, on the pretence of looking for old invoices and ledgers vital for whatever piece of work I claimed to be engaged in. As I was rustling around in a pile of them on the floor, a plaster-cast bust poked the top of its head above them and I stuck it on a shelf to keep me company. It was Lenin, made in memory of his brief residence in Finsbury in 1905. Some 300 yards from Exmouth Market, he'd been a virtual neighbour of my grandad. It was difficult to know, however, what momentary fit of ideology had caused the bust to be cast. The old Labour councillors hadn't thought him appropriate to be displayed in the light of day, hence his presence in the basement. Now the Conservatives were in power, the best he could expect for the future was wiling away the hours in this subterranean municipal safe. I wondered if we'd share the same fate.

A retired major in a careers' advisory office opposite Smithfield Market in the Farringdon Road told me that, if I wanted to 'travel and meet people' as I claimed, I should be an export executive.

This sounded impressive, but turned out to mean a sales rep. A series of job interviews on industrial estates off the A4 came to nothing. These were in almost inaccessible places like Brentford, which I'd assumed had no other existence than to make up the numbers in the Third Division and provide a set of goalposts for Gerry Cakebread to occupy. A furniture and crockery company off the Tottenham Court Road told me with great excitement it had just won its first order – a dinner service for over a hundred people – from the sheikhdom of Kuwait. Alas, someone had sloppily erred in sending the same number of large soup tureens as they had normal plates and bowls. About ninety had been returned, but it was game start. The managing director was less engaged by any interest I might have had in overseas matters, than in what I'd do if I found a work colleague pilfering stock. I avoided suggesting that if it was the buckshee soup tureens, then he was probably doing everyone a favour, and tried to strike a balance: I'd have a quiet word, telling him his actions reflected badly on the honesty of other staff members. The managing director became very angry at this, answering that he'd expect me to come straight to him and that, 'I've never stolen anything in my life'. Fair and virtuous enough, but it called into question the calibre of those upfront in the nation's heroic Balance of Payments struggles. I was packed off the see the office manager downstairs who quietly told me that, if I was looking for work abroad, I'd be lucky at this company to get a daytrip every second year to Brussels.

Two clean-cut types from Proctor and Gamble gleamed a different vision at interviews they were conducting in, by happenstance, the Mayfair Hotel where Blackburn Rovers had stayed. They were British but, obviously, clearly culturally at one with the USA when explaining with the zeal of Mormons on the doorstep how, with their soap products, I could clean up Newcastle. At least, I thought that was what they said – they didn't look the types to tell anyone straight out how they could clean up *in* Newcastle. They took on the judgemental look of southern Baptist priests, however, when I showed no enthusiasm, finding myself more interested in wondering whether in this room the likes of Harry Leyland or, after him, Fred Else might have stayed.

Then, in the first few days of the new year, I went to an interview convened by three types in three-piece suits in a hotel opposite Kensington Gardens. They were back briefly from Scandinavia; a day or so to pick up a new car each – an E-type, a Lotus and a Bentley – before getting back with reinvigorated thrust, and no small measure of smoothness, to Britain's export drive. I suggested I was keen to work in some field fairly remote from the affairs of the parish pump. One of them said: 'You'd be trained in Finland. Are you interested?' As I opened my old school atlas in the evening, my mum said: 'Isn't it Russia?' I said of course it wasn't. But when I looked it up, at least a part of it was. At the eastern extreme of the west of the continent, bordering the lands of Yashin, it was about as far off my line as it seemed feasible to get.

I had two weeks to kill and with the proceeds of my cashed-in council pension bought a plane ticket to the USA. I landed at Kennedy airport the same night I fled down the town hall steps in Upper Street. Near Washington, I attended my friend's classes at Maryland University and, once my accent was detected, was invited to extemporise on the life and times of anyone from Byron to Shakespeare. I ate a lot of French toast, pancakes and hash browns, fun food we didn't have at home. We went to New York and did the sights, in cold but perfect blue-sky weather. Whether at the Statue of Liberty, the Empire State building or walking the length of the Avenue of the Americas, there were no other British people. When the locals heard I was, they fell into raptures of praise and admiration.

Despite their Vietnam War protests, they came across overall as a large and happy team. It was a bit strange how they were such a cheerfully disciplined one. Fiery campus speeches against the draft might well end with a 'Power to the People!' and evoke the audience response of 'Right On!', yet so many people you met just happened to be reading the same book (*Portnoy's Complaint*, say) watching the same film (maybe *The Graduate*) or saying they'd 'always been into ecology' (in Europe I wasn't sure we'd heard of it). They also gave the impression they believed they'd arrived individually at their identical decisions.

They had their formal rules, too. We were due to be having lunch with some other people at a restaurant near the Congress building on what had turned out to be a fine, spring-like day, but my friend couldn't think what to wear. I suggested something white I'd seen her in the previous summer in London only to learn that no woman wore white before May 1. Over an enjoyable meal, I heard several times how charmingly conservative the British were. But that said, and despite the repeated wonderment of anyone new I was introduced to – 'Wow, you're British' – they always spoke in a manner which, at home, would have suggested we were the oldest of friends. There obviously was a 'special relationship'. In a land of one big party, smiling faces said: 'Why don't you come and live here?' I said I'd see what I could do once I'd made some money.

o   o   o

The announcement stated that we were landing at Helsinki airport but outside it looked like a large snow-covered field, with a small hut for a terminal. At the station in the centre of the city, which was dotted with more drunks than King's Cross, St Pancras and Euston combined, I boarded a train, tightly sealed against the sub-zero temperatures. Lenin had been put on his sealed train through Germany, presumably so he couldn't get near the locals and subvert them, his destination the Finland station in St Petersburg. I was heading for the frosty halt of Iisalmi (imagining it might not be big enough to warrant the title station), six hours into the deepest, lake-scoured innards of the country. Any efforts to subvert, or sell to the Finns, would have to take account of their being worthy challengers for the title of the quietest nation in the western world.

On a visit to the country a dozen or so years before, Khrushchev had made himself highly unpopular at a reception at the Soviet embassy when he decided to tell a joke to those invited to meet him there. Three Finns set off into the forest, skiied silently for hours towards some pre-determined destination till they arrived at a fork in the trail. 'This way', grunted one of them as they embarked on another wordless odyssey to reach another divided path. The same guy said, 'This way', and they skiied for another day till it was realised they were hopelessly lost, and the other two turned on him. 'That's the trouble with you,' they said angrily. 'You talk too much.' Khrushchev fell into gales of laughter and the Soviet embassy officials followed suit, but his Finnish audience glared back. I could see the same looks on my journey. Virtually the only language that bore any relation to theirs, of course, was Hungarian, so I wouldn't have understood anything. But unlike the Hungarians I'd sat among, this lot shared hardly a word between them.

Snow fell from a steel-grey sky on to a flat countryside of black fir trees, the dullness of which was relieved only when it got dark at about 2 p.m. There were no hamburgers or hash browns on the menu in my hotel, only tough strips of reindeer. Outside my hotel room, a snow-plough worked within the small pool of light from a streetlamp, getting nowhere in the near blizzard conditions. I'd walked New York's Avenue of the Americas in the sun precisely a week earlier. To the obvious question of what was I doing here, I was hard pushed to come up with any rational answer.

One factor in this was that Finland's largest export commodity was paper. My job was to sell it back to them. One of the guys who had interviewed me had explained the demonstration I'd have to perform. He showed me a thin sheet of filmy blue paper. I shouldn't imagine, he pointed out quickly, that this was the piece of 'carbon paper' it appeared to be. He used the term with great distaste. It did a similar job but was a revolutionary concept in copying materials. Carbon paper was a thin sheet of tissue with coal dust slapped on it. This was made of nylon and contained ink. He put a magnifying glass on it, scratched under it with the end of a biro, as a result of which I could see both the textile's weave and the liquid. The theory was that once areas of its surface were used, the ink from the unused bits flowed to them. It was, thus, more efficient than carbon paper. It was also much more clean. Secretaries loved it because it didn't get their hands dirty. To make this possible we'd produced our own unique ingredient with which to cover the material – 'A special sealing chemical,' he told me, 'which we call Q6.' The formula was secret, of course. I thought, however, that whatever it was, it had quite a familiar smell.

All its special features naturally led it to be expensive, some twenty-five times the cost of mere carbon paper. This meant we could make a lot of money. We went into schools, factories, pharmacies, florists, anywhere that had a typewriter. In provincial Finland, people fell off their chairs, or at least blushed profusely, when, unannounced, a British salesman materialised out of the snow piled by the door. They shook their heads in deep embarrassment to the question of whether anyone spoke English. It didn't matter. You jabbered on regardless and people often bought just to get rid of you.

A nurse in the town of Joensuu near the Soviet border helped me translate my demonstration into Finnish. Other members of the company scorned this. One, who been in the country months, walked into offices with a dictionary which he'd stuff close to the face of whoever he was visiting with his thumb under the Finnish for 'hello'. It helped break the metaphorical ice. What was the point of mastering, or attempting, such a language, when all it would do if people didn't want to buy was encourage them to argue? It was best to stay dumb till they signed on the line.

I worked alone. There was no salary, earnings were entirely on commission. My first week under my own steam was in the port of Kotka, east of Helsinki, a short drive from the Soviet frontier. Its paper mill belched a cellulose cloud which reeked of rotting fish. Those among the locals who spoke said there was a Finnish phrase for it: 'It smells money.' I made £90 tax-free in the week, without taxing myself unduly as I tripped around the old ice stacked on the pavements and in the middle of the streets. At Islington town hall I'd been on £24 gross per week which was held to be quite good money. Now I was getting, once you took their stoppages into account, as much as Banks and Bonetti.

I was pondering this fact on the Saturday morning after I'd completed my first week and had gone to visit the old dacha of Tsar Nicholas II, a large log cabin outside Kotka. No one else was there amid the drifts and the half-frozen streams emptying into the Gulf of Bothnia. Without interruption I was able to work out that I could soon be away from the frozen fringes of capitalism and back into the warmth of ideological HQ. In Washington DC I'd tout the stuff to people who were unable to resist a quaint accent. I reckoned I'd need only three or four months from now to earn a little bit of capital to make the transatlantic move. Where were we, April 11? I was surprised, therefore, when I got back to my hotel and went to check why there was so much noise in the bar, to find the FA Cup Final on TV.

Because of the forthcoming World Cup in Mexico, it was being played a month earlier than normal. I found a stool at the bar just as Peter Houseman's shot went under Leeds' keeper Gary Sprake's body for Chelsea's equaliser, and let out a cheer. This surprised me, the cheer no less than the goal. Sprake had gone down for the ball all wrong, using his feet poorly, then belly-flopping hopelessly. But it was the first time I could remember greeting in such a way a keeper's mistake.

Sprake hadn't turned out to be what he could have been. He was born in the same Swansea street as Jack Kelsey, so had a fair role-model. In one of his early internationals in Cardiff against England, I'd noticed how Ninian Park had risen to acclaim his first high catch from a corner. This was another unprecedented reaction to my knowledge. It seemed to indicate the crowd's relief that here possibly, and some years after he'd been forced from the game, was at last a keeper up to Kelsey's class. There was no doubt that Sprake was a good keeper. Leeds fans would argue that point for years afterwards, despite his being known for often glaring errors. His own goal against Liverpool at Anfield was the first usually recalled by his detractors. He'd made to throw the ball out, tried to check at the last second, and succeeded only in whirling around and hurling it into his net. Keepers had always made silly mistakes, though. The cruel difference now was they received closer attention from endless repeats on television.

But that wasn't the problem. Disappointingly, Sprake's antics suggested he didn't want to be a detached keeper but a fully participating member of the Leeds team and all it stood for. Leeds players were well known for not letting any slight against a teammate go unpunished. Billy Bremner, Norman Hunter, Jack Charlton, they could all look after themselves. When all else failed they called in Johnny Giles. It was an all for one, one for all outfit. The individuals of a squad like Chelsea could be seen flouncing in their spare time in and out of the boutiques of King's Road – George Best at European Cup-winning Manchester United said he'd have loved to join them and be part of the London scene. By contrast, manager Don Revie urged his Leeds players to marry early in order to 'settle down' – it wouldn't have been Best's scene at all. They were a team of down-to-earth northerners, who played housey-housey together on the night before a game.

Sprake was part of it and as far as I could tell just wanted to be one of the bunch. He couldn't resist a lot of unnecessary 'me, too-ism'. He'd get into tangles common to all keepers – a hefty shoulder charge would be made on him, perhaps, as he rose for a corner but instead of 'taking' it, either staring at his adversary with blank-faced contempt or ignoring him completely, his response was to make a big deal of it, rear up, maybe throw a punch. His Leeds teammates were bound to pile in on his behalf. That's what they'd do for each other, why not him? In the ensuing mêlée he could guarantee he'd look a tough, 'no shit' guy. But what was the point of posturing like this? These days, all a keeper had to do in the event of an opponent getting physical, was wait for the ref's whistle in his favour. It showed what had happened: crafting the law in their favour had encouraged keepers to become prima donnas.

In the other goal, Peter Bonetti was a different type. With his slight build, he was a likely target for a clattering, but used his speed to remove himself from most scenes of aggravation. In this game, Leeds were all over Chelsea. David Webb, ex-Leyton Orient, was at right-back. Dave Sexton, now Chelsea manager having given up on the ghost of success ever coming to haunt Brisbane Road, had bought him. Webb was being given the run-around, however, by Leeds left-winger Eddie Gray. Bonetti's brilliance and Sprake's mistake were pretty much what salvaged Chelsea a draw.

For the replay eighteen days later at Old Trafford, Sexton moved Webb into midfield where he would be less exposed to jinky wingers and find the opportunity to make his runs upfield more easily. He scored the winning goal from a Chelsea set piece. Arriving late to meet a long throw-in from the left, he rose, hit it with his shoulder rather than head, but still put it in the net. Bonetti, though injured early on, turned in another display of agile and assured goalkeeping for Chelsea and, with his Cup winners' medal, toddled off for what was likely to be a quiet few weeks as Gordon Banks's understudy in the World Cup finals in Mexico.

I went to work in Norway, leaving Helsinki a few minutes after President Nixon announced the invasion of Cambodia. An American guy who worked with the company and lived in Finland to escape the draft was swearing at the TV as Nixon spoke. I went with the company director with the E-type and we reached the ferry at Turku a little before midnight, just as the ramp was closing. After a sauna I went to bed, my cabin right at the water line. By way of a brief stop in the Åland islands, the boat cut through the ice with the amplified sound of the old machine used by grocers to scythe bacon. We reached Stockholm in the morning and had driven to Oslo by early evening. The next day we got as far as Geilo before catching up with the snow plough. The prospect was that this road wouldn't be open for another week or so till the middle of May, so we found an alternative route through the mountains and across the Sognefjord to our west coast destination of Bergen. Most Norwegians had been prevented by their country's luxury import taxes from previously seeing such a piece of British engineering as an E-type Jaguar in the flesh. A boutique asked us, therefore, no sooner than we'd arrived, to carry a couple of its models on the back in a procession through the city celebrating 900 years of its history. Some seventy-two hours in Norway, and with what seemed to be the city's entire population gathered on the streets, we exchanged waves with the crown prince looking down from the balcony of the Norge hotel, in our role as symbols of Bergen 1970.

Everyone was welcoming. The Norwegians reckoned to have an affinity with the British. They, too, had stood alone. They'd been unable to stop the German invasion but fought back from their mountains. I was personally thanked for giving refuge to King Olav during the German occupation. The annual tree they gave to Trafalgar Square was a small price to pay. They all knew a lot more about us than we did about them. They saw British football live each week, which was more than we did. Norwegian football they hardly mentioned at all, other than to apologise that it was far too inferior to merit much attention.

Working was a lot tougher, however, than in Finland. Bergen wasn't some small port in a remote land, but one where British carbon paper salesmen had rolled in by the dozen off the ferry from Newcastle. In several places on my first day I was told to get out as soon as I'd asked if the receptionist spoke English. An office manager I did get through to apologised for being unable to do any business but said many of the British salesmen had defrauded local buyers, sending them orders of 10,000 or even 100,000 when they'd ordered a box of a mere 1,000. Often these deliveries had been signed for by managers who assumed the mistake must have been theirs and that no one from Britain could surely have been acting in an underhand way. Bad stories had appeared in the business press. In some places, he said, I'd be lucky if the police weren't called.

The solution I found to this was to put on a cod American accent. It fitted the identity I believed I was aiming for anyway. It also turned out to be highly popular and got me into every office. All Norwegians had an uncle who had jumped ship in Brooklyn, or ancestor who'd taken the wagon train to Minnesota and wanted to talk about them. Rather than a special relationship, based on shared language and memories of the nuttier king Georges, theirs was a more obvious blood link. The peculiar thing was that in a city like Bergen, which prided itself on being a big village where everyone knew the affairs of everyone else, I was often recognised in the evenings as one of the Englishmen who had arrived in the E-type. Then during the day people were happy to talk to me about things American. After twenty minutes' pleasant conversation on topics quite unrelated to what I was selling, people were delighted to buy what I had to offer and wave me on my way.

Alf Ramsey had introduced a certain swagger into the England squad. They entered the 1970 World Cup as one of the favourites and as a team not visibly burdened by the crowd's expectations of them. They were in the habit of winning, sometimes without playing particularly well. They raised their game to whatever was required by the quality of the opposition. As a better team than the 1966 winners, it was clear they knew it and this element of arrogance caused resentment. I could tell this when watching their first match against Romania among a group of Norwegians. This was in the main hotel of Haugesund, a small, sleepy town on the south-west coast, though destined for bigger things now that North Sea oil had been discovered nearby. The Norwegians' empathy with British traditions of solitude meant also they were a people with a keen feeling for the underdog. They, therefore, cheered the Romanians. And they jeered when Geoff Hurst slipped in the lucky goal that won the game and turned, one arm raised cockily aloft, to receive the acclaim of his teammates. It was strange watching this, and the first time I could recall a British international team that so relished being overdogs.

In Mexico the England contingent had also angered its Mexican hosts by bringing its own food and drink. Ramsey's bilious episode two decades before in Rio de Janeiro convinced him British stomachs far from home should not be troubled by cosmopolitan incursions into the local cuisine. Quantities of sausages and bottled water had travelled with the England party. The characteristic Mexican image of the English was of eccentric gentlemen, who none the less acted with courtesy, respect and the general signs of a high *educación*. Ramsey's squad enjoyed no such goodwill and, if anything, were seen as acting in the arrogant 'we do things our way' manner of *gringos*, namely Mexico's US neighbours.

Still, it wasn't Alf's problem to worry about petty sentiment. He was a manager not a PR man, whatever that was, whose job was to win matches, rather than friends and influence people. At one stage of the trip, he was advised to give a tip to the Mexican policeman who had been with the team for a number of days. Ramsey was as aghast as if he'd been offered a plate of bull's *machitos* for breakfast. 'You don't tip policemen,' he protested. Whatever were things coming to? It'd never do in Britain to offer inducements. When abroad we should set an example, not pander to local customs.

England's second match against Brazil seemed hardly to matter. Whatever happened, the two countries would progress from their opening group. It was a probable dress rehearsal for when they'd meet again in the final. As such, it was an occasion mainly devoted to gaining the measure of each other. Maybe there would have been an advantage in terms of boosted confidence from winning the game, but then again, it might only have let complacency seep in. Brazil's 1–0 victory could, therefore, have been a blessing. True, it meant England's next round match was to be against the West Germans rather than Peru, but no big problem there. And it might only cause the Brazilians to come unstuck later, in the final. Ramsey's team, on the other hand, would have learned from it, and be better able to peak at the right time.

Not being overly bothered by the match, I almost missed Banks's save. The evening in far northern Europe felt as warm as the commentator said it was at just after midday in Guadalajara's Jalisco stadium. For the previous ten minutes of the game, it hadn't fully commanded my attention. People marvelled at how Banks covered the full width of his goal. As Brazil quickly broke away down the right side of the field, Banks was stationed at his front post in preparation for Jairzinho's cross. He had to turn while the ball swung over and make the 8 yards to his back post in a little over a second. As Pele met the ball with his head, Banks completed the last part of his manoeuvre with a dive covering about half the distance between the uprights. Pele rose, according to one description, 'like a salmon out of white water'. As befitted the greatest footballer in the world, he headed the ball towards the corner of the net hard and down, intending that its bounce just in front of the line should evade the keeper's flailing right arm. As all agreed, it was amazing enough that Banks got near it. Yet the key element of the save most people missed.

A yard, maybe just a touch more, in front of his line, had Banks dived straight he would have reached pretty much where the ball was but found himself deceived by its bounce. Thus, he had the presence of mind to adjust his dive, instantaneously twisting in midair to swoop diagonally. This took him back towards his goalline. From here he was able to get to the ball as it rose on the bounce and to push it up just enough to clear the crossbar. It barely plopped over it, landing gently on the roof of the netting, an explosive moment promptly defused. Covering the width of his goal in the way he had required agility of the utmost brilliance. The real triumph of Banks's save, however, lay in the getting back.

Pele was shouting for a goal from the moment he headed it. He said that when Banks saved it he hated him. Possibly he had to restrain himself from rushing in and hammering the keeper around the shoulders and head. The other Brazilians and the strongly pro-Brazilian Mexican crowd were sent into degrees of disappointment and awe. I heard the commentator remark what a fine save it was, and there was no arguing with that, yet found I wasn't surprised at all. Banks's save didn't shock, it reaffirmed. This was the kind of thing our keepers did, not least the one who, without doubt, was now the best in the world. At thirty-two, Banks had no weaknesses in any aspect of his game. His save in the Jalisco stadium proved to be the high point of British goalkeeping, the perfect combination of the spectacular and safe. At the same time, I didn't see what there was in that to get excited about. For a few moments, England captain Bobby Moore did stand quietly and applaud. Alan Mullery, who had been beaten to the ball by Pele, patted Banks on the head as he stood over him and said,

'Why didn't you catch it?' With a corner to face, Banks got up and got on.

o   o   o

Sabotage was suspected when Banks was struck down by a stomach bug shortly before the team's quarter-final game against West Germany. But it was unlikely someone had spiked the sausages or spring water that Ramsey had brought or, as was hinted darkly, that a waiter 'got at' a bottle of beer. The team played three qualifying games in enervating heat and had lost sleep as hostile crowds gathered outside their hotels to jeer and bang drums. Montezuma's Revenge usually struck soft foreign stomachs at times of tiredness, tension and lowered resistance.

Yet when the late change was announced, for the game to be staged in the small mid-Mexican city of León, there was no need for alarm. Had Bobbys Moore or Charlton, say, dropped out, that would have been different. We had goalkeeping talent to such a degree that Banks was replaced by Peter Bonetti, who was only 'slightly less gifted' than Banks himself, according to such an objective assessment as that of Scottish sports writer Hugh McIlvaney. At twenty-eight Bonetti had won six caps and though he had never played in such a major international game, with Chelsea had regularly proved himself to be a keeper who didn't wilt under pressure. He could have been the first choice of any other nation in the tournament. Unfortunately, he had only an hour to prepare himself mentally for the game and had last played a little under three weeks before.

He'd had very little to do as England went 2–0 ahead by just after half-time. England had dominated a predominantly midfield battle and blocked Beckenbauer's customary fluid service to Gerd Muller up front. Things got undeniably nervy when Beckenbauer, inspired perhaps by his goal in the meaningless Hanover game two years before, decided to strike out on his own. Pushed quite wide to the right of the field he put in a hopeful shot on goal, which bounced in front of Bonetti. It went under his body as he dived. This happened to keepers who had had little to do. The goal was his fault but very untypical of him. He'd made errors in his early days at Chelsea, but then so had Banks in his at Leicester. I'd certainly never seen him make such an elementary mistake before.

It did absolutely nothing for his confidence. Such moments were always difficult – how did a keeper get his mind off the mistake he'd just made and prevent it leading to another? There might be the eery feeling, too, that the fates had turned and were set to work irreversibly against you. But with twenty minutes remaining, all it would need was a bit of extra support from his defence and some luck. Bonetti got little of either. Soon after, the ball ping-ponged around the penalty area, his defenders missing several opportunities to clear it. Their exhaustion showed when it was knocked out hopefully only to reach the German left-back Schnellinger who was advancing up the left-wing. Fortunately Schnellinger was also tired and punted in a poor cross, which headed for veteran Uwe Seeler. At 5 foot and not very much, Seeler was near enough the smallest player on the pitch.

In his book published two years earlier, Peter Bonetti had said that you learned to 'expect the unexpected' from continental players. He had nearly been caught out on one of Chelsea's European tours, when an opponent, to the side of the goal and with his back to it, had tried a sudden overhead kick. From this 'impossible position', the ball had beaten Bonetti and he was thankful to see it sail just past his far post. Coincidentally, the tour had been in West Germany and Seeler the forward concerned.

There was no chance this time of him doing an overhead kick. The ball was far too high and it would be all Seeler could do to get his head to it. Then, Bonetti had said, 'expect the unexpected'. Seeler in the air had one particular forte, which was his strength itself. The one-time apprentice furniture clerk in Hamburg was built to have been taken out on a removal job or two himself and was quite up to shifting heavy chests and armoires down winding staircases in old German apartment blocks. His knack was to rise early for a high ball and take taller defenders with him. Using his muscles, he could hang in the air for the split-second it took for the defenders to be heading down again, thus losing their height advantage. Seeler now did just enough to reach the ball before anyone else. His back to the goal, he executed the headed equivalent of the move which had surprised Bonetti before, a flick backwards off his receding hairline. It sent the ball into what writer Brian Glanville described as a 'remarkable, tantalising parabola'.

The bomb that hit the chimney stack down our street at number 40 must have followed a similar flight path. It was touch and go where it would land but I felt as soon as it left Seeler's head it was bound for the far corner of Bonetti's goal. A keeper from the days of the flat cap standing squarely on his line would have reached such a ball. All he would have to do was stand and wait, skipping at the last moment to tip it over, reassuringly rattling the crossbar for good measure. But keepers weren't on their lines these days. They were always out that extra few feet and yards, in closer touch with the rest of the team. Under most circumstances it was a preparatory move to narrow the angle, but not this one. The ball made for the angle between bar and post, the one part of the goal it was almost impossible for Bonetti to get to. It was a fluke that it found it. Seeler could not have deliberately guided the ball to that area of the net, but he deserved his luck. He'd played as the youngest ever full international at Wembley in 1954 and, at the same venue, in West Germany's losing team in 1966. His effort when he'd played Bonetti in Germany before had narrowly failed to pay off and, as he went for the unexpected again, he reaped fair reward. England's keeper was unable to get back to reach the ball. This wasn't Bonetti's fault. He was in the position dictated by the times. Britain and its keepers didn't know whether they were off their lines or on them.

The goal decided the game. The Germans had the psychological advantage of having hauled themselves back from two goals down and scored the inevitable winner in extra time. Bonetti's defence was at fault for leaving Muller unmarked to volley the ball in but by now England's keeper was the easy target. Many blamed him for all three German goals. 'Bonetti!' The name spoke for itself, he was a 'continental', flash and unreliable. Coming so soon after Banks's save against Brazil, the timing couldn't have been more unfortunate. The last impressions are the strongest and it was easy to believe that Banks had always been so wondrous and Bonetti so susceptible. The defeat left the impression that a more 'British' keeper wouldn't have done such a thing. I still argued with people about this years later but, in truth, it was a feeling that was in us all.

The ripple effect of England's first defeat in a major encounter with West Germany was to go on for years. Harold Wilson had gradually worked his way back to a level of popularity such that opinion polls made him the favourite in the general election to be held a few days later. He had called it in the expectation of England doing well in the World Cup and the government benefiting from the boost in the electorate's morale. The loss in León became the equivalent of Nixon's five o'clock shadow in his US election battle against Kennedy a decade earlier. Psephologists said it was enough to have caused the small swing that accounted for Wilson's marginal defeat.

It was the first time a British football match, let alone the activities of a goalkeeper, had had such an impact on the higher affairs of state. In came Ted Heath and the Tories with promises to cut inflation 'at a stroke', but they soon found themselves in confrontation with the unions over pay. 'Who rules?' demanded Heath, as he went again to the polls. Not you, said defeats inflicted by the coalminers, the electorate, and then Margaret Thatcher as she took control of the Conservative Party with more strident ideas on what to do about the unions and the traditional areas of the British economy where their power lay.

Some years later, I went to León, still a provincial city with paved squares, a few old buildings from Spanish colonial times and clipped Indian laurel trees in its main plaza. It was the nation's shoe-making capital, Mexico's Northampton. Its small stadium had a non-league feel to it, more like that of Bedford Town. In the hot mid-morning, straw-hatted workers watered the pitch with hoses and swept the terraces with witches' brooms. You wouldn't have had any sense of what had happened there. One well-timed leap by a veteran German footballer had done more than the Luftwaffe managed in years of aerial warfare. Uwe Seeler's flick found Peter Bonetti unable to get back to his line and set events on course to the demise of old industrial Britain.

C h a p t e r 12

On *to the* Pole

B razil beat Italy 4–1 in the 1970 World Cup Final in Mexico City's Aztec stadium in one of the finest spectacles of attacking football in the tournament's history. As memorable was the pitch invasion by fans at the end of the game, dancing in unrestrained delight which reflected the way the Brazilian team had played.

The comfortable margin of victory seemed to bear out the predictions that the result had been a foregone conclusion. Italy had rarely impressed in the competition. In the semi-final they had rather luckily beaten the Germans, not least because of the fallibility of the German keeper, Sepp Maier. Yet there was a moment when the Italians had Brazil on the ropes and failed to press their advantage. They'd forced an equaliser at the psychologically important time of a few minutes before the interval. This had led from a mistake by their twenty-year-old right-half, Clodoaldo, who, employing some inexcusably fancy footwork, back-heeled the ball in a deep defensive position and gave Boninsegna a clear run at the Brazilian keeper, Felix – in effect, a clear run at the goal itself.

The Brazilians managed to hold on, then stormed back as if

nothing untoward had happened. The most remarkable thing about their Mexican triumph, both in the final and in all their previous games, was that they achieved it with only ten men. They suffered no especially serious injuries in the championships and, strictly speaking, were rarely in any game without eleven men on the pitch. It was just that Brazil did not play with a recognisable goalkeeper.

It was the habit of many Brazilian footballers to play under assumed nicknames – Vava, Pele, Tostão – hence Felix appeared to have classified himself as another in a line of goalkeeping Cats. Probably this was testament to what he felt were his natural abilities in the role: agility, grace, speed of movement. If so, he was deluding himself, yet would have had a reasonable case for claiming to be a keeper of many lives. By the end of the 1970 competition he had used up most of them, but emerged by general agreement to be the luckiest, and worst, goalkeeper to win a World Cup winners' medal.

The story put around was that he played for one of Brazil's top clubs, Fluminense, but that was only a cunning ruse by the Brazilians to convince everyone they had a better last line than was truthfully the case. It was obvious he had no experience in the position. He'd conceded soft goals against Peru and Uruguay in the quarter- and semi-finals respectively but they were only a part of his problem. Detachment was a natural and necessary feature of the keeping art, yet Felix took it to another level. He watched the game with the fascination of a fee-paying spectator behind his goal, rather than as someone employed to be stationed in front of it. 'Where's that going?' he seemed to say as a dangerous cross ball came over. 'I wonder what that's going to do.' It rarely occurred to him to do anything about it. When he did, invariably it would have been better he hadn't. He had some intuitive grasp of his limitations, however, and so generally left things for his defence to scramble away as best they could.

Gilmar had retired from the game only the previous year after his 100th international. For well over a decade he had dominated a position which many were happy to leave well alone. Brazil had lost the 1950 World Cup on home territory. Keeper Moacyr Barbosa was blamed for Uruguay's winning goal and publicly hounded ever after. Two others, Roberto Gomes

Pedrosa, who had played in the first World Cup in 1930, and Castilho, Brazil's keeper in 1954 in Switzerland, later committed suicide. The position seemed cursed.

Gilmar came to Wembley in 1956, a Latin dandy in his made-to-measure outfit, while otherwise borrowing from another blueprint. His two penalty saves kept the score in England's favour to 4–2 and staved off humiliation. The principal features of his game were calmness and unflappability. Keepers performed that way in Britain, Brazil's old neighbour and roving citizens of which had first brought the game to the country. What better example in an uncertain world for a keeper to follow?

With its backline sewn up, Brazil's football could get on with expressing itself along lines of the national character. In its World Cup victories of 1958 and 1962, it reproduced the exuberance of something akin to the traditional Brazilian street carnival. An infectious phenomenon, carnival urged people to enjoy through participation. Up where the action was, was where everyone wanted to be. Even Brazil's defenders played this way. Their fourth goal against Italy – three minutes from the end and which had the fans straining to get dancing themselves on the pitch – showed this. Pele laid off a ball to his right in the Italian penalty area and Carlos Alberto charged up from the defensive depths of full-back to score with a shot struck as powerfully and accurately as many a forward could have managed. No Brazilian player wanted to be hanging back downfield and away from where it was all going on. As for the one position which had to be, who in this nation of more than 100 million souls could conceivably want to play there?

None but one, judging by Felix. He had a bit of front, you had to hand him that. He took the field with studiedly wrinkled brow, a semi-severity to give a first impression that he was on top of things. This, with his longish sideburns and full-wave of hair at his forehead, give him a similarity to Pat Jennings. Yet Felix was barely worth a few games on Hackney Marshes. As I watched him, I was sure he wouldn't have made the South East Counties League, not even Division Two. But for being born 5,000 miles away, I could have played in goal for Brazil.

England's loss against the Germans in León had left me as fed up as I could remember after a game of football. Walking around the Bergen waterfront over the following days, I reminded myself such a thing should not be taken so seriously. It seemed as good a time as any to do some travelling. I went to work around Stavanger, further south, going into draughtsmen's offices where the plans were being finalised to exploit the oil that lurked between here and the coast of Scotland. On the southern tip of the country, the resort town of Mandal was full of young Swedes and their old Saabs and black Volvos. The blazing heat didn't feel like Norway. This was the country the Arctic convoys had battered around *en route* to Russia, pursued by the *Tirpitz*, in the worst conditions at sea in the war. That was, of course, all the way up its lengthy coast – '*Hammer*-fest, *Trom*-so, Lo-*fo*-ten'. So, I set off in the direction of the Pole.

In Hammerfest, the north's three months of summer daylight were under way. On my first night I went swimming at the town pool – a small lake, reed-encircled on the outskirts – and was bitten by mosquitoes as virulent as anywhere in southern Europe. I couldn't sleep for the seagulls, which screamed through the night, and when I peered through my hotel room's curtains – tightly shut to no useful effect – saw locals out washing their cars at three in the morning. I asked people in the offices I went to visit how they stuck the same period of winter dark. They seemed surprised at this. This was the 'finest place to live in the world', one man told me, then spoiled the recommendation by adding the goalkeeper's dictum: 'someone has to do it.' If people weren't here, he said, the Russians would walk straight in.

I took a boat around the North Cape to Honningsvåg, where Russian whalers were docked in the small harbour. A ferry-load of Brazilian tourists waited sadly to leave, gathered by the rail. Being in such places as this could subdue even the likes of them. Also, people might come all the way from such distant places as Rio Grande do Sul, only to witness a sky covered by thick cloud. They had to imagine the midnight sun behind it. This happened to me on the evening I went the 15 miles by road out to the North Cape. I was about to take the bus back just after midnight when some young Norwegians pulled me into the bar near the edge of the cliff. I should catch the last bus with them at two o'clock, they said, as they set about consuming beer and schnaps at a rapid rate. Luckily enough, the sun broke through at 1.30 a.m. and they waved me outside to take a picture of it, while they remained inside not wishing to miss good drinking time. We sat at the back of the bus for the journey back to town along the bumpy road, rutted by the months of winter. It was all that was needed for them to throw up, to the general disgust of the other passengers. I stayed loyally by them, pretending to be stoically unfussed, but the Germans on board, uncomplicated types in this and many other matters, moved angrily to seats nearer the front.

The deserted border post to Russia near the town of Kirkenes was along a narrow muddy track. A gate barred the way, after which the path disappeared into undergrowth. There was a small town showing no signs of life a couple of miles away at the edge of a hill. The Norwegians said its name was Boris Gleb. It sounded straight out of Ian Fleming and I never found it on any map, so assumed they were making it up. The gate was opened only very occasionally for the ceremonial exchange of ski hats and other things that might have blown over it. I heard the guy at the small Kirkenes tourist office telling a couple of Americans who had come to visit relatives saying somebody had once strayed over the frontier wire: 'He came back in a box,' he said, to the visible alarm of his audience. The north Norwegians loved to talk like this.

Young people in the town would strike up conversations when I was eating in the few restaurants or cafés. They were happy to meet someone from the centres of civilisation and invited me back for hours of drinks and talk in their clapboard houses. I usually ended up walking alongside the small fjords back to where I was staying in the cloudy light of 2 or 3 a.m. Lemmings, all yellow and grey fur and protruding teeth, would suddenly squeal out from grass verges.

Most of the three-hour bus ride alongside the fjord to the town further east of Vardø was in view of the plume of smoke from its fishmeal factory. Generally it streamed away towards the Soviet Union but sometimes turned to engulf the town. I worked there for three days and more or less every office I visited bought from me. The man from the electricity board thanked me for what he said had been forty enjoyable minutes practising his English and then said, 'So, what are you selling? I'll have some.' The bus back to Kirkenes airport left just after midnight. By now the lemmings were not stopping at the verges but dashing out from them and under the vehicle's wheels. The driver didn't flinch. The locals said they were working themselves up into one of their mass suicidal runs and it was zoologically interesting to be witnessing the beginnings of such a thing. I tried to find some deeper significance to it, but concluded there was none. My plane back to the south, and thence to London, left at about 5 a.m.

I prepared for my assault on the main centre of world capitalism by shopping, Chelsea-footballer style, in the King's Road. What with a three-piece tweed suit from the Village Gate, a cutesy accent and a quaintly British product to sell, I could envisage little way the Americans could not succumb. Indeed, in offices in Washington and Baltimore the following week, chief executives and the very presidents of companies fell over themselves to receive me. My Britishness got me in without an appointment and into conversations about their visits to Europe, the trips made by their daughters' college choir to Rome and, in the case of those who hadn't been to where I came from, their regrets at not yet fulfilling a life's ambition. 'I've only flown over London, but it looked great from the air,' one captain of western industry told me.

But when they saw what I was there to sell, they shifted with no notable loss of balance or composure, into another mode. They remained eminently friendly, though looked at me as if I was quaintly mad. With some regret, they pointed out that there was a Xerox machine in every office. In Islington town hall I couldn't recall there having been one in the council's entire finance department, unless the borough treasurer had one secreted away in his office for his own clandestine use. You were compelled to trek upstairs to the legal department and the office of Sid Porrett, the legal clerk who still basked in the glory of having brought Joe Orton to book over the library caper; or you went as far again down to seek the closely controlled photocopying services of Mr Coffin, the stationery manager, along the basement corridor from the cemeteries offices.

To the Americans, carbon paper was from a past long dead and buried. This shouldn't have been in itself the overriding factor. A basic grasp of the selling art said that, once you'd engaged in a fifteen-minute spell of pleasant conversation, you had sufficiently fanagled yourself into the client's personal space to make an order highly likely. Taken with the facts of the distance I'd come and the novelty of having an eccentric foreigner stroll in on their day made a sale near certain. Our shared heritage, the 'special relationship', would absolutely guarantee it.

But they showed themselves not to be people easily deflected by such side issues. No matter how wide-mouthed they appeared, the smiles and chat never clouded for a moment a shrewd awareness of their best interest. With many north European people you had to break the ice, which might well take some time, but once you'd done so the path lay more or less clear to their hearts or, in the case at hand, to a signature on the dotted line. With the Americans the door appeared open from the outset. Detailed discussions on their divorce settlements might precede even an introductory exchange of names, yet the implied intimacy only confused. It didn't mean you were getting anywhere at all and could be put aside as easily as it had been acquired if their interests, as they defined them, were not served. 'Nope, sorry, not interested,' they'd say, with no edge whatsoever in their voices. They would smile as they showed me to the door.

My three-piece tweed became a sweaty burden in the humidity of a Washington summer. I took to hanging around bars on 14th Street rather than endure more cheerily useless calls. Even in the event of finding gainful employment, green cards would also have been a problem. Students who had set up desks at Maryland University to advise each other on how to avoid the draft pointed out that, in the unlikely event of my being given one, the US government would consider my gratitude such that I'd be on the first plane out again to Da Nang. Facing the wrath of the grizzled old Uncle Ho, who probably bore a special grudge against the British from all the time he'd slaved over his hot Haymarket stove, wasn't what I'd had in mind. I drove to California and tripped over the border at San Diego. The green hills of the USA changed to the brown and barren hills of the Mexican side halfway over the bridge. The markets of old Tijuana were my initial sighting of the Third World and I took flight faster than when I'd first seen Naples. But not before a cheeky *piñata* salesman shouted to me: 'Hey, what's your hurry? Come spend your money now, before you get killed in Vietnam.' French toast, hash browns and other happy food had been losing their attraction for a while. Suddenly the process accelerated.

With Europe the only realistic option, a career in carbon paper began to pall. The guy who drove the E-type knocked down a pedestrian on a crossing in Bergen, who died a few days later. As I was working my way towards the bits of the north of Norway I was yet to see, I was arrested after a day on an island near Ålesund and told my documents weren't in order. The policeman who questioned me was no less complimentary about my role in the war than any of his fellow countrymen, though still asked me to leave Norway straightaway. Final disillusion came when I was given more information about the 'special sealing chemical, which we call Q6'. It wasn't made by us at all, but by the plastics factory whose pungent presence had so often accompanied night training at Brisbane Road.

My mother wrote to tell me the press had besieged the luxury flats at numbers 8–10 in our street, at the same time that George Best had gone missing again from Manchester United. Men from the *Mirror* and other papers were knocking at doors and phoning the houses nearby for information on this mystery. They could have done worse than direct their questions elsewhere and towards his Northern Irish colleague, Pat Jennings. They'd made their full international debuts for Northern Ireland together seven years before and were roommates on every occasion they were selected. Jennings said that Best, no less than him, enjoyed nothing more than listening quietly to older players talk of their experiences. Two or three lagers was his intake of alcohol. His jump into the superstar bracket came with the 5–1 win against Benfica in Lisbon's Stadium of Light in 1966, which sparked United's misplaced hopes that year that they were about to win the European Cup. Best began to worry about the pressure of the fans and their disappointment if he didn't run half the length of the field beating three or four opponents every time. He felt he let them down if he didn't deliver. It was the tyranny of mass expectation that did for Best. Hence he'd come to hole up at the Islington home of his latest 'blonde actress girlfriend'.

After the Norwegian police had bid me a polite farewell, I sought refuge in the east, watching the 1971 Cup Final and Arsenal take the double on TV in Helsinki. At the turn of the year Britain had decimalised the pound as practical evidence of its European intentions and the Heath government was resuming efforts to join the common market. Whether the British public could have cared was debatable, but characteristically one of its goalkeepers anticipated the faint stirrings of a new era. In the Cup Final, Bob Wilson for Arsenal wore the continental number 1 on his back, the first time in modern club football the symbol had penetrated the English game's inner temple.

In late spring I made a final swing to the north of Scandinavia, having hitched through Finland with my suitcases in the direction of the retreating ice. When you looked at people more closely, they surprised you. The Finns, the quietest, shyest race in Europe, stopped to give me lifts almost as soon as I'd been set down from my last. They insisted I stay the night or ate with them and their families. One fellow, an air-traffic controller from a small airfield marginally south of the Arctic circle, apologised – in English he'd polished up working at Foyle's in Charing Cross Road – that he wasn't going anywhere but the couple of kilometres to the house of his girlfriend for lunch. The three of us sat in her garden eating egg mayonnaise and Finnish sausage, watching the ice inch down the Tornio river. It was slower and later this year, they said, and the Finnish air force was bombing it upstream to make it get a move on. Large jagged chunks slowly reared up and overhung the banks; the night before, it had stolen off with the wooden hut containing the family sauna from the end of their neighbour's garden. After our meal he put me back on the road. The first money anyone allowed me to spend was for a bus fare to the Norwegian border at Kilpisjärvi, when there'd been fewer cars than reindeer passing on the road.

I crossed again into Norway, worked a month or so around 'Lofoten' and other islands avoiding the local policeman. I ended with a week in Tromsø, my final night out at the fjord where the *Tirpitz* was sunk. The husband of the family I'd rented a room from and I sat by its rusting anti-submarine nets left draped on a grassbank at the side of the road. An heroic action, no doubt, he said, though things were never quite as they were portrayed. The planes that had mounted the raid to sink it had been helped by the Germans in one of their disconnected moments – officers and crew alike were drunk and having a party on board.

When I returned to London my sister told me of a local cab driver who had collected her from our parents' house and asked casually hadn't I 'been away'. Yes, she said, to Scandinavia. That was funny, he replied, he'd never heard it called that before. He and others had happily imagined that I'd been in Pentonville or Wormwood Scrubs. The longer I was away, the worse the assumed offence. It signified a belated acceptance into the squad from south of Danbury Street, most of whom had now gone away permanently.

In the local elections, a younger breed of Labour councillor was voted back into power. Lenin's bust was rescued from its shelf in the muncipal vaults and rehabilitated to the stone staircase in the town hall's lobby. Its stare fixed all those who ascended to the council chamber (until a rabid rightist's attack on it with a pot of red paint prompted its removal to a small local museum where it was thought less of a provocation). In Chapel Market the banana man diversified into red and green peppers. The mile-long Regent's Canal tunnel roof had collapsed but there were plans to shore it up for pleasure craft to come through. Skips appeared outside houses in greater number, though restoration was not without setbacks. An actor from a never-ending soap called in my dad to clean up the mess in his basement. The ceiling was in danger, its support bludgeoned away in the cause of a flighty open-plan kitchen. Cowboy builders were afoot, who wouldn't have known their JCB from their RSJ. The house was sold to the presenter of a late-night current affairs programme who was wont to jog a couple of hundred yards every morning in sagging tracksuit bottoms to get his paper from the Polish newsagent's.

My intention amid such gentrifying improvement was to apply for a course at Sussex University in international relations. Thinking a background on the Cold War's northern border might not be what they wanted, I went on a trip to where things had recently been warmer: the Middle East. As I was in Cyprus, George Grivas smuggled his way back on to the island to renew his Eoka campaign. Archbishop Makarios drove past me in screaming cavalcade, his 'Black Mak' silhouette clear through his car's back window. In Israel the kibbutz I was on had been seized by Arab forces in the 1948 war and was perilously located on the Jordanian border, at the southern extent of the Israeli-occupied Golan Heights. Nothing was happening. I sent letters home describing the tension of the moment at this lone frontier outpost. My mum wrote back to say the IRA had blown up the Post Office Tower. The street had been shaken out of bed.

At home, the gloom mounted as unemployment passed one million a little after Bloody Sunday. The miners struck in the heart of a dismal winter and phased power cuts around the country were the result. By the time West Germany arrived to resume hostilities against England at Wembley, the lights had been going out all over Britain. This qualifier for the European Championships offered the perfect opportunity for a switch of fortune. Not only might it perk up the national spirit but also provide some recompense for the Germans' fluke of a victory in Mexico. The outcome was quite the contrary. The Germans' display proved one of the most impressive from a visiting team. If Günther Netzer wasn't powering down the field, Beckenbauer was strolling across it. Even their goalkeeper Sepp Maier remained calmly untroubled when called upon. The irony of it was, these people had never won till five years ago – their 'pointless' match in Hanover had amounted to their psychological breakthrough. Then they'd followed it with an undoubtedly lucky victory in the provincial outback of León but now, at Wembley, just to make sure everyone could see, they confirmed a superiority which was starting to look long-term.

My dad found me a labouring job, to fill in time before the academic year got under way, on a hotel being built on the M4 at the turn-off for Heathrow. I made efforts to get into the 'ruggedly smiling hero in hard-hat and donkey jacket' role but became disenchanted after an episode on a plunging hoist. The thing fell into rapid and uncontrolled descent as I walked on it at the ninth floor. Fortunately the wheel of the barrow I was pulling caught on the slightly overlapping edge of the landing two floors down and halted the hoist's accelerating course to the ground. The foreman took the trouble to inform me the contractors would have been exonerated in the event of my demise, since I shouldn't have been on the hoist in the first place.

I moved to the New Covent Garden site, the largest in the country, and the first to be closed by the 1972 builders' strike. The bricklayer's sub-contractor I worked for transferred me again, to a new hotel at Shepherd's Bush to be called the Kensington Hilton (the 'Shepherd's Bush Hilton' was not thought flashy enough, or, in terms a bit continental, to have *cachet*). The union insisted everyone should be on no lower than the basic rate of 42p an hour and inquired of my boss why I was the only one on 40p. 'He's a fuckin' student,' was his response. When he was told it was either a 2p rise per hour or the closing of the site, he relented. 'A rise?' he said, give or take a cheerful expletive. 'But, of course.' He gave me a hod and a half-ton of bricks to be loaded by way of a bouncing ladder, on to a scaffold six floors up. I was the first to be sacked when the strike bit nationally. As flying pickets covered the land and the Shrewsbury Three's cause entered the realms of legend, I was quietly martyred as the Shepherd's Bush One. I'd have been entitled to wear the number drawing attention to the fact on my donkey jacket. My shop steward said he was very sorry to see me go and that at any time and anywhere in the future, I could count on our Amalgamated Union of Building Trade Workers. He genuinely meant it but it was with relief I stumbled into the protected world of university.

The course started in October, the month Gordon Banks was involved in the incident which forced his retirement. The four-steps rule was destined to be the nemesis of great keepers in placing a restriction on the use of their hands in the penalty area, but not in the shattering way that applied to Banks. He'd been at Anfield, playing brilliantly in front of the Kop with Stoke 1–0 up when the referee penalised him for carrying the ball more than the permitted four paces. Banks protested and lost his composure for the rest of the game. Liverpool equalised from the free kick and scored again to win. The next day he was running through a replay of the incident in his mind as he drove home and was involved in a head–on car crash. He lost the sight in his right eye and, though he tried to get back into the game, gave up hope of resuming his international career the following summer. He played later in Florida in the North American Soccer League and was good enough to be voted its keeper of the year. He wondered, however, what he was doing there, when ushered on to the field before games on a horse and dressed in a cowboy outfit.

There was no obvious replacement ready. Shilton had made his debut two years earlier against East Germany and, soon after Banks's injury, Ray Clemence of Liverpool was given his first game. Shilton was favoured when England went away to play Poland in the early summer of 1973 in a World Cup qualifier.

England lost 2–0, a defeat which as good as ended Bobby Moore's career. Shilton was unlucky with the goals but did not put on a display brimming with confidence. The defeat also meant England would have to beat Poland at Wembley in the return match in October.

At such a tricky transitional time, England would have been delighted to borrow what Northern Ireland had: Pat Jennings had been made the first keeper since Bert Trautmann to be voted footballer of the year at the end of the 1973 season. With him Spurs had won the FA Cup in 1967, the League Cup in 1971, the Uefa Cup the following year and now the League Cup again. Jennings was less of a martyr than most keepers. Instead of throwing himself at opponents' feet, he'd stay on his as long as possible. In the event of a keeper committing himself early to move one way, his opponent had only to go the other. But Jennings's method meant it was more likely that the man with the ball would be forced to decide. With the pressure of the moment and the crowd on top of him, he might just bodge it. Also, from a standing position rather than already sprawled on the floor, the keeper would be better placed to move and get to the ball.

It was noticeable during Jennings's career that commentators started to compliment keepers for 'standing up well' to a forward. This interpretation attributed an air of macho defiance to what the keeper was up to. Previously it would have been more likely to attract criticism. Keepers would have been accused of holding back from the glorious moment of all-or-nothing goalkeeping: Jack Thomson at Ibrox Park, Trautmann at Wembley, death and broken necks, or at least the risk of having to spit out studs and broken teeth afterwards. In earlier, bloodier times a keeper's heroism had been in the style of soldiers going 'over the top' in the First World War, or charging across Normandy beaches in the Second. The ball was there and you threw yourself on it. It was tough and potentially deadly, though looked at in one way it was actually easier. You made up your mind and you did it, at which point you stopped thinking. Keepers who 'stood up' were playing the thinking game that little bit longer.

Jennings was a huge-handed, quiet revolutionary. He was not bound by the classic, right way to do things. If a shot was near enough to him, for example, he wouldn't dive and risk it going under his body. He'd stick a foot out. It didn't matter what it looked like, whether it was technically the perfect save. The prime objective, he said, was to keep the ball out of the net. His wasn't a purist but pragmatic and lateral 'think on your feet' style, and a step closer to that of the rest of his team. Everyone knew Jennings was a great goalkeeper, few that he was the first of anything so grand as a 'new age'.

And, just in case there was any doubt whether his courage matched up to that of the 'headlong into the tide' traditional school, his fellow Spurs players would have disagreed. The scene in the players' tunnel was often one where tempers were let loose after stormier games, out of sight of the crowd, television and meddling match officials. Jennings's quiet presence had a way of calming them down. It may have had something to do with the fact that before his professional football days he was used to throwing small trees on to the backs of trucks. But amid the post-match excitement on the walk to the dressing rooms, as explained by one his teammates at White Hart Lane, 'Pat looked after things'.

o   o   o

Two Tottenham players, Irish international Joe Kinnear and Ralph Coates of England, were on holiday in the Costa Blanca when I visited Spain for the first time in the summer. New British colonies had arisen on such lengths of Spanish shoreline, bijoux estates on gentle slopes with narrow roads between bungalows, protected at the entrance by a pole raised and lowered by a uniformed sentry in a sweltering box. There were complexes of tower blocks, unattractively named *urbanizaciones*. They were not populated by anything like typical inhabitants of London's urban jungle – who would have found no novelty in them – but richer people who had bought them to visit on an occasional basis. Numerous expats lived in the area, many in early retirement and some who had brought their teenage and younger children. On the face of it they had a dream life but once they'd strolled to the harbour bar and played a desultory set of tennis, there wasn't much to do but shrivel in the heat and boredom.

The torpor was broken once a year when the foreign community faced their local Spanish third division football team.

Invariably the Spaniards won, but this year the expats were confident. The two Spurs players were quietly roped into the team. Given the state of the town pitch, which bore a resemblance to the former stretch of waste ground at the top of our street, their management back at White Hart Lane might not have approved, but it was felt they'd only have to put themselves about at below half-cock, to make the difference. The problem was the goalkeeper. The expats traditionally used Pancho, the town policeman. Off his moped, he stood at 5 feet 3 inches in uniform and boots. Had he been a member of General Franco's elite *guardia civil*, he'd have enjoyed the extra inch of their funny plastic hat. Pancho was not treated by his own, however, as one of the elite and not thought good enough for the Spanish team. This contrasted with his treatment from the expats. A residence permit, or official permission for an extra few tables and chairs outside the café on the town square, might pass through the bureaucracy quicker with the aid of a member of the municipal police. Pancho was invited to expats' parties. No one challenged him when he stole their ashtrays as mementos. His status in the football team he had also come to expect. It was only after intense diplomatic negotiations, therefore, that he agreed to stand down for part of the game. He would take the field in the excitement at the start of the game and play the first half, I'd slip on in the second.

The stadium was full, the first half tightly fought and the score even at 1–1. I was surprised at how keyed-up the atmosphere in the dressing room was. Pancho sat disconsolately in a corner, perhaps resolving to upgrade his kleptomania to more than ashtrays. Others spoke loudly in English around him, which he didn't understand, about how we were now going to win. Play stuck at the other end in the early minutes of the second half as I took up my position midway between keeper's area and penalty spot. This prepared me to narrow every angle – give or take a speculative long shot over my head. Then a character operating in their midfield spotted this and decided to take the risk with a shot from 30 yards. After only a couple of them I could tell from the weight and height of the ball I was hopelessly out of place. It approached with a look about it which said, 'We'll just do enough to evade your fingertips, then deviously dip behind you and under the bar when we have.' Continental balls were designed for this purpose. As I heard it hit the net I wanted to turn and protest at the unfairness of it all, or at least see a sympathetic face. What I looked at was a skinny expat kid with a sunburnt nose, who shouted, 'You're bleedin' useless, keeper.'

Worse was Pancho's magnificent magnanimity as the presentation was made to the winning team at the side of the pitch. He did not have the words, but offered a heart-felt expression: 'Bad luck, it could have happened to any of us', it said. Though I suspected it added: 'Of course, it didn't happen to any of us, *coño*, it happened to you. Yet I, a mere continental goalkeeper, unite with you in your time of humiliation.'

o   o   o

The second year at Sussex got under way with an occupation of the university administration building to protest against lack of student accommodation on campus and in the elegantly tatty squares of Regency Brighton. It was organised by the Broad Left, a well-oiled machine of both ageing and youthful Communist Party members, and others they might co-opt with the promise of a job on the executive of the student union. It was led by an ex-Scots miner, admitted to the university because of his worldly experience. The political fringe sniped for rhetorical advantage wherever it could. Two anarchists appealed for a 'real occupation' and for students to get out into the night streets of Brighton to bring its 'winos and dossers' into our midst. The ex-Scots miner stamped on their suggestion for being ridiculously off-message. One of them was to be later made a Labour baron to counter the influence of the winos and dossers entrenched in the House of Lords, though that was a good many years hence.

England took the field for the return against the Poles at Wembley as the October War raged in the Middle East. Friends I had made in Israel who had grown up in the confident wake of the 1967 war were sent to the Sinai front and badly battered. One was thrown into jail when he got back home for losing his rifle in the rapid retreat. Israeli assumptions of superiority nurtured in the previous six years were blown away when Egyptian forces recrossed Suez. The night before the game, five Arab and an Iranian oil ministers had met in Kuwait where they decided to raise oil prices by 70 per cent and cut production. Not that it was realised at the time, but it was to bring an end to the West's long post-war boom, any realistic hope of a return to full employment and cosy assumptions about ever-improving living standards and the munificence of the welfare state. It was a moment from when things were to be done much more on the terms of others.

England needed to win the game at Wembley to qualify for the 1974 World Cup finals in West Germany. In sporting terms it was serious, but difficult to grasp as such amid the general mood of 'surely not'. In earlier days, we'd done the World Cup organisers a favour turning up for the competition at all. Now we were willingly offering ourselves to take part, it was inconceivable that we, inventors of the game, could be excluded.

Brian Clough called the nation to arms in his now regular television commentary. He had just resigned in a huff from managing Derby County, with whom he had won the league championship the year before, and may have had visions of a bright TV future. In media moods like this, Clough was unrecognisable as the quiet guy, respectful to kids running after him for his autograph on the platforms of King's Cross. Not that he didn't strike a popular chord when he derided the Polish centre-half, Gorgon, largely on the basis of his name and that he was big and lumbering. I read, much later, that his reference to the Poles' keeper, Jan Tomaszewski, as a 'clown' provoked uproar. It may well have done among Clough's no doubt regular viewers in Lodz and Katowice, but in Britain I failed to detect any widespread wave of liberal sympathy on Tomaszewski's behalf. Clough spoke for the nation, the English one at least. Almost by definition, to a country whose keepers were 'the best in the world', a continental keeper like the Pole was a clown.

He didn't do much to destroy the belief in the way he played. He flapped quite a lot in the first half of the game. As well as launching himself into several full-length saves and tips over the bar, he showed an ability to keep the ball out of the net with his elbows and knees. Other shots hit his post and scraped the bar. Though he stopped everything he had to, he never managed to create the impression that he knew how he had done so. For a top-class British keeper, this inability to command and reassure wouldn't have been good enough. Yet as the game went on, the feeling took hold that this might not matter. It was working itself out as one of those games where, for the keeper, the fates were with him. He was enjoying himself and probably laughing as he played.

At half-time Clough said again what we wanted to hear. He by-passed the interviewer and addressed the camera directly: it would be 'all right', he said, in a manner which understood at that moment his national audience's need for therapy. As for that Polish keeper, Clough stood by what he had previously said he was. The second-half outcome was that Tomaszewski staged pretty much a repetition of his earlier gymnastics. His repertoire comprised some great saves and many best described as improvised. You wanted to protest, and say this wasn't right, it was unfair, not at all how the game should be. A keeper disadvantaged by his background and comical style of play should not be coming out on top like this. But it didn't matter how good or bad the saves looked. The objective of all goalkeepers, as no less than the British footballer of the year, Pat Jennings, said, was to keep the ball out of the net. In this, and with only the exception of England's one goal from a penalty, Tomaszewski was spectacularly successful.

At the other end Peter Shilton did what was, by comparison, technically correct. A mistake by Norman Hunter near the halfway line set up a Polish charge on goal and a snappy shot by Domarski from the right of the penalty area. It was a little to Shilton's left. A smart dive, body behind the ball, hands to it, and it would be all right. Unfortunately, Shilton had stood with nothing much to do on a cold, damp night and, therefore, wasn't at his sharpest. He went down but his body and hands didn't get to the ball quickly enough and it went into the net as he dived. He later said that the problem was he tried to make the 'perfect save' – a clean grasp of the ball. A clumsy alternative would have been to knock the ball to the side, in which case it would have gone for a corner. There was also the Jennings, Gaelic-football style possibility of getting a foot to it. Tomaszewski might have tried either and succeeded. Shilton did it right and got it wrong. Tomaszewski did it all wrong and got it right on the night. The national sense of shock was considerable.

Amid the hush of the university library next day I discussed this with a friend who played football with me in games organised on the cinder pitches of the sports centre at the distant, forested end of the campus. These were generally friendly kickabouts – our team was named Apparent Madrid, on the grounds we weren't much like the Real one – among assorted early post-60s types who wanted to indulge their regard for the game out of sight of their political friends. There was no swearing of secret oaths exactly, but those that were uttered were safely lost on the winds sweeping the South Downs. My teammate was big, fair, curly-haired like the Pole's centre-half Gorgon. A few years later while working as a lawyer in the Gulf, he walked into a lift, put his frame between its closing doors to hold it for a friend, but it took off and killed him. Sometimes when accidents like this happened, the fates weren't with you.

But on the morning after England's first failure to qualify for the World Cup finals, and at the very centre of learning in one of Britain's most progressive universities, we agreed: Clough was right, Tomaszewski was a clown. A fortnight later we mounted a last-ditch defence through most of the game we were playing in. This was against the team organised by the Broad Left, the Icepicks, whose Stalinist vanguard reserved their best displays for when they came up against the Trotskyists, but who today were raining blows on us. Between us we made a series of scrambled stops, which included one or two grovelling saves on my knees. These did the job but were, frankly, embarrassing. Peter Grummitt – ex-Nottingham Forest and England Under-23 keeper – and the other Brighton players who trained earlier on the cinder each morning were watching as they strolled to their cars. In the final minute I bundled one ball away over the bar, at which my teammate shouted: 'Shit, this is like England and Poland!' In an earlier epoch (and if he hadn't been the size he was), this might have been worth a smack round the face. As it was, it was a slap on the back and, in a hard world quite capable of its humiliating moments, I was happy to take the acclaim.

We were used to keepers performing last-ditch heroics but they had been our keepers, who did it our way. Seeing someone else do it in his way was tough. It wasn't like Trautmann being lovable because he was 'like us', since the Polish keeper wasn't. Nor was it like foreigners turning up at Downing Street equipped with surprisingly good English, – they at least were still speaking our language. The difficulty was accepting the Pole's as a piece of keeping that was brilliant in its own terms, not ours. Twenty years on, all bar a month, and in the same arena, it was as shocking a lesson as that handed out by the Hungarians. They'd beaten us in our game on our territory. Tomaszewski did all that, and in 'our' position.

During the 1998 World Cup in France, BBC and ITV match commentators and analysts became involved in quite frequent conversations about the virtues and vices of foreign keepers. In one, Barry Davies and David Pleat had recalled several with excitable to clownish tendencies in this and previous competitions. 'And Tomaszewski, Barry,' chuckled Pleat, 'don't forget him.'

Davies replied in his customary tone, suggestive of critical reflection and sudden dyspepsia: 'Ah, but he was a lot better than people gave him credit for.' A quarter of a century on, it still needed to be said.

C h a p t e r 13

Long game

Shortly before the Germans were to receive the world in 1974, startling stories circulated as to who was in charge of their team. Surely their boss was – they were German, after all – whoever that might be. In this case, their manager was the kindly and polite Helmut Schoen who had taken defeat in such good heart on Germany's behalf in 1966. Yet the rumours were that the players had nominated their own man, Franz Beckenbauer, a bit of a smoothie, often refered to as the Kaiser. The sides collapsed into an unseemly row, the players demanding more cash and other benefits in return for their World Cup participation. They buckled down when the management threatened to send the dissidents home and play the reserves. That was more like it.

The Germans could surprise you like this. There they were, a nation which marched in serried ranks with respect for authority, everything, then in a flash it was gone. The order would peel away and they'd become a bit of a rabble. They had come to the 1974 Finals not only as hosts but as the convincing winners of the European Nations Championships from two years earlier, when they'd beaten the Russians by three clear goals. They were up there among the favourites, but at first it was difficult to arouse their interest. Poor in their opening game against Chile, they won thanks to defender Paul Breitner, a bush-haired, moustaschioed Maoist, who took the long route to goal with a shot from 35 yards. Little better against Australia, a nation of cricketers, they then suffered the humiliation of losing in Hamburg to East Germany, the first occasion on which the two countries had played each other. The winning goal was scored near the end, shortly before an announcement over the tannoy wishing the few East Germans allowed to make the trip a safe journey home. You sensed it was made from behind gritted teeth.

But as poorly as they played, they always did either just enough to hang on, or that little extra something to get by. There was an inevitability about them, that somehow they'd slip through. Even the loss against their brothers from across the Wall worked out well – it meant that the East not the West had the difficult task of advancing to a second group consisting of Brazil, Argentina and Holland. It began to look a little clever and calculated. The Germans getting smart like this was a reversal of historical stereotype, at least that which had taken a firm hold in the post-war years. Of course, there had always been an inevitability about them, namely that you could count on them to stamp over those they came into contact with. But then they'd fail. The flawed national character which caused their bullying became their undoing. They overstretched themselves and couldn't see things through. A nation renowned for its consistency, in the end lacked it. The machine went *kaputt*.

It was difficult to put a finger on exactly how West Germany did keep going in the initial stages. Beckenbauer was not at his best, nor Gerd Muller in the forward line. Günther Netzer, having stormed across Wembley so successfully in 1972, had won himself a lucrative transfer to Real Madrid only then to go off the boil. The player who made the difference was their unlikely keeper, Sepp Maier, the Bavarian buffoon.

Maier, of Bayern Munich, had been in the 1966 German squad in England but was put out of the reckoning for the World Cup Final because of injury – luckily for him. The rules protecting keepers hadn't yet seeped so deeply into the consciousness to prevent the German keeper on the day, Hans Tilkowski, being given a fair (or not, as the case might have been) clattering by Geoff Hurst in their midair duels for the ball. He handled them quite bravely, though who was to say they didn't intimidate him from advancing for the crosses that led to two of England's goals.

You wouldn't have fancied Maier's chances of doing any better. Judging by his histrionics against England in León in 1970, he was no braveheart under pressure. He'd thrown himself on the floor after one minor encounter with Francis Lee, head and shoulders smaller than him. Had the fellow no dignity? Against Italy in the semi, Maier was frequently on the ground again, and as the ball bobbled past him into the net. This was similar to the German keeper I'd seen grovelling on the ground in Berlin's Olympic stadium in 1956. They were allegedly a hard people, but you saw at times like this that they weren't.

Maier also looked a joke. He wore ridiculous long black shorts and socks in the same shade which came up to meet them. Probably he didn't want to get cold at those raw times of the season, or was scared his legs would get a bit of a scraping, poor lamb, on days when the goalmouth was hard. The most noticeable feature was his gloves, large padded ones which made his hands look comically large. He wore these under all conditions, not just when it was wet. This was unprecedented and wrong by all established and proven standards. What was the point? Was he worried about the ball slapping his hands, or breaking a nail?

But they worked very well for him in the 1974 tournament. This registered with me when the Germans played Poland in the game that would decide which of them would move on to the final. The Poles had improved to such an extent they were good value to cause another upset. The Frankfurt pitch had been waterlogged by heavy rain. The ground staff soaked a lot of it off but conditions were awful for a keeper. Mud was fine, because it produced the joint effects of glueing down the opposition and making the ball stick in your hands. But surface water on the pitch was another element. The ball skimmed off it like a stone across a pond, seeming to accelerate as it did so. It washed all mud off the ball, making it as handleable as a lively porpoise. It was a struggle to use your feet to get near any threat as it arose. But Maier handled everything impeccably, darting out from his line to make interceptions as if he was walking on the only piece of dry land around. He made a double save from Lato and Gadocha, which was one of the highlights of the World Cup, and Germany went through to the final.

They lined up opposite the Dutch, who had brought their idea of 'total football'. It was a flexible mode of operations, where each player theoretically would cover for any other. The Germans were also exponents of the style but the arch-pragmatist Dutch had refined it. These were the ancient middlemen of Europe. In modern times, they were the continent's truckers, shuttling everyone else's goods from one country to another, the linkers of the parts. You had only to look at their very strange keeper, Jan Jongbloed, initially the Dutch third choice but who stayed once he'd won his chance. If he'd actually ever been a 'youngblood', it would have been back in the spivvy era, because he was thirty-four. A squint suggested he had trouble focusing. He had long sideburns and old-fashioned greasy hair, the type who in the early 1960s you'd have seen hanging around the local snooker hall above Burtons. Maybe someone had organised a street kickabout one day and, in the absence of volunteers, had made him play between the posts. As a sop they let him play 'rush goalie'. He shuttled between the backline of defence and his midfield. You wondered if he would end up in the forward line. He'd scamper back, realising at the last moment he was entitled to use his hands. It worked. When it didn't, his defenders were back to cover for him, in keeping with the dictates of total football. As a form of goalkeeping, though, you wouldn't have said it had any future.

Maier had no one covering for him and had to play far more conventionally. After the Dutch had scored with their penalty in the first minute of the final, the Germans equalised from one themselves, then went ahead 2–1. Maier maintained their tenuous advantage with a classic keeper's plunge at the feet of Johnny Repp near half-time. The Germans then held on, Maier finally saving a full-blooded volley from Jan Neeskens at the far post from a couple of yards out. Henry Kissinger, who was in the stadium, thought he noted a German stereotype from the 1930s at work. He suggested that the Dutch had been the better team but it was the Germans who had summoned the will. The triumph was mainly Maier's. Through the entire competition he made no mistakes. Pat Jennings described him as a 'model of consistency from beginning to end'.

As England's keeper Peter Shilton noted, this quality of consistency was not one readily associated with continental keepers. Maier was obviously untypical of them. From 1966 he didn't miss one game for Bayern Munich till 1979, over 400 in all. A half dozen reserve keepers came to the club and left again without getting a single run-out in the first team. Before the 1974 World Cup finals Bayern had just won the European Cup, and held it for the following two years.

While he was performing with reliability season after season, Maier also managed to be outlandish. As his floppy gloves testified, he was inventive. His general dress sense showed him to be an eccentric. The Germans had given up being a nation of eccentric inventers some time before the Second World War. He could also seem slightly mad. I met him during the 1990 Italian World Cup, in the German training camp as they were preparing for their semi-final against England. He was their goalkeeping coach. While the German players, Jürgen Klinsmann et al., responded to questions on the sunny patio of their hotel, Maier was at a first-floor window shouting jokes and sprinkling water from a glass on to the crowd below. They smiled self-consciously and waved back: 'Ach, that's just Sepp,' they said.

There was a formality to these daily meetings with the media. It was the *Pressestunde*, the 'press hour'. After it one day I approached the German keeper, Bodo Illgner, with a quick query on when he might be available for filming next day. He recoiled at a question being put to him: 'Only in the press hour,' he said anxiously, hoping no one had seen our quite irregular interchange. Maier was without any such inhibition, even during the more sacrosanct moments of training itself. I was standing behind a makeshift goal he'd rigged up one day as he, Beckenbauer and Bertie Vogts put Illgner through his paces. He suddenly danced behind the posts and pulled me into the proceedings. Beckenbauer, accustomed to but still mildly disconcerted by the antics of his old Bayern teammate, looked at Vogts. Vogts looked back before they both shrugged their shoulders: 'Ach . . .' it was just Sepp.

When I spoke to him about his introduction of the gloves for all seasons, he spoke of '*Die Revolution*'. It wasn't a modest choice of words but he said it quietly and matter-of-factly as if, well, that's exactly what it was. When I said it would have been nice if such things had been the convention, say, two or three decades earlier, but that in England sports teachers and other coaches would have banned them under any conditions but rain, he looked confused – as if I was the one from a rigid and inflexible society.

In Germany, after him, Maier clones were spawned, a genera- tion of keepers in long shorts and tight black stockings. The use of all-weather gloves caught on almost everywhere. Our keepers held out with great determination for years, but otherwise it was incredible: a German had set the style in goalkeeping, which was, by right, essentially British. Short of, say, Volkswagen buying Rolls-Royce, nothing more silly could be imagined.

○   ○   ○

In my last year at Sussex a student put himself up for election as president of the student union, walking around campus in a Second World War German army helmet and black leather miniskirt. He'd been the star turn on 'University Challenge' when he had answered several questions on religion. Running against the normal block ticket organised by the Broad Left, he won by a landslide. Some declared this the 'end of the '60s', albeit five years late; others that it was time for a change in the stagnant structure of things, even if it meant voting in a loony.

Mrs Thatcher had not long won the vote to be the new leader of the Conservative Party. As the news had come through, I passed one of my lecturers running from the campus bar to use the phone. 'They'll never get back in now,' he shouted, and we agreed, with no small element of glee. He later went on to become mayor of Brighton, municipal politics being the only area where the Labour Party was to enjoy any association with power for many years. My international relations course, meanwhile, had run up against the antics of the large and clever companies that were operating around the world. What exactly had ITT's role been in the overthrow of Allende in Chile? Firms that concerned themselves with the simple production of bananas were frequently able to change governments in countries like Costa Rica and Panama. But every time you tried to read about them, the academic text was clogged with mysterious equations and economic terms designed to exclude the ill-educated from the club. I went on to find out what they were all about at the London School of Economics. There was no hint of '60s-style barricades, even though for four years unemployment had been over one million, the figure once thought likely to trigger conflagration. But as with German goalkeepers and their floppy all-weather gloves, the 'revolution' was coming from an unexpected quarter.

The system was stumped. When asked why inflation was going up, prime minister Jim Callaghan said, 'Because prices are rising.' The theories of John Maynard Keynes – Bloomsbury Group fellow, lived, what, 400 yards west of the Finsbury borough line? – had been used to run the economy since the war. For densely logical reasons, they stated that inflation and unemployment couldn't happen together. But they were. I'd recently taken a holiday in the USA, where an economics professor at Stanford University whom I'd never previously met, blurted out to me, clearly concerned: 'Do you realize you're inflating at 25 per cent?'

It wasn't something I'd taken full and grave stock of, but serious-minded people in the economics profession had. From the wings, the 'monetarists' said inflation was caused simply because there was too much money sloshing around. Take it out of people's pockets, they said, unpamper them with a dose of austerity and then, when they couldn't buy anything, just watch prices come down. Britons and the world needed to stand on their own two feet, with their backs to the wall and noses to the grindstone. It would put them through some painful contortions at first, but they'd appreciate the benefit eventually.

My LSE lecturers who believed in this walked with a spring in their step, the missionary ring of confidence about them. Keynes was out, Milton Friedman in. We spoke less about unemployment than about the individual's choices between work and leisure. One lecturer pronounced it 'lee-shur'. I assumed he was American and had possibly studied in Chicago under Friedman. It turned out that he came from Nottingham, no nearer to the US Midwest than the English east Midlands. But he was a nice fellow and I'd have said clearly captivated by the land of happy food and people across the Atlantic. He drew a graph which, scientifically as far as we knew, proved the forty-hour week achieved by the unions over years of proletarian struggle was to the workers' disadvantage. An Italian woman taking the course, a member of the Communist Party in her homeland, was dumbstruck. Another lecturer whom we thought was going to teach us never did, though we were required to buy advance, photostated copies of his new textbook. It was breathless stuff. He, a Professor Alan Walters, was away advising Mrs Thatcher on her path to power. The first time I saw a picture of him was many years later when he appeared on the steps of Downing Street amid reports that Mrs Thatcher's chancellor of the exchequer, Nigel Lawson, was going to resign as a result of his interference.

○   ○   ○

In the early to mid-'70s, England and Britain's goalkeepers were performing brilliantly but beginning to look a little passé. As Maier was touting his gloves around the globe, we witnessed Peter Shilton's superb save from Kenny Dalglish of Scotland in the 1973 international at Wembley. The ball flew across him as he flung himself left, but too high for him to reach with his left hand. His right arm, therefore, came round in an arc and palmed the ball away. A photographer captured the instant the ball made contact with Shilton's hand, quaintly clad in black wool.

But, so what? Our keepers remained supreme in our post-Tomaszewskian isolation. There was not only Shilton but Ray Clemence of Liverpool. He was impeccable in the air, as he'd shown in the 1971 Cup Final against Arsenal – he'd be out, catch the ball safely and hang on to it in spite of mid-air collisions. Questions were asked on that day about his modest goalkick, which led a couple of passes later to the winning goal from Arsenal's Charlie George (Islington boy, Holloway school), but his errors were rare. He had what his Liverpool boss, Bill Shankly, called a goalkeeper's 'desperate courage'. After Ramsey's departure from the England manager's job, Don Revie favoured him to Shilton.

Then what of those behind them? Joe Corrigan – at 6 feet 4 inches and 15 stone – had laboured under the weight of popular expectation at Manchester City caused by his following in the footsteps of Frank Swift and Bert Trautmann, but had come through. When his confidence dropped in his earlier days at the club, he was loaned to Shrewsbury, managed by Harry Gregg.

He managed to win nine England caps despite the presence of Shilton and Clemence. Alas, Jimmy Montgomery was never to play in an international. His instinctive double save which won the 1973 Cup Final for Second Division Sunderland against First Division Leeds was what most people remembered him for. Thus, he became England's latest greatest uncapped keeper. There was that feeling again, that wherever you looked at England's keepers, they were all great.

In the middle of England's international exile, its clubs moved to unprecedented success. From 1977 to 1981, Liverpool with Clemence won the European Cup three times, Nottingham Forest with Shilton twice. Aston Villa were European champions in 1982. Keeper Jimmy Rimmer had to go off injured after a couple of minutes – the game was up, you'd have thought. But reserve keeper Nigel Spink stepped in, unknown south of the Watford Gap, to plug the breach. It all came awkwardly close to suggesting that isolation was where England performed best, and belonged. As the national team failed to qualify again for the World Cup (the 1978 finals to be held in Argentina), some of the fans revelled in it. In October 1977, the more radical among them made their first appearance in national colours, as they advanced to beat up mighty Luxembourg.

The scale of the violence on the terraces had captured widescale public attention when Leeds lost to Bayern in the 1975 European Cup Final in Paris. As the Leeds fans ran riot, the French police turned the dogs on them. English hooliganism at the international level, however, was to some extent inspired by that of the Scots. Every second year for some while, it seemed, hairy inebriates in kilts and wrapped in the cross of St Andrew had come to terrorise old ladies in Baker Street station and off-licences within several miles of Wembley stadium. Matters reached a peak for the Scots in 1977. Their post-match demolition of the goalposts earned the denunciation 'animals' from Brian Clough. As with his statements four years earlier about Poland's keeper, what came to pass wasn't wholly desirable. Infuriated at the violation of their turf, England's hooligans were soon engaged in equally bestial acts on a far wider foreign front.

There was one difference. Once England's fans began to give vent to their feelings, they took the form of xenophobia. Every and anyone out there in the great foreign unknown was a target. The Scots were not obvious xenophobes – they only really had a problem with the English. They got on rather well with other foreigners, as they'd proved when in 1974 Scotland had been the only British representatives at the German World Cup Finals. The language barrier was an initial problem but when you'd overcome that with the clinking of glasses, a good time could be had by all.

In 1978, Scotland was again the only British country to qualify for the World Cup. Not so many of their fans as had gone to Germany could make it to Argentina. It was mystifyingly distant. There was some initial suggestion in the Scottish press that their team was now 'off to Rio'. One group of supporters investigated the chances of hiring a submarine to get to wherever on earth it was they were heading. But those hardy souls who did make it were immediately able to make a nonsense of any past 'animal' comments. To any Europeans they met, they could show they were nothing like the English, who had lately been causing so much continental dismay. In the case of the Latin Americans they caroused with, there was a similar if subtly different job to be done. The people of Latin America had the unfortunate tendency to call anyone from Britain *inglés*. The Scots were able to explain how entirely different they were.

The Scottish team were a disappointment. Their send-off to Argentina, when manager Ally MacLeod organised what came across as an advance mass victory celebration, was embarrassing. The huge expectations it placed on the team were far too much to carry, not least by goalkeeper Alan Rough. Anyone who watched him play regularly for his club, Partick Thistle, knew his performances were commendable. But the jump from Maryhill in Glasgow to the World Cup in Argentina was a big one. Nevertheless, the Scots left many friends in their wake. By contrast, England's clubs were unable to stop winning when they took to the international road, while their fans created a welter of bad feeling.

The 1978 World Cup also underscored the far more vaunted prospects for Scottish diplomacy *vis-à-vis* the English. Argentina was not simply the second successive tournament when the Scots had been the sole emissaries of Britain, but also that when they had enjoyed the simple pleasures of going it alone. Their qualification in 1974 and 1978, taken with the small matter of their awareness of how much Scotland was contributing to the British exchequer in North Sea oil revenues, fuelled the Scots' confidence that they were truly ready to go their separate way. Less than a year later in spring 1979, as the last of their straggling fans were probably still making their way back home from Argentina, the site of Scotland's new national assembly was being prepared as the British general elections were called.

o   o   o

Argentina's victory in the World Cup provided the boost to national morale that its military rulers wanted. They were engaged in their 'dirty war' against the country's guerrillas – or anyone who fitted a very wide definition of left-wing – and welcomed the popular distraction. You could see the delight of the normally po-faced president, General Jorge Videla, known as 'the Bone', as he presented the team their winners' medals and gave a stiffly exaggerated thumbs-up. I'd been given a job working on a publication in London writing about Latin America. When its correspondent in Buenos Aires, an Argentine, joined the ranks of those 'disappeared' by the military, people in the office who knew him were in tears. Most of those I worked with were experts on the large or recently topical Latin American countries: Brazil and Mexico, Argentina, Chile in the wake of Allende, Bolivia as a result of Ché. Nothing much was happening in Central America so they gave me, as the new boy, the task of covering it. Nicaragua blew up straightaway.

Its president, General Anastasio Somoza, was pinned back on his line in the capital, Managua. Guerrillas of the Sandinista Liberation Front were closing in, attempting to overthrow his family dynasty which had ruled since the 1930s. He was a busy man and I waited all day to speak to him in his bunker, a line of huts made of one reinforced material or another, in a military compound next to the Inter-Continental hotel. At lunchtime his public relations man took me to eat at an expensive country club, where Argentine-sized chunks of best fillet steak featured on the menu. From the quiet and detached atmosphere, it was impossible to detect there was a war going on. The battle, the PR-man told me, was not of rich versus poor, but the Somoza family's determined struggle against communism. We drove back to the bunker through the ruined centre of Managua, destroyed by an earthquake seven years before and yet to be rebuilt. Quantities of the foreign aid that flowed in for the purpose had failed to elude the safe hands of the Somozas and their friends.

The president saw me in the early evening and apologised for the delay. So much of his time was being taken up, he suggested, because there was the wrong man in the White House. The USA had been Nicaragua's oldest ally against communism but now President Jimmy Carter wittered on about 'human rights'. It needed someone again in Washington who saw the world as it was, sharply divided along lines of 'East versus West'. Nicaragua was part of that crisis and he was prepared to stand and slog it out alone if others wouldn't. After his brief discourse on those priests and other members of the Catholic church in the region who had latched on to the guerrilla cause, I had to leave saying I had a plane to catch to Costa Rica in 20 minutes. His son, dressed in army fatigues and highly polished boots laced over the ankle, in his capacity as head of the elite presidential guard, shouted out to me not to worry as I was ushered towards the fleet of white Mercedes lined up outside the bunker. They'd phone ahead to the airport and have the plane held, he said: 'Call a strike or something.'

Mrs Thatcher won the election a month later, promising a singular slog of blood, sweat and tears on behalf of a beleaguered Britain. Steep-piled rubbish in the streets and unburied bodies in the morgue during the previous winter handed her what she took to be a popular mandate to make war on the carping unions. She would emphasise not the principles of collectivism but of self-reliance and taking the medicine. She decreed we would live by the dictates of neo-classical economics – or looked at another way, the classic values of the goalkeeper.

Peter Shilton had been bought by Brian Clough, manager of Nottingham Forest, two seasons earlier. From Leicester, Shilton had at first followed Banks's path to Stoke for a fee of about £340,000, three times the record for a British keeper. Leicester's 'madness', therefore, at having sold Banks to give Shilton his chance at the age of seventeen, didn't look quite so deranged.

Shilton's performances were reckoned at Leicester to have been worth maybe a dozen league points a season. Clough bought him for £273,000, agreeing to pay him £20,000 a year, more than any other player at the club. Keepers were traditionally undervalued, he said, when eyebrows were raised, and Shilton was entitled to every penny. The word was, however, he'd offered his new signing a salary of £15,000. He'd been chivied, and niggled, into giving more by Shilton's tireless negotiation over detail, 'his extra 10 per cents for this and that'.

Shilton provided ample percentage returns. When Clough claimed publicly that buying Shilton had rescued the keeper from obscurity, Shilton responded that Clough's only success without him would have been the league championship he'd won with Derby earlier in the decade. With Shilton making the difference, Nottingham Forest soon won the championship for Clough again, a clear seven points above Liverpool. They qualified for the European Cup the next season, therefore, and proceeded to win it. Their victory came just a few days after that which brought Mrs Thatcher to power

Shilton was a phenonemon. Keepers before him faced the world in determined fashion but took things more or less as they found them. Some spoke up for themselves. After the war, Frank Swift and Ted Ditchbourn had been advocates of players' rights, appealing for a sense of fairness from the game's overlords to pay players more than a few quid a week. This put their bosses' backs up (nothing wrong with that) but without wheedling much out of them. In the 1960s Bert Trautmann had left the game, a victim of its meanness, after Manchester City's pay offer of £35 a week.

Shilton took responsibility for himself in a manner not seen before. He had the nerve to annoy someone as verbally forceful as Clough but, knowing his worth, made sure to get something out of it. A gambler – to his cost when it came to the horses – he took risks that paid off. And what if he did aim to make a profit? There was no shame in that, he suggested. It was an honest recognition of the times in which we lived. Weren't we all, in the end, in it for the money?

Shilton comported himself in his work in the same way as he bargained. In training he went on and on, long after the other players had left for the day and their lunchtime Wimpy, till he got it right, or till it hurt. Clough adopted his haughty ''ay, young man' tone, ordering him to 'get in the bath, Peter'. Clough's assistant Peter Taylor, a former goalkeeper, tried gentle persuasion. When this got nowhere, he became frustrated and called Shilton an 'obsessive'. Shilton didn't disagree, and carried on.

At the end of the 1980 season, Nottingham Forest won the European Cup again. Opponents Hamburg had Kevin Keegan playing in European footballer of the year form and the odds in their favour. Nottingham Forest slipped in an earlyish goal and then as good as left it to Shilton. It was one, among many, of his most brilliant games and an example of how the sweat and the effort could be made to pay off. Mrs Thatcher, meanwhile, ran the country on four hours' sleep a night, a firm believer herself in the principle of 'if it hurts, it's good for you'. The effect wasn't lost on the country, as unemployment climbed to over two million.

o   o   o

The prime minister honed her accent – as Sir Alf Ramsey had done – to suggest disdain and a bit of culture, and set out to confront her detractors on domestic and foreign fronts. Wherever you looked, the enemy was communism. It was in our car factories and mines. In western Europe you could feel the Soviet Union's pernicious influence seeping through the Wall. So many of the Europeans were social democrats, group people, who loved big corporatist blocs and wasting your money running them. They were naturally inclined towards the European Community – they were communalists. You only had to say the word to hear how suspicious it sounded.

Shilton-style, she chivied the Europeans in her negotiations on the community's budget, insisting on that extra percentage for Britain: 'Half a loaf?' No thank you. At times when they wouldn't agree, it didn't matter because it justified the wisdom we'd acquired from history. Continental Europe caused trouble; we sorted it out. At times when they couldn't understand this, we were happy to step back and let them stew. If we found ourselves in a minority of one, we were well used to that. Mrs Thatcher reported back her simple message: who would rid us of these turbulent Europeans?

'We will, luv,' came the enthusiastic response from the football terraces. 'No worries.' Things had reached such a desperate international pass that England now lost to Norway. It meant possible elimination from another World Cup, the 1982 finals scheduled for Spain. But taking the cue from their leader, the doubtless 'tiny minority' of fans who were prepared to go out on a radical limb said, well, who needed to be a member of anyone else's lousy club anyway? In May 1981 England went to play Switzerland. The Swiss weren't in 'Europe', that was to say the Community, not that we'd have cared or known. They were foreigners and that'd do. When they'd beaten us in Basle a few heads and a lot of their flashy shop windows were kicked in (funny how they looked so much nicer than ours).

On the broad international stage, Mrs Thatcher had found someone she could identify with in Washington. Jimmy Carter's hand-wringing guilt complexes over human rights gave way to Ronald Reagan. He espoused traditional values, those of Main Street in small town USA. The prime minister was from small town England, daughter of a Lincolnshire grocer whose shop wasn't that many turnings away from Grantham high street. The two leaders held comparable views on unions – they were perfectly fine elsewhere, in places like Poland, where Solidarity was taking on the communist regime. Between them, they recognised a communist threat when it was stealthily making for the western goalmouth. Central America's left-wing guerrillas, who had by now seized power in Nicaragua, had prompted a similar uprising in El Salvador. If you looked at the map, President Reagan declaimed, El Salvador was only as far from the US–Mexican frontier, as that border was from Washington DC. My God, the enemy was almost upon us. We had to advance to narrow the angle as it bore down on freedom's net. In El Salvador, the president announced, he'd draw his 'line in the dirt'.

He found sturdy back-up support in the Vatican. Five years on from Tomaszewski, the Poles had carved out the shape of an impressive goalkeeping tradition by getting one of their own voted into the hallowed number one spot in Rome – Karol Wojtyla, Cracow boy, had played in goal as a youth. When the puff of smoke went up, his appearance at the top of the team-sheet was a surprise, but he'd adapted well to the unfamiliar conditions. He was a bit smiley and liked playing to the crowd a lot, which suited the Italian style. He looked with favour on Reagan's support for Solidarity in his homeland. He wasn't one for the young red priests, so-called, who backed left-wing guerrillas in the president's Latin American backyard and he let his distaste be known. Archbishop Oscar Romero of San Salvador, an elderly theologian of no radical origin but who had angered the military in his Sunday sermons on a better deal for the poor, told me in his seminary how he felt the Pope understood him but was constrained, by ecclesiastical diplomacy, from saying so. A year later someone from the military death squads shot the archbishop at his altar. The Vatican condemned the murder but whoever did it felt they had allies in both Washington and Rome.

By 1982 the El Salvador war was at its height. President Reagan insisted it was an East–West issue, Mrs Thatcher agreed and the newspapers and networks followed. The BBC sent their man down from Washington. He wore a light-coloured suit. It was possibly white, and understandably a little grubby in the tropical heat. He told me he'd been sent to find the 'bang, bang', the action of the Salvadorean conflict. A night or so later I found him slumped alone in a hotel bar armchair, disconsolate that ITV's man knew every day where to find the bang, bang, while he seemed to go only in the wrong direction. I put it down to his being spoiled in Washington on State Department briefings and other easy news. Being a war correspondent was probably not his thing.

I went to watch the El Salvador football team train on a university pitch near town. They'd qualified for the World Cup three months hence. The US networks weren't interested, nor anyone else from the UK. The only other media representation there was a crew from a Protestant TV station in Holland. They shot a bit of footage but it was also a night off for them. Later I shared the hotel lift with their reporter; we agreed the Salvadorean team would get slaughtered when they reached Spain. In press conferences he would routinely ask blunt questions of characters like the US ambassador. Given the state of the country and the mayhem wrought by the army, why didn't Washington withdraw support for the military right away? Early next morning, news filtered through that the Dutchmen had had a rendezvous with the guerrillas outside town to spend a day and night or so filming in their camps. The army followed and ambushed them as they headed off the road and into the hills. A couple of hours later, two American photographers and I went to where the 'incident' was said to have happened. There were only a few scraps of food, European-made clothing and a bullet case or two to suggest it had. The army put the bodies on show in the evening, a memorandum to the foreign press that it didn't want the war portrayed in romantic terms of rich against poor, but to reflect the hard realities of the struggle between East and West.

The leader of the Salvadorean right agreed to an interview shortly before I left. Major Roberto D'Aubuisson, 'Blowtorch Bob' as he was known because of his supposed sophistication in interrogation techniques, was a small fellow with a pock-marked face and was thought to know who was behind the death of Archbishop Romero. People who said such a thing were 'communists and criminals', he responded, 'animals'. Once we'd got all that out of the way, he was charm itself. He threw his young kids into the swimming pool by which we'd been sitting amid the bougainvillaea, to make a fetching family scene for a Thames TV camera crew. On football he struck a defiant nationalist pose. 'Just you see if El Salvador meet England in Spain. We will win.' In the pleasant mood and ambience, I took it he was joking and responded accordingly. 'Don't laugh,' he said quietly, and I thought it interesting how quickly I could remove all evidence of mirth from my face.

As with that going on in Argentina, El Salvadors was a dirty war. One of the dirtiest wars he'd come across, said photographer Don McCullin who had seen Cyprus, the Nigerian civil war after the breakaway of Biafra in 1967, Vietnam and others. McCullin (Islington boy, from Yonge Park at the back of the Finsbury Park Astoria) had broken several ribs falling through a roof on the trail of a police operation and had lain for hours until his absence at the hotel was noticed. Our flight back home via Miami was for him an especially long one, though it took only little more than half a day and it was remarkable how the world could change in that time. Central America had been the front-page news, yet for all Mrs Thatcher's willingness to help the US president defend his line, it was not a war to win her an election at home. Facing off an assumed communist threat in an area where Britain had no real interest wouldn't divert the electorate's gaze from the crisis of unemployment. But the very cause and a front-page crisis to drive Central America off the media map had arisen by the time I'd landed back at Gatwick.

It was Argentina that provided it. If anything, it was a country even further away. We'd been getting on rather well, surprisingly, since the stormy game in the World Cup quarter-finals in 1966. Ossie Ardiles and Rickie Villa from Argentina's 1978 squad of world champions had come to play for Spurs. Everyone loved the cutely Latin way Ossie said 'Tot-ten-hum' and how Villa's mazy dribble had squeezed the winner past Joe Corrigan in the 1981 Cup Final replay. Then the Argentine military regime had ruined it.

Actually, scrap-metal dealers had started the trouble. They were always a marginal lot, operating at the fringes of legality. Down our way they made their bundle of cash weighing up lead and copper in the mornings – no questions asked as to how it had been accumulated the night before – then lost it in the bookie's on the corner of Burgh Street in the afternoon. The taxman never had a chance of taking his share. But this lot were operating much further afield than south of Danbury Street and the Island Queen. They'd landed on the remote isles of South Georgia, as if they rather than our queen had sovereignty over them. Argentina's generals followed up by invading the Falkland Islands days later.

The Foreign Office had taken its eye off the ball. The Falklands had always been a relatively easy imperial cross to deal with and the Argentines – for all their occasional bad-mouthing and whining over islands they called the Malvinas – could usually be trusted not to follow through. Lord Carrington, the foreign secretary, resigned with the disgrace of it. Everyone knew it was his FO team that was to blame, that he couldn't possibly be expected to know everything and take all responsibility on his shoulders, but he said he should. It seemed a quaint gesture from a bygone age.

Few Britons knew where the Falklands were. Maps were few and far between. Reports suggested that wily Argentines had been into places like Foyles some weeks before and bought every cartographic representation of Port Stanley and Goose Green there was. Opinion polls showed many people thought Argentina had stormed islands off the coast of Scotland. No small proportion of their number were equally unsure whether anything should be done to save them.

Britain's formal retreat from greatness had begun thirty-five years before with the 'loss of India', so the question was why a stand should be made now over this boggy imperial remnant. But a special Saturday session of Parliament was convened and strong suggestions made that Mrs Thatcher's government would fall if no action was taken. When the arguments were weighed, it was decided there was little alternative but for Britain to advance from its line. The population of 1,500 or so Falklanders didn't want to be ruled by Buenos Aires. This might not have been for the most enlightened reasons – they regarded Argentines, rather as Gibraltarians viewed Spaniards, as dusky, untrustworthy dagos – but advocates of more progressive thinking were outflanked by the simple truth that the Argentine regime was very nasty. They threw tortured leftists out of planes, alive, over the mouth of the River Plate. Their bodies washed up on beaches, even troubling the Argentine and Uruguayan upper middle class on whose behalf such action had been taken. For the Argentine military the populist capital made from the World Cup triumph four years earlier had been exhausted. The generals needed something else to keep them alive and this was it.

It was touch and go, again, whether we'd have to stand on our own. The USA wavered – it often did. It had its Latin allies and interests in the Americas to think of. The Argentine military had sent advisers to support Washington in Central America, which was more than Britain had. Yet Mrs Thatcher had proved the USA's truest ally in Europe. That was the front line of the world's conflict, behind which the USA played backstop (their slowly emerging interest in football had done little to suggest they'd ever have what it took to be called goalkeepers). Henry Kissinger bluntly summarised the axis of world power as running from Moscow, through western Europe to Washington. Was Latin America important? Of course it was, he said: 'like a dagger pointed at the heart of Antarctica.' On the basis of a shrewd definition of where its interests lay, the USA made its decision to back Britain. Much cloudy talk was to ensue of the president and queen's love of horses and other manifestations of the 'special relationship'.

As the task force made its way to the South Atlantic, TV reports were sent back of soldiers relaxing and celebrating on board the ships. They were the first for more than a generation sent to a 'real war', as opposed to the muckier one in Northern Ireland. There were a lot of cheers among the soldiers at the prospect of smashing a foreign enemy – the work, after all, they were contracted to do. They looked and sounded not a lot different from some of England's football fans crossing the Channel to battle things out on the continent. There may well have been more than a few among them with such experience. The overseas battle in support of Mrs Thatcher's world view had taken the fight to the streets of Basle as well as Belfast, Luxembourg as well as Londonderry. Now she'd given her armies a proper job to do.

The world could only lend its support. The Soviet Union conducted a large amount of trade with Argentina but the military government was so awful, that had Moscow rallied to its aid it would have been one of its most startling historic compromises since the 1939 Ribbentrop pact. There was insignificant support from fellow Latin American countries like Venezuela. Others like Mexico tagged along for sentiment's sake, while reminding Buenos Aires how rich polo-playing Argentines had fancied they had more in common with Europe than their own continent. The Argentine junta was abandoned to face the troops yomping across the Falklands mud from San Carlos bay. The final collapse came when they heard the gurkhas, with their kukhris, were on their way, too.

After its withdrawal, the military government in Buenos Aires collapsed and Argentina returned to liberal democracy. Mrs Thatcher won an overwhelming victory at the polls a year later. From the popular British perspective, the Falklands proved how it paid to 'stand up to tyrants'. This was something we'd always felt we stood for – in isolation, when need be. A quarter of a century before, at the time of Suez, there'd been none so deaf as those others who wouldn't listen. They had claimed there was a new way of doing things, the USA's and USSR's way. Each justified itself as vehemently as the other in terms of being anti-imperialist, while seeking to carve up the world between them. In 1956 from both the official British view and that of the majority which supported the defence of 'our territory', there was a set of enduring values which needed to be defended. They'd said then we'd been mad, when from the island standpoint we knew it was the others who were crazy. It took them a while, but 1982 enforced a reckoning and they came round and saw the sense of it. It proved, in the British mind, we had been right all along.

England kicked off at the World Cup in Spain two days after Port Stanley was recaptured. They had made it only because in the qualifying stages, the Swiss, who had been so badly mauled by England's hooligans, retained their neutrality by surprisingly beating Romania in Bucharest. England, therefore, slipped through to the final stages in spite of themselves, though amid speculation of withdrawal should they ever run up against Argentina. With little to choose between Clemence and Shilton, England manager Ron Greenwood alternated them in pre-Spain games. When a choice finally had to be made, the single-minded drive of Shilton won selection. It was, however, to be Pat Jennings, thirty-six, who had the most enjoyable competition of the British keepers, playing well when Northern Ireland caused one of the bigger shocks by beating the hosts 1–0 in Valencia.

A week or so into the competition, I'd gone to Islington to visit some friends, new entrants to the borough. They lived in the formerly shady environs of Chapel Market at the back of the Agricultural Hall. In fact, the area still hadn't changed much but, having mentioned this once, I could tell it was not a fruitful theme of conversation. I resorted to first principles of keeping myself to myself and slipped out between the dessert and coffee to see how Scotland were coping with Brazil.

Since Ronnie Simpson there had been a succession of Scottish keepers who performed well enough for their clubs but didn't make the step up to international class. The only real exception was David Harvey of Leeds who had done well in Germany in 1974. Otherwise, Scottish keepers bore the exaggerated hopes of the fans on their shoulders and, accordingly, stood rooted to the spot as the ball flashed by them. The Scots had been the most convincing of the British teams in qualifying for Spain, and were the first to see their challenge fizzle out when they got there. Their identity revealed over the previous eight years – group types, who related well with the world, as opposed to dogged isolationists who didn't – had been reflected in their goalkeeping. In the four years since the finals in Argentina, they hadn't found anyone to replace

Alan Rough. He was by no means to blame for the actions of his teammates but, at a time when last-ditch heroics were needed, he stood bemused as Brazilian shots zoomed into the net.

My absence from the table had not hampered the flow of conversation. Others present included a former student activist from the barricades of 1968 and, what with the implications to weigh of the Falklands on the configuration of world politics, there was plenty to discuss. 'What's the score?' said the Third World editor of a prestigious national broadsheet on my return. The inquiry was a little breathless for someone who had given no previous indication that she knew who was playing, or in what competition, and so I suspected I was being mildly patronised. The others were far from unfriendly but made no attempt to seem interested, which was fair enough because you knew they weren't remotely.

Shilton gamely conceded only one goal in five matches. England did manage a goalless draw against West Germany but they needed a win and it was the old adversary who went through. Sepp Maier's lengthy career had been ended by a car accident and the Germans had a new keeper in Harald Schumacher. Where Maier had been endearingly eccentric, Schumacher came across as a posturing braggart. His famous flying tackle on France's Battiston in the semi-final did not curb his swagger in the least and his offer to pay his victim's dental bills – Battiston's jaw had been broken – endeared him to no one. Nor did his extravagant claim to be the greatest keeper in the world. The fates immediately contrived his comeuppance in the World Cup Final. The outcome was both a German defeat and an endorsement of the old goalkeeping values of quietness and modesty. Astoundingly, the keeper who displayed them was Italian.

Throughout his career, Dino Zoff's performances were rarely exciting. He was a kind of Gil Merrick of Italian goalkeeping. He'd always known, he said, that he wanted to play the position and it never occurred to him to do anything else. He appeared unflappable and didn't fit the broad category of 'Italian' at all. Geographically he only just made it: he was almost a Slav, from Friuli in the north-east near Gorizia, where Tito's partizans glared down from the hills on to the British troops stationed there after the war. It got pretty cold in that area, and was not a place where relaxed Italian pavement life and expansive conversation was a year-round feature.

Three years after their triumph in Spain, Italy came to Mexico, where I was based, to get some match practice at altitude for the following year's World Cup. Their first game was to be against England, which, originally scheduled as an innocuous friendly, had been transformed into a full-scale healing exercise after the Heysel disaster only a couple of days earlier. The Italian players stood around outside their hotel awaiting their coach to the Azteca stadium. Most chatted, mingled with journalists or, as in the case of Paolo Rossi, beetled off for a few minutes' shopping in Aca Joe's. Zoff, present in a coaching role, stood by the glass frontage of the hotel, managing to be both within the milling group and without it at the same time. He didn't say a word that I saw or heard, signed autographs for any Mexican kids who approached him, then returned to peering above the heads of those around him looking for his route of escape. Nothing would have made him happier than to be on the team bus and gone.

Juventus had bought him for £280,000, a world record for a keeper in 1972, when he'd been playing for Naples. Cold and foggy Turin was his kind of place. He once went 903 minutes for Juventus without a goal going past him. He was said to have no nerves, which annoyed him. He agreed he was calm but his objective, he pointed out, was to appear strong. The implication that this came naturally smacked of people taking him for granted. It was enough to make a keeper glad to let a goal in to show what he did was far from easy. He'd gone 1,143 minutes without conceding a goal in international matches when Haiti, of all countries, managed to get one past him in the 1974 World Cup in Germany. He described it as a 'relief'.

Zoff was written off after the Argentine World Cup in 1978. Two Dutch strikes from far out of his penalty area beat him in the semi-final. The new Adidas ball being used dipped and swerved more than ever and, at thirty-six, Zoff was thought not equal to the challenge. But four years later he was back, in Spain and as Italian captain. His and his team's chances as they struggled in their early games – and were fortunate not to be eliminated by Cameroon – were about as bright as the dull grey sweater he had made his trademark. His career, as successful as it had been with a line of international caps, Italian trophies and European cups, was believed to be in its twilight days.

Pat Jennings, however, had remarked two years earlier how impressed he had been by Zoff's goalkeeping. Jennings had not long been subject to one of those weird decisions which afflict football managers when it comes to goalkeepers. Eamon Dunphy, in his book *Only a Game?* about life as a footballer at Millwall, had said he didn't rate old goalkeepers as trainers since they didn't understand the rest of the team. There was no reason to doubt that, nor, by extension, that players from other positions knew bugger-all about goalkeeping. Why else would Tommy Docherty have thought of replacing Bonetti in his prime with his brief purchase in 1966 of Alex Stepney? And just as Leicester in 1967 had announced to Gordon Banks that they had no further use for him, so Spurs eleven years later told Jennings they were prepared to let him go. Jennings was upset by this and with poetic justice snapped up by Tottenham's north London rival Arsenal, to serve seasons yet of productive time. In 1980 Arsenal had beaten Juventus in the semi-final of the European Cup Winners' Cup, when Zoff in the opposite goal had played superbly. It was 'not only his shotstopping' that was first class, noted Jennings, but also the stuff of which rounded goalkeeping performances were made: 'his handling of crosses and overall command of his goalmouth'.

In the Spain World Cup, Zoff held the backline till the rest of the Italian team decided to stir themselves. When they did, they had to beat Argentina and Brazil. A save Zoff made to stop Brazil equalising in the tense closing stages, when composure must have been nearly impossible to maintain, was breathtaking. Italy won through to the final against the Germans. Zoff kept a consummate cool in an especially tense goalless first half until the Italians gradually asserted authority in the second. Only five minutes before the end did he show signs of wavering. He almost collapsed with the awareness of what he'd achieved – World Cup victory, perfectly timed for the end of his career.

o   o   o

Whatever could have been expected of Zoff, he'd lived up to it. He respected British goalkeepers, whom he said were generally better than their Italian counterparts. He couldn't have spoken more highly of Banks, Shilton and Jennings, but in 1982 he showed he could perform consistently as well as any.

Since I'd first visited Italy in the early 1950s, it had always been a chaotic and relatively poor country. As for its image inherited from the war, it had been the unserious enemy, the one that had never wanted to put up a fight, the one for which the number 1 on the back of the jersey really was substitute for a backbone. If out of that and its chaos it could produce a goalkeeper to match ours in matters of the long game, there were no tellings what it might get up to next.

Four years later the Italians took a closer look at their national accounts and decided they'd got a few of their figures wrong. In the depths of southern Europe, they weren't so poor at all. There was that chaotic 'black economy' of theirs, the small undeclared businesses, Lambretta workshops, Marlboro sellers by the Neapolitan harbour gates and myriad fiddles no one declared but for many comprised a living. When they estimated what it was worth, added it in and compared their figures to those of the world's oldest industrial society, they found – right in the middle of Mrs Thatcher's economic miracle – that the Italian economy had surpassed that of Britain. '*Il Sorpasso*', they called it, a special term to mark the moment, which showed they thought it something well worth celebrating.

Chapter 14

Um Goleiro Inglês

On the new runway, built by the Cubans, at Point Salines airport in Grenada, US troops waited to be loaded on to the large transport carriers that had come to take them home. Above the scream of the jet engines, they cheered when one of their commanding officers shouted to them: wouldn't they like to drop in on Havana on the way? I asked the general in charge whether for the USA the successful outcome of the invasion of the island in October 1983 had healed the scar of Vietnam. He said it had, 'not that there was any scar' in the first place. Then he added, surprised: 'You're British! . . . I love your accent.' (I hadn't thought there were still Americans who said this.) 'And we still love your "Iron Lady", even though she got it wrong on this one.'

Mrs Thatcher's hopes for an alliance of the English-speaking peoples both to push ahead with the Cold War and to counter distasteful involvements with the babbling continentals, were far from new. Churchill had wanted it, as had Macmillan in the thrusting days of Kennedy. We were relatively old and doddery, but wise and could advise. There was an implicit dignity to

273

this, a response to those who scurrilously suggested we acted like nothing more than the fifty-first state – even though the feasibility of such an arrangement had allegedly been pondered by one of Harold Wilson's Labour governments. Mrs Thatcher's grandiose post-Falklands notions had gone the way of all flesh, however, when she tried to assert Britain's role as goalkeeper of the Caribbean.

In Grenada, at the southern extent of the Windwards, Maurice Bishop's New Jewel Movement had pushed out the old government of Eric Gairy in 1979. Gairy, a veteran trade union leader, took over when the British departed, though he was to spend a good deal of time away from home attending international summits on unidentified flying objects. With his gaze distracted, his opponents had seized power. Bishop and the NJM were a funky mix of nationalist and left-wing policies and comprised a generational rebellion against the Caribbean leaders who succeeded the British. These were diligent, church-going people, many of whose age group had come to settle and work in Britain from 1948, but they were relatively conservative, take-it-as-you-find-it types whom Bishop enjoyed annoying. Tom Adams, prime minister of neighbouring Barbados, he refered to as 'Uncle Tom'.

He annoyed Washington, too, with his plans for the new airport. For its living Grenada depended on such crops as nutmeg and the regular visit to St Georges' harbour of the white refrigerated ship sent by Geest to take its bananas to Europe. Tourism was underdeveloped, said Bishop, as he sought funds for the airport in the west, failed to get them and accepted the Cubans' offer to build it. At the same time, not wishing to make the same mistakes as post-revolutionary Cuba and Nicaragua, namely of needling the USA so much that it made life virtually unbearable thereafter, he sought to maintain half-decent relations with the West. On his sometimes impromptu visits to London, he drew large audiences to his meetings, which might only have been arranged at the last moment, with notice passed by word of mouth. He often spoke of the awkwardly isolated course he was trying to steer internationally between the sides. 'You can clap with one hand,' he said. A group of kids with a synthesiser, operating perhaps out of a basement in south-east London, should have set the line to music in his memory – the Maurice Bishop Rap.

It meant only that he bought it from both sides. A group of left-wing ideologues in his cabinet mounted a coup against him while he was away on a diplomatic swing through the Americas. Their implication was that he'd gone soft on bourgeois imperialism. One of the group's leaders had studied at Sussex, obviously when it was experiencing a 1960s', or '60s-style, spasm. They may have seen themselves as sharpening the contradictions of capitalism, assisting history's inexorable march towards final victory. How having Bishop shot on his return to the island assisted their plans was not easy to see.

Concerned parties turned up to see what had happened. Friendly links had developed between the NJM and like-minded thinkers in Islington. One of the borough's Members of Parliament visited the island while I was there. I was driven around by a kindly reporter from one of the heavier Sunday papers, who had a larger expense account than I did and had hired a car. A new Islingtonian himself, he lived in the street by the gardens where the barrage balloon had flown, and was keen to discover whether this was another example of the 'socialist republic of Islington' wasting taxpayers' money. His council rates' bill, he said, was enormous and he wanted me to get in touch with the MP: 'You're *Guardian*, he'll speak to you.' I left a message at his hotel reception, but he didn't respond before I had to leave for London.

The outcome of the killing of Bishop was to pass Grenada's mini-revolution straight into the hands of the Reagan administration. After his success in fending off communism, real or imagined, from the edge of his 6-yard box in El Salvador, the US president was on the lookout for other likely areas in which the USA could assert itself. Thus, US rangers stormed the island after, as President Reagan described it, the 'slaughter of the legitimate prime minister', not mentioning that for the better part of Bishop's four-year rule Washington had been trying to destabilise him. A few men in uniforms were rustled up from the Caribbean and led by the USA in a regional peace force. The old leaders of other islands were also prevailed upon to request the intervention. In line with established protocols on such matters, the USA didn't invade Grenada, it was 'invited'.

Mrs Thatcher had already tried to intervene herself. It wasn't that she liked Bishop's type any more than Reagan did, but

Grenada had been British and this was a British sphere of influence, the Commonwealth. She brought Britain's ancient wisdom to bear and counselled caution of the US president, her friend. In one way or another, we'd handle matters ourselves, she said. Washington, however, had its own agenda. After the impotent Carter years, the American public was being treated to the sight of its power on the march again. This was the US interest as defined at that moment, and that was what counted, not the 'special relationship'.

Mrs Thatcher's hopes that the Falklands victory represented a new thrusting beginning for British diplomacy, therefore, had realistically to be ditched. The point, though often ignored, was that the USA was very useful as a kind of distant penfriend – someone you could happily communicate with from afar, without having to bother maintaining a friendship with near at hand. Grenada confirmed the shocking reality that, as far as finding someone with comparable interests was concerned, there wasn't much of an alternative on the world stage but to come to terms with those awful Europeans.

For the time being, that conclusion could be avoided, thanks to the useful diversion of war, this time one brewing on the home front. Arthur Scargill had been fired by the successes of the coalminers in the early 1970s and imagined he could do it again. His arguments that the government was keen to run down the British coal industry proved entirely correct but how he went about winning them never felt right – it was like England going into matches in the 1950s, with first the Austrians, then the Hungarians with their clever tactical moves; or ancient Balaklava-type battles that were arranged by appointment between the sides, where both lined up and one charged gallantly into the guns of the other. The coalminers' strike was one of the more telegraphed events of Mrs Thatcher's administration. She was well prepared.

Scargill was very brave and pushed ahead, possibly motivated by something like the 'desperate courage' of goalkeepers. Legend may have played too strong a part in it. One of the more famous incidents of the 1970s had been the battle of Saltley gate, with Scargill at the front of the action, arms linked with his comrades as the police tried to break their line. Now he committed himself to another glorious confrontation, but as if he was engaged in a conventional, rather than guerrilla war. This time the government was playing the thinking, tactical game. The 1970s' conflicts had been in winter. Now it was early spring, the worst of the weather over, and coal stocks were high. It was a classic one-to-one, the odds tipped against the miners. As his adversary advanced with the ball at its feet, Scargill threw himself at it, the presidential guard sacrificing himself on the exploding grenade. Mrs Thatcher and her government played it differently – they were the ones who 'stood up', who made the Jennings move of letting the other side commit, telegraph its intentions, fluff it. Over a year in advance of its end, the outcome felt predictable. On the day the miners' strike began, I went to Mexico.

o   o   o

My customary position was on the edge of an unmade bed, in an echoing room, wires attached to my head. These ran from a set of earphones and were jacked into a stripped–down wall socket, electrocution a distinct possibility. It was funny what turned people on. Pleasing Bush or Broadcasting Houses could be difficult. 'You're sounding a bit bathroomy,' shouted the people fiddling with the knobs back in London. They still had to edit the piece you were about to send, with only a couple of minutes to go to the radio newsreel. I'd explain I'd retreated towards the bathroom to get away from the traffic noise outside the window.

'Yes, we can still hear too many of those Bob Jobbins sound effects in the background,' they shouted. Jobbins was the correspondent in Cairo. British people with their grasp of things Egyptian from the days of Suez knew that Cairo was clogged with traffic – that was the kind of chaos countries fell into when they got rid of us. It also meant that only Jobbins was allowed to get away with them. They were felt to add to the atmosphere. But they weren't from Mexico City, the largest city and urban disaster in the world. 'Couldn't you tell them to shut up for a few minutes?' With the top of the hour approaching, one friendly editor came on the line, making an admirable effort to keep calm, and advised that, in his days in the field, he'd found putting a towel over his head and microphone often did the trick. Either that, he added, or a cardboard box.

Richard Burton's death in the summer of 1984 led the newsreel.

There were excerpts of him deeply intoning lines from *Under Milk Wood*. Laurence Olivier followed with stirring tribute in 'Sir Larry' manner, while slipping in that Burton was at his best when he stuck to the serious things, not the flashy stuff he went after in Hollywood. I was surprised to find I was up next, delivering a piece on the world population conference in Mexico City. To be in such company was deeply flattering. I'd filed my report ten minutes earlier at the height of the Mexico City evening rush hour. It was the rainy season; the city, perched at an altitude of 8,000 feet, always felt that bit nearer the crashing thunder. But who would have known? Not the people who tuned in to the World Service, from Gabon to Guyana, Samarkand to Sulawesi. When they heard the newsreader's words 'This is London', articulated in the emotionless tones which said 'need we say more?', they expected a distillation of order from chaos, presented by stiff-backed Lord Reith-types in dinner jackets. I read my report crouched on my knees, mouth and microphone two inches from the floor and with both a bathtowel and a box over my head.

To make any kind of living I had to file on average one report a day – freelance correspondents were paid by the piece, unlike salaried staff, who might disappear off the radar screen for weeks at a time. This was easy if there was another round of Central American peace talks, or a gas installation had blown up at dawn on the outskirts of town killing 1,500 people. Otherwise there was a problem. The trick was to reflect matters East–West. A story like 'Mexico demands payment for oil shipments to Costa Rica' would guarantee to have the night shift yawning around the Aldwych. If you contrived it, however, in terms of how Costa Rica, the only democratic country in Central America, yet badly strapped for cash, may now have to kow-tow for money and oil to Washington, then there were the makings of something. This isolated refuge of neutrality, sheltered behind its volcanoes, this 'Switzerland of Central America', might well be forced to tone down its opposition, in the UN and elsewhere, to President Reagan's claims that Russians were rampant from Guatemala to the Panama canal. 'East–West' was the frame-work within which we understood things, and through which we channelled so much of our thinking. When I received my monthly Bush House payments, I found such pieces had been used up by anyone from the Somali service to the Merchant Navy programme.

England, managed by Bobby Robson, arrived in Mexico in mid-1985 for a World Cup warm-up one year before the tournament proper. They landed as the Heysel disaster happened on 29 May in Belgium, and 39 Juventus fans were killed when Liverpool supporters charged them before the European Cup Final. The terrace nutcases had pursued their policy of British isolation from Europe beyond the point Mrs Thatcher was prepared to stomach and she summoned FA chairman Bert Millichip back for talks in Downing Street, no sooner than he'd checked into his Mexico City hotel. He wasn't being 'summoned' by anyone, he said, as I buttonholed him in the lobby. I thought he also seemed a little irked – though it could as easily have been the altitude and jet-lag – when I asked whether he thought English clubs would be thrown out of Europe. 'We won't wait for that,' he answered, with a note of historical drama, 'we'll go on our own.'

Over the next few days Bobby Robson faced hostile questions from the Mexican press. Their basic drift was that if England's players found they weren't winning a game in the World Cup, would their fans be let loose on the opposition instead? But it wasn't the supporters, so much as the stigma of Alf Ramsey's sausages that still lingered. Robson handled all hostile questions very diplomatically, saying to the Mexican masses that this time England, after the host squad itself, of course, wanted to be 'your team'. Playing only a couple of days after Heysel, England also diplomatically lost to Italy, 2–1. They had the pleasure of going on to beat West Germany (for the first time in a decade), by a clear margin of three goals, but this was a largely meaningless result before a 10,000 crowd in the Azteca stadium, capacity 114,000. Shilton saved a penalty. At the other end, Harald Schumacher appeared a reformed character from his days of jaw-war with Battiston, slapping opponents on the back and seeming as delighted as they were when they scored. It wasn't, however, a very good German team. What with their now being managed by 'Kaiser' Franz Beckenbauer, the imperial smoothie of them all, you couldn't help but think the scheming dastards were saving their powder, much scanter than normal, for a year hence when it really mattered.

Before the England party and media pack left, we put on a couple of cricket matches for them. In one, Gary Lineker, young, virtually unknown given he played for Leicester, and almost too shy to open his mouth in public, killed off the game with 70-odd runs cracked through the thin air. In the other I nearly killed Terry Venables. He hit a dolly catch to me at cover, looked very pissed off and began his long walk to the changing tent as I lobbed the ball back in the direction of the wicketkeeper. Unfortunately it slipped from my hand early, at too high a point of the arc of my arm. It went into a very high loop and the key question, at that Uwe-Seeler-moment, was where would it drop? As far as we could tell, it was bound right for Venables's downcast head. The ball was on its accelerating plunge through Mexico City's atmosphere and we all stood silent. If we'd shouted, there would have been no time for him to get out of the way. 'Oh, *fuck* it!' he said, in one last gesture of disgust at the limp nature of his dismissal and banged his bat hard into the ground. His head jerked forward, as, in *The Day of the Jackal*, an unknowing de Gaulle's did for the assassin's bullet to pass behind it. The ball thudded dully into the ground to the rear of Venables, leaving him none the wiser. Days before he'd become the virtual king of Catalonia by coaching Barcelona to the Spanish championship. I tried to work out how many BBC broadcasts at £22.50 a time it would have taken to meet their compensation claim.

The matches were staged on the luxurious grounds of the Reforma Club – boasting the highest grass cricket pitch in the world – established by nostalgic wanderers from the British Isles around the time of the Mexican revolution. This part of the world had never been the empire and it was surprising how many expats there were in the city: what with those from the Commonwealth, enough available males of vaguely games-playing age to make up four cricket teams alone. There were also, for example, several hundred Mexican Macgregors, who traced their heritage back to a single adventurer who pitched up, probably for a punch-up, around the time of Zapata and Pancho Villa. You'd meet them at the Caledonian Ball on or around St Andrew's Day. They knew the moves of every fling and Gay Gordon, though they were Mexican and often spoke English with a strong accent. Someone from Scotland itself would begin the night's proceedings with a toast 'to the land in which we live'. I couldn't recall many Scots, however, joining the ranks of agricultural batsmen and dodgy off-spinners at the weekends. That had been the thing about them. They'd been the empire builders, the engineers and railway planners, but when they travelled they'd merged and mingled much better. The English turned up and laid a cricket pitch.

This entitled the visiting England footballers to privileges straight out of the Raj. Foreign teams scampered for good training facilities when they came to Mexico City. England bowled up, as if of right, to the Reforma Club. I went to watch them, especially their keepers, coming to grips with the conditions. Gary Bailey of Manchester United, whose dad had kept goal for Ramsey's championship winners at Ipswich in 1962 and later emigrated to South Africa, had been used to the conditions of the high veldt. But your lungs never tightened nor the ball flew in Johannesburg to quite the extent they did here. The three goalkeepers were really having to work at it, he told me, as he took a momentary break. I could see what he meant from the sight of Peter Shilton right by us, though he just kept going.

Once he'd ground himself, Bailey and third-choice Chris Woods through his regime of shot-dive-recovery, shot-dive-recovery for a couple of hours (much less in reality but that was what it felt like watching it), Shilton turned to concentrating on the cross. Ball after ball was pumped high from the wings at each keeper, at virtually every height and angle. Shilton had developed his own method of dealing with them. He'd advance towards the airbound ball till he was almost too far under it and begin his jump when it seemed too late. It would have been, had he tried to catch the ball directly above him. Instead, he'd take it marginally behind his head, when it had dropped in height the bare inch or so needed to make the catch feasible.

Shilton catching the ball after it had gone past him was quite disconcerting to look at, as if he was having to throw his shoulders out of joint or hang like a gymnast on the rings. Shilton was quite used to suspending himself in such a fashion. When he was a schoolboy he was thought too small for a keeper, so he put himself through a range of exercises in order to stretch and grow, one of which was to hang by his arms from a door frame. Had he been around in the days of the Spanish Inquisition, Shilton would have worried Torquemada by volunteering for the rack. Still, it did his career no harm because he grew to 6 feet 1 inch. The other thing about taking the ball like this was the slide-rule precision required. He was getting his hands to it when it had as good as passed out of his sight. I never once saw him drop it and you'd have counted on Shilton hardly ever to do so. The advantage of the method was it meant not only was he taking the ball at its highest possible point, but also that his body was claiming the yard or so of airspace in front of his catch. This was where an opponent might try and steal in with a glancing header, or just jump to try and put him off. Of course, it would have required an exceptionally tall or high-flying jumper to beat him in such a way – or so you would have thought. Shilton, though, was a perfectionist who covered all possibilities and his method made him near unbeatable in this most important aspect of goalkeeping. Shilton had become the absolute master of the cross.

Three months later, Mexico City had one of the worst earth-quakes known to man, registering 8.1 on the Richter scale. My office and apartment were in the centre of town but I was coming in from the southern outskirts, the area of the Ajusco mountain. It was on a slightly different fault-line from the city centre, not to mention on solid rock. By contrast, the centre was on the old dried-out bed of Lake Texcoco, the biblical house built on sand. From its epicentre some 300 miles away off the Pacific coast, the earthquake increased in power, therefore, as it hit Mexico City. It left maybe 30,000 dead, though no one knew precisely. The scenes of people evacuating what belongings they'd rescued on horse-drawn carts, of rubble piled on the streets and of half-shells of buildings looked the equal, and worse, of any pictures or film I'd seen of the London Blitz.

The city had about a hundred aftershocks in the following month or so. When the worst had passed, I reported for the *Guardian* that an engineer inspecting the city's main stadium had found hairline 'cracks in the Aztec'. With the World Cup scheduled to start in May, ITV followed this up and I travelled around the country with Kevin Keegan, who was presenting a preview of the competition. In the hot flatlands of Monterrey in the northern desert, where England were due to play, the city's police chief received me at his desk with his unholstered revolver on a shelf behind him. He anticipated few hotheads among the travelling supporters, he said, whom he imagined would generally act like characteristic English gentlemen, 'the David Niven type'. If not, his men were prepared. With this he leaned to the side of the desk and spat calmly into a metal wastepaper basket.

In the Jalisco stadium in Guadalajara, where Northern Ireland and Brazil were to play, a stadium official pointed out to me that 'it was in that goal that Banks made his save in 1970'. I wondered if he was, Mexican-style, just being hospitable to guests, but he'd said it unprompted and I was happy to take it as evidence that it wasn't only the English who had built the save into the stuff of legend. While the camera crew was shooting Keegan strolling meditatively in the centre circle, I stood around in the goalmouth running through the save's details, though I resisted going into the final dive. A group of groundsmen painting white lines in the penalty area eyed me suspiciously.

This led to the offer of a job for ITV on the World Cup, which, while it meant crossing over from the BBC, I could do in addition to my newspaper work. The details were unclear but it would require some general setting up of interviews and getting camera crews around Mexico City. I was directed to work with Gary Newbon, a reporter from Birmingham. 'I'll probably embarrass you a bit,' he told me on the morning he arrived. A piece had already been dreamed up for him to do and we went straight to the stadium used by the South Korean team for their training. This was next to Mexico City's main bullring, where D. H. Lawrence had written passionately of the gaudy spectacle, and I imagined, to set the scene for the viewer at home, this fact might be worth a mention. The piece, however, was for the Saint and Greavsie programme and to focus on the 'funny names' of the South Korean team: 'seven Kims, four Chos, two Parks and a Bum', as our reporter put it. When the camera swung down the line of players, their coach introducing each of them, I took care to be out of shot, in case anyone from the *Guardian* was watching.

With the competition about to begin, the Brazilian TV network in the next office asked us if they could borrow someone to tell them anything about Northern Ireland, their first-round opponents. I was volunteered for what turned out to be an interview being beamed back to Brazil and introduced as 'one of the leading experts on Northern Ireland football'. Sammy McIlroy, a key team member, I referred to as Jimmy, his dad, who as a player with league title challengers Burnley I'd chased after at Euston station over twenty years earlier. Apart from stuff about how the players of this small and divided nation achieved heightened strength and unity from the act of pulling on their green international shirts, I spent most of the time talking about Pat Jennings. The Brazilians asked how could they possibly repay me. I said not to bother, I was only in the next room anyway, then as I was walking out the door one of them said, perhaps we might like an interview with Pele. They'd signed him up as their chief analyst, and he was due in Mexico tomorrow.

Pele arrived as in stately progress. A horde of Latin American journalists surrounded him for the 400-yard walk from the car park at the TV centre to the studios, stuffing their tape recorders under his nose for a greeting or his prediction of who would win the tournament. After they'd got the few syllables they needed, they'd peel away from the mob and, clearly moved, bark, almost sob, into their machines: 'You have just heard the exclusive words of Pele, *El Rey*!' (the King!). After the Northern Ireland interview, I'd been directed to arrange our pay-off through the urbane, grey-haired Professor Julio Mazzei, a longstanding technical adviser to Brazilian national teams and here more or less acting as Pele's PR-man. Pele was ushered into a studio, composed himself and slipped from talking in Spanish and Portuguese straight into what he excused as his 'poor English'.

He sometimes spoke in the third person: 'Pele knows from his twenty-five years in football, that it is not good to argue with the referee.' It increased his air of grandeur but came with a disarming smile. It was impressive how he, originally a poor kid from the depressed environs of Minas Gerais, had educated and re-created himself. By sad contrast, the Scots TV crew I was with had been discussing how Jim Baxter had slipped from as near as he could get to being pronounced king of his country, at Wembley in 1963, to a life of near poverty in Glasgow. What was to stop our best footballers when they retired at taking even a modest crack at 'doing a Pele'? The likes of Jimmy Greaves, at least with their TV careers, were now having a try.

We managed a week or so later to eke out a second interview

with him (albeit after this one he told his network there was no good reason why he was providing his services so freely to the British). This was in his downtown hotel, though only after we had extricated ourselves from a bad case of Mexico City gridlock to reach it. No one would say exactly what his room number was in the high-rise block and, when we found the right floor, it was a question of knocking on every door. Our reporter got lost in the process. 'Look, you said you'd be here at four o'clock,' Pele barked as we walked in forty-five minutes late, a still respectable time by most Latin American standards but not his. 'I have had these Japanese people waiting here.' He waved to a TV crew from this emerging football nation, where a lot of cash was sloshing around to finance its development. He fixed me with a glare which I imagined he'd given Banks after the save in 1970.

Of course, he did the interview. Before it, our presenter asked if he recalled when they'd met some years before in a restaurant. During the course of that interview the presenter had contrived to break the glass table top. Pele said he didn't want to lie that he did remember, but he'd think about it. The question was slipped in at the end. 'Ah, yes,' beamed Pele, faces may have escaped his memory but not incidents like that. And all the people watching in Britain would be able to see, he said, with an expansive gesture to the empty table in front of him, how this time he'd cleared all cups and glasses away. The fellow was a professional. By contrast I spent much of the interview thinking how I'd ask for his autograph. It was an uncool thing for TV people to do. I was also in the company of Billy McNeil, former captain of Celtic and Scotland who was working with us. But at the end of the interview, McNeil, first man to lead a British team to victory in the European Cup, was first to ask. Pele had a stack of photos waiting for such demands, anyway.

Brazil scored initial victories over Northern Ireland – Jennings's last international – Algeria and Spain, which convinced their huge entourage that they were but a step from the World Cup itself. All their four major TV networks had decamped *en masse* to Mexico, walking around in their yellow replica international shirts, and, what with the press and radio staff they'd brought along, the Brazilian media presence totalled several hundred. Certain of their invincibility, they challenged the

Rest of the World to a game under lights at a Mexico City stadium.

A young Mexican brought the sheet of names of volunteers for the Rest of the World squad to our office. 'Load of bollocks,' said one of the senior producers, lighting another cigarette. Running around in shirt and shorts for an hour or so in the evening was both a threat to the health and a waste of potentially good pulling time in the hotel bar. Several dozen names were pencilled in on the sheet, including Bobby Charlton and Trevor Brooking from the BBC. 'You will not be able to play in goal all of the game,' he said, apologetically. 'We also have a . . .' He hesitated as he checked the lengthy list of names, all of them outside his historical frame of reference. 'We also have a Señor Yashin.'

'See, they're taking the piss,' was the considered view in the ITV office. Lev was in Moscow, where he had had a leg amputated. At best what was being billed by the Brazilians as a big game would shake down to a friendly kick-about between a few of the lesser lights of the media world. This appeared to be confirmed in the dressing room. Shirts had been printed in the names of Charlton and Brooking but they had found prior engagements to occupy them.

I bent to tie my boots with ITV's Martin Tyler and Jim Rosenthal on my left. Our teammate immediately to my right was struggling to get his left foot and aged boot remotely near each other. So we had geriatrics along as well. Not wishing to be impolite, I looked up discreetly from my laces, to see a squat character built like one of the long-distance lorry drivers who used to lodge in our street at the house of Mrs Fox – only if they'd had anything like the size of this bloke's stomach, it would have been many a year since they'd squeezed behind the wheel. He had a square and lined faced. His hair was thinning and plastered back. And there was something familiar about that centre-parting.

I turned to Tyler with a look which made every effort to delete alarm and expletives and came out with something like: 'Oh, I say, we appear to be about to take the field with Puskas.' But, a TV person, he stayed studiedly cool. I had only about five seconds to take stock of the fact that here at my right arm was the man who had abruptly ended the popular concept of British supremacy and empire, when there was a commotion at the dressing-room door.

Professor Julio Mazzei, Brazil's manager for the night, burst in. A crisis had arisen within their squad. They had hundreds of willing takers to choose their team from and no one could imagine how such a thing could have happened, but Brazil had forgotten to turn up with a goalkeeper.

Such had been Brazil's fate since the days of Gilmar. It was how they'd ended up with Felix in 1970: 'Anyone fancy a quiet game between the posts?' they'd shouted. He'd since merged back into the crowd, humbly working for his son-in-law's motor repair business in São Paulo. I'd reckoned that even making it as far as the unhallowed turf of the London Transport ground at the Crooked Billet would have qualified me to play for Brazil, but for the small detail of not being born there. Now, by biding my time, playing it long, the chance had arisen.

My services were volunteered by our team. This was within the amicable spirit of the occasion, if a little too readily, I thought. Maybe someone had heard about that 9–2 defeat against Spurs at Cheshunt. For his part, Professor Mazzei was nothing except grateful as we walked on the pitch. Some 5,000 throats acknowledged our arrival. OK, it may have been nearer half that, but they made a sound equal to when the emergence of Cyril Lee, Sid Bishop and Dave Dunmore from the Brisbane Road tunnel could rattle every tobacconist's window to the Baker's Arms.

The rest of the Brazilian team were gathered in the centre circle, and in some disarray. The ace up their sleeve had failed to show. No one quite knew what had happened to him but the supposition was that Pele had a more promising PR opportunity elsewhere in Mexico City. Mazzei was doing his best to lift their spirits and thought the process might be aided by pointing out he'd found a goalkeeper. This didn't cause much of a stir. One or two nodded and smiled, offering a few friendly words of welcome, and possibly condolence for drawing what was, by their lights, the short straw. 'No, no,' he corrected them, telling those that could to 'speak to him in English'.

The initial effect was to shut them up immediately. Several looked at each other, confused. Mazzei's language directive surely wasn't the problem for most of them. As media types they travelled frequently to and from the USA; a number had just returned from covering the Indianapolis 500. Then one said quietly, but with weight, deliberation and no small measure of awe in his voice: '*um goleiro inglês!*' Another followed up, almost shouting, in Portuguese to the rest of the group: 'We have an English goalkeeper!'

They were making the usual Latin American, and English, error of saying 'English' when they meant British. In their case, all of them experts in the rise of Brazilian greatness in the game, they were just looking back through history. In 1958, when Brazil had first won the World Cup, they'd failed to get past McDonald of England, did so only with great luck against Kelsey of Wales, and seen Northern Ireland's Gregg outvote Gilmar as the keeper of the tournament. The line continued up through Banks in 1970 and they'd just waved Jennings off in his final international. As far as they were concerned, Britain had the finest goalkeepers in the world. Whether or not this was a myth propagated by us, it showed others were perfectly disposed to accept it. Dangerously, however, they were susceptible – not least in this moment of need now Pele had deserted them – to believing all British keepers were great. It got worse when Mazzei introduced me by Christian name: 'Sheel-ton!' they cried.

'They are mostly a young team,' Mazzei said confidentially, drawing me aside. 'They get a little excited.' He introduced me to our captain, quieter, grey-haired, Clodoaldo. This was the young shooting star of the 1970 Cup-winning team who had been profligate in handing Boninsegna a free run on goal for Italy's equaliser, though as it turned out that was just to keep the outcome of the game briefly in suspense. 'We need to talk to them for a few minutes before the game starts,' Mazzei went on, 'so you don't need to stand here.' He nodded towards another older guy in a Brazil shirt, standing with a ball at his feet on the edge of the group. He had the sort of bushy moustache favoured by Parisian taxi drivers. 'You go and practise with Mr Rivelino.'

I said, 'Of course', as if I did this every second Tuesday – a few moments of spare time to kill, a swift call to São Paulo to arrange where and when, and there we were, a quick bit of practice with Mr Rivelino. He twitched his moustache in greeting, and we jogged towards one end of the field, he stopping some way outside the penalty to juggle the ball while I made for my line. From the pantheon, this was the co-star with Pele of the team that had cruised to victory in 1970. Earlier Brazilians like Garrincha, or

Pepe, who had fooled Banks in his first taste of real international football in 1963, were probably the pioneers of the banana shot, yet it was Rivelino who had stretched it to new frontiers. It was why they'd named a square after him in São Paulo. The fellow could bend the ball around it.

But, come on, son, it was too easy to get intimidated by these people. They were in awe of us, too – we were British goalkeepers, after all. When I turned to face him, he was at least 25 yards away. There was little doubt he could really ping it from that range. He'd scored about the fastest goal ever known to man from the halfway line in Brazil once. From the kick-off, the ball was side-footed to him a yard away and he hit it straight in the net. He'd spotted the opposing keeper, not the type who believed we were ultimately alone in this world, on his knees saying a marginally belated pre-match prayer. The goal took a mere three seconds. I made him wait longer while I pulled on my gloves. I'd bought them that afternoon; not having quite accepted that anyone really needed to play in big floppy things, I'd gone half way by buying a pair in fetching white leather with pimpled black rubber strips on the palms and digits for grip. On a dark night they looked like something out of the 'Black and White Minstrel Show', but they'd do. This year's rainy season had hit with an vengeance earlier than usual and Rivelino was standing in no less of a bog out there than I was in my goalmouth. Drizzle was slanting through the lights, some hours after the afternoon's storm. These were a keeper's conditions, more Walthamstow than Me-hi-co.

Rivelino swung his left leg through a low arc, gracefully, powerfully at the ball. From the moment it left his boot it was clear he had hopelessly miscued. Not to be caught out like Banks at Wembley – I wasn't about to run madly this way then hopelessly that – I had advanced the now statutory few yards from my line to neutralise any late outswing in his shot. This proved entirely unnecessary. As I looked up, the ball was flying high and wild above my head in the sparse Mexico City air and I let it pass without even the courtesy of a casual hop, let alone a full-bodied jump. On a sharp twang from behind me, however, I turned to see the ball ricochet hard from the underside of the metal crossbar and down into the net.

After a couple of minutes of the match, Puskas got the ball just outside my penalty area. He had the chance for a shot at goal and I almost shouted at him to hit it with his left foot. My defenders thought I was telling them to get out the way and did so to make his view only clearer. If I'd saved the ball, there'd have been the glory. If he'd scored, where'd have been the dishonour in that? There was a large and esteemed band of goalkeepers who had conceded a goal to Puskas. But he was too old for it now, wiggled his stomach from side to side to wrong-foot us a couple of times and contented himself with a short pass to someone younger.

Shots rained in on the Brazil goal. I failed to hold any, which was embarrassing, but mysteriously won praise as they bounced off various bits of my body to safety. The clean catch didn't seem to matter. The Brazilians were perfectly happy with a rusty old bit of 'shotstopping'. A chance to show what true keeping was about came when our opponents won a corner-kick on the right. It fell from a great height, out of the slanting rain and the floodlights which weren't much better than those on the cinder pitch by Brisbane Road. It was within my area and I moved out for it, screaming loudly, 'keeper's ball!' I thought this would convey a sense of confident command but, for all I knew, to the Brazilians it was a cry of despair. I watched the ball all the way into my gloves. In slower motion, I watched it all the way out again. It landed in the mud in front of me and I, too, was now afflicted by what Bill Shankly had called 'desperate courage'. I flopped on top of it, mindless of any flailing feet. To have conceded a goal after fluffing such a simple catch would have been shaming indeed. I expected to look up to see my defence shaking their heads in disapproval. Then, these were people who recalled the soaring majesty of Felix – they slapped me on the back, by comparison a veritable master of the cross.

'Just give it to Rive,' they had told me before the start. I attempted to, every time I had the chance to kick or throw the ball out. He scored very quickly, then rattled bar and post with shots that dipped and swung. We were still 1–0 up with not much more than fifteen minutes left, when Rivelino had the chance to finish it. He received the ball unmarked 6 yards out, shook his hips and sent the keeper slithering towards one corner of the net, before sidefooting it casually in the direction of the other, but past the post. From my distant end of the pitch, I laughed, this being a friendly game. Behind his moustache, Rivelino looked a little sheepish and tried to smile. His team looked on the point of homicide.

At this point, the Rest of the World's supremacy of numbers came into the reckoning. They had an array of substitutes, ex-French, Italian and German pros, whom we heard had been forced to retire early from their careers but were quite up to storming around for the late stages of this occasion. They scored three, Clodoaldo predictably allowing them in for the equaliser, that turned the game. Soon after, Rivelino slapped the glum French referee around the face. Clodoaldo followed with a kick in the shins and miraculously got away with only a yellow card. By the time of the final whistle, the crowd was hysterical. Brazil left the field in uproar.

'Oh, that fucking Rivelino,' said Professor Mazzei to me after, showing an impressive command of dressing-room vernacular. 'How did he miss that one in front of the goal?' The rest of the team looked equally upset but effusively thanked me for having played. Whoever's fault it was that they'd been humbled, it would never have occurred to the Brazilians to heap anything but acclaim on *um goleiro inglês*.

Taking a leaf out of Gordon Banks's autograph book after he'd played the Rest of the World in 1963, I nipped round to the other dressing room with a sheet of paper to catch Puskas on his way out, alone and largely unrecognised by the crowd. I told him, scarcely exaggerating, that it had been good to play against him.

'*Zank* you veery much,' he replied. And who did he think would win the World Cup?

'*Zank* you veery much.' My Hungarian had never been up to much, so I left it at that.

o   o   o

Of the British nations, only England made it through their opening qualifiers. Ascending from the northern desert to the saturated upland basin of Mexico City and the Azteca stadium they successfully negotiated their way through the second round by beating Paraguay 3–0. In the quarter-finals they were to face Argentina. Four months earlier Argentina's elderly president, Raul

Alfonsin, civilian successor to his nation's shamed military, had passed through Mexico City, prompting an invitation to foreign correspondents to breakfast with him at the Argentine embassy. He began to answer our questions with a hesitant, gentlemanly grace as we munched our grapefruit. Yet mine – asked in a BBC capacity and an unshocking request for him to outline his views on the prospects for Falklands peace – gripped him with a sudden vigour. He stabbed the table with his finger, rattling, if not the sabres inappropriate for this transitional moment in Argentine history, then at least his embassy's silver cutlery set elaborately before us. Mrs Thatcher was being entirely 'intransigent', was a reasonable summary of his argument. It was a point tough to disagree with, but one it seemed he felt obliged to trot out to someone who was obviously an agent of the Thatcherite state.

Given England and Argentina would be playing each other for the first time since the 1982 war, therefore, I didn't expect the Argentine journalists in the TV centre to be especially accommodating when I asked for information on how to get close to their football team. In fact, they couldn't have been more helpful, giving me not only the precise location of the Argentine camp and the squad's training times (an exactitude not to be taken for granted in Latin America) but also whom to mention their names to in the event of there being any problem with the policeman at the gate. The most senior of them, José Maria Muñoz, quiet, polite and wearing a white shirt buttoned to the wrists, presumably as protection against the sun, had been following Argentina's games for as long as anyone could remember. At some forgotten time, he had been credited with inventing the cry of 'Gol-l-l-l-l-l-l-l!' One of those quirkily Latin things, it now celebrated even the most feeble of scores from Tijuana to Tierra del Fuego. You knew it could never catch on in Britain.

Overnight rain had flooded the Mexico City *periférico* almost to the point of cutting off the Argentine camp. It hadn't deterred the 200 Latin American journalists gathered there, however, none of whom was troubled to mention anyone's name at the gate. Anglo-Saxons who volunteered to do so, on the assumption this would guarantee them immediate transit to the stars, only invited their *bona fides* to be checked at bureaucratic length. By the time we got in, all 200 were stationed by the door of the creosoted wooden huts used by the squad as dressing rooms, awaiting the appearance of Diego Maradona. The rest of the Argentine players were out limbering up or lolling around on the grass, steam rising from it in the clear morning sun.

Our advantage was that whereas everyone else seemed to be operating alone for one Latin American radio station or another and equipped only with a tape recorder, we had cameraman, soundman, associated equipment which could clear a path through any crowd if run at hard enough, with a few sets of elbows to follow up. Once Maradona had dealt with a southern Italian journalist's sentimental nonsense about whether he had any special message for the people of Naples, his club of the moment, we were next in the horde and with the only question relevant to the times. At least, it was the only one I'd been specifically directed to ask. I thought I'd better warm up with something gentler: was there any truth in the claim Argentina were just a one-man team? This caused him to frown. Then with the cameraman getting impatient, I hit him with the hard one: to what extent would the 1982 war be in his thoughts as he took to the pitch in three days' time?

Predictably, he blew up. The cameraman was directed to have me out of shot and home in on Maradona waving his arms around. The Argentines, as personified by him, were a volatile bunch. Everyone at home knew that and here it was confirmed. The game would have nothing to do with politics, he said. It would be '*solo futból!*' Just in case we hadn't got the point he shouted it again. It would be 'only football'. Of course, politics or no politics, he lied.

It took him a full forty-five minutes to see off other questions. His last public duty was to have his picture taken with Bobby Charlton, arms around each other's shoulders. His teammates greeted his arrival among them with ironic, but friendly, applause. British journalists had also gone hunting for a quote from Argentina's centre-midfielder, José Luis Brown. He turned out to have had an Irish grandfather, a daughter still at the British school in Buenos Aires but not a word of English himself. He did say everyone at home had lost someone in 1982.

When the team's training was under way, I wandered over to the separate pitch and the Argentine goalkeepers. Nery Pumpido, the first choice, agreed that the war would provide him with a 'special motivation'. Apparently so. At first I couldn't imagine what he was preparing himself for, an hour or so's practice goalkeeping or a hefty bit of sparring with some prancing pugilist about to appear from a creosoted hut. He was having his hands strapped with elastic bandage, as if boxing was his real game. So much of the stuff was applied I couldn't see how it would be feasible for him to handle a ball cleanly. When he fitted on his keeper's gloves, compactly over the bandage, and his training got under way, it became obvious that that was not the point.

Shot after shot was banged at him and his understudies. From every angle and every height, the unwitting objective was to defy the Camus theory of life as goalkeeping, that no ball ever came at you the same way twice. If you spent long enough at it, the more the chances were that it would. Despite the thickness of Pumpido's gloves, without the extra shield beneath them, the bones in his hands would not have survived the onslaught. But when it was over, that was largely it. He and the others did a few stretches, a sprint, a brief jog, took off their gloves, unwrapped the bandages and made for the shower. Balls punted from the wings and across the goalmouth had not detained them. In a sense this was understandable. The completely non-leather ball dated back to the 1960s but Mexico 1986 was the first time it had been introduced by Fifa to the World Cup. It swung at angles and went at speeds not seen before and seemed to require a new kind of keeper, one oriented almost entirely towards the stopping of shots. This was an important component of the goalkeeper's game, but not its art. It was a virtual denial of the cross and what it stood for.

The game between England and Argentina brought Shilton and Maradona together as adversaries and opposing captains. The mood in the stadium was subdued, given there were over 100,000 present, and attemptedly diplomatic. A banner saying 'Exocet Lineker' was removed from the crowd before the start.' Whether it was an English offering, comparing the centre-forward with the missile used to awful effect in the Falklands war, or an Argentine suggestion that this was what should happen to him, was unclear. Shilton and Maradona exchanged flags in the middle. Soon after the match began, the English keeper was hit hard by two Argentine forwards as he came out fast to gather a ball. At the other end, the outcome would have almost certainly been a shoving match as other players bundled in. Shilton got up and shook hands all round. As for Maradona, contrary to his confusion when I'd asked him about Argentina as a one-man team, he became the target for just about every pass his teammates could manage. He flicked, back-heeled and distributed deftly and England began to look mesmerised. Thanks to him, Argentina were getting on top. Shortly before the end of the goalless first half I wrote in my notes that Shilton was fielding and catching superbly everything that came near him.

But the Mexican police were not as prepared as they might have been for the 'David Niven' types that came to grace their shores. Supporters weren't segregated in the enormous stadium, which was all very pleasant initially, as England fans conga-ed from one end to the other and back. But at half-time fights broke out – by chance within spitting distance of a Chelsea banner – which the police had to quell. As the players came out near the scene of this incident for the second half, it appeared as if fans from both sides had agreed to wave their flags together. Then one clashed with another, others were ripped from hands and a larger running battle ensued till the riot police belatedly moved in. It gave the impression that it would only take some further minor incident to set the Azteca in uproar.

Yet the odds were not on anything much arising from the first minor piece of action in the second half. A deflection off a defender's boot sent the ball looping high towards Shilton's 6-yard box and he moved confidently to take it. He'd perfected his own method of taking such crossballs, of course, but on this occasion there was no competing jump from a lanky opponent. Only Maradona was running towards him. Like Uwe Seeler in 1970, the Argentine was just about the smallest man on the pitch. OK, so we knew it was always as well to expect the unexpected of these continental types – Maradona, like so many of his countrymen, had Italian roots – but what chance did he have? Shilton was the master of the cross. Maradona, except when he was doing one of his clever, exhibition juggles, hardly headed a ball in his life.

'*Solo futból!*', only football, he'd said. And in the diplomatic, healing mood of the times, we wanted to believe him. After Maradona had jumped, it was mystifying how the ball had ended in the net. In the commentary position we had to look at the replay on the monitor to get a clear view, by which time the referee was signalling a goal and ignoring the England protests. You'd have thought the Bulgarian linesman was perfectly in line to see what went on, but there we were. It wasn't 'foot-ball' at all. Quite likely Maradona rationalised what he'd done in the political terms he said so vigorously the game would have nothing to do with – certainly it was an upraised hand, he'd have admitted privately, but surely that was only fair dues, the most minimal recompense, no more, for such as the sinking of the *Belgrano*. The 'hand of God', in his own words, had had its way.

The chances now were of a stadium punch-up. This risk of full-scale fighting in the steep and unsegregated rows of the Azteca prompted one of the more depressing moments I could remember, in sport or otherwise. Then Maradona scored his second goal two minutes later, weaving down the field from his own half past umpteen England players. It was as clear that this was one of the greatest goals anyone there was likely to witness, as it was that the first was one of the most dubious. More fights did break out, but these were because of anger at Maradona's initial strike. When full stock was taken of his second – and a large part of the crowd yelled in unison, '*Fuera! Fuera!*' ('Kick 'em out!') at the brawling fans – the stadium consensus was that it had seen a bit of sporting history. The effect was to calm things down.

England came back well, with Lineker scoring once (and nearly again two minutes from the end), but you had the feeling it was all over when Glenn Hoddle had a free kick midway through the second half. From some 25 yards, he struck and curved it beautifully to Pumpido's left. The keeper swooped full length to put it around his post. At practice, I'd seen him make this save on at least three, maybe half a dozen, occasions. The theory was wrong, then; the ball *could* come at you in the same way twice. Pumpido had covered all possibilities and made the match-winning save. In a game, the first real action of which had seen a sacrilegious hand – two fingers, in effect – raised to our majesty on the cross, the last bow had gone to a piece of 'shotstopping'.

At the final whistle, I saw the Argentine reporters babbling into their microphones. I thought of angrily butting in but recalled how helpful they had been, waited a few moments and managed a feeble 'congratulations' as I walked past Muñoz in his buttoned-up shirt. He looked at me astounded, tears starting to swell, seized a microphone from his colleague and gasped: 'Ladies and gentlemen, it is with a deep sense of emotion I have to tell you that a British colleague has come to give us his good wishes.' With this, he shoved it under my nose with an instruction to speak directly to the Argentine people.

We'd had our doubts about the first goal, I mumbled. Yes, he interrupted, it was handball but didn't Maradona's second 'count for two in its own right?' He'd got me on that one. Reaching for something like a Latin American flourish to conclude with, I pontificated that 'at least with this result our two countries could now forget their recent history of problems'. Not to be out-flourished, Muñoz signed off by kissing me extravagantly on the cheek. As a piece of radio it would have made better television but, to the listening millions in Jujay and Comodoro Rivadavia, it was a peace of sorts between Britain and Argentina.

Brazil went out, too, in the quarter-finals. This was against France in a penalty shoot-out, the first time it had been used as a method of elimination at world level. France's 'winner' hit the post and rebounded off the diving keeper's back into the net. It shouldn't have been allowed – the ball was technically dead once it struck the upright – but refs and everyone else were hazy on the rules.

Ron Atkinson, Manchester United manager and ITV analyst, opined how keepers could adapt to the penalty shoot-out. They had only to stand still, he said, and the law of averages would see at least one of the five opposition efforts hit straight at them. I didn't like the sound of this at all. It was the first time I could recall hearing the suggestion that a keeper should save a penalty. Previously it was believed the odds were so stacked against him, that any save was a near miracle. Now the penalty shoot-out was removing one of the easiest bits of potential glory there was. The crowd would soon be expecting a keeper to make a save, to 'do his bit' as a member of the team, rather than retrieve a situation he'd inherited from the misdeeds of others: 'Come on, surely, you can save one of them,' they'd be bellowing.

Throughout the competition Atkinson baulked at coming to Mexico City or anywhere that kept him too long from the beaches of Puerto Vallarta, 'PV', with his wife Maggie. 'All I know is I've got a tracksuit and pair of underpants,' he said, 'and am being shunted around this pox-ridden country.' He was tempted to the capital for the final, where a poor West German team mustered their resources to come back from the dead, and 2–0 down yet again. 'You can never write the Germans off,' Ron said, as their late equaliser went in. 'You've got to fancy their chances now.' We all did, as Maradona laced through the pass to Burruchaga which led to Argentina's winner. German keeper Schumacher blamed himself for all three Argentine goals. He had completely missed the cross which allowed José Luis Brown in for the first. This and two successive defeats in World Cup finals indicated that the fates were now piling it on a bit for that Battiston incident and Schumacher's claim to be the best in the world. I felt sorry for him.

The following day I was reverting to my normal *Guardian* duties and flying to cover the crucial state elections in Chihuahua. After the final whistle, I asked Ron what he'd be up to. 'Off to PV again for a few days,' he said. 'Great Place. Then maybe Las Vegas.'

Nation *of* Shotstoppers

After three years abroad, the decision lay between going home or joining the ranks of permanent expatriates to the Third World. Membership was dotted with sad characters who were neither reconciled to the conditions in which they chose to live – but found themselves seduced, as it were, by their maids, dollars and bougainvillea – nor to the certainty that their distant homeland had changed from the idyll of some earlier day. I went home, concluding that as fine as it was to operate at the edge of and beyond the box, it was better to maintain some grip on what was happening nearer my own back line.

At Her Majesty's pleasure, the Kray twins had been off their patch for the past twenty years and one morning I received a letter, written in the spidery hand of Reg Kray, inviting me to inspect his maximum security lifestyle in Gartree prison. The TV programme I was working on in Birmingham was thinking of doing an item on whether the twins, now they'd served two-thirds of their thirty-year sentence, should be released for good behaviour.

It took weeks to get official permission for the visit. In the meantime, several inmates grew tired of such procedures and escaped in a helicopter which had landed in the exercise area. Other prisoners held back the guards trying to get at them and tension between the jail's staff and customers, I was told, had since been high. Guests and inmates sat in an area about the size of an average school classroom, with a tea-bar at one end and, in a corner at the other, a slightly raised platform with a desk and seated guard. Individual groups sat around tables, an extended Kenyan or Ugandan Asian family at one, visiting a small middle-aged man. What had he done, fiddled his VAT returns on a string of newsagents or petrol stations? It must have been quite some fraud to have got him into Category A, Gartree.

Reg Kray bounced through the door from the cells, lean, with closely clipped grey hair and in a tracksuit. He looked like one of the post-war PT boys, smaller than the average goalkeeper even from those days, but he'd been a boxer. Things had since moved on – he did yoga every morning before dawn. He pointed to another table; some of the Birmingham Six. It was very sad because everyone knew they were innocent. As for Ron and him, remission would be only fair. To make them serve out their sentence, when there were far worse people doing less, would be no more than society's revenge: 'retribution'. People today were more forgiving than that.

They had always been so in the East End, he insisted. The locals recognised that what Ron and Reg had done had only been among villains – George Cornell at the Blind Beggar on the Whitechapel Road, Jack 'the Hat' McVittie, in a basement where east London met gentrifying Stoke Newington. Old friends like Barbara Windsor would go on TV and say as much. People accepted things more generally than you'd think; homosexuality, for instance. I suggested only tough people like his brother Ron could have got away with being so openly gay in the East End. He said no, there'd been a lot of people who were and known to be. I wasn't convinced but though he'd said I should say if I disagreed about anything in our discussion, I didn't argue.

Broadmoor was relatively easy to get into. They put my call through to a phone on an echoing corridor, and an orderly shouted: 'Ronnie Kray, there's someone here wants to visit you. When can he come in?' After some muffled background sound, the person came back to me. 'He says next Tuesday. Is that OK?'

He wore a dark blue suit, hair brushed back, possibly with Brylcreem, and was as bulky as in the 1960s photos of his brother and him by David Bailey. When we'd shaken hands and said hello, he asked me if I had a light. The first thing I had to say to Ronnie Kray was 'no' to something he wanted. It felt awkward. 'No, s'alright,' he said, in the same faint and high voice of his brother, we'd get one in the canteen. He wouldn't let me see the bill for my tea and his four cans of Barbican, and screwed it up in his hand, in the tradition of East End hospitality.

He corrected me: yes, he had been sent down for the murder of George Cornell, but also, with Reg, for that of Jack 'the Hat'. The victims were people who were no good. He and his brother had been respected. Unprompted, he mentioned Lord Boothby. As for his own preferences, he put the record straight once more: he was bisexual. This was news to me but, again, where was the need to dispute? Yes, of course, it would be right to be let free, though he didn't push the point and I thought he seemed more content with his circumstances than his brother. He insisted Reg should be out of prison. Otherwise, it was true, it would only be 'retribution'.

When we finished he said, 'Good visit, wasn't it?' He got up and, as we shook hands, moved away from our table, which was towards the middle of the room, to sit on a chair with his back to the wall. Before I'd left, his attention was already focused on others in the room and surveying things before him.

The programme, based in Birmingham, was tabloid television of the 'Donahue' type popular in the USA. It hadn't had much of a run in Britain but, on a Friday night, was thought one way of tempting people to watch when they came home from the pub. The studio was packed with invited guests and audience, and issues thrashed out at eleven minutes per item. It generated more heat than light, as was the frequent complaint, but it was remarkable how people were prepared to come out and express themselves – transvestites, HIV-positive prostitutes, celibate wives and husbands, a guy from Watford who, one of a rare handful nationwide, had been driven by unemployment to become, of all things, a male stripper. I'd been to several interesting places in the world, from Siena to San Salvador, yet never before to Birmingham. At the 1956 Cup Final, Birmingham fans hadn't had a song of their own, so the stadium ground out the strains of 'Keep Right on to the End of the Road'. Today's audience, which came every week from England's second city or towns nearby, vigorously bashed around every chosen subject. Participants directly involved in the items came from all over the country. I hadn't realised British people were like this. Maybe they, or many of them, had always been.

A fellow from the *Daily Mirror* came on to discuss 'obsession'. Other invitees had a problem with drink and excessive cleaning. His was supporting Newcastle United. Since the days when Ronnie Simpson was in goal for their 1950s' Cup victories, they hadn't won a thing and were languishing in the Second Division. They drove him mad and he agreed to hypnosis. I assumed his involvement was a bit of cooked-up media showbiz to lighten the item. Then a few months later when I was working on the Seoul Olympics, a colleague told me he had a problem with Rotherham. He might – on a south Yorkshire impulse – find himself driving hundreds of miles to watch them in, for instance, Plymouth. He wondered why. So did I. Perhaps this was more characteristic of people who'd played on the field. A keeper could detach.

I had begun to wonder during the 1988 Cup Final. Dave Beasant's penalty save for Wimbledon was brilliant, a full-length dive to his left to parry the ball for a corner. It was the first ever in a Wembley final, and his celebrations were as noteworthy. There was still a game to be got on with, yet Beasant and his mates went into their high fives. The ref held up the game till they were ready. This was a change from the days when keepers used to scowl and wave their teammates away. Beasant also took a lot of the Wimbledon free kicks, some far outside his penalty area. Wimbledon were an 'all for one' team, however, with limited money and resources, which meant they had to work for each other more than normal. It was a form of total football brought on by necessity, not by choice in quite the same way as the trucking Dutch. I assumed Wimbledon and Beasant were a one-off. So was the Cup Final for him. He was transferred to Newcastle United for nearly a million pounds, raising the British keepers' record fee from the £750,000 Manchester United had recently paid Aberdeen for Jim Leighton. It didn't much help Beasant or Newcastle, who continued playing in a way that must have made the *Daily Mirror* man want to do things which would only land him in Broadmoor with Ron Kray.

A month after the Cup Final the programme sent me to join the England fans at the European championships in West Germany. They were smashing up Düsseldorf as I arrived on a hot night in a cloud of tear-gas. For a 'tiny minority' among the mass of decent fans, there were a lot of them. While only a few might put the boot in, there were many more who were happy to tag along. They loved their next stop, Frankfurt. Its medieval quarter of Sachsenhausen had either escaped much of the wartime bombing or been so well restored that there was a mass of small bars to congregate in off its cobbled streets. This was a great place, said a fellow from a Nottingham group I was tracking, and he pondered for a moment to provide colour and context, 'As good as Lloret'. Once British people would have been able to make comparisons only as between the piers of Southend and Brighton, or assert that the chips in Blackpool were the best of them all. Today's frame of reference as good as spanned the western continent. In one way or another, we'd all become seasoned Europeans.

Some of them agreed to appear on the programme live from Frankfurt. One of their mums was brought into the Birmingham studio, harangued her son on air, said she didn't know what she was going to do with him, but he only had to wait till he came home. He looked very sheepish, as if it only needed a few more like his mum in any police force to end the problem. Paul Scarrott, an east Midlands guy well into his twenties and media-styled 'king of the hooligans', had been thrown out of Germany and phoned in to say he wanted to be on the programme. Scarrott said he was fed up with the hassle, all the press and TV people camped on his doorstep, bothering his girlfriend and the like. He was thinking of retiring from it all. Later he did and ran away to Spain where, living as a vagrant, he drank himself to death.

In one Sachsenhausen incident, a group of south-east London nasties were said to have hit a young German woman in the face with a glass. By the time I arrived the police had everyone out of the bar and gathered in a group on the cobbles. They were letting a young German bouncer built for the marines move into the crowd, yelling, grabbing by the collar each of those he identified as the guilty parties. He threw them one by one into the back of a police van, though on the way ran them face first into a very resistant wall. No nose would have survived the impact of this summary German justice. Within the hushed ranks of the quaking crowd, a fellow standing near me, and well away from the bouncer, bravely shouted what should have been a rhetorical question but one which came out sounding like a plea: 'Come on, lads, are we just going to stand here and take this?' As the bouncer bellowed and the helmeted police stood rhythmically slapping their night sticks into the palms of their hands, the silence kind of gave you the answer. It was one of those moments that was almost comical. Maybe, in its way, it was also seminal.

A member of a leading London firm of hooligans I met some years later (he was plastering our kitchen) was indignant that Mrs Thatcher claimed to have solved their problem. After the ninety-six people crushed to death at Hillsborough in the spring of 1989, the Taylor Report and the concept of the all-seater stadium, she took credit, he protested, where little was due. Serious fighters had found the police were getting too clever. He'd been arrested on occasions by people of the same age, in jeans and trainers, whom he and his mates thought were part of their crowd. He'd been threatened with a possible sentence of several years. But he did underline how, in keeping with the principles of Thatcherism, a number of his mates had turned to entrepreneurship, namely bashing out illegal pills and compact discs. It was ecstasy and the sound of music that had led them to no longer want to fight; the 'summer of love' and the European championships of 1988 had been the last run of the serious hoolie. There was still some trouble. Some picked up what they identified as the nation's ball and ran with it, as they had in Dublin in February 1995, with their cries of 'smash the IRA'. But most of the trouble had been pushed outside the sophisticated urban centres, almost to the northerly line of civilisation itself. These days it was caused by kids from places like Carlisle.

In eastern Europe, Gorbachev was the first non-exiled Russian since Lev Yashin whom we liked and with whom we could, as Mrs Thatcher said, 'do business'. To end the Cold War, it just needed that extra threat from Washington to break the Soviet economy if it had tried to keep up with Star Wars. President Reagan had scratched his line in the dirt in El Salvador but Berlin was its true location. The Wall came down.

For the 1990 World Cup in Italy, I went with ITV to chart the progress of the Irish team. In their first game they'd been drawn to play England in Sardinia. The collective mass of the Irish press and TV and the team's good-humoured fans in the stadium were very excited about it, presumably for historical reasons; as Mexico would with the USA, so the Republic of Ireland always welcomed the chance to take a pop at its overbearing neighbour. But to me the game didn't feel like an international. This had nothing to do with the Irish having an English manager in Jack Charlton, or several players who had been brought up in England, but that games with Ireland felt more like a domestic kickabout. The Irish weren't 'foreign'. That was how we'd got away with hanging on to our record of never having lost at home to foreigners when we'd been beaten by them forty-odd years before.

Such games couldn't generate the excitement they used to. Once upon a time the most important thing in the world on a dull Wednesday afternoon was to know, say, how England had fared against Wales at Ninian Park, Cardiff, or the Racecourse Ground, Wrexham. But that was in the days when the major contests were between us, we who had invented the game. Matches against the Republic were outside the home international championship, but only slightly. To be drawn together in a world competition like this felt as if it was a formality we had to run through, conserving resources for the really big games against more exotic foes, and not duffing each other up unduly on the way. The 1–1 draw in Cagliari, therefore, seemed a reasonable compromise.

Before Ireland's game against Egypt in Sicily, we filmed the crew of an Egyptian naval ship in Palermo harbour. In their white uniforms, the sailors comprised their team's travelling support. They received us on board with tea and courteous talk of 'the history of our two great nations, from which mutual respect and friendship had grown'. We went back a long way, they pointed out. They drew against Holland and were unlucky not to win. 'I thought the gyppos played well,' noted Ron Atkinson, former 1950s National Serviceman.

The Italians had presented the World Cup with their customarily sharp eye on style and design. TV coverage came with lots of shots of the country, its medieval spires, leaning towers and Luciano Pavarotti warbling 'Nessun Dorma' over all. In Italy the game had long been more broadly integrated between the social classes. Thanks to the Italians' packaging, suggestive of a bit of culture, an important link was made to the audience in Britain between football and loftier things.

Once the Irish were eliminated by the host nation in Rome, our crew was dispatched to be with the Germans in the north. Their hotel, near the shores of Lake Como, was an ancient pile which looked as if it might have been a castle built in the style of nutty King Ludwig. Sepp Maier fitted in reasonably well. Aside from the rigours of the *Pressestunde*, our job was to film the Germans in their camp, Mrs Beckenbauer topless by the pool and anything else a commercial television network required to build up atmosphere for the semi-final against England.

Turin's Stadium of the Alps was half empty. Later stages of the World Cup had a habit of being like this. Fans of the teams and a few dignitaries came, but by now many others had gone home or weren't bothered. Had US marketing techniques been deployed, as they would be in four years' time, there'd doubtless have been a sell-out. A colleague and I sat in an underpopulated part of the stadium, an upper tier with a fine sweeping view. We had a night off to watch the game, another crew burdened with the task of shooting it. Hence we didn't have to jump up every few minutes to check post-match access to the players' tunnel, whether Brian Moore had a ticket to get into the stadium, or why the police wanted to throw Gary Newbon out. In the absence of tension, it was funny to think this was a World Cup semi-final.

After about twenty minutes my neighbour said: 'Gazza's storming it.' Paul Gascoigne was and continued to do so. The German goal was lucky, and came from another high-rise deflection. There was a monotonous regularity to the way this kept happening: Seeler's flick in 1970, Maradona's knuckle in 1986 and now this, off an England defender's foot, which caught Peter Shilton, forty, some yards in front of his bar. He couldn't get back before the ball fell beneath it. I wondered if four years earlier he might have. A little after Lineker had scored the equaliser, Gascoigne tackled a German player, who, an apparent alumnus of RADA's Berlin branch, hit the turf like a grouse in mid-August. Beckenbauer, and the rest of the Germans on the bench, sprang into the air as if clad in tights and cod-piece. Here they were again, members of a society stereotyped as a tireless machine – *Vorsprung durch Technik* – who forged ahead through precision and application, yet who suddenly reduced themselves to shameless dramatics. Their protests and fist-shakings at the referee got Gazza the yellow card. With that he'd incurred in another game, it meant he wouldn't have played in the final had England reached it. He shed a tear. You could just make it out from our distant seats. 'Ah, look,' we said, 'poor Gazza's crying.'

At this moment the TV director was just doing his job. He ordered his camera to zoom in for the people at home. Little did we know how many of them were watching. Since we'd been away for weeks, cut off in one World Cup training camp or another, we had hardly any idea how much domestic excitement was being generated, and that England's streets were now, as we later heard, 'deserted'. Thus, the camera moved in and brought the moment into almost everyone's homes. Gascoigne shed what was difficult to discern in northern Italy as anything other than a private tear. About 800 miles away, a nation wept.

The penalty shoot-out saw the Germans defy Atkinson's law of spot-kick physics: 'Stand still and one in five will come straight at you.' They reverted to superior *Technik* and each German effort arrowed into a corner of Shilton's net. He had no chance with any. The outcome, while disappointing, was familiar. It was a setback but one with the attendant glories of a determined and heroic performance. Were we not at our best in our darkest days? The struggle only continued, things were never 'over'. Least of all when the fat man sang. As the game ended in tears, the TV credits rolled to 'Nessun Dorma': 'No one sleeps . . . I'll win at dawn.' In essence it was saying, 'never mind, we'll be back', a goalkeeper's anthem, if ever there was one. At home it was loved by everyone, keepers all in spirit. For the footballing masses it had a catchily posh something, while for those of a non-football bent it rounded matters off nicely – it was a bit flash, a bit continental. Suckered by the Pav and Gaz routine, working and middle classes united to create the moment modern football was born. In the Stadio degli Alpi you'd never have known.

The world and football had come in from the cold. Goalkeepers were fairly quick to succumb. It had been inevitable since the collective had reached out its hand of fairness more than thirty years earlier over assaults on the keeper. The back-pass law was introduced in 1992: if the ball was kicked back to the goalkeeper by his own team, he couldn't pick it up and had to kick it. The awful effect was to pull him out of isolation and make him play with his feet. He became an additional member of what had been his defensive back four, another one of the team. The aim was to encourage open, attacking play. The virtues of defence were to be downplayed. They were no longer so relevant.

New technology compounded the problem. The old goal-keeper's guild, with its strict laws on demarcation of job responsibility, had seen its power eroded and so, too, had the print unions. Eddie Shah was sent in as the stalking-horse, took an expensive hit with the colourful pages of *Today*, but made headway for the cause. My uncle Keith, born just before the war, who had followed my grandad into a job in the print, stood on the picket line at Wapping for a year but Rupert Murdoch rode through it to claim the prize. Apart from the many pages that could be added to newspapers without troublesome printers seeking extra payment, there were a lot of column inches spare now all the affairs of the Cold War had passed. New satellite TV channels also created large amounts of extra airtime, Murdoch foremost again.

The nation's majority sport was to fill the vacuum. Football was war by other means. Expanded reporting on the game's ins and outs and its personalities were just right for the celebratory post-Cold War emphasis on leisure and entertainment. Advertising and other businesses were attracted by the game's suddenly discovered cachet. Not only the rich signed up. People who hadn't spent more at a football match than what it took to buy a programme and bag of Percy Dalton's roasted peanuts shelled out welfare benefit and credit they didn't have on Newcastle season tickets or Manchester United away shirts in umpteen colours a season. For an extra £5 – a bargain at only 50p a letter – they'd write 'SCHMEICHEL' on it for you.

Something still wasn't quite right. Previously it hadn't been the done thing among 'thinking' people to have a public interest in football. Individual thinkers risked being written off as a 'football boy', abandoned like a keeper stuck on the pitch peering into a January fog while his team was already back in the dressing room. It was Nick Hornby who provided the philosophical framework many required to express a liking for football. Earlier, the problem had been that you simply liked the game. The dilemma now was you might not like it enough. It was essential to be 'obsessed'. People who found themselves inexplicably roaming to see Rotherham or niggled by Newcastle suddenly were everywhere.

In Islington's Liverpool Road, not 200 yards from where I'd been to dinner in 1982 and where fellow guests those years before could not have cared less about the Spain World Cup, I was sitting in a restaurant when the chef burst out of his kitchen and began speaking animatedly to his customers. I imagined he was in the modern tradition of wild-haired lords of cuisine, given to lashing into those who provided his living for their over-use of the salt. Nothing of the kind – he was after everyone's assessment of that afternoon's football results and the latest league standings. The colleague I'd been with in Grenada after the US invasion in 1983 I saw pictured, sad-faced, in the *Telegraph* magazine, Arsenal scarf bundled around his neck as if advertising Fisherman's Friends. He'd crossed the continent missing boats and trains, only to see Arsenal beaten in the last minute of the 1995 European Cup Winners Cup Final by Nayim's hopeful halfway-line punt over David Seaman's head. He had arrived back exhausted and somewhat clueless as to what made him do it. But would he do it again? Oh, yes. When we'd been in the Caribbean we had discussed a number of things, not least a shared connection with Islington. Its football never got near our agenda. He spoke well, had a double-barrelled name and I'd had him down as a rugby man.

David Mellor, a former cabinet minister turned media-ham, said he recalled when it was easier in polite company to talk about child sex than football. He was right – at the end of the 1970s, when it was reasoned that paedophiles were in line for a liberal break. Lately, 'Who do you support?' had become the statutory first question in personality interviews. Jools Holland, a talented musician, answered he wasn't interested in sport and risked appearing odd, a true goalkeeper of our times. Andrew Lloyd Webber turned up at Elton John's fiftieth birthday bash in a Leyton Orient outfit. It was a red strip and I doubted he'd known it had ever been blue. Looking at the picture of him waving gleefully to the crowd, I wondered if he'd been put up to it by his Orient-supporting brother, Julian, an internationally acclaimed cellist, but who somehow never quite won the same level of credit. If so, it had certainly helped balance the books. By the most reasonable assessment, Baron Lloyd-Webber looked an absolute berk.

Advertisers moved in both to exploit the situation and to edge it along to their advantage with slogans like 'You think it's a religion. We do, too'. People who thought others might have it – this football thing – would hover around each other if uncertain, tempted to come up and touch the comparably afflicted. Their looks said 'yes, we know'. The great thing about being, or professing to be, obsessed was that it gave you a 'condition'. Conditions had once been shunned as intolerable phenomena which got in society's way. Now, in keeping with the new mood for Britain gently encouraged by Reg Kray, and tenaciously fought for by Diana, Princess of Wales – a less judgemental Britain, which replaced retribution with forgiveness – a 'condition' had to be cherished. 'I have come to accept,' wrote a *Guardian* journalist about a friend of hers (an 'artist and father of three') who after Manchester United's loss to Everton in the 1995 Cup Final, 'went up to the bedroom, drew the curtains, lay on the bed and cried in the darkness'. There was an alternative, of course. She, or for decency's sake someone closer to him, could have strode in, let in the light and, having tipped him off the bed, told the sensitive soul to get out and, say, campaign for the poor in Mauretania. But that would have been from a far less tolerant age

Crying used to be for times like becoming aware at the age of nineteen you were being sent to war or hearing of the death of Manchester United's young players at Munich in 1958. At the death of Bobby Moore in February 1993, Geoff Hurst doubted he could appear on television to talk about his old West Ham teammate and England captain without crying, but managed to. Malcolm Allison, hard-bitten ex-coach who had discovered Moore, did shed a tear. The fact that Moore, at fifty-one, was too young to die and had led the most famous English (arguably, British) sporting victory, moved people beyond the game itself. It prompted a *Guardian* editorial, which asked whether we were pining for lost and possibly mythical days of achievements past.

More recently, many people were surprised at the level of their emotions when Elton John sang at the funeral of the Princess of Wales. Amid the extraordinary clamour of the occasion, the crowd's conclusion was that they'd appreciated the rebel, the one who refused, or for some reason failed, to hitch up with the team.

Goalkeepers today, therefore, find themselves in a far more expressive and understanding world than they were ever used to. How do they shape up? Well, they are quite different physical specimens. Joe Corrigan at 15 stone and 6 feet 4 inches was jeered at by crowds for his bulk when he'd kept goal for Manchester City in the 1970s and '80s. Now such dimensions are routine among keepers who train with weights and achieve fitness unknown to the PT boys of the 1940s and '50s. Frank Swift had been a post-war giant of a man at 6 feet 2 inches yet, in a recent assessment I read of Newcastle and Ireland's Shay Given, the one question raised against his qualities was that he was a gnome-like 6 feet 1 inch. The baby boom years of NHS cod liver oil and grainy, concentrated orange juice make it near impossible to recall that 1950s/early '60s keepers hovered around the 5 feet 9 inches mark.

All keepers also have their floppy gloves. If you don't have hands like plates from birth, you can buy them at your local sports store. I wished I'd had them at school and the Orient, but only finally acquired a pair in 1992. This was for a rare appearance for Chelsea Casuals – for whom Brian Glanville continued regularly to turn out in his sixties – against a Sunday team of gas fitters out somewhere north-west of Brentford. We lost, though on the few occasions I got my hands near the ball to any useful effect, it stuck.

Buying the gloves implied another sign of the keeper going soft. I alleviated my discomfort by narrowing my choice to those endorsed by Neville Southall or by Steve Ogrizovic. As a world-class Welsh goalkeeper, Southall was the inheritor of Jack Kelsey's cloak. He'd have looked smarter if he'd worn it, but his preference was for the collar of his undershirt stuck half in, half out of his jersey and his shin-guards strapped outside his socks. He'd slowly risen up through the ranks of Bury and Port Vale to an array of Welsh caps, two league championships and FA Cups and a Cup Winners Cup for Everton. While his teammates celebrated their Cup Final wins at lavish London receptions,

Southall slipped away to drive home alone, across country to his family. Ogrizovic had been stuck as understudy at Liverpool to Ray Clemence. The first-team spot was then awarded to Bruce Grobbelaar, ex-Rhodesia, latterly of Zimbabwe, an instinctive, often brilliant keeper, if liable sometimes to have required the help of his defenders to sort out a tricky predicament. Often safer on the high ball, Ogrizovic only established himself when he moved on to plucky Coventry. I chose the Southalls, but in either case there'd have been little risk of form winning out over substance.

Towering modern keepers, with their physical and psychological advantage of enormous hands, you'd have thought, must surely constitute a safe and commanding presence around their 6- and 18-yard lines. Strangely, however, they don't. David Seaman, of Arsenal and England, having recovered from a loss of confidence during the early '90s under Graham Taylor's international management, is one such character. Beyond him, the quest becomes tougher. Nigel Martyn, often regarded as Seaman's number two, is fondly remembered by Crystal Palace fans as an old-style British keeper, and for some inexplicable spasms once or twice a season on the edge of his penalty area. He didn't entirely lose the habit when he moved to Leeds. Still, everyone is fallible, and many others far more so. The impression in the British premier leagues, let alone in the lower divisions which once produced strong enough backline characters to face the world, is of keepers who advance, panic and, oh my god, flap.

The keeper may only be rebelling against the tyranny of mass expectation. In principle, this is thoroughly commendable and the result of the goalkeeper's unique standpoint of being able to survey and question the collective's tendency to madness. As for what the crowd expects on the field of play, it has been long assumed the goalkeeper would take the crossball without acknowledgement. His dropping it may be just a way of showing what a tough job he has. On the other hand, his susceptibility fits with contemporary debates on 'rights and responsibilities' which feature in weighty newspaper leader pages: are people, for example as the *Daily Telegraph* might thunder, more keen to demand their right to state support, than to fulfil a responsibility to look for work? While leading footballers, or their agents, declare their right to £50,000-plus a week, do they not see it as a duty to avoid expulsion from the field in important World Cup matches? Rule changes many years ago, which in Thatcheresque time would have earned the 'nanny state' tag, handed the keeper in Britain the same right as those on the continent, namely not to be challenged on the high ball. Along the way he has just relinquished responsibility to catch it.

There has to be good reason for this. The first is easy to find: an old-fashioned, continental conspiracy. In days of yore, foreign hosts simply fixed the ball and British teams rolled up off the ferry with their own to counter it. But from the 1950s the continentals became more devious, paradoxically by being above board: they formally introduced a new ball. We first tried it at home with the Belgians in 1952 – you could usually rely on them not to do the dirty, since we'd often entered wars to keep them safe. But we had allowed a white ball for that apocalyptic Hungary game in 1953. It couldn't be said we weren't fair people, and much good it did us. Balls since have swerved and flown at increasingly alarming angles and speeds. For the keeper, they have been like foreigners themselves – perpetually difficult to grasp.

The cross has also become rarer. This was noted, again, as far back as the Hungarians in the 1950s. Continentals used the long ball less than British teams and weren't in the habit of pumping it in from the wings towards a big centre-forward. Combined with the fact that balls have boomed and swung, it meant keepers became less the dourly advancing takers of crosses, and more the flighty reactive types. They have developed into 'shotstoppers'.

'Shotstopping' has stealthily crept into the vocabulary. Maybe I was suffering an unfortunate bout of adolescent deafness, but I don't recall it existing on the training grounds of the 1960s. Had a manager appeared from his office to ask his trainer, 'What's the lad in goal like over there?' and been told he was a good shotstopper, he'd have responded, 'Well, what do you think he's meant to be?' in earthily rhetorical form.

The term has become common currency as efforts have been made to move goalkeeping's status from that of a mystical art to a graspable science. Once few people thought about what keepers did and they were sent to train alone at whatever they thought fit. Then avid students of the backline game pioneered as goalkeeping coaches: Alan Hodgkinson, formerly of Sheffield

United and England, who was inspired to bring new techniques into the British game after he'd stood, in his teens, on the Wembley terraces watching the Hungary spectacular; Bob Wilson, formerly of Loughborough College, Arsenal and Scotland. Others followed, like Joe Corrigan, Ray Clemence and Peter Bonetti, when he'd returned from purdah as a postman on the Isle of Mull. All internationals, they broke down what they knew, like scientists would, into goalkeeping's component parts: cross-taking, distribution – composed of throwing and kicking – and, fatefully, shotstopping.

Since shotstopping is so dependent on reflexes, it doesn't actually require much thinking. When the ball is hit, you have little choice but to get into your save without pondering the matter, and then suddenly, dramatically, it is over. Great to look at and do, it follows that it may conceal what isn't to be found underneath. To hear a commentator or anyone remark knowledgeably of a keeper that he is 'a good shotstopper' can be as much a cause of concern as contentment. It raises the legitimate question: 'Yes, and how well does he take a cross?'

Where stopping the ball going in the net is the ultimate function for which the keeper is responsible, the cross is when he takes responsibility. He has to weigh up quickly whether that high loop winging towards his area of play is the 'keeper's ball' or his defence's to deal with. He must work out when he will start to come for it: too fast, and he'll have to check stride, wait and have others crowding his eventual jump, or he'll find he has come too far and the ball is too high to reach; too slow, and others will reach it first. There may be seconds – not many, but more than enough – for the keeper to think and worry: has he got his timing right, who is running in on him, is he going to collide with one of his own team and, on a bad day, is his confidence up to catching the ball at all? All this necessitates a great deal of keeping cool. Today, however, keepers are less the introverted cross-takers, separate from the crowd and prompting its murmured approval without it quite knowing what it is he is doing; they are more engaged with the crowd, doing the reactive, excitable stuff that all can identify with. They express themselves more openly, representatives of a nation of shotstoppers.

Goalkeepers now turn to receive the salute of the crowd. The penalty shoot-out is a case in point, when even the most mediocre of saves has a keeper running around like a truly mad person, before ending up under a bundle of his teammates' bodies. In Genoa in 1990, Ireland's World Cup game against Romania went to penalties. Packie Bonner's was the deciding save, a good one, not as fantastic as he'd ever made but it did the job. He was the shyest man in the Irish camp, not unlike his counterpart from the north, Pat Jennings. Even Bonner when he'd made his save went into a few leaps of joy, albeit as if he expected to be tapped on the shoulder and told to calm down. I spied similar constraint from David Seaman, after he'd performed in the shoot-out to give England an otherwise undeserved victory over Spain during the 1996 European championships. His celebratory leaping didn't quite let go. He looked slightly embarrassed.

It may on the other hand have been his outfit. After the roll-neck gave way in the 1950s, the round-neck jersey in green became the standard for at least twenty-five years. Now keepers are wearing garb which, under floodlights, is as difficult to look at as a flashing strobe. Novelist A. S. Byatt alluded to the new style during Euro 96. Her presence itself indicated who was likely to be at a football match these days. Dr Germaine Greer was also in the Wembley crowd, sniffily noting the levels of heaving manhood. Ms Byatt was more at one with them, to the point of carnal ecstasy when the crowd reached its chorus of 'Football's Coming Home'. Gasping for air, she described Seaman as 'resplendent like a scarlet lord'. I wondered whether he'd live it down. But two years later, there he was, England's unpretentious keeper, at the Elle Style Awards ceremony in London, being voted the most stylish sports star of the year. Seaman did have the decency to say he was very surprised.

Clad in luminous shirts, goalkeepers are now the subject of enlightenment philosophies from football's progressives. Enlightened clubs in Europe, said Andy Roxburgh, the former Scotland manager turned technical director of Uefa, were teaching young keepers to be part of the defence. He cited clubs like Ajax of Amsterdam, who were training boy goalkeepers to use their feet to intercept balls 'more than merely catch them'.

'Merely' sounded like a nifty bit of rationalisation of all those years Scotland have endured jibes from Jimmy Greaves over their keepers. Who cared if they dropped the ball once in a while?

Where was the big deal in merely catching it? There was a historic resonance in a Scot's singing of continental praises. As anciently illustrated by the ill-fated Mary, queen of that people, they have long wanted to circumvent the English with their European alliances. Oft classified as dour, with the English crowding their space, the Scots have shown they have an outgoing streak in them. In the empire they were always the ones who got out there to mingle and merge, and their football fans also made a much better job of it. But of more uncomfortable significance was that Roxburgh cited a club from Holland. Goalkeepers of tomorrow, it seemed, were to be from the tradition of shuttling Dutchmen – Jan Jongbloed reincarnated, squinting and sprinting upfield and back. The future was the playground rush goalie.

And the continent is coming to meet Britain whether or not Britain likes or invites it. Upwards of a dozen continental keepers have lately been playing in the English and Scottish Premier Leagues, for a number of reasons. Pressure is on managers and boards of directors to provide quick success, not least because the stock markets that many clubs are listed on require instant returns. Short-termism dictates there is little time to nurture young keepers. When they do emerge, their own stock is so rare they command multi-million-pound transfer fees. Managers seek cheaper options, looking abroad for an off-the-peg Czech or Estonian.

There are some rare others, too. At Leicester City, Kasey Keller, an American, has occupied at length the goalmouths where stood Gordon Banks and Peter Shilton. Mark Bosnich, from Australia, a land of cricketers, established his career at Aston Villa. The most successful overseas keeper, Peter Schmeichel, was bought by Manchester United after Denmark's surprise success in the 1992 European championships. Initially he had to curb his preference for punching the ball to meet the demands of the British game, but was so successful that he was regarded by many as the best in the world. Gordon Banks, no less, argues that British keepers should have been learning more than they have done from the likes of Schmeichel, at his best, on how to get off their lines and come for the cross.

The problem may simply be that, wherever they hail from, all are reared in a context where the goalkeeping pace is set by the enlightened kickers of footballs, not the mere catchers of them.

Liverpool's goalkeeping coach Joe Corrigan insists that priorities remain what they were and that the cross is the most important aspect of the keeper's art. Yet if that were the case, would David James's career have survived the huge loss of confidence he suffered soon after he was rewarded with his first England call-up three seasons ago? Corrigan and James's manager, Roy Evans, stuck with him as he went through an awful series of spills. This might not have been the case in an earlier era. There were suggestions the Liverpool keeper had a Nintendo habit and was trapped for wasted hours fiddling with things like cybernetic hedgehogs. Yet as a condition, it was forgiven. It raised the question of how, for example, would Peter Shilton have passed the time in the event of a confidence collapse? Likely he'd have been at the ground after the others had left for lunch and the rest of the day, physically wrestled the bog brushes from the hands of the apprentices and made them pump crosses at him into the late evening hours. But then, the 1990s were no longer the prime times of Shilton.

In December 1996 I went to Leyton Orient to see his 1,000th league game. That tally was quite aside from the 125 appearances Shilton, now forty-seven, had made for England, his myriad FA and European Cup games, and assorted others. At the Brisbane Road door they said the press box was full but they'd find me a seat – I let it slip that I'd been a Junior at the club some blue moons previously. Shilton was the latest in a line of memorable Orient keepers: Dave Groombridge, Frank George, Bill Robertson, John Jackson, not to mention Pat Welton and Mike Pinner. Conceivably, with average crowds down around 3,000, he was also the last.

The game was against Brighton, who, for reasons chiefly financial, were under threat of dropping out of the Third Division entirely, and gave him little to do. In the Portacabin where the press conference was held, I asked him which was the best of the thousand. He couldn't remember. I suggested Leicester's 1–0 victory over Spurs at White Hart Lane in 1967, shortly after he'd taken over from Banks. To all visible intents and purposes his teammates had, apart from their one effort on goal, stayed in the dressing room, leaving Shilton, at the age of eighteen, to handle Tottenham on his own. No, he couldn't remember that game. Not unreasonably, there were just too many. He said he felt he still had it in him to play for England, and that there weren't too many good keepers around any more. There came a time, though, when you thought you could go on, yet suddenly realised you couldn't do it quite as you used to.

The next April the decision was taken out of his hands. Orient manager Tommy Taylor said Shilton's services were no longer required. The reason: Shilton couldn't kick the ball far enough. It left Shilton mystified. He didn't see anything wrong with his kicking. Besides: 'I thought keepers were supposed to be judged on their goalkeeping.' A scandalous whisper among Orient supporters claimed that, once having seen off the exciting publicity opportunity presented by Shilton's 1,000th game, the club had coolly assessed it could no longer pay the wages he required. Whatever, the fact stood that Orient had said a goalkeeper who had 125 England caps, and who since 1967 had put a foot wrong no more than a half dozen times that anyone could remember, was not equipped to turn out for a club placed seventeenth of twenty-four in the lowest division of the English league . . . because he was lacking a few yards in his kick. That Orient could dream of saying such a thing, in the remotest belief there might be an audience out there to listen, was a sign of where British goalkeeping stood.

○　　○　　○

As Britain has moved towards continental merger, so its keepers have moved the same way. Europe and war are not the threats they were, so isolation is not the splendid thing the British imagined it to be. A society that values coming out of itself, no longer sanctifies the ethos of standing alone, or keeping ourselves to ourselves. The British are more prepared to group with others, relate, have a great time.

To some extent this is a rediscovery of the past. In Shakespeare's time, the British, or at least the English, were regarded as what might be understood today as the Latins of Europe, good-time people. Whatever the karaoke classics of the Shakespearian age, the groundlings in the Globe theatre were in the habit of singing them. The later reserve which was built in to the character was probably a result of hundreds of years of wars and military discipline. The Conservative Party failed to spot the signs as the 1997 elections approached, and allowed their scepticism about Europe to reach levels far above that of the population. Britons weren't exactly doing the Grand Tour again – the Circus Maximus and the Parthenon – but they knew their Tossa and Lloret del Mar.

The upshot was that the 'once dingy backwater' of Islington seized the commanding heights of power. The canal tunnel roof had been renovated and pleasure craft chugged through. The threat of weeds ensnaring and pulling local children beneath the water wasn't what it was, and willows brushed the faces of bankside strollers. Community newsletters had circulated around my parents' way for some years. I'd seen articles on 'how things used to be', glorying in how Grandma Snow, with her front-parlour flower business down the street, used to wheel her cart to Covent Garden market at three in the morning, then back before breakfast. The Polish church around the corner in Devonia Road was thriving but St Peter's just along from it, where I'd last been for my grandad's funeral in 1979, had closed for lack of custom and been converted into expensive apartments. By way of places to eat, Upper Street had once boasted not much more than the Blue Kettle near the old Lyon's Corner House at the Angel, the Wimpy facing Islington Green and a Cypriot café opposite St Mary's church. Now it was no surprise to find places serving Cuba Libres on tap, stuffed chiles, whether mild or piquant, and the finer specialities of the Eritrean kitchen.

Social democracy had sat out the Thatcher years in the likes of Gibson and Myddelton Squares. The force itself arose from Barnsbury. Not in the form of a mob outside the school gates to beat up our centre-forward, but an individual sent to exchange headers in a kids' playground in Brighton with Kevin Keegan. Tony Blair's house was a couple of streets away from where my great-cousin had been killed in the wartime bombing, and just the right side of the Caledonian Road to command premium prices. The Labour leader was measured about Europe during the election campaign but, in general, preached an unsceptical view. A few weeks after his overwhelming victory, the final retreat from greatness came with the passing of Hong Kong. Unencumbered by empire we could stride purposefully into Europe, like Peter Schmeichel at Old Trafford pacing upfield for a late corner.

But in the manner of Schmeichel pulling a hamstring on such

occasions, our progress stalled abruptly. Yes, yes, we had said we wanted to be in there with them all, participating far more keenly than before, but a few details had yet to be worked out. It was all about being on different economic cycles. We'd peddle for a while longer on our own, rather than in tandem, if they didn't mind, especially on the united currency. We were Europeans, just unready for the euro. We asked if we could be in on the meetings of great continental minds scheduled to supervise its introduction – a classic 'of but not in' the team, that left other European Union members aghast. But if they wouldn't see sense, that was their problem.

They needed our dispassionate guidance. Italians, Spaniards, Portuguese, they wouldn't have known how to form a bus queue, but give them a group to join and they couldn't resist it. They just wouldn't think the implications through. The French would be in it, as long as they could lead. Look how they were trying to smuggle their man late into the central bank job, when everyone had agreed Europe's money was better off initially under the control of a Dutchman. Even the Germans couldn't be trusted. You'd have thought them reliable in dull monetary matters, since the horrors of 1920s hyper-inflation still played such a part in their thinking. But now they'd hit upon the idea of revaluing their gold reserves – an accountancy fix – in order to meet the Maastricht criteria. Thanks, but, for the while, no thanks. We always had our special relationship to tide us over. Indeed, after the election, there were the Clintons and Blairs together in sunny London, all smiles, visits to Shakespeare's renovated Globe and, if appearances were anything to go by, the oldest of friends.

Signs of the ancient nation's detached greatness were discernible during the 1998 World Cup in France. This was not always for the best reasons. Some of our boys went on the rampage again, this time in Marseilles. It was to loud condemnation, yet not from everyone. Some political and journalistic thinkers defended them, pointing out how these were the ranks from whom we historically recruited our foot soldiers. You couldn't expect them both to behave, and be ready for potential calls to arms. Their aggression was sometimes unfortunate but had been so often gloriously employed in our extraordinary fighting past.

It hovered, too, over the tournament's goalkeeping. Among

the analysts and commentators lively discussion was aired on the subject, particularly as it concerned foreign keepers. The Paraguayan José Luis Chilavert excited much of it – captain, free-kick specialist and penalty-taker, he was lauded as one of the keepers of the competition. I didn't recall it being mentioned, but he also personified where goalkeeping's future was likely bound. British keeping was not discussed at great length, at least in a direct sense. But the general impression was conveyed that we did it right and others didn't. Conversation returned again and again to studied contemplation of the cross – how others handled it and to what extent they brought calm and comfort to their defence.

The Tunisian in England's first match, Chokri El Onaer, didn't have what it took. Taffarel of Brazil was game, but no Gilmar. Jorge Campos of Mexico showed a mix of agility and first-class handling but didn't inspire confidence, not Alan Hansen's at least: 'What can you expect from a keeper who's 4 feet 6?' From Europe, the veteran Spaniard Andoni Zubizarreta was suspect in several aspects of his game and Andreas Köpke in the German goal looked unusually shaky. Fabien Barthez, for the hosts and eventual winners, smiled a lot but more in a way to suggest good fun and entertainment, than someone upon whose shoulders you'd rest responsibility for your life savings.

Of the British World Cup contingent, David Seaman had little of note to do. Jim Leighton, signing off from world competition at forty, had a fine first half's shotstopping in Scotland's game against Brazil. In a way, though, their presence was immaterial. What was important was that behind and over it all was a kind of phantom British keeper. Through the century he had set the standard on how to do it right, a standard others rarely matched. He was a mix of characters: the old fellow in the flat cap, watching the ball loop down towards him, rattling his crossbar as he followed it over the top; Swift getting up and on with it; Kelsey, Banks, Shilton, Clemence and any number of others coming out to claim the high ball; Jennings 'standing up'. This was strange because the species was no less endangered at home than on these foreign fields. Soon it was as likely to be history as the empire and other central features of what Britain once believed constituted its greatness. Yet for now the feeling persisted that as long as the British goalkeeper was there – if only in mind – then there was still something left.

Banks, Gordon, *Banks of England* (Arthur Barker, 1980)

Bartram, Sam, *Sam Bartram by Himself* (Burke Publishing, 1956)

Bonetti, Peter, *Leaping to Fame* (Stanley Paul, 1968)

Clemence, Ray, *Clemence on Goalkeeping* (Lutterworth Press, 1977)

Dunphy, Eamon, *Only a Game?* (Kestrel Books, 1976)

Encyclopaedia of Sport (Sampson Low, Marston and Co., 1959)

Glanville, Brian, *The History of the World Cup* (Faber and Faber, 1984)

——(ed.), *The Footballer's Companion* (Eyre and Spottiswoode, 1962)

Gregg, Harry, *Wild About Football* (Soccer Book Club, 1961)

Hamilton, Ian, *The Faber Book of Soccer* (Faber and Faber, 1992)

Hazlewood, Nick, *In the Way!* (Mainstream Publishing, 1996)

Jennings, Pat, *Pat Jennings – An Autobiography* (Willow Books Collins, 1983)

Kelly, Stephen (ed.), *The Kingswood Book of Football* (Kingswood Press, 1992)

Kelsey, Jack, *Over the Bar* (Stanley Paul, 1958)

Lahr, John, *Prick Up Your Ears* (Penguin, 1980)

——(ed.), *The Orton Diaries* (Methuen, 1986)

Leatherdale, Clive, *England's Quest for the World Cup* (Methuen, 1984)

Merrick, Gil, *I See it All* (Museum Press, 1954)

Miller, David, *Stanley Matthews – The Authorised Biography* (Pavilion Books, 1989)

Moynihan, John, *The Soccer Syndrome* (Sportspages Simon and Schuster, 1965)

Pele, *My Life and the Beautiful Game* (New English Library, 1978)

Shilton, Peter, *The Magnificent Obsession* (World's Work, 1982)

Stepney, Alex, *Alex Stepney* (Arthur Barker, 1978)

Swift, Frank, *Football from the Goalmouth* (Sporting Handbooks, 1948)

Trautmann, Bert, *Steppes to Wembley* (Robert Hale, 1956)

Wilson, Bob, *You've Got to be Crazy* (Arthur Barker, 1989)

Aberfan disaster 186
Acland Burghley school 164
Africa 50, 84, 118; *see
    also* North Africa *and*
    South Africa
Agricultural Hall, Islington 5,
    268
Ahab, Captain 76, 209
Ajax, Amsterdam 315
Algeria/Algiers 26, 42,
    189, 285
Allen, Reg 41, 72
Allende, Salvador 253, 258
Allison, Malcolm 310
Amalgamated Union
    of Building Trade
    Workers 239
America/Americans/USA/
    United States 35, 43, 46–9,
    57–8, 70, 74–5, 82, 87,
    120, 126–7, 144, 152–3,
    159–60, 163, 167, 197–8,
    210, 213–15, 219, 221, 227,
    233–4, 254, 262–8, 273–6,
    278–9, 301, 304–6, 309, 316
Amsterdam 208, 315
Anderson, Stan 146
'Apparent Madrid' 246
Ardiles, Ossie 265
Argentina 181, 249, 256–8,
    265–8, 270–1, 291–8
Argyll, Margaret, Duchess of
    101
Armfield, Jimmy 135, 147

Armstrong, Neil 210,
Armstrong-Jones, Anthony
    177
Arsenal 14, 15, 31, 41, 73, 86,
    90, 96, 105, 121, 138, 150,
    209, 237, 255, 271, 309,
    312, 314
Asher, Jane 177
Ashurst, Len 146
Astle, Jeff 139
Aston Villa 19, 45, 87, 118,
    256, 316
Astor, Lord 149
Atkinson, Ron 297–8,
    305, 307
Atlético Madrid 168
Attlee, Clement 50, 52–3, 58
Australia/Australians 80,
    249, 316
Austria/Austrians 55–8, 61, 63,
    64, 82, 183, 207, 276
Azteca stadium 279, 282–98

Bacigalupo 32
back-pass law 308
Baghdad Pact 101
Bailey, Gary 281
Baily, Eddie 40–41, 170–2
Balance of Payments crisis 196,
    197, 213
Balewa, Sir Abubakar
    Tafawa 119
ball (leather/plastic,
    brown/white, continental)

20, 55, 64, 71–2, 176–7, 242, 270, 294, 313

bananas 47, 274

Banks, Gordon 141, 147–8, 154, 164, 182–3, 187, 191, 202, 217, 222–6, 239, 259, 271–2, 283, 285, 288–91, 316–17, 321

Barbados 186, 274

Barbosa, Moacyr 229

Barcelona 92, 280

Barnsbury 5, 106, 111, 150, 162, 177, 319

Barthez, Fabien 321

Bartram, Sam 24–5, 30, 35–36, 70, 96, 113

Battiston, Patrick (*see* Schumacher)

Baxter, Jim 147, 152, 284

Bay of Pigs invasion 127

Bayern Munich 249–53, 256

Baynham, Ron 79, 81

BBC 12, 14, 17, 99, 101, 118–19, 159, 161, 179, 247, 263, 277–86

Beasant, Dave 302

Beatles, The 136, 177, 194–5, 210; *see also* Lennon, John; McCartney, Paul

Beattie, Dick 138–9, 165, 176

Beckenbauer, Franz 205, 224, 238, 248–53, 279, 306–7

Bedford/Bedfordshire 4, 6, 51–2, 86; *see also* Sandy (Beds)

Bedford Town 179, 227

Belfast 160, 267

Belgium/Belgians 20, 29, 54–5, 87, 206, 279

Belgrade 49, 91, 98, 200

Belo Horizonte 46–9

Benfica 200–4, 235

Berlin 12–17, 22, 43, 79, 85, 210

Berlin airlift 43

Berlin Wall 128, 210, 249, 305

Berry, Johnny 90–1

Best, George 200, 218, 235

Bexley 167

Big Freeze (1963) 143–4

Biggs, Ronnie 150

Bikila, Abebe 118

Bikini island 70

Bilbao 86

Birmingham 54, 87, 105, 283, 299–302

Birmingham City 19, 35, 52–4, 76–7, 106

Bishop, Maurice 274–6

Bishop, Sid 287

Bishop of Stepney 140

Blackburn Rovers 105, 134, 152, 213

Blacklaw, Adam 170

Blackpool 14, 22, 46, 59, 134, 136

Blair, Tony 317–20

Blanchflower, Danny 19, 125, 170

Blanchflower, Jackie 87

Blitz, the 5, 8, 14, 26

Bologna 29, 30

Bolton Wanderers 58–9, 84, 96, 105, 142

Bomb, the 34, 57, 70

Bonetti, Peter 136–7, 163–4, 192, 202, 217, 219, 224–7, 271, 314

Bonner, Packie 315
Bootham Crescent 96
Boothby, Lord 179, 301
Borghi 47–8
Bosnich, Mark 316
Bournemouth 15, 45
Bozsef, Jozsef 63
Bradford/Bradford City 138
Brady, Ray 200
brainwashing 74, 98
Bramall Lane 96
Brand, Ralph 121
Brazil/Brazilians 15, 45–9, 71,
    78–9, 99–101, 107, 118–19,
    131–3, 139, 148, 164, 180,
    186, 222–3, 228–230, 249,
    268–9, 271, 283–97, 321
Brentford 138, 213, 311
Brighton 243, 247, 253, 303,
    317, 319
Brisbane Road 131, 149, 151,
    155, 158, 165–179, 208,
    235, 289, 318
Bristol Rovers 131
British Drug Houses (BDH)
    11, 87, 93, 198
British Guyana (see Guyana)
Broad Left 243, 246, 253
Broadfoot, Joe 201
Broadmoor 300, 303
Brocket Hall/Lord 9, 10
Brooking, Trevor 286
Brown, Bill 100, 125–6,
    147, 166
Brown, José Luis 293, 298
Buchan, Charles/*Charles
    Buchan's Football
    Monthly*/album 31,
    135–42, 155

Budapest 63–4, 81–3,
    100, 207–8
Burgess, Ron 40, 146, 179
Burgin, Ted 96
Burnley 14, 98, 141, 170, 284
Burton, Richard 277–8
Burton's 125, 251
Bury 141, 311
Busby, Matt, 'Busby Babes' 23,
    86, 90, 191, 200–4
Butler, Rab 108
Byatt, A.S., on Euro 96 315

Caiger, Arthur 76
Cakebread, Gerry 138, 212
Caldow, Eric 121
Callaghan, James 197, 206, 254
Cameroon 270
Campos, Jorge 321
Camus, Albert 189, 202–3,
    294
cap (keepers) 8, 23, 112
Cape Town ('Winds of
    Change') 116
Carbajal, Antonio 99
Cardiff 73, 102, 218, 305
Carey, Johnny 33, 131, 152
Caribbean 273–6, 309
Carlos Alberto 230
Carter, President Jimmy
    259, 262
Caserta 28, 133
Castilho 230
Celtic, Glasgow 21, 26, 191,
    200, 285
Central America 253,
    258–9, 262–5, 274,
    278
Chadwell Heath 173

Challoner, Detective
   Inspector 189
Chamberlain, Neville
   26, 33, 47
Channel, English 20, 49, 79,
   99, 104, 132, 148, 163, 267
Chapel Market 5, 110,
   185, 237
Charles, Mel 124
Charles, Prince of Wales
   101–2
Charlton, Bobby 91, 105,
   122–3, 152, 159, 161, 180,
   200, 224, 286, 293
Charlton Athletic 24–5, 30, 35
Ché (Guevara) 258
Chelsea 26, 72, 96, 136–7,
   163–4, 173, 202, 209,
   218, 233
Chelsea Casuals 311
Cheshunt 168–76
Chesterfield 182
Chilavert, José Luis 321
Chile 46–7, 131–2, 153,
   249, 253
Chokri El Onaer 321
Churchill, Winston 6, 28,
   33–5, 44, 53, 57, 73, 144,
   176, 194, 211, 273
Clapton, Eric 178, 190
Clemence, Ray 237, 255–6,
   268, 312, 314, 321
Clinton, Bill and Hillary 320
Clodoaldo 228, 288–91
Clough, Brian 96, 145–6,
   244–7, 256, 259–61
Coates, Ralph 241–3
Cold War (*see* East/West)
Coldblow Lane 139, 202

Common Market (*see*
   European Union)
Commonwealth 102, 144,
   197, 276, 280
Communists/Party 31, 50, 63,
   163, 243, 254
Comunale stadium (Florence)
   29
Conservative government/
   Party 53, 147, 149, 162,
   199–200, 212, 227, 253,
   265–8, 318–19
Cornell, George (*see* Kray,
   Ron and Reg)
Coronation 11, 60, 101
Corrigan, Joe 255–6, 265, 311,
   314, 316
Costa Rica (*see* Central
   America)
Coventry/City 14, 54, 79,
   146, 312
Cowan, Jimmy 39
Cowan, Sam 23
Crabb, Commander Lionel
   'Buster' 74, 88
Cripps, Harry 201
cross, dealing with 100–1,
   160, 164, 175, 281–2,
   294–6, 312–18
Crystal Palace 138, 146, 312
Cuba/missile crisis 127, 140,
   153, 273–6, 319
Cubs (31st North London)
   75, 85–6
Cullis, Stan 30, 42
Cyprus/Cypriots, 80–1, 106,
   111–12, 118, 128, 140,
   147–8, 189, 237, 264, 319
Czechoslovakia 3,

31, 87, 100, 132, 206

Dadachanji, Dr 53, 67
Daffodil 107
D'Aubuisson, Major Roberto ('Blowtorch Bob') 264
Davies, Barry 247
Davies, Reg 139
Davis, Harry 121
Dean, James 74
de Beauvoir, Simone 203
decimalisation 235
de Gaulle, General/President Charles 144–5, 186, 197, 200, 280
Dei Marmi stadium 29
Delany, Ron 82
Delfont, Bernard 131
Den, The 139
Denmark 82, 87, 316
Denning Lord/Report 149
Derby County 32, 136, 244
devaluation/£50 limit 196, 206
Diana, Princess of Wales 310–11
Dick, Johnny 125
Didi 78, 100
Ditchburn, Ted 30, 32, 37–42, 45, 70, 75, 81–3, 181, 260
Docherty, Tommy 124, 136, 163, 173, 181, 202, 271
Domarski 245
Doncaster Rovers 15, 89
Double, the (League and Cup) 86, 168, 171, 235
Downing Street 33, 57, 73, 198, 246, 279

Drake, Ted 96
Drewry, Arthur 33, 47
Drinkwater, Ray 138
Dundee 100, 125
Dunkirk/Spirit 48, 104, 180, 196
Dunlop, Albert 140
Dunmore, Dave 287
Dunphy, Eamon 271

East End (London) 110, 131, 140–1, 149, 151, 158, 165, 179, 185, 299–303
East/West crisis (Cold War) 153, 183, 210, 237, 267–8, 273–6, 278–9, 304–8
Eastham, George 124
Eden, Sir Anthony 73–4, 81
Edward I, King 109
Edwards, Duncan 16, 85–6, 90–1, 212
Egypt/Egyptians 73, 81, 243, 277, 305
Eintracht Frankfurt 117, 203
Eire (*see* Ireland)
Eisenhower, General/President 28, 120
Elizabeth II, Queen 101–2
El Salvador (*see* Central America)
Else, Fred 213
Empire, departure/retreat from greatness 34–5, 68, 81–4, 87, 102, 118–19, 162, 178, 198, 266, 276, 319, 321
Empire and Commonwealth Games 102
Empire Day 11, 87
Empire Loyalists 162

England 12–17, 19–21, 29–36, 37–50, 52–68, 71–4, 78–9, 81–5, 89, 96, 98–100, 105, 118, 131, 135, 144–7, 152, 164, 168, 180–3, 191–2, 200, 202, 205, 221–7, 243–53, 256, 262–4, 267–9, 276, 279–97, 303–7, 312, 318, 321

Entertaining Mr Sloane (Joe Orton) 188

Epstein, Brian 194

Eton Manor 165–7

Europe/Europeans 56–7, 63, 75, 152–3, 180, 234, 316

European Cups and competitions 72, 86, 90, 117, 132, 145, 153, 168, 176–7, 191 , 200–5, 235, 238–9, 248, 256–7, 259–61, 271, 285, 303–4, 309, 311, 315–16

European Union/Integration/ EEC/Common Market 73, 84, 144, 186, 197, 235–6, 243–7, 261–2, 276, 318–20

Eusebio 152, 200–4

Evans, Roy 317

Evening News 65, 77, 135, 167, 177

Evening Standard 63–4, 135

Everest 60–1

Everton 22, 30, 45, 135, 140, 310–11

Exmouth Market 4, 6, 57

Falkland Islands/Malvinas 265–8, 274, 292–6

Farm, George 105

Farrell, Peter 45

fascism, British (*see* Mosley, Sir Oswald)

fees (goalkeepers' transfer/ signing-on) 41–2, 89, 136, 146, 150, 182, 193, 259–60, 270, 302, 316

Feisal II, King 101

Felix 228–30, 287–90

Fenton, Benny 152

Ferguson, Bobby 193

Festival of Britain 52

Fifa 61, 294

Filbert Street 192; *see also* Leicester City

Finland/the Finns 207, 213–20, 235–6

Finney, Tom 58

Finsbury 4, 5, 7, 8, 57, 80, 116, 212, 254

First World War 20, 25–6, 46, 48, 59, 130

Fleet Street 5, 7, 23, 56, 77, 198, 200

Florence 29, 30, 33, 58–9, 79, 95

Football Association/FA 48, 58, 61, 73, 86, 152, 210, 279

Football League 77

Footballer of Year (Britain/Europe) 76, 152, 240

Foulke, Billy 'Fatty' 20, 36

Foulkes, Bill 91

four-steps rule 195–6, 239

France/the French 20, 42–3, 45, 49–50, 73, 84, 87, 103,

108, 144–5, 148, 163, 181, 247, 297, 320–1
Fulham 89, 91–2, 94–5, 125, 164

Gagarin, Yuri 126, 153
Gaelic football 44, 191–2
Gaetjens, Joe 47–8
Garrincha 132, 288
Gartree prison 299–300
Gascoigne, Paul 306–7
George, Charlie 126, 255
George, Frank 317
George V, King 23–4
Germany/Germans 12–17, 26–7, 34, 41, 44, 56, 61, 72–3, 75–8, 84–5, 87, 107–8, 117, 130, 144, 150, 152, 154, 197, 200, 205, 220, 224–30, 236, 238, 248–54, 269–71, 279, 297–8, 303, 306–7, 321
Germany/Germans, East 128, 208, 210–12, 249
Ghana/Gold Coast 84, 162
Gibraltar/Rock of etc 92, 266
Giles, Johnny 218
Gillies, Matt 192–3
Gillingham 15, 37, 139
Gilmar 78–9, 99–100, 131, 229–30, 288, 321
Given, Shay 311
Glanville, Brian 226, 311
Glasgow/Glaswegians 14, 21, 34, 121, 138
Glazier, Bill 138, 146
gloves (goalkeepers') 23, 91, 93–5, 112–13, 250–5, 294, 311–12

Godwin, Tommy 44
Gomes Pedrosa, Roberto 229
Goodall, Roy 30
Goodison Park 43–5
Gordon Walker, Patrick 167
Gorgon 244–6
Grade, Lew 131
Graham, George 136
Great Britain (football team) 118, 126, 191
Great train robbery 149–50, 178
Greece/Greeks 81, 118, 130, 147–8
Green, Pete 190
Greene, Geoffrey 64–5
Greenock/Morton 26, 39, 149
Greenwood, Ron 268
Greer, Dr Germaine, on Euro 96 315
Gregg, Harry 15, 89–91, 93, 97–8, 100, 122–3, 159, 160, 200, 255, 288
Grenada/Caribbean 273–6, 309
Grobbelaar, Bruce 312
Groombridge, Dave 317
Grosics, Gyula 63, 160
Groves, Vic 124
Grummitt, Peter 134, 246
Guardian 275, 282–3, 298, 310
Gurkhas/kukhri 60, 267
Guyana/British Guyana 78, 186, 278

Hackney 133, 142
Hackney Downs school 150
Hackney Marshes 47, 151, 165, 195, 230

Hackney Road children's
  hospital 53, 70
Haffey, Frank 126, 191
Haley, Bill 85
Haley's Comet 161
Hall, Jeff 106
Halliwell, Kenneth 188, 194–5
Hammerfest 129, 231
Hamburg 72, 225, 249, 261
Hampden Park 117, 164, 203
Hanover (Germany) 205
Hanover school 10–11, 93,
  106, 113–14, 116, 198, 205
Hansen, Alan 321
Hardy, Sam 19–20, 34
Hargitay, Mickey 115
Harvey, David 268
Hastings, Battle of 63–5, 182
Haverty, Joe 124
Hayes, 'Judo' Al 199
Haynes, Johnny 89, 91, 125–6
Heath, Edward 227
Helsinki 62–3, 215–19
Henderson, Willy 137
Hendrix, Jimi 189–90
Heysel 270, 278
Hibbs, Harry 19–21, 25,
  34, 42, 53
Hidegkuti, Nandor 63–6
Highbury 21, 38, 49, 52,
  63, 85, 90, 92, 94–5, 102,
  121, 123–4, 126–8, 151,
  163–4, 209
Highbury school 106,
  108–12, 120, 127–8,
  128–30, 139–40, 149, 151,
  162–3, 177–8
Hill, Jimmy 89, 91, 125, 146
Hillsborough 304

Hilton, Kensington/Shepherd's
  Bush 238–9
Hoddle, Glenn 296
Hodgkinson, Alan 84–5,
  96, 313–14
Holland, Jools 309
Holland/Netherlands/the
  Dutch 87, 208, 249–51,
  263, 270, 302, 315–16
Holloway school 109, 126,
  150, 162
Hollywood 54, 115, 278
Home international
  championships 20, 39, 45,
  65, 84–5, 89, 125–6, 159,
  164, 305
Honeypot Lane 173
Hong Kong 50, 319
Hooliganism 256–8, 261–2,
  270, 278, 283, 295–6, 303–4
Hopkinson, Eddie 84,
  97–8, 142
Hornby, Nick 309–10
Houseman, Peter 218
Howe, Jack 32
Huddersfield Town 20, 30
Hungary/Hungarians/Magyars
  15, 17, 62–8, 71–2, 81–3,
  115, 160, 206, 216, 247,
  276, 313–14
Hunter, Norman 218, 245
Hurst, Geoff 125, 155, 182,
  221, 250, 310

Ibrox Park 22, 34, 240
Iceland 26
Illgner, Bodo 252
India/Indians/the Raj 34, 38,
  50, 67, 266, 281

inflation 254
Inter-Milan 176, 191
Ipswich 144–5, 281
IRA 237, 304
Iran/Iranian 243; *see also* Persia
Iraq 101
Ireland (North) 19, 39, 43–4,
    55, 89, 98–100, 131, 146,
    159, 235, 238 (Bloody
    Sunday), 267, 268, 283–5
Ireland (Republic) 19, 43–4,
    83, 124, 128, 131, 304–6,
    311, 315
Ironmonger Row baths 7
Irwin, Cecil 146
Island Queen (public
    house) 11, 265
Islington 1–12, 105–7, 113–14,
    116–19, 129, 130–1, 133,
    151, 177–8, 187–9, 235–7,
    255, 264–5, 268–72, 275,
    309, 319–20
Islington borough council
    10; libraries 76, 130–1,
    147; town hall 184–214
    passim; 233
Islington Gazette 127
Israel 35, 237–8, 243
Italy/Italians 4, 16, 26, 28–9,
    31–4, 45, 58, 61, 69, 76,
    79, 88, 95–6, 104, 118, 132,
    168, 228, 254, 262, 272,
    279, 305–7
ITT 253
ITV 99, 161, 247, 283–6,
    297–8

Jackson, John 317
Jairzinho 222

Jalisco stadium 222–4, 283
Jamaica 108, 118, 190
James, David 317
Japan/Japanese 27, 70, 97, 285
Jay, Douglas 186
Jay twins 186, 198
Jennings, Pat 146, 166, 179,
    191–2, 130, 135, 139–40,
    245, 251, 268, 271–2, 277,
    284–5, 288, 315, 321
Jobbins, Bob 277
John, Elton 309, 311
John Mayall's Bluesbreakers
    178, 190
Johnson, President Lyndon B.
    197
Johnston, Harold/Harry 65–6
Jones, Paul 177
Jongbloed, Jan 251, 316
Jönköping 39, 100
Juventus 31, 105, 270–2, 279

Kafka, Franz 183
Kagan, Joe 198–9
Kay, Tony 164
Keegan, Kevin 261, 282, 319
Keeler, Christine 148–9
Keller, Kasey 316
Kelsey, Jack 15, 73–4, 96,
    100–2, 105, 112, 123–4,
    131, 136, 139, 155, 161,
    218, 288, 311, 321
Kennedy, President
    John F. 120, 153, 159,
    227, 273–4
Kenya/Kenyatta, Jomo,
    President 50, 57, 162
Kevan, Derek 98
KGB 154

Khrushchev, Nikita 74,
    153, 215
Kilmarnock 193
Kinnear, Joe 241–3
Kirkenes 232
Kissinger, Henry 251, 266
Köpke, Andreas 321
Korean War 49–50, 53, 198
Kray, Ron and Reg 179,
    299–303, 310

Labour government/Party
    50, 52–3, 57, 167, 177,
    199–200, 212, 237, 243,
    253, 319–20
Laika 88, 153
Laker, Jim 80
Latin America/South America
    16, 47, 59, 61, 257–8,
    262–8, 288
Law, Denis 147, 200
Lawrence, Tommy 176
Layne, David 'Bronco'
    138, 164
Lee, Cyril 287
Leeds United 218–19, 256,
    268, 312
Leek, Ken 193
Le Flem, Flip 134
Leicester City 43, 142, 148,
    164, 182, 192, 259–60,
    271, 316–17
Leighton, Jim 302, 321
Lenin V.I. 57, 211–12,
    215, 237
Lennon, John 195
León 224–7, 230
Leslie, Lawrie 126
Lesotho/Basutoland 186

Leyland, Harry 105, 213
Leyton County school 146
Leyton Orient 110, 131, 133,
    146, 149–52, 155–9, 160–1,
    165–76, 183, 208, 218, 287,
    309–11, 317–18
Liedholm, Nils 99
Lineker, Gary 280, 294–6, 306
Lisbon 200, 235
Liverpool/Liverpudlians
    14–15, 19, 29, 131, 147,
    176, 200, 218, 239, 255–6,
    279, 312, 317
Lloyd Webber, Andrew
    309–10
Lofoten (Islands) 129, 231, 236
Lofthouse, Nat, 'Lion of
    Vienna' 58, 96–8, 170
London County Council 10
London School of Economics
    (LSE) 200, 254
London Transport/LT ground
    150, 155, 168–79, 287
Loot (Joe Orton) 189
Lowe's 3–4, 95, 102, 115, 119
Loxley, Bert 139
Luton/Luton Town 36, 51,
    79, 86, 107, 141
Luxembourg 167, 256

McCartney, Paul 177
McCullin, Don 264
McDonald, Colin 98,
    100, 288
McIllveney 47
McIlroy, Sammy 284
McIlvaney, Hugh 224
Mackay, Dave 147
MacLeod, Ally 257

Macmillan, Harold 116, 149, 179, 273–4
McNeil, Billy 285
McParland, Peter 87
Macedo, Tony, 'Rock of Gibraltar' 92–5, 125, 164
Maestri, Mario 12, 16, 194
Maier, Sepp 228, 238, 249–53, 269, 306
Maine Road 86, 120
Makarios, Archbishop 80, 111, 118, 162, 237
Malaya/Malayan emergency 50, 57, 152
Malvinas (see Falkland Islands)
Mansfield, Jayne 115–16
Maracana stadium 47
Maradona, Diego 293–8, 306
Martin, Con 44
Marx, Karl 57
Manchester 14, 75–6, 80
Manchester City 22–5, 35, 74–8, 86, 102, 120, 134, 142, 165, 255–6, 311
Manchester United 16, 41, 44, 72, 85–7, 89–92, 94–8, 120–3, 131, 134, 141, 146, 148, 191, 200–5, 209, 235, 281, 297, 302, 308, 310, 316
Manfred Mann 177
Mao Tse-tung/Maoism 162, 198, 249
Marquee 178, 183, 189
Marseilles 103, 320
Martin, Con 44
Martyn, Nigel 312
Marwood, George 108, 130
Maryland, University of 210, 214

Matthews, Reg 13–17, 79, 81, 93, 107, 136, 209, 212
Matthews, Stanley 13, 46, 48, 59, 66, 71, 97, 134
Mazurkiewicz, Ladislao 180
Mazzei, Professor Julio 284–91
Medwin, Michael 117
Meisl, Willy 61, 64
Mellor, David 309
Mercer, Joe 30
Merrick, Gil 52–8, 60–8, 71, 76, 96, 113, 160, 162, 269
Metamorphosis (Franz Kafka) 183
Mexico/Mexicans 99, 180, 219, 221–27, 234, 258, 262, 267, 270, 277–99, 305, 321
Middle East 74, 81, 101, 237
Middlesbrough 96
Milan 28, 79, 168, 184
Millichip, Bert 279
Millwall 30, 139, 141, 201
miners' strikes 227, 238, 276–7
Minto, Ronnie 113–14
Mirror 114, 130, 163, 202, 235, 302
Moby Dick (Herman Melville) 76, 209
Mods and Rockers 166, 196
Montevideo 59
Moore, Bobby 155, 173, 177, 223–4, 239, 310
Moore, Brian 306
Moreland Street school 116–17
Montgomery, Jimmy 145, 256
Mortensen, Stan 32
Moscow 50, 74, 81, 98, 266
Moscow Dynamo 34, 46, 153
Mosley, Sir Oswald 9, 54, 105

Moynihan, John 71, 164
Muller, Gerd 224, 226
Mullery, Alan 223
Munich 90, 98, 122,
   206–7, 310
Muñoz, José Maria 292–7
Murdoch, Rupert 308
Murphy, Peter 77
Mussolini, Benito 21, 28, 184

Nagy, Imry 81
Nairobi 50, 128
Naples 28, 132–3, 234,
   270, 293
Nasser, General/President 73,
   82
National Coal Board 186
National Health Service
   (NHS) 9, 89, 311
National Service 101, 128–9,
   182, 305
Nayim 309
Nep stadium 71, 208
Netherlands (*see* Holland)
Netzer, Günther 238, 249
Newbon, Gary 283, 306
Newcastle/United 124,
   126, 145, 173, 191, 302,
   308–9, 311
News Chronicle 31
News of the World 5, 6, 149
New York 82, 107, 214, 216
Nicaragua (*see* Central
   America)
Nigeria 119, 264
Ninian Park 218, 305
Niven, George 121
Nixon, President Richard 120,
   219, 227

Norman, Maurice 132
Norrköping 39
North Africa 26–7, 30, 33, 69
North America Soccer
   League 239
Northampton 227
North Sea/oil 107, 230, 258
Norway/Norwegians 16, 40,
   87, 129, 219–37, 262
Nottingham Forest 107, 134,
   256–61, 303
Notting Hill 105, 149
Notts County 139
Nureyev, Rudolph 153
Nyerere, Julius 162

October War 243
Ocwirk, Ernst 'Clockwork'
   56–8, 207
Ogrizovic, Steve 311–12
Old Trafford 86, 90, 92, 319
Olivieri, Aldo 95
Olympic Games 12, 22, 39,
   62–3, 82–3, 118, 126, 153,
   212, 302
Only a Game? (Eamon
   Dunphy) 271
Orient (*see* Leyton Orient)
Orton, Joe 187–9, 194–5, 233
Owens, Jesse 12, 22, 118, 212
Owen's school 7

Palio (Siena) 80
Palmer, Harold 63
Pancho 99–100
Paraguay 291, 321
Paris 43, 49, 145, 200, 203
Partick Thistle 257
Partizan Belgrade 200

Partizans 49, 269
Pavarotti, Luciano 306–7
Pele 100–1, 131, 181, 222–4, 229, 284–8
Pentonville prison/Hill 108, 142, 234
Pepe 289
Persia 73
Peru 222, 229
Petts, Johnny 123
Philip, Prince 147
Pinner, Mike 118, 160–1, 316
Pleat, David 134, 247
Poland/the Poles 12, 82, 87, 94, 111, 130, 237, 239, 243–7, 250, 256, 262–3, 319
poliomyelitis 18, 107
Ponomoreva, Nina 81, 83
'Pop music' 105
Portsmouth (Pompey) 22–3, 74, 88, 100, 127–8, 138–9, 165, 167
Portugal 152, 181–2, 200–4
Possibles (England) 25
Prague 31, 206
Prater stadium 58, 207
Preston North End 14, 124
Preud'homme 29
Probables (England) 25
Proctor and Gamble 213
Profumo, John 140
PT boys 38, 42, 54
Pumpido, Nery 293–7
Puskas, Ferenc 15, 17, 63–8, 82, 117, 152, 154, 207, 286–91

Queen's Park Rangers 40–1, 138, 173

Rainham 151
Ramsey, Alf 40, 47, 62, 144–5, 148, 170, 180–2, 192–3, 202, 221–4, 255, 261, 281
Rangers, Glasgow 22, 34, 121, 137, 147
Ray, Johnny 70–1, 74
Reagan, President Ronald 262–75, 278–9, 304–5
Real Madrid 86, 117, 203, 246, 249
Reforma Club (Mexico City) 280–1
Regent's Canal 5, 8, 75, 82–3, 88
Rest of Europe 40, 95, 131
Rest of the World 61–2, 95, 152, 286–91
Revie, Don 218, 255
Reynolds News 135, 145
Rhodesia 178, 312; see also Zimbabwe
Rice Davies, Mandy 149
Richards, Gordon 60
Rimet, Jules 45, 48
Risinghill school 111
Rivelino 288–91
Robertson, Bill 317
Robson, Bobby 91, 125, 279
Romania 221, 268, 315
Rome 118, 132, 262–3
Romero, Archbishop Oscar of San Salvador 263–4
Ronan Point explosion 200
Roosevelt, President Franklin D. 6
Rosenthal, Jim 286
Rossi, Paolo 270

Rotherham 302, 309

Rough, Alan 257, 269

Roxburgh, Andy 315–16

Russia/Russians/Soviet Union
34, 43, 46, 50, 56, 58, 70,
75, 81–3, 87–8, 98–100,
101, 103, 126–7, 129, 132,
140, 148–9, 152–4, 159,
183, 206–8, 215, 217, 230,
248, 261, 266–8, 304–5

Saint (*see* St)

Salvoni, Elena 12, 194

Sandinista guerrillas (*see*
Central America)

Sandy (Beds) 6, 8–9, 26, 28,
34–5, 38, 44, 79, 86–8

São Paulo 131, 229, 288–91;
see also Brazil

Sartre, Jean Paul 189, 202

Scandinavia 39, 213

Scargill, Arthur 276–7

Schmeichel, Peter 308,
316, 319

Schoen, Helmut 248

Schroiff, Wilhelm 132

Schumacher, Harald 269,
279, 298

Scotland/Scots 20–1, 30–1, 39,
71, 84–6, 99–100, 109, 121,
125–6, 137–8, 146–7, 149,
164–6, 200, 256–8, 265–6,
268–9, 280–1, 284–5,
315–16, 321

Scott, Elisha 19, 20, 34

Seaman, David 309, 312,
315, 321

Second World War 1, 3,
6–14, 21, 26–38, 41–4, 49,
53–9, 62, 72–4, 81, 87,
97, 116, 132–3, 152, 154,
183, 240

Seeler, Uwe 72, 152, 225–7,
280, 306

Selectors 33–6, 54, 72, 79,
81, 84, 145

Sexton, Dave 173, 218

Shah, Eddie 308

Shamrock Rovers 44

Shankly, Bill 255, 290

Sheffield United 20, 84,
96, 313–14

Sheffield Wednesday 118,
134–8, 164

Shilton, Peter 193, 239, 245–7,
252, 255–6, 259–61, 268–9,
272, 279, 281–13, 288,
294–6, 306–7, 316–18, 321

shotstopping 294–6, 312–8,
321

shoulder barging 72, 87,
97–8, 195

Siena 28, 59, 79–80,
132–3, 186

Simpson, Ronnie 126, 191,
268, 302

Smith, George 139

Smith, Ian 178

smog, London 69–70, 79,
133, 143

Soccer Star 135, 139

Somoza, President
Anastasio/Nicaragua; *see*
Central America

South Africa 13, 116

Southall, Neville 311–12

South America (*see* Latin
America)

South East Counties League 59, 157, 167–76, 230
Soviet Union (see Russia)
Spain/Spaniards 3, 20, 48, 61, 86, 92, 192, 205–8, 241–3, 264, 266–71, 281, 285, 315, 321
Special Relationship (see America)
Spink, Nigel 256
Sporting Life 5
Sprake, Gary 218–19
Springett, Ron 131, 138, 145
St John, Ian 147, 283
St John's Church/school (Islington) 2, 113, 116
St Luke's Church (Finsbury) 8
St Martin's Art School 189
St Mary's Church (Islington)
St Pancras station/town hall 36, 109, 134, 136, 141–2, 215
St Peter's Church (Islington) 94, 319
Stadium of Light (see Benfica/Lisbon)
Stalin 159, 246
Stamford Bridge (see Chelsea)
Standen, Jim 105, 155, 161
Stepney, Alex 200–4, 271
Stiles, Norbert/Nobby 121–3, 182, 200
Stinka 117
Stoke City 133–4, 259
Streten, Bernard 52, 96
Suez Canal 73–4, 82, 267, 277
Sunday People 164–5
Sunderland 145, 256
Sussex, University of 149, 186,

190–1, 237, 243, 245–6, 252, 275
Swan, Peter 164
sweater, goalkeeper's, roll-neck to modern 8, 74, 78, 82–3, 100, 187, 236, 315
Sweden/Swedes 39–41, 43, 61, 100, 122, 152, 202
Swift, Frank 22–5, 30–6, 37–43, 45, 75–6, 90–1, 96, 113, 154, 160, 255, 260, 311, 321
Swindin, George 96
Switzerland/the Swiss 15, 31, 38–9, 71–2, 84, 96, 262, 268, 278

Taffarel 321
Tanganyika (Tanzania) 162
Taylor, Hugh 21–2
Taylor, Peter 261
Taylor, Tommy 318
Taylor Report 304
Teddy Boys/Teds 74, 82, 85, 105, 128
Telegraph magazine 309
Test Ban treaty 153
Thames TV 264
Thatcher, Margaret 227, 253–4, 259–62, 272–7, 292, 304–5, 313
Third Lanark 191
Third World 234, 269, 299
Thomson, Jack 21–2, 240
throwing (the ball) 24, 160–1
throwing (the match) 165, 176
Thurlow, Alex 75
Tilkowski, Hans 249–50
Tilson, Fred 23

Times, The 64, 211
Tirpitz 129, 231, 236
Tito 29, 49, 269
Today programme 119, 179
Tomaszewski, Jan 244–7, 255, 262
Topical Times 135, 147
Tottenham Hotspur/Spurs 30, 38, 40, 62, 82, 132, 144, 147, 150, 166, 168–73, 191, 239–42, 265, 271, 287, 317
Trautmann, Bert 74–8, 102, 120, 142, 154, 157, 165, 239, 245, 255, 260
Trinder, Tommy 92, 125
Tromsø 129, 231
tuberculosis 75
Tunisia 26, 321
Turin 31, 270, 306–7
Tyler, Martin 286

Uprichard, Norman 100
Upton Park 125
Uruguay 48, 59, 71, 180, 229, 266
USA (*see* America)

Valley, the 35–6
Vassall, John 140
Vava 131, 229
Venables, Terry 136, 280
Vienna 56, 58, 96, 98, 160
Vietnam 163, 234
Villa, Pancho 280
Villa, Rickie 265
Villa Park 55, 105
Vogts, Bertie 252

wages 21, 24, 38, 125, 146,
150–1, 165, 171, 217, 260, 312, 318
Waiters, Tony 168
Wales/the Welsh 15, 30, 39, 40, 47, 62, 73, 82, 99–102, 105, 109, 128, 131, 146, 218, 305, 311
Wall Street Crash 20
Walsall 41–3
Walter, Fritz 13, 16
Walters, Professor Alan 255
Walthamstow 110, 131, 150, 166, 168, 289
Wapping 308
Ward, Stephen 149
Warsaw Pact 81
Washington DC 153, 214–15, 217, 262–8
Waterlow's 6, 59
Watford 146, 166, 173, 179
Webb, David 165, 173, 218
Welton, Pat 110, 317
Wembley 15, 20, 22–4, 39, 54, 56, 59, 61–8, 72, 79, 84–5, 87, 89–90, 100, 125–6, 146–8, 152, 154, 159, 177, 182, 202–4, 230, 243–7, 256, 289, 302, 314–15
West, Gordon 135, 140, 158
West Bromwich Albion 91, 98
West Ham United 125–5, 155–8, 161, 173, 193, 310
What the Butler Saw (Joe Orton) 194
White, John 147, 166
White City 81, 211
White Hart Lane 40, 45, 90, 125, 166, 170, 193, 209, 241

Who, The 178
Williams, Bert 41–50, 52, 54–5, 71–3, 76, 87, 96, 112, 136, 164
William Tyndale school 107, 150, 184
Wilson, Bob 236, 314
Wilson, Harold 167, 178, 186, 196–8, 227, 274
Wimbledon 302
Winchester Cup 155, 173
'Winds of Change' speech 116
Windsor, Barbara 300
Winterbottom, Walter 47, 58
Wojtiya, Karol, Pope John Paul II 262–3
Wolstenholme, Kenneth 99, 145
Wolverhampton Wanderers 13, 30, 41–3, 72, 96
Wood, Ray 72, 79, 81, 87, 89, 97
Woods, Chris 281
World Cup 15, 17, 19, 29, 31, 45–9, 59, 62, 71–2, 96, 100–1, 122, 131–2, 145, 153, 180–3, 200, 205, 217, 221–30, 239, 243–53, 256–8, 263–5, 268–71, 282–98, 305–7, 313, 315, 320–1
World Youth Cup 146
Wrexham 47, 305
Wright, Billy 40, 47, 63–7
'Wunderteam' 56, 61

Xerox 233

Yashin, Lev 83, 98–100, 132, 152–5, 183, 214, 286, 304
York City 96
Younger, Tommy 15
Yugoslavia/Yugoslavs 29, 49, 61–2, 79, 82, 90–1, 98, 269

Zamora, Ricardo 21
Zanzibar/Sultan of 162
Zapata (Emiliano) 280
Zeman, Walter 58
Zimbabwe 312
Zoff, Dino 269–72
Zubizarreta, Andoni 321
Zussman, Harry 131